DATE DUE

OCT 2 0 1993	
MAY 0 2 1994	
DEC 0 5 1994	
MAR 2 1 2002	

BRODART   Cat. No. 23-221

BRAND EQUITY & ADVERTISING
Advertising's Role in Building Strong Brands

ADVERTISING AND
CONSUMER PSYCHOLOGY
A series sponsored by the Society for
Consumer Psychology

AAKER/BIEL • Brand Equity & Advertising: Advertising's
(1993)　　Role in Building Strong Brands

CLARK/BROCK/STEWART • Attention, Attitude, and Affect in
(in press)　　Response to Advertising

ENGLIS • Global and Multi-National
(in press)　　Advertising

MITCHELL • Advertising Exposure,
(1993)　　Memory, and Choice

THORSON/MOORE • Integrated Communications:
(in prep.)　　Synergy of Persuasive Voices

BRAND EQUITY & ADVERTISING
Advertising's Role in Building Strong Brands

Edited by

David A. Aaker
University of California at Berkeley
Alexander L. Biel
Alexander L. Biel & Associates, California

LEA LAWRENCE ERLBAUM ASSOCIATES, PUBLISHERS
1993   Hillsdale, New Jersey   Hove and London

Lawrence Erlbaum Associates, Inc., Publishers
365 Broadway
Hillsdale, New Jersey 07642

Library of Congress Cataloging-in-Publication Data

Brand equity & advertising : advertising's role in building strong
    brands / [David A. Aaker and Alexander L. Biel, editors].
        p.   cm.
    Includes bibliographical references and index.
    ISBN 0-8058-1283-0. — ISBN 0-8058-1284-9 (pbk.)
        1. Brand name products—Valuation—Congresses.   2. Advertising—
    Brand name products—Congresses.   I. Aaker, David A.   II. Biel,
    Alexander L.   III. Title: Brand equity and advertising.
    HD69.B7B72   1993
    659.1—dc20   92-40963
                                                                        CIP

Books published by Lawrence Erlbaum Associates are printed on acid-free
paper, and their bindings are chosen for strength and durability.

Printed in the United States of America
10   9   8   7   6   5   4   3   2   1

Contents

Preface   ix

1 Brand Equity and Advertising: An Overview
       David A. Aaker and Alexander L. Biel   1

Part I   A Global View on Building Brands

2 The Landor ImagePower Survey®: A Global Assessment
       of Brand Strength
       Stewart Owen   11

3 Building Brands Across Markets: Cultural Differences in
       Brand Relationships Within the European Community
       Jeri Moore   31

4 Branding in Japan
       Hiroshi Tanaka   51

v

Part II The Brand Personality and Brand Equity

5 Converting Image Into Equity
Alexander L. Biel   67

6 The Brand Personality Component of Brand Goodwill:
Some Antecedents and Consequences
Rajeev Batra, Donald R. Lehmann, and Dipinder Singh   83

7 Can Products and Brands Have Charisma?
Norman Smothers   97

8 Beyond Brand Personality: Building Brand Relationships
Max Blackston   113

9 The Value of the Brand: An Anthropological Perspective
Grant McCracken   125

Part III The Role of Advertising in Creating Brand Equity

10 Advertising, Perceived Quality, and Brand Image
Amna Kirmani and Valarie Zeithaml   143

11 Asking the Right Questions:
What Do People Do with Advertising?
Judie Lannon   163

12 Expansion Advertising and Brand Equity
Brian Wansink and Michael L. Ray   177

13 The Impact and Memorability of Ad-Induced Feelings:
Implications for Brand Equity
Julie A. Edell and Marian Chapman Moore   195

14 Varieties of Brand Memory Induced by Advertising:
Determinants, Measures, and Relationships
H. Shanker Krishnan and Dipankar Chakravarti   213

Part IV   Perspectives on Brand Equity

15   Decomposing a Brand's Consumer
        Franchise into Buyer Types
        Josh McQueen, Carol Foley, and John Deighton   235

16   Cognitive Strength of Established Brands:
        Memory, Attitudinal, and Structural Approaches
        Curtis P. Haugtvedt, Clark Leavitt, and Wendy L. Schneier   247

17   The Dual Structure of Brand Associations
        Peter H. Farquhar and Paul M. Herr   263

Part V   Perspectives on Brand Extensions

18   Advertising Claims and Evidence as Bases for
        Brand Equity and Consumer Evaluations of
        Brand Extensions
        Kent Nakamoto, Deborah J. MacInnis, and Hyung-Shik Jung   281

19   Brands as Categories
        David M. Boush   299

20   Fit and Leverage in Brand Extensions
        Edward M. Tauber   313

Part VI   Case Studies and a Commentary

21   The Role of Corporate Advertising in Building a Brand:
        Chevron's Preconversion Campaign in Texas
        Lewis Winters   321

22   Are Brand Equity Investments Really Worthwhile?
        David A. Aaker   333

23   Brand Equities, Elephants, and Birds: A Commentary
        William D. Wells   343

About the Contributors   357

Author Index   365

Subject Index   371

Preface

This book consists of a set of papers delivered at a conference on advertising and building strong brands that was held in May 1991—the 10th annual advertising and consumer psychology conference. Our concept is based on the idea that much can be gained by combining advertising and marketing professionals with academic researchers in advertising, marketing, and consumer behavior. Professionals can gain an insight into the new theories, measurement tools, and empirical findings that are emerging. Academics can benefit from the insights and experience that professionals describe and the research questions that they pose.

When we were asked to co-chair the 10th conference, we selected the area of branding because of the intense interest in it both in academia and in the "real world" and because of our own continuing fascination with brands as strategic assets. We then strongly encouraged people who we knew had exciting ideas or research efforts to participate. The result is an extremely strong set of authors and papers. The lead piece where the Landor study of brands is described in detail for the first time will be worth the price of the book for many, but it is but one of 22 selections.

There are many who deserve thanks. The Consumer Psychology Division of the American Psychological Association and its president Tim Brock are the prime force behind the annual conference. The other conference sponsors, the Marketing Science Institute and the Haas School of Business, provided support when it was needed. Valerie York, who was the administrative chair-

person of the conference, is an incredible talent and was the reason the conference ran smoothly. She deserves our admiration and appreciation. Finally, the
enthusiasm and competent support of Lawrence Erlbaum Associates were wel-
come, indeed.

David A. Aaker
Alexander L. Biel

Chapter 1

Brand Equity and Advertising: An Overview

David A. Aaker
University of California at Berkeley

Alexander L. Biel
Alexander L. Biel & Associates, California

Brand equity, a concept born in the 1980s, has aroused intense interest among marketing managers and business strategists from a wide variety of industries. The Marketing Science Institute, a consortium of over 50 leading firms, considers brand equity one of its top research priorities. For this reason, substantial research effort has been channeled into defining, measuring, and understanding the antecedents and consequences of building strong brands. This book is one result of that effort. The topic is prominent because of (a) the financial community's interest in placing a value on brands, and (b) reaction against the frequency of short-term price competition that dominates many industries.

The financial community has placed extraordinary prices on the value of established brands, treating them as intangible assets with the potential to grow in value rather than depreciate. As a result, interest in a company's portfolio of brands has been elevated from the marketing department or product group to the executive floor and boardroom.

Philip Morris purchased Kraft for more than six times its book value. In his 1989 keynote address to the Advertising Research Foundation, Hamish Maxwell, the man behind the acquisition, emphasized that he was buying strong brands. Philip Morris sought brands that (a) had a loyal consumer franchise, (b) could convert the pull of that consumer franchise into leverage with the grocery trade, (c) could be extended, and (d) most importantly, could guarantee the successful diversification of Philip Morris outside the tobacco business.

In some ways, Nestle's recent acquisition of Perrier for $2.5 billion represents the quintessential tribute to brand equity. As a sparkling mineral water, Perrier is as undifferentiated from its competitors as a product can be. Yet, as the long-established, category-defining brand, Perrier brings something quite valuable to Nestle.

A second impetus for interest in branding is the debilitating price competition that has occurred in industry after industry, from TV sets, to airlines, to automobiles, to coffee, to frozen food. The percentage of advertising/promotion mix that is diverted to brand-building advertising shrank from 90% in the 1950s to 25% in the early 1990s. The balance is spent on trade (nearly 50%) and consumer promotions. This has resulted in a tendency to compete on prices, an accompanying reduction in loyalty, and often a focus on costs while sacrificing product improvement and quality standards.

What is the route away from a reliance on prices as the primary competitive arena? Many believe the answer is brand equity—building brands that are strong enough to resist the pressure to compete largely on price. The emphasis would then turn from the short-term pay-offs of price promotion to longer term strategy.

We must first determine exactly what the concept of brand equity means. A consumer perceives a brand's equity as the value added to the functional product or service by associating it with the brand name. A company may view it as the future discounted value of the profit stream that can be attributed to the price premium or enhanced loyalty generated by the brand name. From a managerial perspective, it is a set of assets—including brand awareness, brand loyalty, perceived quality, and brand associations—that are attached to a brand name or symbol (Aaker, 1991). This book expands on these views and suggests others.

There is a broad consensus that advertising is a major contributor to brand equity, and many of the papers in this volume explore that contribution. Other papers explore issues related to the broader questions of how brand equity should be created and managed:

- How can/should the asset value of a brand name be measured?
- On what is brand equity based?
- How can it be developed and enhanced?
- How can brand equity be exploited through brand extensions?

The book contains six sections, plus this introduction and a concluding commentary by Bill Wells. In the first section, three chapters present a global view of branding. The second section discusses brand personality. The third section deals explicitly with the role of advertising in creating brand equity. The fourth provides three different perspectives on brand equity. The fifth delves into brand extensions, and the sixth includes several case studies.

A GLOBAL VIEW ON BUILDING BRANDS

There is, with good reason, intense interest in branding issues as firms grapple with developing and implementing global branding strategies. In this context, the three chapters that open the book provide timely insight into the area, each from a very different perspective.

The lead chapter in this section, by Owen at Landor, is "The Landor ImagePower Survey—A Global Assessment of Brand Strength," which includes perceptions of hundreds of brands in Europe, Japan, and the United States, determined along esteem and awareness dimensions. In our view, this survey is a useful empirical effort to study brand power. The survey methodology and results have never been published in as great detail as they are here.

The ImagePower survey provides a specific operational view of what brand strength is and how it should be measured so that brands can be compared. It identifies how brands perform along these measures, a first step toward learning how strong brands become strong and why weak brands are weak. Of special interest is the existence of side-by-side data in Europe, Japan, and the United States. Thus, we can observe which types of brands are strong in each market (e.g., car brands tend to be stronger in Europe). We also explore how foreign brands fare in each market.

The next piece, by Jeri Moore of DDB Needham, "Building Brands Across Markets: Cultural Differences in Brand Relationships Within the European Community," describes a survey of brand strength for 93 brands in 13 product categories across five countries, conducted by DDB Needham. The awareness dimension is similar to the Landor measure, but esteem is replaced by *brand affinity* ("brand I like," "suits me," "brand I trust") and brand perceptions ("leading brand," "worth the price," "excellent quality").

Moore also explores cultural factors that may contribute to the ease with which a brand can build its equity within a particular market. These factors, combined with graphic examples of how actual brand equities vary, by dimension, across markets, suggest the dangers of using a common marketing strategy across markets within the European Community.

The next selection, by Tanaka of Dentsu, "Branding in Japan," is a rare paper by a leading Japanese researcher that discusses why advertising in Japan is so different. Tanaka describes the extent to which Japanese advertising relies upon mood advertising and proposes reasons for this. His arguments provide true insight into the Japanese culture and advertising environment. He discusses the role of new product velocity and its impact on the corporate brand in Japan. Tanaka reviews nine empirical studies sourced in Japan, basing his theories on sound evidence.

BRAND PERSONALITY AND BRAND EQUITY

A number of chapters in this book explore brand personality in the context of equity. Brand equity is a newcomer to the lexicon of marketing, whereas brand personality has been around for some 40 years. Martineau, writing in the early 1950s, was an early champion of the concept. The chapters in this section take a new look at brand personality, brand image, and their relationship to brand equity.

In chapter 5, "Converting Image to Equity," Biel presents an overview of the brand image concept. Noting the easily confused terminology for brand image and brand equity, he argues that brand equity is driven by consumer choice. Choice, in turn, is driven by brand image. Biel notes that functional differences between brands are becoming ever more trivial. As a consequence, he suggests that the "soft" concepts of brand personality and brand relationships (see Blackston, chapter 8) are likely to be far "harder" and more effective in creating brand equity than most marketers realize.

In "The Brand Personality Component of Brand Goodwill: Some Antecedents and Consequences," Batra, Lehmann, and Singh explore the impact of brand personality on the extendibility of a brand. They present the results of a pilot study and speculate about some of the ways in which advertising contributes to brand personality.

Smothers notes that a brand, like a person, can have a personality. This well-known concept leads to a similar analogy to explain the extraordinary loyalty enjoyed by a few brands. Are certain commanding, almost magnetically appealing brands—like certain people—charismatic? If so, what implications can we draw about how these brands attained their enviable position? In his chapter, "Can Products and Brands Have Charisma?" Smothers draws on the sociological literature to develop the implications of this unique concept.

Blackston, on the other hand, is concerned that brand personality alone does not adequately explain the interaction of people with brands. For example, he notes that those who like a brand and those who do not often describe a brand's personality in much the same terms. This led him to develop the concept of *brand relationships*, which he explores in "Beyond Brand Personality: Building Brand Relationships." Specifically, Blackston advocates a very different perspective on brand relationships, going beyond asking consumers to describe the personality of brands to determining what they believe that brands (as people) think of them. Blackston, who won the coveted British Market Research Society prize for a paper discussing this subject, argues that this concept helps to explain brand equity.

Whereas Smothers looks at brands through the lens of sociology, McCracken approaches brand equity from the anthropological viewpoint. His thesis is elegantly simple: Brands have value because they add value. In "The Value of the Brand: An Anthropological Perspective," the author focuses on the cultural meanings of brands: How do they get there and why are they important to consumers? A particularly interesting construct in McCracken's paper is the process he calls *meaning transfer*.

McCracken suggests that cultural meanings are constantly drawn from the general culture, transferred to brands and product categories by advertising, and then transferred from brands to consumers. Strong brands, he notes, are rich "storehouses of the meanings" that consumers use to define their actual and aspiration selves.

THE ROLE OF ADVERTISING
IN CREATING BRAND EQUITY

Advertising, along with personal experience, is an undeniable force majeure in creating brand equity. But how, exactly, does advertising impact equity? What is the mechanism involved? Biel notes that advertising drives brand equity by creating or enhancing brand image. The chapters in this section represent the latest, best thinking on how advertising contributes to equity.

In Aaker's *Managing Brand Equity* (1991), one of the four dimensions of equity is perceived quality. Work by The Ogilvy Center using the Profit Impact of Market Strategy (PIMS) data base suggests that advertising affects profits by amplifying a brand's relative perceived quality. In turn, perhaps the most robust of all PIMS findings is the clear relationship between quality and ROI.

Kirmani and Zeithaml, in "Advertising, Perceived Quality, and Brand Image," develop a model of perceived quality while exploring the relationship between intrinsic and extrinsic cues, and how they relate to perceived value. Of particular interest is their conceptualization of perceived value as the contrast of what is received compared to the cost in both monetary and nonmonetary terms.

The conventional U.S.-originated conceptualization of advertising is expressed in terms of its effect on consumers. But Lannon, one of the most prolific writers on this topic in the United Kingdom, turns this idea upside down. "What do consumers do with advertising?" she asks. In her contribution to this volume, "Asking the Right Questions," Lannon shows that these two essentially different models produce very different kinds of advertising.

Lannon argues that advertising styles depend not only on the intuitive choice of models, but also on the evolution of advertising style. Utilizing a semiological approach, Lannon describes the evolution of advertising styles in developed markets from what she calls "the manufacturer speaks" to "the brand creates its own language code."

In "Expansion Advertising and Brand Equity," Wansink and Ray examine advertising's ability to increase the frequency of usage for an established brand. However, encouraging frequency of use is not without its risks. For example, advertising encouraging people to eat Campbell's soup at breakfast, an inappropriate time, could evoke negative overall attitudes toward the brand. Experimental data on two alternative approaches to extending use contexts is reported, one using a situation-specific frame, the other a product-specific frame. Each has a place, the authors argue, but the conditions favoring each vary.

Edell and Moore, in their chapter on "Impact and Memorability of Ad-Induced Feelings: Implications for Brand Equity," demonstrate that the feelings induced by advertising exposure are stored in memory as part of the ad trace. In addition, the authors show that ad-induced feelings and brand claims are equally well recalled. Importantly, the ability to retrieve these feelings can be facilitated with a number of different retrieval cues.

Krishnan and Chakravarti, in "Varieties of Brand Memory Induced by Advertising: Determinants, Measures, and Relationships," are interested in how memory is created. In particular, they focus upon implicit memory, where the consumer is unaware of the role of advertising in affecting memory even though it has an impact. After reviewing several theoretical bases for the phenomenon, they discuss how it might be measured using indirect tests.

PERSPECTIVES ON BRAND EQUITY

This section contains three very different perspectives on brand equity that provide new insight into the construct.

Efforts to measure brand equity are often based on survey data in which consumers were asked to appraise brand names. In the first selection of this section, McQueen, Foley, and Deighton, a practitioner/academic research team, take a very different approach.

Their chapter, "Decomposing a Brand's Customer Franchise into Buyer Types," is based on behavioral rather than survey evidence. As their title suggests, they categorize people into five unique buyer types on the basis of brand purchase behavior over time. For example, one group buys only one brand consistently; another chases deals. The authors argue that identifying and understanding these buyer types can help the marketing manager develop strategies. They also suggest that segmenting by purchase pattern will result in very different calculations of lifetime value of customers and will provide leverage in allocating marketing assets.

In their wide-ranging chapter titled "Cognitive Strength of Established Brands: Memory, Attitudinal, and Structural Approaches," Haugtvedt and his co-authors Leavitt and Schneier suggest that managers are not well served by their overreliance on primitive measures of brand strength. They review a variety of supplementary measures to help explain strong brands. The authors suggest that not all strong brands are alike. Some have a simplex structure; others have a structure they characterize as multiplex.

Haugtvedt, Leavitt, and Schneier point out that a simplex structure may be easier to achieve, but ultimately more vulnerable to competitive attack or, even worse, gradual changes in how the product category is used. A strong brand with a multiplex structure, however, although harder to build initially, is less likely to be susceptible to competitive attack.

Understanding and managing brand associations are at the heart of brand equity. Farquhar and Herr note that it can be important to consider the direction of the associative links. The ability of a brand to suggest an association (such as a product class, user, or attribute) may be very different from the ability of an association to stimulate a person to think of a brand. The authors discuss ways to measure the strength of these links and show how the concept of a directional link can be useful for building brand strength and determining how to extend a brand.

PERSPECTIVES ON BRAND EXTENSIONS

Because new brands are expensive to create and cannot guarantee success, brand extension has become the strategy of choice with increasing frequency. It is no surprise, therefore, that a number of contributions to this volume focus on extending currently successful brands.

In the chapter by Nakamoto, MacInnis, and Jung, "Advertising Claims and Evidence as Bases for Brand Equity and Consumer Evaluation of Brand Extensions," the authors speculate, based on an experiment, that when the strength of the original brand is based on the specific attributes of the brand, any transfer of equity to a new product is likely to be successful but limited to products in adjacent fields that share common attributes. However, the authors also find that when the parent brand's equity is based on a general or an overarching characteristic such as quality, it is easier to extend the brand to a wide range of disparate categories.

In "Brands As Categories," Boush raises the novel idea of considering brands as categories. Although he proposes this new paradigm to supplement rather than replace the more conventional notion of product category, Boush makes an intriguing argument for the value of a paradigm shift. His chapter shows an interesting relationship to Tauber's idea of leverage, which follows.

Although others have argued that advertising is often the most important contributor to brand image, it is interesting to note that one of the world's strongest brands, as shown by Owen (chapter 2), is Sony. Yet Sony has historically been a low spender in advertising. One possible explanation for this exception may have to do with Sony's new product strategy: By expanding into closely adjacent fields, the brand's new products have clearly leveraged Sony's expanding concentric circles of expertise.

This observation is particularly interesting in light of Tauber's discussion in his piece entitled "Fit and Leverage in Brand Extensions." Tauber argues that leverage is a greater consideration than fit in building successful extensions and implies that a brand with broad fit potential is likely to have little to offer in the way of leverage. He suggests that a brand that fits many categories well is usually deficient because it brings little or no leverage to the party. He argues that too often marketers chase fit at the expense of leverage. Noting that they are somewhat inversely correlated, he suggests that marketers and researchers would be well advised to work at understanding the meaning of the established brand and then to seek situations where a unique image offers leveragable potential.

CASE STUDIES

Two chapters provide case studies that illustrate the actual brand strategies and their result. Winters provides another of his series of in-depth case studies of brand advertising in his chapter "The Role of Corporate Advertising in Building a Brand." In this case, he details how Chevron built a corporate name in Texas, to be used as a platform for a brand launch. The story is complete with campaign selection and postcampaign tracking.

Aaker, in "Are Brand Equity Investments Really Worthwhile?" discusses the short-term pressures that inhibit investments in brands. He describes a series of four case studies to illustrate how brand management decisions can dramatically affect the fortunes of a brand and can actually result in large changes in shareholder wealth. The cases involve the Datsun-to-Nissan name change, the lack of customer support at WordStar, the vision of Weight Watchers, and the fall of Schlitz beer caused by a change in ingredients and process.

A COMMENTARY FROM BILL WELLS

It is always a treat to have Bill Wells (long-time DDB Needham advertising strategist, now a University of Minnesota professor) provide his insight. We are pleased to have his commentary provide the capstone to the book. He observes that, like the blind men interpreting an elephant by feeling different parts, marketers too often generalize from an atypical segment. He suggests that the thoughtful use of the right taxonomy will reduce the problem. Seven such taxonomies are proposed and discussed. For example, potential customers and brand-loyal customers can be very different from the total population; salience and trust are very different characteristics of personalities used in advertising. In this final chapter, Wells refers to many other chapters in the book, positioning them in a larger context and adding insight to their message.

REFERENCE

Aaker, D. A. (1991). *Managing brand equity*. New York: The Free Press.

A Global View
on Building Brands

The Landor ImagePower Survey®: A Global Assessment of Brand Strength

Stewart Owen
Vice Chairman, Landor Associates

Discussions of brands and branding have become increasingly common in recent years. The subject weighs heavily on the minds of managers and executives in corporations, agencies, and consulting firms around the world. A subject that was traditionally the province of brand managers in a few major packaged goods firms has become of central concern to everyone in the business community.

Not surprisingly, an avalanche of speeches, books, seminars, corporate task forces, articles, and conferences has focused on the dos and don'ts of effective branding. Interest in the topic is intense, but much of the information fueling the discussion has been anecdotal, and the heros of one season's books quickly become the goats of the next.

Given this, we develop a true branding database. Our objectives for the database are clear: We want to evaluate the strength of brands around the world, across categories, and over time. Our objective is to answer such questions as: "Which are the strongest brands in this category?" or "in that market?"; and "Which brands are gaining in strength?" "Losing strength?" The Landor ImagePower Study® was conducted in 1988 and 1990 as the first step to developing just such a database.

WHY WE CONDUCTED THE STUDY

Our objectives necessitated a novel methodological approach. Normally, companies, products, and services are all evaluated within very narrow parameters. A given company is tested within the context of its direct competitors and among its target customers. The questions asked about the company generally focus very specifically on the attributes and features which are considered important to success in that particular category.

Obviously, these kinds of research studies are important and critical for companies to conduct. However, they would not have provided the kind of information we wanted. Interestingly enough, they do not always provide all of the information that is important to the management of many of our clients. What has changed?

New Threats

Traditionally, each product category and each geographic market in the world operated as a self-contained universe. Detergent marketers worried about and competed with other detergent brands; German companies competed primarily with other German companies or, at most, other Europeans. Increasingly, however, companies have found themselves under attack from brands and companies which began in other markets around the world or in product categories other than their own.

Manufacturing Efficiencies

The need to maximize economic and marketing efficiencies has begun to push many companies toward a more global competitive stance.

Brand Extension

The ever-increasing expense of brand creation, coupled with the rising failure rate of new product introductions, has caused companies to try to maximize the value of their existing brands through line extensions, good–better–best systems, brand/subbrand relationships, and so on.

Merger, Acquisitions, and Joint Ventures

The merger and acquisition fever of the 1980s spurred many companies toward the need to better understand the value of their current brand properties, as well as the value of existing merger/acquisition candidates. The increasing occurrence of joint ventures has also resulted in linking brand names that traditionally would never have been linked.

Ineffectiveness of Traditional Media

The increasing communications clutter and fragmentation of media channels have resulted in a consequent degradation of communications effectiveness. This loss in effectiveness means that, more and more, all brands are now competing against all other brands for share of mind among consumers.

Lack of True Product Differentiation

The difficulty of achieving and then maintaining real technological/product advantage means that even companies outside of the traditional packaged goods arena have begun to look to other means of product differentiation.

Need For Consumer Pull

In the past, many companies have not felt a need for consumer pull, perhaps because they marketed only within narrow business-to-business channels, sold on price, OEMd to others, or manufactured and developed products which existed only as an element in someone else's finished goods. In recent years, many of these companies have begun to feel the need to move "up the food chain" and have realized the corresponding need for consumer pull. Even those companies with no intention of selling to the general public have begun to realize the value of having a positive image among the community at large.

Changing Spending Mix

Pressures on advertising budgets and the increasing role of trade and consumer promotions have weakened many traditional brand loyalties. Companies caught in this high-pressure double bind have begun to look for new, nontraditional means of building brand image.

All of these pressures and changes in the marketplace have created an interest in a broader evaluation of brands than that offered by traditional research studies.

The Landor ImagePower Survey® was conducted in 1990 to measure the strength of more than 6,000 consumer and corporate brands in 14 countries around the world. Its comprehensive coverage of industries and markets and the resulting ImagePower® rankings provide a broad perspective on branding and the importance of managing brand equity consistently over time.

HOW WE MEASURED BRAND STRENGTH

The elements that make up brand strength are complex and multifaceted. They are dependent on the category in which the brand operates, the culture and attitudes of the target audience, the competitive mix, and the positioning and functional attributes of the product and brand itself. Obviously, no general study can measure all of the elements that make up a brand's profile.

Given this, we made a conscious decision to develop the simplest and most elegant brand model possible. Like all general models, its simplicity means that some of the details seen in a more narrowly focused study are absent; in exchange, we offer many new and additional insights, made possible only with the juxtaposition of so many brands and markets.

The simple assumption behind the ImagePower Survey® is that in order to be powerful, a brand needs to be both well known and well regarded; that is, people must be familiar with the brand and must also feel good about it. Although both of these dimensions are undoubtedly the result of a myriad of individual factors, familiarity and esteem can best be seen as the ultimate result of effective management of a product's many individual product, service, and communications elements. The ImagePower® measure gives equal weight to both brand familiarity, measured by our Share of Mind (SOM) dimension, and positive brand regard, measured by our Esteem dimension. The total ImagePower® rank is then calculated by taking a simple average of a brand's Share of Mind and Esteem scores.

HOW THE SURVEY WAS CONDUCTED

To insure consistency of the data from market to market, we used an identical, self-administered questionnaire format in each of the 14 countries included in the research. The countries were chosen so that the world's largest "branded" markets could be represented. We focused on three primary regions: (a) The United States, (b) Japan, and (c) eight western European countries (Belgium, France, West Germany, Italy, the Netherlands, Spain, Sweden, and the United Kingdom) representing the European region.

In addition to these ten countries, we also conducted a limited version of the survey in some secondary markets, represented by Poland, Hungary, the USSR, and Hong Kong. Because these markets are not yet on a par with the markets represented by the three primary regions, their results are not included in the global rankings shown later in this chapter.

Because brands representing over 70 product categories were included in the survey, from high-end luxury products to mass-market discount retailers, a similarly broad sample of respondents was needed to accurately assess the power of each brand. We recruited a demographically representative sample of adults ages 18 to 65 across each of the 14 counties in which the survey was conducted.

The sample sizes varied from country to country according to the size of each country's brand list, yet each sample was large enough to allow the rankings to be divided by basic demographic breaks (sex, age, income, etc.). All fieldwork was conducted from February through August, 1990. Total sample structure is shown in Table 2.1.

Regardless of market, each respondent rated a total of 800 brands. A series of questionnaire rotations were used to increase the effective number of brands rated, so that in the United States, for example, a total of 2,000 brands were rated using this method. In some markets, the total number of brands rated was 800 or less, necessitating no rotation.

TABLE 2.1
Total Survey Sample Structure

	North America	Europe	Asia
Belgium	—	500	—
France	—	500	—
Hong Kong	—	—	200
Hungary	—	200	—
Italy	—	500	—
Japan	—	—	1,000
Netherlands	—	500	—
Poland	—	200	—
Soviet Union	—	200	—
Spain	—	500	—
Sweden	—	500	—
West Germany	—	500	—
United Kingdom	—	500	—
United States	5,000	—	—
	5,000	4,600	1,200

Each respondent rated brands along the two test measures—Share of Mind and Esteem. The ratings were conducted using five-point scales and a multistep question process. These ratings were then used to generate a composite score for each brand on Share of Mind and Esteem; the two scores were then averaged to create the ImagePower® Score. These three scores were then ranked independently to create the rankings used for all of the brand analysis.

Total number of brands evaluated in each market were as shown in Table 2.2.

TABLE 2.2
Total Number of Brands Evaluated

	Number of Brands
Belgium	800
France	1,421
Hong Kong	400
Hungary	400
Italy	1,024
Japan	800
Netherlands	800
Poland	400
Soviet Union	400
Spain	935
Sweden	798
West Germany	1,127
United Kingdom	1,600
United States	2,000

FACTORS INFLUENCING BRAND STRENGTH

Table 2.3 shows the ImagePower®, Share of Mind, and Esteem rankings for
the top 25 brands in the United States, Europe, Japan, and the world.

The brand names you might have expected to do well in a survey of this
kind, generally did well. However, the rankings often resulted in real surprises,
with a few seemingly humble brands coming in high on the lists and a corresponding range of major marketers with relatively weak performances.

Upon closer examination, there were several key factors shared by the high-
ranking brands, regardless of their having a luxury or mass-market positioning. Many strong brands did not share every one of the factors listed, but they
serve to characterize and differentiate the stronger name from the weaker ones.

None of these factors, taken in isolation, can be considered a new finding,
but careful attention to maintaining these brand characteristics, as a group,
is crucial to a brand's continuing success. Specifically, we consider the following factors to have the most influence on the ImagePower® of a brand:

Longevity.   Being around for a long time helps. Being the first to enter a
category is even better. Many of the brands occupying positions in the top
100 in a given market have been there for 25 to 50 years, or even longer. Brand
equity, just like financial equity, is built up over time. Brands that have maintained a consistent presence over the years are better able to utilize the familiarity and understanding a customer has with their products to build momentum
and power. Brands such as Coca-Cola, Levi's, GE, Betty Crocker, and so on
have such a long history that the brands have become a part of American culture as well as commercial symbols. Given the incredible cost of media today,
building a new brand is a difficult and problematic process. The lesson is clear:
Brand strength is a long-term investment. First, build and protect the strong
brands you already have.

Product Category.   Some product categories are simply more involving than
others. They tend to create higher awareness of the offerings and often higher
esteem. Thus, a brand's product or service category can be a great help or
hindrance in its overall ImagePower® rating and is particularly important in
determining the relationship between its Share of Mind and Esteem rankings.
Brands in categories such as entertainment, food, soft drinks, and automobiles all tend, as a group, to be ranked highly. As a result, examining an individual brand's performance should always include a consideration for whether
the brand over or underperforms its category.

Quality.   Although this factor may seem obvious, this study reminds us
that quality and reliability are at the base of every brand's credibility with the
public. Whatever else a company or product stands for, it must first "do what

TABLE 2.3
Top 25 Brands in the United States, Europe, Japan, and Worldwide

	United States Brand	US SOM	US Esteem	Europe Brand	EU SOM	EU Esteem	Japan Brand	JP SOM	JP Esteem	World Brand	W SOM	W Esteem
1	Coca-Cola	1	5	Coca-Cola	1	10	Sony	1	4	Coca-Cola	1	6
2	Campbell's	6	1	Sony	3	1	National	4	9	Sony	4	1
3	Disney	10	2	Mercedes-Benz	8	3	Mercedes-Benz	50	2	Mercedes-Benz	12	2
4	Pepsi-Cola	4	11	BMW	11	2	Toyota	9	18	Kodak	5	9
5	Kodak	8	4	Philips	2	6	Takashimaya	5	25	Disney	8	5
6	NBC	3	16	Volkswagen	4	7	Rolls Royce	100	1	Nestlé	7	14
7	Black & Decker	15	3	Adidas	6	9	Seiko	21	14	Toyota	6	23
8	Kellogg's	9	7	Kodak	7	8	Matsushita	18	20	McDonald's	2	85
9	McDonald's	2	84	Nivea	5	14	Hitachi	6	44	IBM	20	4
10	Hershey's	22	6	Porsche	18	4	Suntory	8	42	Pepsi-Cola	3	92
11	Levi's	18	10	Volvo	16	12	Porsche	118	3	Rolls Royce	23	3
12	GE	14	14	Colgate	9	24	Kirin	17	32	Honda	9	22
13	Sears	5	79	Rolls Royce	28	5	Hotel New Otani	78	8	Panasonic	17	10
14	Hallmark	32	9	Levi's	21	13	Fuji TV	7	81	Levi's	16	8
15	Johnson & Johnson	35	8	Ford	15	31	Snow Brand Milk	19	45	Kleenex	13	16
16	Betty Crocker	26	12	Jaguar	38	11	Imperial Hotel	109	7	Ford	10	24
17	Kraft	24	13	Fanta	10	51	Coca-Cola/Coke	3	119	Volkswagen	11	26
18	Kleenex	20	19	Nescafé	13	56	Mitsukoshi	20	48	Kellogg's	14	30
19	Jell-O	16	26	Black & Decker	25	20	Japan Travel Bureau	13	63	Porsche	27	11
20	Tylenol	28	18	Esso	17	42	Disney	55	19	Polaroid	15	44
21	AT&T	12	62	Michelin	29	21	Aunomoto	12	74	BMW	32	12
22	Crest	31	28	Lego	41	15	Kikkoman	14	70	Colgate	21	51
23	Duracell	39	20	Bosch	43	16	All-Nippon-Airlines	28	49	Seiko	33	15
24	IBM	46	17	Peugeot	19	50	Honda	30	50	Nescafé	19	64
25	Fruit of the Loom	25	41	Audi	36	22	Yamaha	38	34	Canon	35	17

it is supposed to do.'' It should be noted, however, that quality is not necessarily synonymous with luxury. Some prestige products such as Mercedes-Benz and Rolex did rank high on the list, whereas other luxury brands like Cadillac and Yves St. Laurent did not do very well. Many nonprestige brands like Windex and Jell-O actually outperformed these venerable names. In the context of the survey results, quality can best be expressed in terms of the ability of a product to meet customer's expectations consistently over time. This is demonstrated by the extraordinarily high U.S. rankings given to such basic brands as Campbell's and Black & Decker. Again, the lesson is clear; there is no substitute for performance.

Media Support.   The brands ranked highest in Share of Mind generally spend the money to make sure they stay visible. Visibility in itself, apart from media dollars, also plays a large part in strong Share of Mind rankings. A brand such as McDonald's, with its retail ubiquity, gains visibility through a strongly branded physical location in addition to its massive advertising budget. Of course, some brands with large advertising budgets (e.g., Burger King, Oldsmobile) did not do well and others with miniscule spending came out high on the lists (e.g., Rolls Royce, Windex). But in general, the message is again clear, brands must be supported over time to remain strong.

Personality and Imagery.   Ideally, a brand should do more than just identify the product. Many of the most powerful brands in the survey have clear enough images to become almost synonymous with their product category, or are able to differentiate their offering on the basis of the brand name alone. Brands such as Kleenex, Hallmark, and Levi's are good examples of defining the category on their own; Disney manages to brand a form of entertainment. For example, it is reasonably easy to define the target audience for a Disney movie and what characteristics it might have, regardless of the actual title of the film. Can the same be said of Warner Brothers, Paramount, or Universal? Strong brands usually stand for something in the minds of consumers.

Continuity.   Even if a brand has not been around for 100 years, a sense of heritage or continuity is necessary for a brand to have relevance from one year to the next. The key here is continuity of message, not sameness of execution. We can see examples of strong message continuity in how McDonald's evolves its advertising slogans from one campaign to the next; each theme is executed toward a range of customer targets around a single core message—and that message does not change radically from year to year. This has produced a clear image over the years of what McDonald's represents, and clarity of image helps to produce a strong brand.

Renewal.   The opposite side of the coin is also true. Strong brands must constantly renew themselves, making themselves relevant to each new generation of consumers. The study is replete with once great brand names that failed to renew themselves (e.g., Lucky Strike, Bell & Howell, Philco). To a new generation of consumers, these once great names now mean very little.

Efficiency.   Companies that operate in a wide variety of product categories have several options for branding their product families. Those that take the umbrella branding approach, endorsing a variety of individual brands under a parent or "super brand," generally rank higher in ImagePower® than those that take a strictly stand-alone brand approach. Both are certainly viable marketing plans, but it appears that brands such as Kraft, Johnson & Johnson, and Nabisco successfully funnel the impressions of dozens of individual brands (e.g., Philadelphia Cream Cheese, Tylenol, or Oreo) toward a common source, the parent brand. This is an extremely powerful means of creating leverage, either in extensions of existing brands or to enter new product categories via the parent brand's established credibility. In a marketplace where brand clutter and pressures on advertising budgets have worked together to make efficient communications difficult, the ImagePower® study suggests that focusing marketing dollars on fewer rather than more brands is probably the most effective way to go.

THE WORLD'S MOST POWERFUL BRANDS

Table 2.3 shows the 25 brands that ranked highest in Global ImagePower®, combining the three major regions included in the survey. Coca-Cola was the strongest brand in the world in ImagePower, just as it was in the 1988 pilot version of the survey. Interestingly, no single market or product category can be said to dominate the list. There are American, Japanese, and European names among the top ten. The list includes electronics, computers, and automobiles, but also soft drinks, fast food, film, and chocolate.

The list includes brands from all markets, but twelve of the top 25 names are American. Considering the top 100 (shown in the Appendix), or 200 brands globally (not shown), roughly half of the list is American. Despite this continued strength in world markets, the international performance of many American brands seems to be based more on Share of Mind (SOM) than on Esteem. Perhaps this SOM strength is a result of the U.S. marketers' early focus on global markets.

The two brands near the top that showed the greatest increase between our 1988 pilot and 1990 were Sony and Disney. Each of these has dramatically increased its presence in Europe over the last few years. Equally interesting is IBM, a company that, for most of its history, has sold nothing to the general public. Despite that, the strength and clarity of its historic image and culture have created one of the world's strongest brand names.

There were a number of similarities among the U.S., European, and Japanese results. Brands such as Coca-Cola, Sony, Disney, McDonald's, Levi's, Kodak, and Mercedes-Benz did well outside their home markets. In all three areas, the local television networks did well (the NBCs, CBSs, Fuji TVs, NHKs, and BBCs of the world). In the United States and throughout Europe, the leading chocolate marketers performed well (e.g., Hershey's, Cadbury, Nestlé, Marabou). We suspect that chocolate has become the world's most acceptable indulgence.

Strongest Brands in the United States

The higher ranks of the American brand list are populated largely with a broad range of basic, no-nonsense consumer products that appeal to a wide range of consumers. This love affair with the everyday products of the commercial world appears to be peculiarly American; the results in Europe and Japan are quite different. The top 25 U.S. brands are shown in Table 2.3.

When we look at the source of strong U.S. brands, the results may be surprising. The overwhelming number of strong brands are American in origin, with only automotives, electronics, and a few luxury brands offering many non-U.S. names. The highest ranking Japanese brand is Sony at 37, followed by Panasonic at 55, Toyota at 83, and Minolta at 223. The highest ranking European brand is Nestle at 30, followed by Mercedes-Benz at 106, and Rolls Royce at 189. There may be a substantial segment of "buy American" U.S. respondents who prevent foreign brands, especially Japanese brands like Toyota, from being ranked high on Esteem.

There can be substantial differences across segments such as age. Table 2.4 shows the differences in the ImagePower® rankings by age. Note that Disney, McDonald's, Levi's, and Tylenol have their strength among the young. In contrast, Black & Decker, GE, Sears, and Jell-O are very strong among the older group and much less so among the young; perhaps this is a bad omen for the future.

Despite the ongoing homogenization of tastes and culture across the United States, regional brand differences were still alive and well. An extreme example of such a variation was Wal-Mart, which was the 2nd strongest brand in the study in its home West–South Central Region and was not even among the top 200 brands in the U.S. rankings. Another is Crest, 22nd in the U.S. rankings, which was in the top 10 in the Middle Atlantic, West–South Central, and New England regions. Still another was Chevrolet, only 26th in the U.S. rankings, but among the top 10 in the East–South Central rankings.

In general, the results among men and women are quite similar. However, when we isolate only those brands that are ranked quite differently between

TABLE 2.4
Top 25 U.S. Brands, by Age of Consumer

	Brand	18–29	30–39	40–49	50–59	60 +	Baby Boomers
1.	Coca-Cola	1	2	1	2	2	2
2.	Campbell's	2	3	2	1	1	3
3.	Disney	6	1	4	9	12	1
4.	Pepsi-Cola	4	4	3	4	7	5
5.	Kodak	5	5	5	5	15	4
6.	NBC	7	8	7	7	6	7
7.	Black & Decker	10	10	6	3	3	13
8.	Kellogg's	15	7	9	6	8	11
9.	McDonald's	3	6	10	16	17	12
10.	Hershey's	13	12	11	8	22	10
11.	Levi's	8	11	8	25	48	8
12.	GE	33	20	13	10	4	15
13.	Sears	19	17	14	11	5	31
14.	Hallmark	21	25	15	13	18	17
15.	Johnson & Johnson	16	15	22	18	27	18
16.	Betty Crocker	14	14	21	21	25	22
17.	Kraft	18	16	17	19	62	24
18.	Kleenex	29	22	20	14	13	23
19.	Jell-O	30	24	19	12	14	30
20.	Tylenol	9	18	24	24	42	20
21.	AT&T	43	36	31	28	21	27
22.	Crest	11	9	12	20	19	6
23.	Duracell	27	26	28	41	43	36
24.	IBM	40	29	30	42	69	9
25.	Fruit of the Loom	26	30	25	32	26	46

genders, a dramatic and interesting pattern emerges. The female-only brands are all personal care products and are consistently focused on adornment. They include L'Oreal, New Freedom, Sure & Natural, 9 West, Almay, Clinique, Bali, Cover Girl, and Naturalizer. The male-only brands revolve around sex, sports, and violence, what might be called the testosterone effect. They include Playboy, Fram, Motorcraft, Louisville Slugger, Smith & Wesson, Winchester, Briggs & Stratton, Buck Knives, and NFL.

As we reviewed the data, we found that a number of brands were highly controversial; their Esteem rankings were far below their Share of Mind rankings. Generally, these brands received low Esteem rankings because of very bipolar responses, with some people positively disposed toward the brand but others very negatively disposed. Fast-food restaurants and automobiles were notable entries in this category. Consider the relative rankings of fast-food and automobile brands as shown in Table 2.5.

A similar finding for fast foods appeared in Europe and Japan, but automobiles generally garnered higher esteem ratings in both Europe and Japan.

TABLE 2.5
Ranking of Fast Food and Automobile Brands

Brand	ImagePower	Share of Mind	Esteem
McDonald's	9	2	84
Burger King	43	11	170
Pizza Hut	77	34	190
Kentucky Fried Chicken	82	17	325
Chevrolet	26	7	107
General Motors	36	13	116
Ford	64	21	205
Toyota	83	41	178

The group of high Share of Mind and low Esteem brands included cigarette brands, such as Marlboro, Winston, Benson & Hedges, and Camel, and alcoholic beverage brands such as Pabst, Old Milwaukee, Schlitz, Colt 45, and Jack Daniels. Other brands in this category included Playboy, National Enquirer, Exxon, National Rifle Association, Amway, Jane Fonda Workout, Mary Kay, MTV, U.S. Sprint, The Emmy Awards, No Doz, Nutri System, and the World Wrestling Federation.

There was also a set of brands for which Esteem was much higher than Share of Mind. These included Disney, Black & Decker, Hershey's, Hallmark, Johnson & Johnson, IBM, Fisher Price, Crayola, National Geographic, Sesame Street, Maytag, WD-40, Mercedes-Benz, and 3M. In general, categories such as luxury goods, toys, and baked goods all tended to have higher Esteem responses than Share of Mind.

In the United States, the relationship between Share of Mind and Esteem scores is also quite different than in much of the rest of the world. In the United States, Share of Mind and Esteem are highly correlated. For example, among the top ten Share of Mind brands, five are also top ten in Esteem—Coca-Cola, Campbell's, Disney, Kodak, and Kellogg's. The results for individual European countries and the Japanese show far greater independence between Share of Mind and Esteem.

Strongest Brands in Western Europe

The top 25 brand list in Europe is quite different from the American list. Both include Coca-Cola and Kodak, but the Europeans also include eight automotive companies (Mercedes-Benz, BMW, Volkswagen, Porsche, Volvo, Rolls Royce, and Ford) and two electronics manufacturers (Sony and Philips). The Americans include no companies from either category.

Although this may indicate some differences in interests and values among Europeans, it is probably driven as much by historic marketing patterns. Automotive and electronics companies were among the first manufacturers to market pan-Europe rather than to a single home market. In fact, outside of the automotive category, American and Japanese brands appear to have a real advantage in developing European-wide brands. Slightly more than half of the top 100 pan-European brands turned out to be American or Japanese in origin. Again, this is probably the result of the American and Japanese focus on all of Europe rather than on a single "home market."

The strongest foreign brands across Europe again resulted in the same global names. The top U.S. brands were Coca-Cola (1), Kodak (8), Colgate (12), Levi's (14), Ford (15), and Fanta (17). Interestingly, the American brand Fanta did much better in Europe than it did in the States. In Europe, Fanta has become one of the major soft drink brands, although it remains a minor player in its home market. The Japanese brands were not as established in Europe as the U.S. brands—the top Japanese brands were Sony (1), Honda (32), Toyota (37), Canon (51), and Yamaha (52).

Age, again, makes a difference. For example, among those 40 years of age or older, the single strongest pan-European brand was the Dutch electronics manufacturer Philips. Among those under 40 years of age, the strongest brand was the Japanese electronics firm Sony. The results may be indicative of a longer term changing of the high technology guard. With respect to automobiles, the older group favored Mercedes-Benz and Volkswagen; the younger group rated BMW higher.

When we look at the results within individual European countries as shown by Tables 2.6a and 2.6b, the results are quite different from those for Europe as a whole. Among the major countries (France, United Kingdom, Germany, Italy, Spain, and Sweden), the top of the lists are dominated by local brands (i.e., the number one brand in Germany is Mercedes-Benz; in the United Kingdom, it is Marks and Spencer; and in France it is EDF-GDF). The specter of common European-wide brands does not emerge in Tables 2.6a and 2.6b. In fact, there are few brands that appear among the strongest brands across Europe. Sony and Kodak may be the exceptions, but neither is among the top 25 brands in Germany or Sweden. Coca-Cola is another, but it is missing in France and Germany. Is the concept of strong European-wide brands a myth or simply still around the corner?

Strongest Brands in the Soviet Union and Eastern Europe

A shorter version of the survey was used in Poland and the Soviet Union just before the Eastern Bloc alliances began their collapse and realignment. Thus, an opportunity to measure the strength of 400 major brands in a premarket environment—an environment in which brands generally did not exist; or where they already existed—was not readily available. The results are shown in Table 2.6a.

TABLE 2.6a
Top 25 Brands in Spain, Sweden, Poland, and USSR

	Spain			Sweden			Poland			USSR		
	Brand	SOM	Esteem	Brand	SOM	Esteem	Brand	SOM	Esteem	Brand	SOM	Esteem
1	Sony	6	1	Volvo	1	1	Sony	1	1	Sony	5	1
2	Nescafé	4	7	Ikea	2	3	Volvo	7	2	Adidas	4	4
3	Cola Cao	5	6	ICA	4	7	Mercedes-Benz	10	3	Ford	7	3
4	Nestlé	8	3	Marabou	8	5	Adidas	3	9	Toyota	13	2
5	Coca-Cola/Coke	2	15	SAS	5	9	Toyota	5	7	Mercedes-Benz	6	6
6	La Casera	1	28	Wasabröd	10	6	Ford	4	10	Fanta	2	11
7	El Corte Ingles	3	20	Orrefors	25	2	BMW	17	4	Pepsi-Cola	3	12
8	Mercedes-Benz	34	4	Electrolux	14	10	Philips	15	8	Volvo	15	5
9	Bimbo	18	22	Kosta Boda	34	4	Porsche	20	5	Fiat	16	7
10	BMW	60	5	Coca-Cola/Coke	9	26	Honda	14	11	Panasonic	18	8
11	Aspirina Bayer	23	14	Lego	28	11	Sanyo	8	15	Sharp	17	10
12	Levi's	38	10	Husqvarna	23	15	Panasonic	19	12	Marlboro	8	14
13	Adidas	31	11	Findus	17	29	Opel	12	16	Christian Dior	19	9
14	Philips	22	27	Gevalia	21	18	Volkswagen	13	17	Coca-Cola	9	16
15	Nivea	14	46	Hennes & Mauritz	6	71	Rolls Royce	27	6	Aeroflot	1	35
16	Sanyo	25	24	Nivea	24	19	Kodak	22	13	McDonald's	12	17
17	Fanta	7	112	Colgate	22	24	Coca-Cola	9	26	BBC	14	19
18	Volkswagen	36	18	Adidas	27	16	Lego	23	14	Stolichnaya	10	20
19	Porsche	75	8	Mercedes-Benz	47	13	Pepsi-Cola	6	34	Boeing	20	15
20	Fontaneda	26	29	Bregott	19	40	Nivea	21	22	Chanel	22	13
21	Kodak	27	25	Philips	30	20	Boeing	24	18	Zenith	11	29
22	Renault	20	39	Rörstrand	78	8	Fiat	2	56	Puma	21	18
23	Rolls Royce	119	2	Pripps	13	63	Audi	26	19	Disney	24	21
24	Colgate	17	52	Kungsörnen	32	23	Marlboro	11	47	Levi's	23	27
25	Bayer	54	17	Melitta	31	32	Wrangler	16	39	Philips	25	22

TABLE 2.6b
Top 25 Brands in the UK, France, Germany, and Italy

	United Kingdom			France			Germany			Italy		
	Brand	SOM	Rank Esteem	Brand	SOM	Rank Esteem	Brand	SOM	Rank Esteem	Brand	SOM	Rank Esteem
1	Marks & Spencer	2	1	EDF-GDF	1	1	Mercedes-Benz	2	1	Sony	5	1
2	Kellogg's	4	2	Antenne 2	3	4	Volkswagen	4	5	Barilla	3	2
3	Cadbury	5	3	Vittel	4	5	Bosch	7	2	Fiat	1	11
4	BBC	1	8	SNCF	2	6	ZDF	1	12	Mulino Bianco	16	5
5	Nescafé	3	9	La Poste	11	3	BMW	9	4	Canale 5	2	33
6	Heinz	9	4	Sony	20	2	Siemens	8	7	Kodak	20	6
7	Boots	10	7	Peugeot	8	8	ARD	3	11	Bic	6	23
8	Mc Vites	11	5	TF1	5	18	Aldi	5	10	Algida	11	14
9	Yellow Pages	8	14	Philips	17	9	AEG	6	9	Yomo	17	12
10	W.H. Smith	17	11	Evian	12	15	Adidas	10	6	Fanta	4	30
11	Sony	25	10	Orangina	6	29	Daimler Benz	15	3	Volkswagen	25	8
12	Duracell	29	12	FR3	9	24	Langnese	23	8	BMW	39	4
13	Rolls Royce	62	6	Renault	18	14	Nivea	11	14	Coca-Cola/Coke	7	44
14	Kit Kat	14	24	Bic	7	35	Oetker	12	15	Lancia	30	10
15	Kodak	24	17	France Telecom	21	10	UHU	16	17	Olivetti	24	13
16	Dulux	31	13	Larousse	39	7	Eduscho	25	18	Ferrari	45	3
17	Persil	16	25	Lesieur	10	33	Grundig	37	16	RAI	9	43
18	Coca-Cola/Coke	7	48	Kodak	31	12	Lego	41	13	Ferrarelle	19	20
19	ITV	6	78	Yoplait	15	27	Tchibo	26	24	Perugina	13	29
20	Sainsbury's	21	26	Carrefour	13	32	Lufthansa	34	19	La Reppublica	18	25
21	Mars	15	33	Adidas	36	11	Dr. Oetker	21	30	Buitoni	27	19
22	Black & Decker	30	22	Danone	32	20	Miele	36	22	Alemagna	23	31
23	Hoover	23	28	Air France	33	19	Porsche	30	25	Alitalia	26	27
24	Ford	19	40	Leclerc	16	38	Milka	39	20	Porsche	56	7
25	Lego	66	15	Chambourcy	34	21	Sparkassen	18	43	Alfa Romeo	28	22

As might be expected, relatively fewer brands were recognized by the respondents in these countries. However, across all three markets an amazing number of brands were, in fact, known. Some of the known brands, like Pepsi-Cola, Adidas, and McDonald's, had some distribution in the Eastern Bloc. Others, like Marlboro and Levi's, were apparently available largely through the black market. Still others, like Sony, Panasonic, and Mercedes-Benz, are brands which we expect are rarely seen but highly aspirational. Finally, there are brands that are reasonably well known in Eastern Europe, like Honda and Toyota, for which we have no readily available answer. It is hard for us to believe that very many people have ever seen these products.

These results, we think, speak to the amazingly global nature of many of these major brands, which are now known even in countries in which they are not legally available. The results also speak to the tremendous pent-up demand that exists throughout the world for consumer goods and for the iconic value of success and plenty that brands have come to represent.

There were variations from country to country in brand-awareness levels. The Polish respondents were less familiar with brand names than Hungarians but more familiar than the USSR where the average respondent was aware of only about 25% of the list of 300 names. As awareness levels decreased, respect for American brands increased. This may be an ominous relationship with respect to the future of American brands in these new markets.

Those brands that did manage to register both Share of Mind and Esteem in these countries tended to be in the categories of automobiles, consumer electronics, and, interestingly enough, athletic shoes.

Strongest Brands in Japan

Results in Japan (Table 2.3) showed a number of differences from other markets as well as a number of similarities. As in the United States and Europe, Sony and Coca-Cola both performed very well. However, the top 20 list included an industrial company that does not even market under its own name, Matsushita. In general, corporations performed better in Japan than they did in the United States. The top 25 brands also include two hotels—the New Otani and the Imperial Hotel—as well as the country's major travel agency—the Japan Travel Bureau (JTB).

In addition, many of the traditional rules and limitations for branding do not apply in Japan, where huge trading companies (Mitsubishi, Suntory, Matsushita, among others) operate in dozens of product categories simultaneously under the exact same brand name. There are few corollaries in the west for such tremendous brand stretch. Of course, this also makes it more difficult to attribute a brand's strength to any single product or service.

Although the Japanese top 100 is dominated by Japanese brands (see Appendix and Table 2.3), there are a number of European and American brands that do perform well. In general, the high-performing European brands are luxury products like Mercedes-Benz (3), Rolls Royce (6), Porsche (11), Chanel (31), Rolex (35), and Pierre Cardin (47); the high-performing U.S. products sell Americana—Coca-Cola (17), Disney (20), Saran Wrap (28), Kentucky Fried Chicken (51), and McDonald's (69).

The Japanese fascination with European luxury products becomes particularly apparent when we look at the Esteem rankings, which are dominated by luxury brands from Europe. One wonders if this fascination with branded luxury will continue unabated as the Japanese become more confident about their place on the world stage.

WHAT WE HAVE LEARNED FROM THE IMAGEPOWER SURVEY®

In the beginning, it is always the company—the organization that creates, manufactures, and sells its products and services to the marketplace. Next comes the product—the physical reality, with its basic features, functions, and attributes, which defines and characterizes what the company is offering for sale. Then comes the long-term communications elements of the brand, or the brand identity, if you will—the positioning, names, symbols, colors, tag lines, and other long-term communications devices, which are created by the marketer to help define the offer. Finally come the short-term communications executions—the individual advertising campaigns, promotions, and so on, which fuel and build the brand over time.

Together, from the parent company to its individual communications executions these elements make up the life and the history of a given brand. Day by day, individual consumers are exposed to these brand manifestations, and taken in total, they create the perception each consumer has of that brand.

If we distill all of the lessons gathered from the ImagePower study, in the end the message is quite simple. Strong brands are the result of careful long-term management of every aspect of the product–consumer interaction. When there is message consistency from product attribute to packaging to advertising and so on, the chances of success are greatly increased. Successfully managing each of these steps is what brand strength is all about.

APPENDIX

TABLE 1
Top 26–100 Brands in United States, Europe, Japan, and Worldwide

	United States			Europe			Japan			World		
		Rank			Rank			Rank			Rank	
	Brand	SOM	Esteem	Brand	SOM	Esteem	Brand	SOM	Esteem	Brand	SOM	Esteem
26	Chevrolet	7	107	Gillette	24	40	Fujitsu	42	35	Sprite	18	87
27	M&M's	30	33	Renault	20	69	Toshiba	16	83	Jaguar	40	19
28	Colgate	23	45	Martini	22	66	Saran Wrap	44	41	Lipton	24	45
29	Nabisco	40	25	Ferrari	52	17	Nissan	37	52	Nissan	22	57
30	Nestlé	38	35	IBM	47	18	NTT	10	148	Yamaha	26	47
31	RCA	37	43	Nestlé	32	45	Chanel	143	11	Cadillac	30	33
32	Tide	33	53	Honda	31	47	Glico	15	127	Nike	45	25
33	Goodyear	36	47	Pepsi-Cola	12	144	Seibu	31	75	Shell	25	76
34	Lipton	45	36	Ajax	27	70	Bridgestone	69	36	Rolex	72	18
35	Quaker Oats	47	32	Opel	26	72	Rolex	178	5	Adidas	41	39
36	General Motors	13	116	Bic	40	48	Canon	82	30	Minolta	50	28
37	Sony	60	27	Toyota	33	77	Shiseido	27	102	Volvo	47	34
38	General Mills	55	29	Shell	35	68	Yakult	26	128	Gillette	38	32
39	7 Up	29	70	Duracell	54	27	CALPIS	25	134	Chevrolet	29	70
40	UPS	58	30	Christian Dior	57	25	Japan Airlines	45	80	Chanel	54	35
41	Philadelphia Cream Ch	52	38	Grundig	45	41	Fuji	87	46	Visa	31	52
42	Polaroid	43	54	Kellogg's	48	37	Nescafé	29	136	Ferrari	71	20
43	Burger King	11	170	Schweppes	42	54	NEC	71	64	Del Monte	44	46
44	Planters	63	37	Palmolive	34	85	Asahi Chemical Indust.	66	67	American Express	28	82
45	Sunkist	62	40	Alfa Romeo	44	53	Renown	81	58	Lego	79	13
46	Heinz	56	42	Lacoste	60	32	KAO	34	118	Christian Dior	62	42
47	Del Monte	69	34	Nike	71	19	Pierre Cardin	124	29	Sunkist	43	77
48	Reader's Digest	44	59	Braun	58	36	Volkswagen	134	27	Duracell	86	7
49	Fisher Price	116	15	Panasonic	56	39	Lion	33	123	Johnson & Johnson	48	73
50	Rubbermaid	99	21	Citroën	30	117	Wacoal	113	38	Audi	58	59

No.			Brand			Brand			Brand			Brand
51	77	31	Crayola	69	26	Canon	24	179	Kentucky Fried Chicken	82	38	Pioneer
52	103	22	National Geographic	46	62	Yamaha	104	55	Toto	94	29	Nikon
53	65	49	Q Tips	23	155	Fiat	2	447	NHK	52	72	Sharp
54	57	60	Crisco	39	93	Ariel	40	129	Sapporo	42	114	Mitsubishi
55	76	51	Panasonic	14	239	McDonald's	157	22	Hotel Okura	36	119	Mobil
56	19	171	Kmart	70	29	Chanel	112	53	Panasonic	39	160	7 Up
57	53	67	Lifesavers	55	65	Moulinex	65	91	Mizuno	34	162	Suzuki
58	74	61	Oreo's	91	23	Pioneer	51	107	Kuroneko Yamato	67	40	Goodyear
59	61	73	Windex	67	55	Disney	39	141	Morinaga Milk Indust.	69	58	Xerox
60	94	46	Pillsbury	62	61	BASF	190	13	Christian Dior	53	81	Bic
61	84	56	Sara Lee	51	91	Knorr	57	104	Nestlé	46	108	Mazda
62	141	23	Sesame Street	53	89	Mars	46	138	Kanebo	59	90	Hitachi
63	86	55	Minute Maid	68	60	Kleenex	56	110	Sumitomo Bank	99	31	Harley Davidson
64	21	205	Ford	61	86	Heineken	62	105	Dai-ichi Kangyo Bank	83	49	Hilton
65	27	165	MasterCard	50	108	Polaroid	48	139	Meiji Milk Products	55	67	General Motors
66	101	48	Birdseye	65	80	BBC	88	85	Nintendo	63	83	Fuji
67	151	24	Maytag	84	44	Bennetton	119	60	Crown	56	93	Scotch
68	71	75	Gillette	49	122	Lux	63	113	Mitsubishi Industries	84	55	Pierre Cardin
69	68	78	Eveready	59	102	Johnnie Walker	22	237	McDonald's	92	36	Michelin
70	78	69	Clorox	89	46	Seiko	53	131	Victor	60	111	Toshiba
71	110	44	Band Aid	110	28	Rolex	181	21	Yves St. Laurent	51	121	Pampers
72	72	77	Snickers	85	57	Siemens	67	115	Asahi	68	88	Wrangler
73	81	68	Nike	64	110	BP	59	132	Fuji Bank	87	60	20th Century Fox
74	87	66	Ritz Crackers	105	38	Yves St. Laurent	23	244	Yomiuri Newspaper	105	53	Yves St. Laurent
75	54	89	Oscar Meyer	111	33	Cartier	77	109	Citizen	70	118	Philips
76	92	65	Hunt's	63	123	Suzuki	197	17	Dunhill	66	126	Lux
77	34	190	Pizza Hut	83	88	Olivetti	52	147	Meiji Seika	120	27	TDK
78	42	140	Visa	66	135	Nissan	84	108	Kokuyo	93	74	Casio
79	120	52	General Foods	95	73	Rover	137	61	Kikokuniya (Groceries)	102	71	Dunlop
80	97	76	ABC	98	67	Saab	11	349	JR	61	129	Kit Kat
81	66	111	JC Penney	94	79	Dunlop	238	6	BMW	97	61	Paramount Pictures
82	17	325	Kentucky Fried Chicken	107	59	AEG	43	184	Mitsubishi	74	130	Nivea
83	41	178	Toyota	101	75	Goodyear	110	84	Sumitomo (Group)	80	115	Kawasaki

(Continued)

TABLE 1
(Continued)

	United States			Europe			Japan			World		
		Rank			Rank			Rank			Rank	
	Brand	SOM	Esteem	Brand	SOM	Esteem	Brand	SOM	Esteem	Brand	SOM	Esteem
84	Green Giant	118	63	Lancia	80	107	Yamazaki Baking	35	220	Kraft	81	128
85	Ziploc	122	64	Wrangler	82	111	Cadillac	166	33	Cartier	128	41
86	Johnson's Baby Shampoo	113	72	Mitsubishi	76	119	Sogo	41	202	Reebok	133	21
87	Cheerios	64	135	Nikon	124	35	TDK	126	78	Black & Decker	90	78
88	WD-40	183	39	Puma	96	87	Lipton	68	158	Chrysler	64	147
89	Holiday Inn	51	168	Lamborghini	136	30	Allinamin	73	151	Sanyo	78	163
90	Milky Way	80	118	Marlboro	37	281	Nihon Denki	111	90	Johnnie Walker	77	146
91	Duncan Hines	149	58	General Motors	90	100	Louis Vuitton	218	12	Heinz	89	91
92	Zenith	114	83	Mazda	73	139	Band-Aid	103	101	MasterCard	73	120
93	Energizer	136	74	Sprite	72	160	Mitsubishi (Group)	89	122	Renault	85	139
94	Morton Salt	100	103	Kawasaki	92	114	Q.P.	95	117	Esso	75	157
95	Bisquick	142	71	Cadillac	99	103	Daimaru	47	205	Bayer	91	107
96	Gold Medal	185	50	Harley Davidson	123	49	Hanae Mori	163	43	Lamborghini	141	37
97	Miracle Whip	85	131	Electrolux	100	101	Seibu (Group)	102	116	Fanta	76	192
98	Dairy Queen	79	145	L'Oreal	103	94	Matsuzakaya	74	170	M&M's	107	75
99	Procter & Gamble	105	102	American Express	75	164	Kleenex	133	96	CBS	95	103
100	Sprite	73	167	Visa	78	156	YKK (Yoshida Kogyo)	153	65	Boeing	98	164

Building Brands Across Markets: Cultural Differences in Brand Relationships Within the European Community

Jeri Moore
DDB Needham Worldwide

By December 31, 1992, the 12-member European Community (EC) is scheduled to complete its plan of creating the world's largest trading bloc. Since 1958, when six initial members, Belgium, France, Italy, Luxembourg, the Netherlands, and West Germany, signed the Rome Treaties, there has been a European Economic Community or Common Market. Since that time, Britain, Denmark, Ireland, Greece, Portugal, and Spain have joined. The end of 1992 marks the projected time for removing all remaining barriers to free trade among these countries. The EC will then compose a single market of 320 million people, and will generate an estimated $2.4 trillion a year in gross domestic product ("A Survey of Europe's Internal Market," 1988). The size of this market can be emphasized by comparing it to the United States, which has 247 million people and an economic output of $3.9 trillion.

The coming of the EC has led to rapid changes in marketing in Europe. One change is a proliferation of new competitors in many product categories. In earlier, simple times, a typical fmcg (fast moving consumer goods) product category might have included only a few local and national brands competing for shelf space and market share. With the coming of the EC, manufacturers have been aggressively expanding their marketing territories. Decisions are now being made about protectionist barriers to trade with countries outside the EC (such as the United States and Japan). These decisions will control the influx of new brands from outside the EC. Even if the EC passes tariffs on external trade, there will probably be considerable expansion of foreign manufacturing facilities in Europe ("Reshaping Europe," 1988). The net result will surely be much greater competition in most product categories and in every country.

A second important marketing change that is expected—and indeed beginning—to occur in the EC is an increased intensity of advertising. An important contributor to this increase is the rapid expansion of the number of brands, particularly those that already have a history of strong advertising support in their home markets. In addition, the advertising media available in many countries is expected to increase greatly. Media growth is already visible in the broadcast industry. For example, in the beginning of the 1980s, Europe had only 28 major commercial television channels. By 1990, there were 56 (Daser & Richey, 1990). By 1995, there may be as many as 120 channels (Daser & Richey, 1990). Thus, the potential for broadcast advertising will increase by 400%, and the crowd of newly available brands in each country will quickly fill the advertising time as it is made available.

The increasing number of brands and the expanding advertising environments create a challenging combination of problems and opportunities. On one hand, companies and entire industries that have thrived behind protectionist barriers are likely to be wiped out by their more efficient competitors both within and outside the EC ("Europe 1992," 1988). Indeed, economies of scale will become critically important. Although the market will become much more dangerous for the small and the unprepared, there will also be the potential for tremendous gains. The EC estimates that the streamlining of trade laws, transportation, banking, and business laws will reduce consumer prices in Europe by 6.1% by the end of 1992 (Holden & Dowd, 1990). This, in turn, will give Europeans increased spending power, which is expected to spur a 5% to 7% increase in community-wide gross domestic product and create as many as 2 million new jobs ("Europe 1992," 1988). There will be much more money available for spending on brands, and it will be much more efficient to market those brands. Thus, the potential for profit is impressive.

The growth in the number of brands, the amount of advertising, and the potential for profitable marketing have already precipitated increased attention to brands within the marketing community. Questions of brand equity, brand performance, and the dynamics that underly changes in both of these areas are becoming far more important. This is further complicated by the belief that the French, British, Spanish, and many other groups of Europeans exhibit tremendous cultural variations in their perceptions of, knowledge about, and attitudes toward brands and even entire product categories.

Unfortunately, there has been little research on European brands, and even less work on comparing brands across countries. In an effort to address this void, the DDB Needham Brand Equity Pilot Study was developed and implemented. Before the design and the results of the study are presented, however, some basic conceptions about brands and their meanings must be discussed, at least briefly.

Brands and Brand Equity

The most fundamental question here, of course, is what constitutes a brand. Because other chapters in this volume analyze this issue in detail, we treat it very simply and briefly. A brand is basically a name that refers to the product of a particular manufacturer in a particular product category. A brand includes tangible or intrinsic qualities (Preston, 1975), such as its physical appearance, performance data, package, and the guarantees or warranties that are attached to it. Perhaps more importantly, a brand involves aspects that the consumer attributes to it, beyond its tangible features (Farquhar, 1989). These aspects may include attitudes toward the company that produces the product or toward the brand itself, beliefs about the brand in relationship to self and others, and so on.

It is often argued that, for the consumer, the brand eases the problem of choice and purchase. A consumer can quickly recognize brands indicating a particular product category. The brand may provide confidence to the consumer about the quality of the product and gratification of image of self (Achenbaum, 1972). Based on this conception, brand equity can be defined as "everything the consumer walks into the store with" (Farquhar, 1989). In other words, equity is the value added to the product by the fact that it wears a brand name and has a history in the mind of the consumer.

One of the most important aspects of this definition is the fact that brand equity lies in the minds of the consumers, who carry fairly complicated sets of assumptions and beliefs about their roles (Holbrook, 1987). Given the variety in cultures across Europe, it is likely that general orientations toward brands would vary just like specific brand attitudes. Thus, any study of brand equity in Europe must look at responses to specific brands as well as a more general feeling for, reliance upon, or degree of cynicism toward brands in general.

Some argue that, for certain consumers, all brands are perceived alike or at parity with each other. Clearly, this general perception of brands will vary across people (and perhaps whole cultures), and it will also vary within people (BBDO Worldwide, 1989). Although consumers may hold a general concept of brands and what they mean, they certainly hold specific concepts of particular brands.

The performance of a particular brand often depends on: (a) how long the brand has been in the market in a particular country; (b) the competitive arena in which the brand operates in each country; (c) aspects of the distribution of the brand; (d) the advertising and marketing pressure that supports the brand; and (e) cultural receptivity to the content of the brand's advertising and marketing programs.

With these background assumptions in mind, a number of research questions can now be articulated:

- Can a set of standard measures be developed to determine brand performance in a variety of markets?
- Does the salience of entire product categories vary by country?
- Is that variance associated with brand equity in those product categories?
- Are there cultural variations that influence consumers' propensities to form brand relationships and commitments?

METHOD

Sample

The sample for this study included 500 European Community consumers in five countries: Britain, France, Germany, Spain, and Italy. All respondents were female primary grocery shoppers, aged 20 to 50. Respondents were interviewed individually by a native speaker of their own country. All interviews took place during November, 1990.

Brands Tested

The questionnaire in each country included fmcg (fast moving consumer goods, known in the United States as packaged goods) brands, both local and national, in 13 product categories. Brands selected for each of the countries included: (a) established multinationals, (b) emerging multinationals, and (c) major local brands. Across the five countries, a total of 93 major brands were tested. Within each country, approximately 30–34 brands were represented.

Translations

The original questionnaire was developed in English. In each of the non-English-speaking countries, market research firms translated the questionnaire into the language of their own country. To insure accurate and consistent translations, the local offices of DDB Needham "back translated" the questionnaires into English. These were compared to the original version, and discrepancies were examined and corrected.

Dependent Measures

Respondents received an initial screener to establish their age, employment, and their role as primary grocery shopper.

Awareness of brands was indexed by handing respondents a set of cards, each picturing a brand name/logo treatment. Each respondent sorted the cards into three piles: (a) those which she had used, (b) those she had heard of but never tried, and (c) those with which she was unfamiliar. Perceptions of and feelings toward the brands were measured by asking those who had heard of a particular brand to rate the brand on a series of 10-point scales. Liking for the brand was indexed by asking respondents how much they liked the brand (10-point scale anchored by *like–dislike*.) Other characteristics used a 10-point scale on which the anchor points were *describes very well* and *does not describe at all*. The characteristics rated in this manner were:

- a leading brand;
- worth the price;
- excellent quality;
- suits me well;
- a brand I trust.

Next, respondents were asked about their attitudes and habits vis-à-vis brands and shopping. For example, on 6-point scales anchored by *definitely agree* and *definitely disagree*, they responded to statements such as "I always check prices, even on small items"; "I usually buy the same brands every time I shop"; and "Before going shopping, I always sit down and make out a complete list." These items are listed in Table 3.1.

Finally, respondents were asked demographic, product usage, and media habit questions.

TABLE 3.1
Three Dimensions of Propensity to Form Brand Relationships

Item	Factor Loading
Brand Differentiation	
All brands are about the same.	−.79
The quality of a store brand is just as good as the quality of nationally advertised brands.	−.76
Risk Aversion	
I often buy things on the spur of the moment.	−.77
I am usually among the first to try new products.	−.71
Before going shopping, I always sit down and make out a complete list.	.54
I always check prices, even on small items.	.55
Loyal Buying Behavior	
I buy my favorite brands regardless of what's on sale.	.82
I usually buy the same brands every time I shop.	.73
I would go to another store to get my favorite brand if I couldn't get it at my usual store.	.50

RESULTS

Brand Equity Scores

For each of the brands in the study, a brand equity score was calculated as the multiplicative product of Brand Awareness × Brand Liking × Brand Perceptions. Again, brand awareness was based on visual recognition of the brand-named logo treatment. Brand Liking was indexed with the single 10-point *like–dislike* item. Brand Perceptions included the five diagnostic attributes (leading brand, brand I trust, suits me well, excellent quality, and worth the price). These attributes reflect the basic brand equity components of attitudes toward the product brand and beliefs about the brand in relation to self.

Each brand equity score was standardized. The average score was fixed at 100, and above or below average scores were adjusted accordingly.

The Three Classes of Brands

The original conception of three kinds or classes of brands was established by three different patterns of brand equity scores across the five countries. Figure 3.1 shows examples of two established multinational brands, Kodak and Duracell. Both of these brands have above average brand equity scores in each of the five countries sampled.

Figure 3.2 shows the brand equity scores for an emerging multinational brand. Evian is a French mineral water that is also marketed in the United Kingdom, Germany, Italy, and Spain. As shown, Evian has high brand equity scores for France and the United Kingdom, but much lower scores in the other countries—markets in which it has yet to fully establish itself. An emerging multinational brand, then, can have a strong brand equity profile in at least one country and slightly weaker profiles in a number of other countries, often where it has been introduced more recently.

Figure 3.3 shows the competitive situation for Evian. In France, its home country, Evian's closest competitor, Vittel, has equally high brand equity. In the United Kingdom, its major local competitor, Perrier, has a lower brand equity score. But in Germany, Italy, and Spain, Evian's brand equity is considerably lower than each of its major competitors.

Figure 3.4 displays the main components of the brand equity measures for both Evian and Vittel in France. Awareness, Liking, and Brand Perceptions are virtually identical for both of these competing brands in France.

The situation for Evian is quite different, however, in the United Kingdom. Figure 3.5 shows that awareness of Evian in the United Kingdom is not as strong as that of Perrier, but its Liking and Brand Perceptions scores are higher than its competitor among those who are aware of it. The situation for Evian shows a further differentiated pattern in Germany (Fig. 3.6). Here, awareness

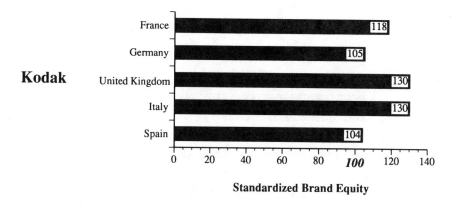

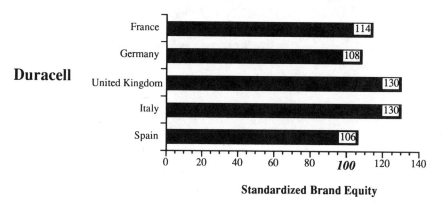

FIG. 3.1. Brand equity scores for two multinational brands.

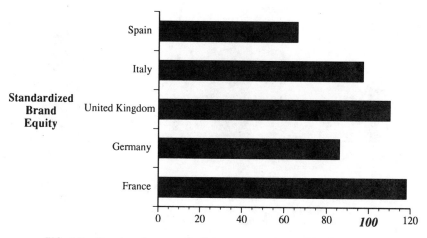

FIG. 3.2. Brand equity scores for Evian, an emerging multinational brand.

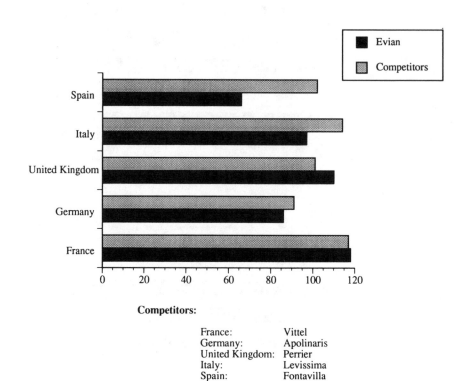

Competitors:

France:	Vittel
Germany:	Apolinaris
United Kingdom:	Perrier
Italy:	Levissima
Spain:	Fontavilla

FIG. 3.3.   Brand equity scores for Evian and its major competition in each country.

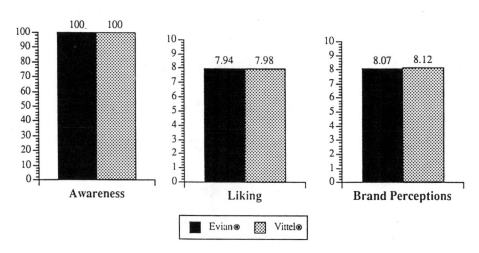

FIG. 3.4.   Components of Evian and Vittel brand equity in France.

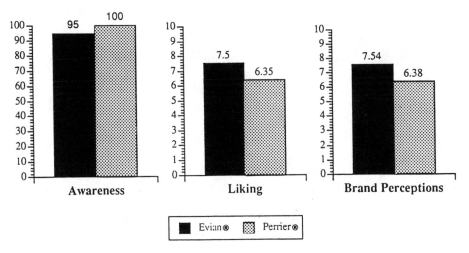

FIG. 3.5. Components of Evian and Perrier brand equity in the United Kingdom.

of Evian is much lower than that of its largest competitor. Furthermore, it is less well liked than the local brand, Apolinaris, among those who are aware of it. However, and intriguingly, Evian's Brand Perceptions are much higher than those of the local competitor.

Figure 3.7 shows that in Italy, Evian lags behind the local competitor, Levissima, on all three measures. The lag in Spain is even more pronounced (Fig. 3.8), and indeed, in Spain, Evian is a minor brand with awareness among only 22% of the sample, versus 99% awareness for Fontavilla, the primary local competitor.

It is apparent that the brand equity performance of true multinational brands

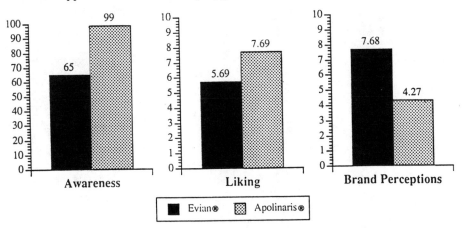

FIG. 3.6. Components of Evian and Apolinaris brand equity in Germany.

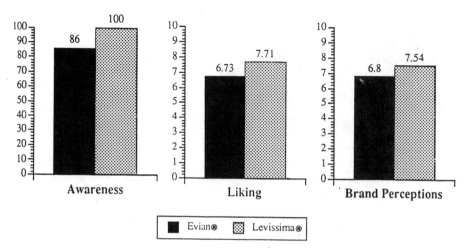

FIG. 3.7.   Components of Evian and Levissima brand equity in Italy.

and emerging multinational brands show very different patterns across the individual markets. Because purchase reinforcement (maintenance) strategies are generally quite different from trial (growth) strategies, the relative strengths of local brands can be important considerations for marketers who compete across markets in the EC.

Salience of Product Categories in Five Countries

The second area of exploration in this research is category salience. In other words, are there variations in the importance consumers place on product categories that can be observed and explained?

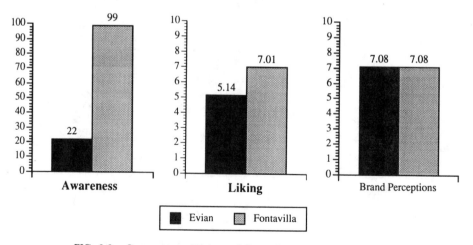

FIG. 3.8.   Components of Evian and Fontavilla brand equity in Spain.

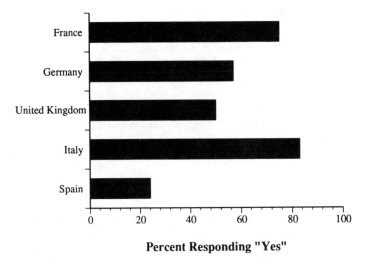

Percent Responding "Yes"

FIG. 3.9. Use of bottled water in five European countries.

As an example of market variation, Fig. 3.9 shows the percentage of respondents indicating that they ever use bottled water. France and Italy show much heavier use of the category than the other three countries. In fact, in Spain, only about 22% of the respondents indicated ever using the product. It can be hypothesized that selling bottled water in Spain will be a much more difficult task because the people are less accustomed to the product category itself.

Why are there such differences in the use and presumed salience of product categories in these countries? Figure 3.10 shows the use of tea in the five countries. The United Kingdom, as one might expect, has the heaviest concentra-

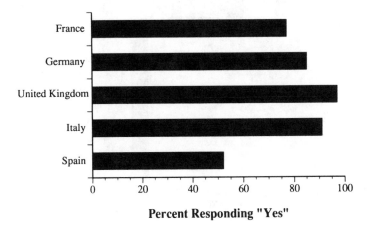

Percent Responding "Yes"

FIG. 3.10. Use of tea in five European countries.

tion of tea users. Italy, France, and Germany are next highest, but Spain is quite low.

Figure 3.11 suggests that product usage and brand equity for the brands in the tea category are related. Both France and Spain, which show low tea usage, also exhibit low tea brand equity scores. In contrast, the United Kingdom and Italy, with much higher tea-usage scores, also show much higher tea brand equity scores. The fact that those countries in which consumption is greater have stronger brands may be due, in part, to more aggressive advertising in higher potential markets. However, some of this variation might also be caused by differences in consumers' "openness" to brands, based on category salience.

Figure 3.12 suggests that lifestyles may also be related to product usage and salience. In countries where the percent of working women is higher than the European Community average, frozen meal use is much higher than in the two countries where the percent of working women is below the average. The only exception to the observed pattern is France, where the tradition of quality

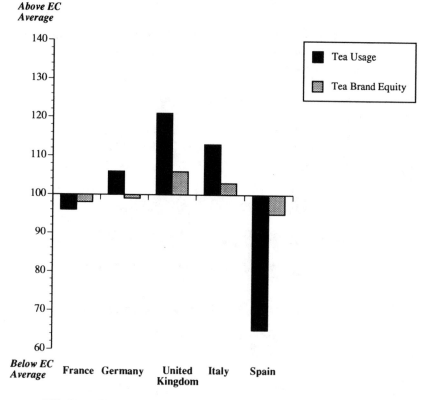

FIG. 3.11.   Tea usage and brand equity indexed to five-country average in five European countries.

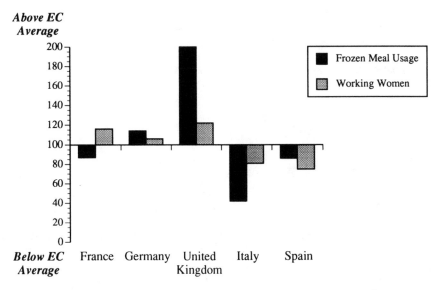

FIG. 3.12.   Frozen meal usage and percent of working women indexed to five-country average in five European countries.

cooking, or perhaps dining out rather than using frozen meals, may mitigate against the relationship between working women and frozen meal consumption. It seems reasonable that in countries where lifestyles include many working women, the convenience of using frozen meals would lead to heavier usage of them.

Figure 3.13 provides further evidence for the link between lifestyles and product category consumption. It shows that the percent of working women is highly correlated with breakfast cereal usage. This link is true even in France, the one country whose use of frozen foods did not fit the predicted lifestyle pattern.

Cultural Orientations Toward Brands in General

The third research hypothesis suggests that there are cultural variations in orientations toward brands in the five countries, and that these cultural orientations influence consumers' propensities to form brand relationships and commitments across product categories. To index propensity to build brand relationships, a series of 6-point, *agree–disagree* statements were presented. These items are shown in Table 3.1. Factor analysis of these items identified three dimensions. These factors, together with the items composing them and their factor loadings, are also shown in Table 3.1. The factors are: (a) perceptions of brand differentiation, (b) risk aversion, and (c) loyal buying behavior.

Figure 3.14 shows these cultural variations for the five countries. In terms

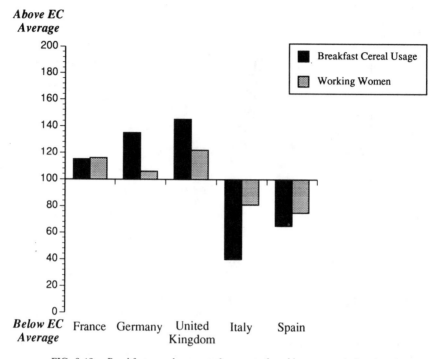

FIG. 3.13.   Breakfast cereal usage and percent of working women indexed to five-country average in five European countries.

of brand differentiation, Italy showed the highest scores, with Germany and Spain intermediate, and France and the United Kingdom the lowest.

Although the present study was not designed to gather evidence about why brand differentiation perceptions vary by country, considering the fact that France and the United Kingdom have had more advertising for longer than in the other three countries, consumers in France and the United Kingdom may simply be more sophisticated about brands. Indeed, as brands proliferate in countries, there appears to be greater perceived parity among those brands (BBDO Worldwide, 1989).

There are also differences in levels in risk aversion across the five EC countries, with Spain, Italy, and France showing high levels of risk aversion. In Germany and particularly in the United Kingdom, risk aversion scores are considerably lower. It is likely that higher levels of risk aversion cause consumers to exhibit greater brand loyalty (i.e., sticking with what they know). It can also be hypothesized that strategies used to communicate with risk-averse consumers would differ from those employed against more risk-taking targets.

Finally, the degrees of loyal buying behavior also vary across the five countries: Mean loyal buying scores are higher for Italy and Spain than for France,

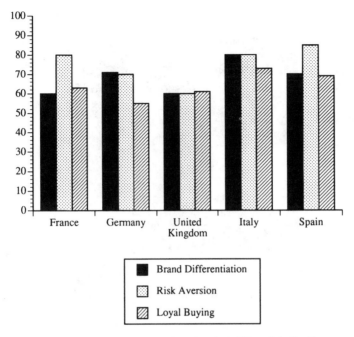

FIG. 3.14.   Cultural variations in orientations toward brands in five European countries.

Germany, and the United Kingdom. This pattern mirrors the one for brand differentiation reasonably closely, and is therefore consistent with the notion that there is more consumer sophistication and perhaps more brands from which to choose in the United Kingdom, Germany, and France than in the two more southern countries.

The differences in propensity to build brand relationships are summarized in Fig. 3.15. For each of the three components of brand receptivity, the level of agreement is shown for each of the five EC countries. The figure shows that Italy is high on all three measures, and Spain is high on two. Thus, these two countries are expected to have fairly stable sets of strong brands, with newer brands having a more difficult job in achieving successful entry. In contrast, the picture is much different in the United Kingdom, where two components of brand propensity show low ranges of response, and only loyal buying shows responses in the middle range. Thus, in the United Kingdom, and to some extent in France and Germany, building brand equity might be more difficult.

The brand propensity findings lead directly to the next question: Are there differences in these five countries that could explain or contribute to the observed variation in their brand receptivity? Answers were not directly available in the data set reported here, but perusal of other databases about EC

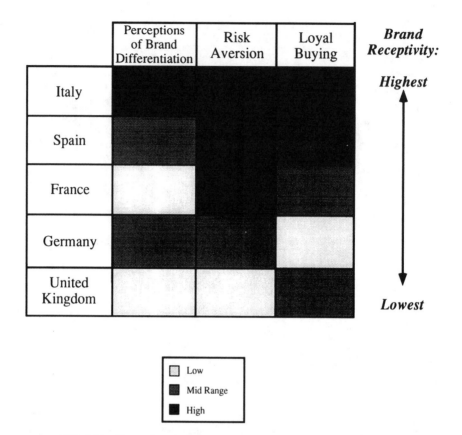

FIG. 3.15.   Propensity to build brand relationships in five European countries.

markets yielded some reasonable clues. Data reported in the United Nations Demographic Yearbook and Reader's Digest's Eurodata suggest that there is variation in the degree of traditionalism in the five countries. Table 3.2 lists four indicators of traditionalism: (a) demographics, (b) product usage tendencies, (c) beliefs regarding women's roles, and (d) orientation toward organized religion. Countries with higher brand receptivity have larger families and fewer working wives. They hold more traditional beliefs about the appropriate roles for women in society, and they express a stronger confidence in the church as an institution. They report higher purchases of traditional cooking ingredients (such as cooking oil) and less use of more "modern" convenience foods (such as prepared entrees).

Trust of authority is another dimension that varies across the five countries. In those countries with higher brand receptivity, more confidence is expressed toward advertising, the press, the broadcast media, and international business.

TABLE 3.2
Value Indicators in Five European Countries

Indicators of Traditionalism	Higher Brand Receptivity	Lower Brand Receptivity
Demographic Characteristics	Larger families	Smaller families
	Fewer working wives	More working wives
Beliefs Regarding Women's Roles	Traditional	Liberal
Express More Confidence in . . .	The Church	
Product Usage Tendencies	Cooking ingredients	Convenience foods
Trust in Marketing Practitioners		
Express more confidence in . . .	The advertising industry	
	The press	
	TV, radio media	
	International companies	
Media Reliance		
Dominant Medium	Television	Newspapers

Finally, the five countries also vary in terms of the media on which they report reliance. In countries with higher brand receptivity, there is more reliance on television; in countries with lower brand receptivity, there is more reliance on newspapers. Media reliance is an important indicator of the degree to which countries are urbanized and industrialized (Ball-Rokeach & DeFleur, 1975). There is also evidence that people who report the broadcast media as their source of information tend to be less well informed than print users on a variety of issues (Wade & Schramm, 1969).

Why are these three factors—traditionalism, trust, and media usage—related to brand receptivity? Of course, the findings here are only correlational and it would be dangerous and inappropriate to conclude causation in either direction. However, we might hypothesize that as cultures modernize, and women shed traditional values and behaviors, they become more "sophisticated," and likely more cynical, consumers. As countries become urbanized, more people read, and there are more newspapers and magazines available. With these developments, consumers may become less willing to accept the idea that brands are differentiated. Indeed, a recent advertising agency report (BBDO Worldwide, 1989) suggests that the greatest challenge to marketers in highly developed societies is to produce parity-breaking advertising.

SUMMARY AND DISCUSSION

Although preliminary, these results lead to some conclusions:

1. For individual brands, extreme variations in brand equity values are present as a function of several important factors. Brand managers will make serious errors in strategic direction if they assume that a brand's awareness, its liking, or perceptions of its quality are identical in EC markets. Particularly if a brand is an emerging multinational, responses to it are likely to vary drastically from one country to another within the EC.

2. The salience of various product categories may also vary drastically from country to country in the EC. There is reason to believe that historical and lifestyle variations account for at least some of these differences in salience. It is most important for brand managers to realize, however, that the salience of the category to which their brand belongs may play an important role in the development of brand equity and brand loyalty.

3. There appear to be important variations in receptivity to brands, generally, at least in the five EC countries tested in the present study. Countries such as Spain and Italy show high receptivity; Germany, France, and the United Kingdom show much lower receptivity. The marketer, therefore, must consider different introductory, growth, or defensive strategies in each of these different markets. Before these strategies can be defined, it is critical to develop equity profiles for the brand in each of the EC countries in which it is to be marketed.

These findings are intriguing, but much more research is clearly necessary. We need to develop cross-cultural category salience measures beyond those used here. We need to confirm and expand the findings on variations in receptivity to brands and to administer these measures in other markets beyond the five included in this study. Finally, we need to explore the relationship between media, cynicism, and brand equity and loyalty.

REFERENCES

Achenbaum, A. A. (1972). Advertising doesn't manipulate consumers. *Journal of Advertising Research*, *12*(2), 3-12.

Ball-Rokeach, S. J., & DeFleur, M. (1976). A dependency model of media effects. *Communication Research*, *3*, 3-21.

BBDO Worldwide (1989). *FOCUS: A world of brand parity.* New York: Author.

Daser, S., & Richey, B. (1990, July 19). U.S. broadcasters stand to gain as European TV market grows. *Marketing News*, p. 10.

Europe 1992: Danger or opportunity? (1988). *Editorial Research Reports*, *1*(2), 18-27.

Eurodata: A consumer survey of 17 European countries. (1991). The Reader's Digest Association, 1991.

Farquhar, P. H. (1989, September). Managing brand equity. *Marketing Research*, pp. 24-33.

Holden, A. C., & Dowd, K. M. (1990, July 9). EC directives change rules for marketing in Europe. *Marketing News*, p. 12.

Holbrook, M. B. (1987). What is consumer research? *Journal of Consumer Research*, *14*(1), 128-132.

Preston, I. (1975). *The great American blow-up: Puffery in advertising and selling.* Madison, WI: University of Wisconsin Press.

Reshaping Europe: 1992 and beyond. (1988, December 12). *Business Week.*

A survey of Europe's internal market. (1988, July 9). *The Economist.*

United Nations Demographic Yearbook 1988 (40th ed.). (1990). New York: Author.

Wade, S., & Schramm, W. (1969). The mass media as sources of public affairs, science, and health knowledge. *Public Opinion Quarterly, 33,* 197–209.

Chapter 4

Branding in Japan

Hiroshi Tanaka
Dentsu Inc.

INTRODUCTION

The objective of this study is twofold: (a) to identify characteristics of Japanese marketers' brand-building strategies in their domestic markets and (b) to discuss possible factors which explain the characteristics of branding strategies in Japan. The focus here is to analyze the strategies from consumer and corporate behavioristic viewpoints, rather than from a cultural viewpoint.

A resurgence of international marketing debate was observed during the 1980s (Levitt, 1983). One of the major issues in this "globalization vs. localization" debate was whether globalized marketing strategies are possible in the current internationalization trend. In this debate, standardized advertising was a point of great contention among the global marketing issues. However, *standardization* itself is a vague concept which can only be defined on a continuum (Moriarty & Duncan, 1991) because there are several levels of standardization (e.g., strategy, concept, theme, visual, copy, and medium). In addition to the terminological problem, the globalization debate had another weakness: The idiosyncracies of each individual market had rarely been studied in their specific marketing contexts.

A good example of this is Japan, which has received significant attention in international business studies. Many scholars and practitioners have studied Japanese management, distribution systems, and negotiation styles; they have, however, sometimes neglected Japanese consumer marketing. Although there have been studies related to Japanese marketing (e.g., Lazer, Murata, & Kosaka, 1985), they did not emphasize consumer marketing or branding.

This chapter describes how the Japanese consumer marketing system, particularly the brand development system, differs from that of the United States. We explain the difference from a marketing point of view (i.e., from the consumer and corporate behavior point of view) rather than from cultural perspectives.

This study is a conceptual one, presenting a research framework on Japanese marketing and advertising. It includes existing comparative data between the United States and Japan and it aims to stimulate future research in global marketing.

ADVERTISING STRATEGY

There is no need to emphasize the importance of advertising in modern marketing. Advertising is persuasive communication which conveys verbal messages as well as emotions and feelings. It not only increases consumer awareness of the brand name, but also nurtures the long-term viability of the brand by providing both functional and emotional values to consumers.

Although the branding function of advertising may not differ between Japan and the United States, past studies have revealed differences in advertising expressions.

Journalists and practitioners frequently point out (Kishii, 1987; Reed, 1985) that Japanese advertising appears "softer," with more of a "mood" orientation, than its Western counterparts. This notion has been empirically supported by content analytical studies (Hasegawa, 1990; Hong, Mudderrisoglu, & Zinkhan, 1987; Mueller, 1987; Tanaka, 1984), although Madden, Caballero, and Matsukubo (1986) and Hong et al. (1987) found that Japanese magazine advertisements are at least as informative as their American counterparts. Tanaka (1984) reported that cultural values appear equally as frequently in both countries, but functional values are used more frequently in U.S. magazine ads. Hasegawa (1990) analyzed the content of Japanese and American TV ads and found that Japanese advertisers utilize softer appeals (Table 4.1). Soft sell is defined as "mood and atmosphere conveyed through a beautiful scene or the development of an emotional story or verse. Human emotional sentiments are emphasized over clear-cut product-related appeals" (Mueller, 1987).

Another notable characteristic of Japanese advertising is its "irrelevance" (or at least its seeming irrelevance) to the product and consumers. MacMaster (1985), then president of J. Walter Thompson in Japan, raised the question of relevance, stating that a Japanese advertising campaign is qualitatively underdeveloped because of its lack of relevance to its target consumers (i.e., the communication appears to concern neither the target customers nor the products).

TABLE 4.1
Proportion of Hard- and Soft-Sell TV Commercials

	Japan (n = 380)	United States (n = 432)
Hard-sell commercials	26.3%	49.1%
Soft-sell commercials	73.3%	50.9%

$x^2 = 44.257$ ($p < 0$).

Note. From Content Analysis of Japanese and American Prime Time TV Commercials by K. Hasegawa, 1990. Adapted by permission.

Holmberg (1985) examined Japanese print advertisements and reported that almost half of the sample (47%) used foreign models, many of whom were Westerners. Another indication is that Japanese advertising does not appear to be directly related to their target consumers.

In summary, Japanese advertising can be characterized by its emotional/soft-sell nature of execution and its seeming irrelevance to products and/or consumers.

The question, then, is why Japanese advertising is different from that of the United States. Many of the authors of the already cited content analysis studies have attributed the difference to Japanese culture.

However, it should be pointed out that this *culture-affect-ad* hypothesis has not yet been fully substantiated. There are several reasons why this thesis may be suspect:

1. Mueller (1987) interpreted the high usage of the soft-sell appeal as a reflection of the indirect and nonverbal communication of Japanese people. However, as Mueller herself admits, the *ad-reflect-culture* thesis does not always succeed in explaining advertising expressions. For example, *group consensus* appeal, regarded as one of the basic elements of Japanese culture, rarely appears in Japanese magazine advertising.

2. Marquez (1975) also found that the advertisements of developing Asian countries often reflect Western cultural values rather than indigenous ones.

3. Research evidence has not yet been submitted to support the assumption that a soft-sell appeal is more effective than a hard-sell one for consumers in Japan. For example, Matsui (1991) reported that there were no differences in the communicative effectiveness on brand awareness and purchase intention scores between direct and indirect executions. This is counter to the previous notion that indirect execution is more effective.

Although the advertising as reflection of culture hypothesis is a promising concept, its theoretical basis, operationalization, and validation methods should be carefully developed for further advancement of the field.

Thus, rather than cultural perspective, let us look at the consumer behavioral aspect of the Japanese people in order to explain the executional differences between Japanese and U.S. advertising.

Regarding consumer behavior, there are two major differences between Japanese consumers and their U.S. counterparts: (a) purchasing behavior (frequent purchase and in-store decision making) and (b) information processing.

Japanese consumers shop and buy more frequently; Manabe (1990) compared the purchase behavior of American and Japanese housewives and found that Japanese housewives go to their primary stores more frequently than Americans (Table 4.2). There are several possible reasons for this:

1. Organization for Economic Cooperation and Development (OECD) statistics suggest that Japanese consumers purchase more fresh foods than Western consumers.
2. The limited space within the Japanese home means that refrigerator and storage spaces are not large enough to hold a week's food.
3. Another reason may be that the percentage of Japanese housewives working outside the home is not as high as that for America, even though the number of working women has increased enormously in recent years.
4. Japanese retail outlets are highly accessible. There are more retail stores in Japan than in the United States (Tajima & Miyashita, 1985), which means that stores are conveniently located for consumers.

To study Japanese purchasing behavior, we must also look at the point at which the purchasing decision is made. Otsuki (1982) surveyed Japanese consumers' purchasing habits and found that Japanese consumers tend to choose which items/brands to buy in the store rather than prior to their shopping trips (Table 4.3). In other words, Japanese consumers are likely to be in-store decision makers.

TABLE 4.2
Frequency of Product Purchase: Japan versus United States
(Percent responding "Buy almost everyday" at primary store)

	Japan (n = 1,100)	United States (n = 776)
Meats	15.8%	1.4%
Fish/shellfish	12.2%	0.9%
Vegetables/fruit	32.5%	3.5%
Frozen foods	0.6%	0.4%
Milk/dairy products	16.5%	2.6%
Bread/rice	11.1%	0.9%

Note. From Kokoku no shakai-gaku [Sociology of Advertising] by K. Manabe, 1990, Tokyo: Nikkei Kokoku Kenkyu-jo. Copyright 1990. Adapted by permission.

TABLE 4.3
Planning Consumer Purchases

Japan	Type of Market (1981)			
	Large Supermarket (%)	Small Supermarket (%)	Convenience Store (%)	Liquor Store (%)
1. Specifically planned	3.5	13.5	6.8	30.4
2. Generally planned	15.9	14.5	30.6	25.1
3. Substitute	0.4	0.9	5.5	2.4
4. Unplanned	80.2	71.6	62.0	42.2
In-store decision making (2) + (3) + (4)	96.5	86.5	93.2	69.6

Note. From Shodo-gai ha naze okoru-noka? [Why does impulse purchase occur?] by H. Otsuki, 1991, in Shohi to Ryutsu. Adapted by permission.

These two characteristics of Japanese purchase behavior are interrelated. Japanese housewives go to the supermarkets so frequently—everyday or every other day—that the need to decide which items/brands to buy before shopping is lower because the purchase volume per trip is presumably small enough that most of the items can be remembered without a shopping list. Such regular shopping habits, with less purchased per shopping trip, may result in quick and flexible decision making inside the stores (i.e., Japanese consumers decide what to buy at the point of sale).

The characteristics of Japanese advertising—soft-sell and nonverbal messages—contribute to information processing in the minds of Japanese consumers because image-related or emotional information is thought to be more easily retrieved than cognitive/rational information.

Another explanation for soft-sell and irrelevant Japanese advertising is based on how Japanese consumers process information or change attitude. In this regard, the results of two previous comparative studies are particularly important:

1. Yamamoto (1987) tested two TV advertisements, one image and one nonimage, in Japan and the United States. The average response time taken to evaluate the image items of each commercial was measured after exposure. The Japanese subjects reacted in less time to the image-style commercials than the Americans; on the other hand, there was no difference in reaction time for the nonimage ads (Table 4.4). Yamamoto concluded that Japanese consumers tend to process information "top down," rather than take a "bottom-up" approach. Top-down information processing refers to the development of a whole impression of the target object first (e.g., whether it is "good" or "bad"). Bottom-up information processing refers conversely to the gradual development of a total impression by first focusing on the individual features of that object.

TABLE 4.4
Top-down versus Bottom-up Information Processing

Average Response Time to Image Items (Unit: 1 millisecond)

	Japan	U.S.	t-test	
Image ad (Tire)	1,396	2,004	$p < .001$	(Top-down)
Nonimage ad (Video Camera)	1,651	1,679		(Bottom-up)

Rank Order of Fast-Response Ad Evaluation Items

Tire ad		Video Camera ad	
Japan	United States	Japan	United States
High class	Good function	Light	Portable
Like	Tough	Large	Small
Good function	Easy to use	Easy to use	Good design
Unique	Sloppy	Portable	Advanced technology
High speed possible	Reliable	Expensive	Autofocus

Note. From "Shakai-teki joho-shori Katei no hikaku bunka teki kento: Kokoku joho no shori ni kansuru kento" by M. Yamamoto, in *Josei Kenkyu-shu*, 1987, Tokyo: Yoshida Hideo Kinen Jigyo Zaidan. Adapted by permission.

2. Fields (1984) showed comparative data of finished commercial test results for Japan and the United States (Table 4.5). He found that there is a significant difference in copy point recall between these two countries and that the persuasion score (arousal of purchase intention) reached the same level in both countries. Batra and Stayman found that creating a mood in advertising affects the amount of total cognitive elaboration and stated, "the effect is greater when the reader has a low need for cognition and when the ad contains weak message arguments" (1990, p. 203).

In summary, Japanese mood advertisements assist consumers' decision making by reducing the need for cognition because they do not feel a strong need

TABLE 4.5
ASI Test Results: Foodstuff Commercials (Japan vs. United States)

	Japan	United States
Interest	573	557
Brand recall	66%	75%
Involvement	19%	29%
Copy point recall	9%	56%
Brand selection shift	+11	+12
Persuasion (Increased desire to purchase)	71%	72%

Note. From "Kokoku hyogen no nichi-bei hikaku" by G. Fields, in *Amerika no kokoku hyogen*, 1984, Tokyo: Nikkei Kokoku Kenkyu-jo. Reprinted by permission.

to spend much of their energy on advertised products. Top-down information processing of advertising is considered an appropriate mode to assist the purchase decision-making process. The nonverbal communication style of the Japanese people also contributes to this advertising processing and decision making at the moment of brand choice.

THE USE OF CORPORATE BRANDS

Visitors to Japan will notice that many Japanese broadcast advertisements carry corporate trademark logos, sometimes accompanied by corporate messages, at the end of the commercial film.

Yamaki (1990) reported that Japanese and Korean TV commercials display corporate identity logos more frequently than the United States and West Germany. The corporate name is regarded as one of the key elements in branding development for Japanese marketers.

Let us look at the brand system of Aji-no-moto, a leading food manufacturer (Table 4.6). Many Aji-no-moto items, such as cooking oil, are crowned with the corporate name AJI-NO-MOTO. In Western marketing scenes, brands are more likely to be independent; Procter & Gamble (P & G) would rarely use its corporate name to endorse its brands.

We observe more examples of the corporate branding system in other consumer product categories. KIRIN, the largest brewery company in Japan, markets KIRIN Lager Beer, KIRIN Draft Beer, and KIRIN Orange Juice. Kirin's competitor Suntory owns Suntory beer lines as well as Suntory whiskey lines; the latter dominates the Japanese whiskey market.

TABLE 4.6
Ajinomoto Brand System

Seasoning	Ajinomoto
	Hi-me
	Hondashi
	Cook-do
Oil	Ajinomoto Salad Oil
	Ajinomoto Corn Salad Oil
	Marina
	Ajinomoto Mayonnaise
Soup stock	Ajinomoto Consommé
	Knorr
Frozen food	Ajinomoto Frozen Food
Cornflakes	Kellogg

Kao, Japan's leading toiletry manufacturer and P & G's archrival, applies its name to a wide range of products across different markets: Kao Attack (detergent), Kao Merit (shampoo), Kao Sofina (skin care), Kao Cooking Oil, and even Kao Floppy Disk!

One could argue that too much extension of a brand name can damage that brand's image and weaken the brand values.

Another point of view is that the Japanese corporate branding system is derived from an important aspect of Japanese culture, namely harmony (*wa*), in which consumers tend to rely on names of good reputation and to purchase a large corporation's branded products because they make the consumers feel more comfortable and secure.

Unfortunately, few empirical studies have explored the relationship between corporate image and Japanese consumer attitudes. Nishio (1989) reported that a good corporate image, including "reliability" and "planning capabilities," affects the evaluation of a product's attributes, not attitude toward the brand directly. This study also suggested that, in a successful marketing case such as Asahi Dry Beer, corporate image tends to influence brand purchase intentions. Although Nishio's survey results have limited generalizability, it may be safe to conclude that corporate image is not always powerful enough to directly influence the Japanese consumers' brand choice.

Instead, I would like to suggest that the corporate branding system be viewed from the perspective of Japanese corporate behavior. The key is in the new product syndrome of Japanese companies.

As shown in Table 4.7, Japan and the United States launch relatively the same number of new products annually, taking population size and GNP into account.

Shimaguchi and Ishii (1989) stated that quick model change is one of the most important features of Japanese manufacturers, providing corporations with a beneficial edge in a highly competitive market place. For example, Japanese automobile manufacturers regularly launch new car models every four years, which is far more frequently than Western manufacturers. Within such

TABLE 4.7
New Product Launches by Sector: Japan versus United States

Product Type	Japan	United States	Index
Beverage	720	642	89
Food	1,294	3,489	269
Health/beauty aids	1,106	1,578	143
Household products	269	451	168
Reference: (population/million)	123	248	201
GNP ($billion, 1989)	$2,867	$4,811	168

Note. From *Nikkei New Product Ranking*, 1991, and *Product Alert*, 1991. Adapted by permission.

fierce market conditions, incessant new product launches employing corporate branding are usually a better option than choosing an independent branding system.

Here are two possible reasons for Japanese marketers to adopt a corporate branding system:

1. Under a single, strong corporate name, it would be easier to perform the quick scrapping or building of subbrands. If a company adopts an independent branding strategy, quick scrapping and building results in a higher marketing cost than taking a corporate brand strategy. In this regard, it is understandable that Western advanced technological industries, such as IBM and Philips, tend to use corporate branding systems like the Japanese, because technological development is so quick in these markets that it is hard to nurture a strong independent brand in a longer time perspective.

2. Because Japanese firms are enthusiastic about expanding their product lines under competitors' pressures and distributors' requests, corporate branding is likely to form a useful pact among marketers, distributors, and consumers (i.e., no matter what the product category is, that product is regarded as reliable in quality as long as it has a famous, well-known corporate name).

The question is, then, why are Japanese companies forced to launch so many new products year after year?

According to a recent Japanese government survey (Table 4.8), Japanese companies, more than their U.S. counterparts, believe that launching new products is an effective way to defend their market share against competitors. Behind this belief is a strong market-share orientation among Japanese companies (Table 4.9). American companies tend to think that profitability and/or ROI are the most important company goals. Stockholder demand is one issue that forces U.S. companies to focus on profit. In the United States, increase in the stock price as a reflection of corporate profit is the strongest demand of stockholders, whereas in Japan, growth of the enterprise is paramount (Ta-

TABLE 4.8
Companies' Preferred Means of Defending Market Share

	Japan (n = 201)	United States (n = 56)
Price discounting	29%	41%
Nonprice sales promotion	37%	41%
New products	69%	47%
No special measures	5%	7%

Note. From *Nichi-bei no kigyo kodo hikaku* by the Ministry of International Trade and Industry, 1989, Tokyo: Nihon Noritsu Kyokai.

TABLE 4.9
Comparison of Company Goals
(Average of rank-order score)

	Japan	United States	
ROI	1.24	2.43	***
Market share	1.43	0.73	***
New product ratio	1.06	0.21	***
Increase in share price	0.02	1.14	***
Efficiency of production	0.71	0.46	**
Equity/debt ratio	0.59	0.38	
Improvement of product portfolio	0.68	0.50	
Improvement of working conditions	0.09	0.04	**
Improvement of public image	0.20	0.05	**

** = statistically significant at .01 level.
*** = statistically significant at .001 level.

Note. From *Nichi-bei kigyo no keiei hikaku* by T. Kogano, I. Nonaka, K. Sakakibara, and A. Okumura, 1983, Tokyo: Nihon Keizai Shimbun-sha. Adapted by permission.

ble 4.10). A comparison of the two countries' branding strategies is summarized in Table 4.11.

Many management scholars have pointed out that Japanese companies take a longer term view of corporate management than their American counterparts (Kotler, Fahey, & Jatusripitak, 1985). Ironically, as far as branding strategy is concerned, Japanese marketers are more likely to take shorter term views on managing their brands (more precisely, subbrands) in order to gain market share more quickly.

The Japanese Ministry of International Trade and Industry (MITI) interviewed 10 leading home electronics manufacturers on the cycle of model renewals (1992). This survey revealed that during the fiscal year 1991, these companies launched new models of home electronic appliances almost every year. As for TV sets, a model is likely to last only 12 to 13 months before being replaced by an updated model. The average cycle of a new model VCR is even shorter:

TABLE 4.10
Shareholders' First Priority

	Japan (n = 202)	United States (n = 54)
Dividend increase of	6%	4%
Stock price increase of	12%	42%
Growth	56%	15%
Stability	24%	4%
Social responsibility	2%	0%

Note. From *Nichi-bei no kigyo kodo hikaku* by the Ministry of International Trade and Industry, 1989, Tokyo: Nihon Noritsu Kyokai. Adapted by permission.

TABLE 4.11
Strategic Branding Priorities: Japan versus United States

	Japan	*United States*
Company goal	Share	Profit/ROI
Brand system	Corporate brand	Independent brand
	Short term	Long term
Major issue	How to cope with the changing environment	How to maintain the brands' life cycle
Communication	Familiarity	Reward–benefit
Ad tactics	Tag (corporate ID) Common tonality	Theme/campaignability

9 to 10 months. MITI has called on manufacturers to use longer model change cycles, claiming that too-short model cycles are typical of excessive and non-productive competition. Consequently, this rapid introduction of new models ends up as a flood of new subbrands under an umbrella corporate brand.

This Japanese corporate branding system provides ample flexibility in coping with quickly changing environments, such as technological development and market growth. For example, because the KAO corporate brand has a well established and trusted general home product image among consumers, KAO has successfully extended its brand lines from detergent to floppy disks under its corporate name.

To maintain this corporate branding system, there are some observable devices in advertising:

1. Corporate familiarity, rather than specific product merits, is emphasized in advertisements to preserve the psychological tie between corporations and consumers.

2. Consistency of tone and manner is visible throughout leading advertisers' advertisements. For example, advertisements for Suntory whiskey lines usually have the same mature and sophisticated atmosphere and are easily associated with the product lines.

3. Many Japanese TV commercial films carry corporate logomarks at the end to identify the products' mother brand.

On the other hand, the top-notch Western companies appear to concentrate on raising brands through longevity. They try to establish a brand franchise among consumers using unique and consistent brand personalities and visual symbols. Lux toilet soap and shampoo is a good example of a global brand. Famous actresses are associated with the brand symbol to demonstrate the special creaminess and shining hair concepts as major benefits of the product. Each brand does not usually have any direct nominal connection to its corporate parents. Their motivation to maintain this independent brand system is derived from their profit orientation; long-life brands can stand "milking" for a longer period.

CONCLUSION

The emotional soft-sell approach of Japanese advertising is related to Japanese consumers and their purchasing habits, such as regular shopping frequency and in-store decision making.

Corporate branding, another characteristic of Japanese marketing, is probably due to Japanese corporate behavior, which focuses on achieving the best market share. As a result, Japanese corporations launch many brands that are integrated under a central single corporate brand system. This system enables Japanese corporations to launch new products and new models one after another within a short time period.

In summary, although the Japanese corporate branding system approach may seem odd to Western marketers, it is most likely the result of adaptational behavior in the highly competitive, quickly changing market environment.

As noted earlier, this chapter intends to stimulate global marketing debate by examining one specific marketing environment and to explain the characteristics of Japanese marketers within their own marketing context.

ACKNOWLEDGMENTS

The author would like to thank Ms. Gillian Wellstead and Mr. Erik Newton for their help in revising this paper. Thanks are also extended to Professor David Aaker and Mr. Alexander Biel for their insightful comments.

REFERENCES

Batra, R., & Stayman, D. M. (1990). The role of mood in advertising effectiveness. *Journal of Consumer Research, 17*, 203–214.

Fields, G. (1984). Kokoku hyogen no nichi-bei hikaku [Comparison of advertising execution between Japan and the U.S.]. In *Amerika no kokoku hyogen* (pp. 127–159). Tokyo: Nikkei Kokoku Kenkyu-jo.

Hasegawa, K. (1990). *Content analysis of Japanese and American prime time TV commercials.* Unpublished master's thesis, Department of Radio and Television, Southern Illinois University, Carbondale, IL.

Holmberg, E. R. (1985). *Foreign images in Japanese advertising: An overview with historical and sociological perspectives.* Paper submitted to International Division, Waseda University, Tokyo, Japan.

Hong, J. W., Mudderrisoglu, A., & Zinkhan, G. M. (1987). Cultural differences and advertising expression: A comparative content analysis of Japanese and U.S. magazine advertising. *Journal of Advertising, 16*(1), 55–68.

Kagono, T., Nonaka, I., Sakakibara, K., & Okumura, A. (1983). *Nichi-bei kigyo no keiei hikaku* [A comparison between Japanese and American corporate management]. Tokyo: Nihon Keizai Shimbun-sha.

Kishii, T. (1987). Message vs. mood: A look at some of the differences between Japanese and Western television commercials. In *Dentsu Japan Marketing/Advertising 1987* (pp. 51-57). Tokyo: Dentsu Inc.

Kotler, P., Fahey, L., & Jatusripitak, S. (1985). *The new competition.* Englewood Cliffs, NJ: Prentice-Hall.

Lazer, W., Murata, S., & Kosaka, H. (1985). Japanese marketing: Towards a better understanding. *Journal of Marketing, 49*, 69-81.

Levitt, T. (1983, May-June). The globalization of markets. *Harvard Business Review*, pp. 92-102.

MacMaster, N. A. (1985, March). *A question of relevance: Must Japanese advertising be different to be successful?* Paper presented at the International Education Center Forum, Tokyo, Japan.

Madden, C. S., Caballero, M. J., & Matsukubo, S. (1986). Analysis of information content in U.S. and Japanese advertising. *Journal of Advertising, 15*(3), 38-45.

Manabe, K. (1990). *Kokoku no shakai-gaku* [Sociology of advertising]. Tokyo: Nikkei Kokoku Kenkyu-jo.

Marquez, F. T. (1975). The relationship of advertising and culture in the Philippines. *Journalism Quarterly, 52*, 436-491.

Matsui, M. (1991, January). Shin-shohin no shijo donyu to shohisa maindo [New product introduction and consumer attitude]. *Asahi Ad Monthly*, pp. 10-15.

Ministry of International Trade and Industry. (1989). *Nichi-bei no kigyo kodo hikaku* [A comparison of corporate behavior between Japan and the U.S.]. Tokyo: Nihon Noritsu Kyokai.

Moriarty, S. E., & Dunkan, T. R. (1991). Global advertising: Issues and practices. *Current Issues and Research in Advertising, 13*(1&2), 313-342.

Mueller, B. (1987). Reflections of culture: An analysis of Japanese and American advertising appeals. *Journal of Advertising Research, 27*(3), 51-59.

Nishio, C. (1989). Burando sentaku no kitei-yoin ni kan-suru kenkyu [The effect of corporate image on brand choice]. *Marketing Science, 13*, 37-43.

Otsuki, H. (1982). Shodo-gai ha naze okoru-noka? [Why does impulse purchase occur?]. *Shohi to Ryutsu, 6*(4), 153-160.

Reed, J. D. (1985, November 4). Does the soft sell still sell? Japanese ad executives concentrate on *kanjo. Time*, p. 24.

Shimaguchi, M., & Ishii, J. (1989, January). Moderu chenji no sekkyoku-teki tenkai [Aggressive utilization of model change]. *Diamond Harvard Review*, pp. 49-58.

Tajima, Y., & Miyashita, M. (1985). *Ryutsu no kokusai hikaku* [International comparison of distribution]. Tokyo: Yuhikaku.

Tanaka, H. (1984). *Cultural values in U.S. and Japanese magazine advertising: A comparative content analysis.* Unpublished master's thesis, Journalism Graduate Studies, Southern Illinois University, Carbondale, IL.

Tsusan chosa: choki-ka yobikake e [MITI study calls for shorter model change cycle]. (1992, March 11). *Nihon Keizai Shimbun.*

Yamaki, T. (1990). *Kokoku kokusai hikaku to gurobaru senryaku* [International comparison of advertising and global strategies]. Tokyo: Sanno Daigaku Shuppan-bu.

Yamamoto, M. (1987). Shakai-teki joho-shori katei no hikaku bunka-teki kento: Kokoku joho no shori ni kansuru kento [A comparative cultural analysis of social information processing: An examination of advertising information processing]. In *Josei Kenkyu-shu* (pp. 138-158). Tokyo: Yoshida Hideo Kinen Jigyo Zaidan.

The year in numbers—1990. (1991, January 7). *Product Alert*, p. 4.

Part II

The Brand Personality and Brand Equity

Chapter 5

Converting Image into Equity

Alexander L. Biel
Alexander L. Biel & Associates, California

Ever since David Ogilvy focused attention on the concept of brand image in the 1950s, marketers have struggled to come to grips with the idea. Ogilvy declared, ''Every advertisement must be considered as a contribution to the complex symbol which is the brand image—as part of the long term investment in the reputation of the brand'' (1951, p. 178). Although Ogilvy identified advertising's contribution to image, he also recognized that advertising was not the only source of imagery for a brand.

Whereas there has been general agreement that brands—at least some brands—do have images, there has been far less consensus about what images are, whether they can be measured, how they are formed, and, ultimately, what they are worth.

There is also a good deal of confusion about the relationship of brand image to a relative newcomer to the lexicon of marketing—positioning.

This paper offers some insights about the nature of brand images and explores the relationship of image to the concept of brand equity.

''BRANDSCAPE'' AND PERSONAL BRANDSPACE

Anthropologist John Sherry (1987) noted that brands have become so ubiquitous in 20th-century America that we could say we are living in a rich ''brandscape.''

From this brandscape of availability we select a personal brandspace in which to live. My personal brandspace suggests a proximity—both positive and negative—to the plethora of brands available to me. For example:

From the Crest toothpaste I brush with each morning to the Remy Martin cognac that ends my day, I move in a perceptual space richly furnished with brand symbols.

It's raining, so I take my L.L. Bean raincoat and my Knirps umbrella. As I get into my Subaru to go to the office, I must decide whether Shell, Texaco, or Chevron will be the gasoline I buy, whether *The San Francisco Chronicle* or *The Wall Street Journal* will fill me in on the news, and whether I'll grab breakfast at McDonald's or the Hilton. In either case, I'll pass a Burger King, a Wendy's, and a Jack in the Box before I eat.

As I get on the freeway, I notice a Mercedes just ahead of me; a U-Haul trailer is about to switch lanes behind me. Between my home and my office, I pass Wells Fargo, Security Pacific, and Bank of America branches, as well as billboards for Winston's, Coca-Cola, and Sapporo Beer.

My secretary comes in wearing a pair of Levi's and Nikes. She tells me she got a great deal on Rossignol skis, but is thinking of taking up biking. Do I know anything about Cannondale?

At lunch, I choose a Becks beer; my Marlboro-smoking guest considers a Diet Coke, but then opts for a glass of Mondavi Zinfandel with his meal, and a Perrier to start.

I could go on, but the point is inescapable. And I haven't even turned on my Sony TV to watch the advertising!

Indeed, from the brands I use, and other brands that are adjacent to me, you may have started to develop a mental picture of me, an idea of what I'm like, and expectations of how I might behave. Brands not only furnish the environment in which I live, but they also enrobe me, and by doing so, help define who I am.

Further insight comes with visiting another city for the first time: Familiar brands create a feeling of security for the visitor. Holiday Inns once based an advertising campaign on "no surprises" and that, of course, is a strong brand's generic promise.

But there is more to it than that. When sociologist Louis Wirth described the ennui of life in the city, he noted that although one lived, played, worked, and prayed with the same people in small towns, the inexorable march toward urbanization and relocation brought far more fragmented relationships.

For some consumers, how they feel about brands and expect to be treated by them yields a pleasing degree of comfort. As one moves through a daily routine, there is a certain measure of reassurance in the familiar advertisements, signs, and logos that one encounters.

Finally, on a very practical level, consumers like brands because they package meaning. They form a kind of shorthand that makes choice easier. They let me escape from a feature-by-feature analysis of category alternatives, and in a world where time is an ever-diminishing commodity, brands make it easier to store evaluations.

What is a Brand? Revisited

The first brands were developed by industrial concerns over 100 years ago to wrest control of sales of products from retailers. Although brands originated in the field of consumer goods, today the concept of brand has spread to a far wider range of "purchasables." Service brands abound; so do brands in the business-to-business field. Indeed, the utility of paradigm shifting is such that it is not uncommon for sophisticated marketers in tourism to refer to ski resorts, cities, and countries as brands, for movie makers to refer to films as brands, or for utility managers to describe their firms as brands. I suspect that when it comes to attracting students, recruiting faculty, or winning grants, it is surely not inappropriate to think of universities as brands.

EQUITY: THE VALUE OF BRANDS

Although the definition of brand equity is often debated and the term is frequently confused with brand image, we see a clear distinction.

Brand equity deals with the value, usually defined in economic terms, of a brand beyond the physical assets associated with its manufacture or provision.

Whereas brand image is a concept originated and "owned" by marketers and advertising specialists, the idea that a brand has equity that exceeds its conventional asset value is a notion developed by financial people. Underlying a brand's equity is the concept of a brand's *consumer franchise*, the loyalty or fans it commands. Brand equity can be considered the additional cash flow achieved by associating a brand with the underlying product or service.

In the case of a brand acquisition, it is the expectation of the future cash flow that commands a premium over the cost of developing the plant and infrastructure required to bring a new, competing brand to the market.

It is useful—albeit incomplete—to think of a brand's equity as the premium a consumer would pay for a branded product or service, compared to an identical unbranded version of the same product/service.

It also follows that stronger brands will have more equity than weaker competitors. A good example of this comes from the field of personal electronics, where it is not unusual for several marketers to share the same production facilities. Sony, Nikon, and Ricoh market an identical camcorder, alike in all respects except for brand name and price. The Sony version sells for an average price that is about 10% higher than the Nikon, yet it outsells the latter. The Ricoh retails for about 8% less than the Nikon, but enjoys a smaller share of market.

The controversy about whether to include brand equity on a company's books is not yet resolved, but the fact that this is a debatable issue has already drawn attention to the financial properties of brand values.

STRONG BRANDS

What is a strong brand? Interestingly, marketers are not particularly articulate in identifying the characteristics of brand strength beyond share of market. However, when asked to identify strong brands with no supporting guidelines, there is a great deal of agreement about which brands are strong and which are not.

Rolex, for example, is consistently described as a strong brand, as is Alka Seltzer. Not surprisingly, so are IBM, Pepsi, Green Giant, Kleenex, Volkswagen, and *The New York Times*. Winston, however, is not. Neither is Canada Dry, nor *The New York Daily News*.

Several attributes characterize brands marketers describe as strong, including salience with respect to the product category. Leavitt (1987) noted that strong brands are more likely to have shape and substance. They evoke a more extensive, richer set of associations. Visual images and words or phrases linked with strong brands are likely to be more easily retrieved from memory. Finally, strong brands are held in high regard.

Interestingly, strong brands often have high market shares, but market share alone does not distinguish them from other brands.

BRAND IMAGE DRIVES BRAND EQUITY

Brand equity stands for a financial concept associated with the valuation placed on a brand. It is useful to recognize that the equity of a brand is driven by brand image, a consumer (or customer) concept. Schematically, the relationship is represented in Fig. 5.1.

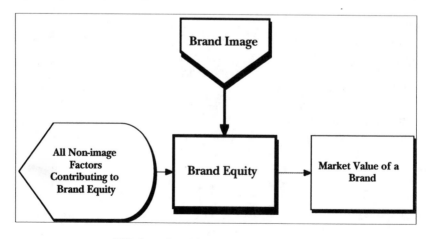

FIG. 5.1.   Brand image drives brand equity.

Any expectation of the cash flow premium enjoyed by a successful brand ultimately depends upon consumer behavior, which is, at root, driven by perceptions of a brand. Although behavioral measures of purchase describe the existence of equity, they fail to reveal what is in the hearts and minds of consumers that actually drives equity.

Brand Image Defined: Associations Linked to Brands

If brand equity is the added value brought by a brand, how can we most usefully define brand image? A good starting point is to describe the image of a brand as that cluster of attributes and associations that consumers connect to the brand name.

These evoked associations can be *hard*—specific perceptions of tangible/functional attributes, such as speed, premium price, user friendliness, length of time in business, or number of flights per day.

They can also be *soft* emotional attributes, like excitement, trustworthiness, fun, dullness, masculinity, or innovation. A brand like Apple might be associated with youthful ingenuity, whereas IBM might be linked to efficiency. Prudential may evoke thoughts of stability; Allstate may conjure up care.

THREE COMPONENTS OF IMAGE

The image of a brand has three contributing subimages: (a) the image of the provider of the product/service, or corporate image; (b) the image of the user; and (c) the image of the product/service itself. However, the relative contribution of these three elements varies by product category and brand. In the case of Marlboro, the corporate reputation of Philip Morris plays hardly any role at all in forming the brand's image. The product image itself contributes, but perhaps the strongest contributor is the impression people have of the brand's users.

Gray Poupon plays heavily on the image of the user, a little on the image of the product, and not at all on the reputation of the manufacturer.

All three components of image are operating for the leading brands in the personal computer field. Image of maker, product, and user each clearly contribute to the brand image of Macintosh or IBM's PC.

This is represented schematically in Fig. 5.2.

Personality and Character

Clearly, the user component of brand image can be described in terms of imputed personality. Consumers have little difficulty describing the person who might smoke Marlboro cigarettes, serve Gallo wine, or wear Calvin Klein jeans.

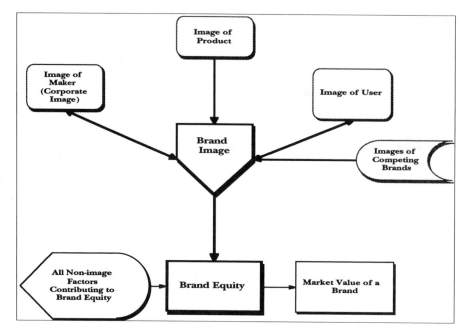

FIG. 5.2.   The three components of brand image.

By employing sufficiently sensitive questions, researchers can elicit rich, consistent descriptions of the personality and character of the brand itself. Consumers have little trouble describing brands as selfish or generous, dull or sparkling, charming or stiff. Some brands are considered responsible, distinguished, sentimental, or righteous; others are described as slippery, sophisticated, careless, or arrogant. Although brand personality studies have heretofor been largely ad hoc in nature, some progress is being made in the development of standardized, transnational brand-personality measures.

More recent research suggests that brands can evoke feelings as well as associations. Some brands make one feel happy; others, confident or safe. Still other brands evoke feelings of boredom, confusion, or amusement.

Although conventional wisdom implies that consumers are blank tablets upon which marketers etch images, some investigators have suggested that the dialogue is two way. Lannon (see chapter 11 of this volume) believes that consumers interact with brands. Blackston (see chapter 8 of this volume) proposed the idea of brand relationships by showing that consumers describe not only the way they see brands, but also the way in which brands see them.

Visual Representations

Brand images also have a strong nonverbal component. The unique symbols long associated with many brands—especially strong brands—are automatically accessed from memory as soon as the brand is shown. For some, the pictorial image of silver-wrapped kisses comes to mind when the word Hershey is presented; others see the silver-on-chocolate-brown wrapper. When Green Giant is mentioned, people see the Giant himself in their mind's eye. For some, the red field with a yellow shell appears when Shell is mentioned. The distinctive batwing shape alone evokes identification of its owner, Levi jeans.

Indeed, King (1989) suggested that the use of a well-chosen visual metaphor can capture, through association, desirable values associated with a brand. The visual metaphor can provide a powerful set of symbols that are particularly important in service categories, where there is no tangible product per se. Examples include the Wells Fargo stagecoach (symbolizing a bank that comes through for its customers), Merrill Lynch's bull (denoting optimism), and the visual representation of "the way is clear" for Germany's Volksbanken Raiffeisenbanken (suggesting a high level of service).

Visual representations also have some unique advantages. Whereas counterargument is sometimes elicited by verbal messages, visual representations are processed differently and are not subject to the same logical scrutiny employed for verbal propositions. As a consequence, they are more likely to be accepted. If the Green Giant, for example, symbolizes *fresh from the farm*, this is less likely to be challenged by the viewer than a verbal claim stating that a brand of canned vegetables is farm fresh.

Hard and Soft Attributes

There has long been concern among marketers that the softer attributes of brands have little impact on purchasing behavior. However, recent research evidence suggests that this is not necessarily the case.

A BBDO study (1988) that asked consumers to estimate the extent to which leading brands in a category were truly different or pretty much the same revealed that consumers were far more likely to find differences in categories that rely on emotional appeals, such as beer and cigarettes, than those utilizing predominantly rational appeals, such as cleaning products.

A possible explanation may be that functional differences between many brands today are at best marginal; most or all detergents, for example, claim they clean better than the competition. In any event, technological progress is so rapid that any advantage is short lived.

However, the so-called softer characteristics of image, such as brand personality, are often far more differentiated because they are less constrained by the physical attributes of the underlying products. The metaphorical and symbolic vocabularies available are much richer. Bank of America and Security Pacific may be locked in combat about who offers the best rates and points on mortgages. However, they cannot today "own" the spirit of the West, with its strong values of dependability and commitment, that Wells Fargo has so effectively pre-empted.

Brand personality has two other advantages:

1. Although features can change and today's advantage can become tomorrow's liability, brand personality, if it taps more enduring values, has a far better chance of achieving longevity.
2. Brand personality encourages more active processing on the part of the consumer, suggesting the he or she can interpret a brand's image in a manner that is more personally meaningful.

Figure 5.3 represents the ways in which associations drive image, which in turn drives equity.

Sources of Imagery

In addition to direct and indirect (e.g., word of mouth, media reports, etc.) personal experience with a brand, media advertising is an obvious source of image, both reflecting and forming the brand's gestalt. Morris the Cat for Nine

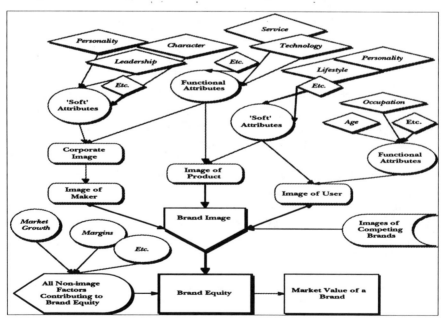

FIG. 5.3. The multiple attributes of image.

Lives cat food, the Friendly Skies of United, Karl Malden for American Express Cheques, the man with the eyepatch for Hathaway shirts, and Budweiser's Clydesdales are all examples of the residua of well-established campaigns. This is not, of course, a new phenomenon. The Doyle Dane Bernbach advertising for a plain-to-the-point-of-ugliness car, the Volkswagen Beetle, was so uniquely effective that one could argue that the advertising actually became a product attribute. By purchasing the car, a buyer also obtained "bragging rights" to the sophistication of the car's advertising. Buyers evolved from being simply practical, to being clever, in the know, and smart.

Some marketers treat media advertising as the sole source of brand image, but this is not always the case. In fact, it is a dangerous assumption because the sword of image obviously cuts both ways. Other sources include:

Direct Response

Direct mail contributes, but not always positively. Interestingly, most direct marketers place heavy emphasis on the behavioral response that their efforts obtain, but neglect its impact on image. As a consequence, whereas the sophisticated Annie Liebowitz print ads for the American Express Card induce me to think of the card as prestigious, the direct mail pieces that clutter my mailbox urging me to sign up suggest a company that's certainly not above hustling me.

Sales Promotion

Sales promotion can also contribute, both positively and negatively, to image. For example, a company that constantly runs price promotions tends to reduce perceptions of quality; consumers feel that the brand is worth less because it is always on special.

On the other hand, an Ivory soap promotion that gave awards to consumers who found specially made bars of Ivory that didn't float moved the product and found a fresh way to reinforce the purity associations of the brand's image.

Brand Name

Names can contribute strongly (e.g., Eveready batteries, Formula 44 cough medicine, Orville Redenbacher popcorn, Compaq computers, and IBM) or they can dilute image. For example, Purolator found that their name served them less well than did Airborne's when they tried to compete with Federal Express. When a company called Documents Handling Limited entered the international package delivery business, they changed their name to DHL. Kentucky Fried Chicken has just changed its name to KFC to help shed today's negative associations with frying.

Corporate Identity

Corporate identity, design, and packaging are also contributors. The Campbell Soup can label and the classic shape of the Coca-Cola bottle are both unmistakable examples of packaging's contribution. The Rock of Gibraltar has long stood for Prudential and its rock-solid stability.

The golden arches identify McDonald's, San Francisco's pyramid building symbolizes Transamerica, and the "good hands" mean Allstate Insurance.

Even here, the sword can cut two ways. In an effort to expand its overnight delivery service facilities in Europe, Federal Express bought a trucking company in Germany. Along with trucks, the company owned a barge company. The acquisition was duly rebranded. As a consequence, passersby see boats bearing the Fed Ex logo, leisurely plying the Rhine.

Michael Purvis of the design firm SBG suggests that some brands, through their packaging, have come to "own" certain colors; competitors usurp those colors at their peril. Purple and orange belong to Federal Express. IBM owns dark blue in business machines. Yellow belongs to Kodak in photography. For batteries, Duracell owns bronze and black. Tiffany claims light blue through their unique packaging. Red and white belong to Campbell.

Public Relations

A firm's relations with its public can also contribute to image. Tylenol, in the long run, won respect for its proactive handling of package tampering. The brand added to its image of integrity. In contrast, Perrier damaged its credibility by vacillating over explanations about how traces of benzene had gotten into the product. AT&T's efforts to force a takeover of NCR paints a more predatory picture of the company than the view most consumers previously held.

McDonald's is a firm with an uncommonly good understanding of the way public relations contribute to image. It would be hard to justify the opening of a unit in Russia on the basis of revenue generation alone, but the media coverage of a unit opening in Moscow made the firm seem a little more international, a bit more forward looking. Their public commitment to reducing environmental pollution increases the perception of the company as a good citizen, as do tray liners offering tips for conserving water in drought areas. Introducing a lean hamburger—despite (or perhaps because of) the fact that it is not expected to be a big seller in the short term—says that the firm is concerned about the health of its customers.

Staff

For service-oriented businesses, the firm's employees are significant channels of image communication. Berry, Bennett, and Brown (1988) noted that the job of the chief marketing person in a company marketing things is to purchase and organize outside resources, such as advertising; the equivalent marketer in a service business has the primary task of getting everybody in the firm to do marketing.

One consequence is that corporate culture can indirectly play an important role in image development. The Avis "we try harder" theme exemplifies a firm that tried to involve employees to impact perceptions of Avis. More recently, General Mills' Olive Garden restaurant unit has successfully motivated staff to deliver a consistently high service level, subbranded Hospitaliana.

BRAND POSITIONING

Another term in the lexicon of marketing is positioning, or more completely, brand positioning. This refers to both the process and end result of building (or rebuilding) an image for a brand relative to a target market segment. The American Express card, for example, has been positioned as the appropriate method of payment for travel and entertainment for upper income consumers. Miller Lite was positioned as the beer that gave heavy beer drinkers "permission" to drink more. American Airlines is positioned as the businessman's airline.

It is not always necessary to specify a distinct market segment in positioning a brand, but a market target is usually implied by a successful positioning strategy.

BRANDING RESEARCH: WHERE WE STAND

In the past, research on branding has focused on the identification of brand image and on the monitoring of changes in image. Studies of this type were usually descriptive in nature.

Today, the key issues in branding research, from a practitioner's point of view, focus on two themes:

1. Quantification of brand equity.
2. Identification of brand image elements that are likely to impact changes in consumer behavior and lead to changes in brand equity.

THE QUANTIFICATION OF BRAND EQUITY

Econometric modeling approaches decompose brand value using the market value of a firm's stock as the dependent variable. Other investigations reflect measures that are closer to consumer behavior.

One intriguing approach utilizes a two-factor trade-off between brand and price through time in an attempt to gauge changes in equity as a consequence of marketing activities.

RELATING BRAND IMAGE TO BEHAVIOR

Assessing brand image involves two goals: The most obvious is simply revelation and understanding. 2. A more action-oriented goal addresses modification of the brand's image. The technology for accomplishing this second goal is also more complex.

Recently, however, there has been encouraging progress. For example, Morgan and his colleagues at Research International on both sides of the Atlantic have demonstrated a promising model known as Pilot/Locator. As the name suggests, Pilot/Locator is a micromodel of an individual's brand image that relates that image to the person's preference structure. In other words, the marketer can now work with an actionable link between changes in brand image and brand choice.

By simulating changes on a disaggregate basis, the micromodel predicts the effect of shifts in brand image on brand preference. Studies of this type are particularly appealing to the practitioner in the sense of providing prescriptions for brand positioning.

The following two examples, necessarily sanitized to protect the proprietary interest of clients, demonstrate how this approach is operationalized:

1. The first example involves a brand in the food service field. To capture preference, a standard constant sum preference exercise was conducted among the dominant brands in the client's product field. In many fields—especially those where the exogenous variables are relatively weak or can be effectively accounted for—there is a strong relationship between the preference obtained in the constant sum measure and share of market, and in this example the relationship obtained.

Separately, but among the same consumers, a description of the brands was undertaken, using 10-point Likert scales covering 32 image items known to be important to the product category. These data provided the input for a perceptual map of the images of the brands competing in the market.

Since Pilot/Locator is a micromodel, the investigators were able to model each consumer, based on images of each brand in the respondent's salient set and the dependent variable derived from the constant sum exercise.

Through a series of simulations, it was possible to determine which of the 32 image variables, if improved for the client's brand, would be most likely to lead to an increase in overall brand choice. Once this is done for a single variable, it is possible to continue the process to look for the next contributor,

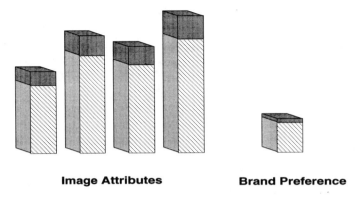

Image Attributes   **Brand Preference**

FIG. 5.4.   Changes in some brand image attributes drive changes in brand share.

and so on. By editing the image scores on a respondent-by-respondent basis, it is also possible to create a new map on the assumption that the prescribed image improvements can be achieved.

In this particular exercise, a group of 4 critical attributes was identified. A 20% improvement in any one of these 4 out of the 32 image attributes would increase the brand's share of preference by about 11% (Fig. 5.4).

2. The second example is drawn from a nonfood fast-moving consumer goods (fmcg) category. This category could be described as "commodity like" because prior research indicated that consumers made very few functional distinctions between brands.

Because of this, all 28 of the independent variables were personality descriptors. Examples included family-oriented, responsible, rugged, peaceful, and masculine. Again, Likert scales provided the independent variables, and a constant sum preference task contributed the dependent measure.

Figure 5.5 shows the initial perceptual map that was generated. It displays the brands relative to each other and to the personality variables.

Each independent variable was increased 20% to determine the importance of the variables in determining share of preference. Indexed scores ranged from +182 to −50 relative to the mean.

The first Pilot/Locator simulation (Fig. 5.6) shows changes for the client's brand, which we have called "Chaser," if it were to successfully modify brand personality based on improving its image on the variables most likely to increase its share of preference. To do this, it would need to become more family oriented, dependable, and responsible. It would also need to be more traditional and all-American in character. The second bar shows what would happen instead if Chaser were to enhance its personality to be more like the brand "Leader," which is the dominant brand in the market. This strategy would require making Chaser's image more gentle, peaceful, and feminine, but also a bit more fancy.

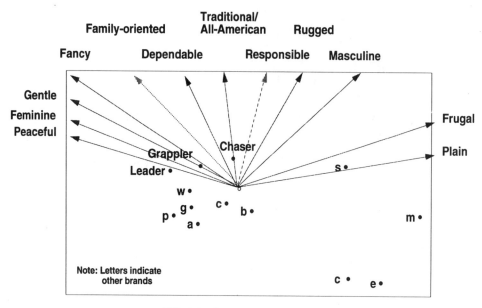

FIG. 5.5. Brand personality map.

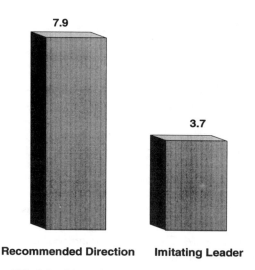

Recommended Direction   **Imitating Leader**

FIG. 5.6. Change in preference share for chaser.

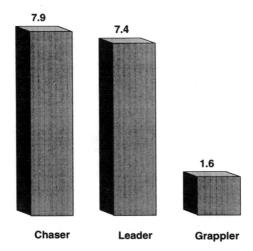

FIG. 5.7.   What if Leader or Grappler imitated new Chaser? Changes in share
of preference.

Clearly, the data suggest that following Leader would not, in the end, do
as much for Chaser's share of preference.

Figure 5.7 shows Pilot/Locator's prediction of what would happen if Leader and the second brand in the market, "Grappler," were to adopt the strategy recommended for Chaser.

We can see that the strategy would work for Leader, but not for Grappler. However, Leader's current success suggests that it would be unlikely to
change. Conclusion: Competitive imitation of Chaser's strategy would not be
a threat.

BUILDING STRONG BRANDS: A SUMMARY

The market has clearly declared that brand equity is alive and well. We demonstrate the relationship between brand image and equity, identify attributes of
image, and suggest sources from which a brand develops an image.

Future research will continue to explore the connection between elements
of a brand's image and the equity that the brand commands. In the main,
most firms currently develop brands by refining and recombining functional
attributes. The increasing speed of technological change shows that there are
better opportunities for developing stronger, more erosion-resistant brands by
allocating a larger share of resources to the so-called softer side of image than
is currently the case.

REFERENCES

BBDO Worldwide. (1988). *Focus: A world of brand parity*. New York: BBDO.

Berry, L., Bennett, D. R., & Brown, C. W. (1988). *Service quality: A profit strategy for financial institutions*. Homewood, IL: Richard D. Irwin.

King, S. H. M. (1989). Branding opportunities in financial services. In *Proceedings of the (British) Market Research Society Conference on Advertising and Marketing Financial Services*. London: MRS Press. See also Brand building in the 1990s, *Journal of Marketing Management, 7*[1]. (See also 3–13.)

Leavitt, C. (1987). *Understanding brand images: A theory and methodology* (Working paper). San Francisco: The Ogilvy Center for Research & Development.

Morgan, R. (1990). *The Pilot image attribute micro-model: A brief outline of background and practice* (Working paper). London: Research International. (See also Roe, M. M., & Morgan, R. (1990). Predictive brand image—Using the Pilot model to assess the effectiveness of global marketing. *Proceedings of EMAC/ESOMAR Symposium*, Athens.)

Ogilvy, D. (1951). Speech to American Marketing Association annual meeting, *AMA proceedings*. Chicago: American Marketing Association.

Sherry, J. (1987). Paper presented at XIV annual conference, Association for Consumer Research. Toronto: Association for Consumer Research.

Chapter 6

The Brand Personality Component of Brand Goodwill: Some Antecedents and Consequences

Rajeev Batra
University of Michigan

Donald R. Lehmann
Columbia University

Dipinder Singh
Ogilvy & Mather, New York

Brand names are regarded among the most valuable assets owned by a company. A well-known and well-regarded brand name—one with a high level of *equity* or *goodwill*—can often be extended into new product categories, in a way that saves the extending company many of the expenses of establishing a new brand name (Aaker & Keller, 1990). As a consequence, companies acquiring others pay significant asset valuation premiums for the portfolio of brand names that are acquired.

This chapter presents a study on the importance of a brand's personality in extending a brand name across product categories and the nature of the categories into which it can be extended. We then discuss several antecedents of brand personality and identify aspects of brand personality creation through advertising that warrant further research attention.

Before we present the study, we briefly review what we mean by *brand image* and *brand personality*. The terms are often used interchangeably. However, it has been argued that brand imagery is a more encompassing term, including within it not merely brand personality but also the attributes and benefits or consequences that the user associates with the brand (Plummer, 1985). Gensch (1978) wrote that "the term 'image' . . . is an abstract concept incorporating the influences of past promotion, reputation and peer evaluation of the alternative. Image connotes the expectations of the consumer" (p. 384). Reynolds and Gutman (1984) listed the following ways in which image has been opera-tionalized: (a) general characteristics, feelings, or impressions, (b) perceptions of products, (c) beliefs and attitudes, (d) brand personality, and (e) linkages between characteristics and feelings/emotions. They provided another opera-tional measure based on a means–end chain (further developed in Reynolds & Jamieson, 1985). Whatever method of operationalizing image is used, it is generally specific to a particular application (e.g., Gensch, 1978; Sirgy, 1982).

When we speak of a brand's personality, we mean the way in which a con-sumer perceives the brand on dimensions that typically capture a person's personality—extended to the domain of brands. There are many approaches to conceptualizing and measuring human personality (Mischel, 1986), but we shall use the *trait* approach attributed to Allport, Eysenck, and Cattell, in which a human or brand's personality is a pattern of traits (Guilford, 1973). A trait is defined variously as "any distinguishable, relatively enduring way in which one individual differs from others" (Guilford, 1973, p. 23) or "the basic qual-ities of a person" (Mischel, 1986, p. 116). Typically, the trait approach classi-fies or scales people using trait terms from everyday language (e.g., friendly, aggressive, honest, etc.). Anderson (1968) provided a rich source of trait terms through a likableness rating of 555 traits.

A great deal of work has been done in the identification of trait-based dimen-sions for personality measurement (e.g., Eysenck & Rachman, 1973). Many studies conclude that five stable personality dimensions emerge when humans are measured through lists of trait words, such as those by Anderson (Dig-man, 1990). These five dimensions (with illustrative bipolar scales) are:

1. Extraversion/introversion (e.g., adventurous–cautious, sociable–reclusive).
2. Agreeableness (e.g., good-natured–irritable; gentle–headstrong).
3. Conscientiousness (e.g., responsible–undependable; tidy–careless).
4. Emotional stability (e.g., composed–excitable; calm–anxious).
5. Culture (e.g., artistically sensitive–insensitive; intellectual–unreflective).

It seems reasonable that these five dimensions of human personality meas-urement could also apply to the personality of brands, although not all brands need to have strong ratings on all these dimensions. However, brand person-alities should also go beyond these five. Although the basic demographic charac-teristics of a human being, such as age, gender, and social class, need not appear in such personality dimensions (because they are visible or easily inferred) the demographics of a brand are often its most salient personality characteristics. Prior research on brand or retail store personality (e.g., Birdwell, 1968; Jaco-by & Olson, 1985) showed that brands or stores are often perceived by con-sumers as "old" or "young," "masculine" or "feminine," "upscale" or "downscale."

This is not surprising; consumers seek brands with personalities that are congruent with either their own or their sought-after (aspirational or ideal) personalities (for a review of this extensive literature, see Sirgy, 1982). This process follows from the idea that consumers use a brand's personality to help define, both for themselves and for others, their sense of self (Belk, 1988; Grubb & Grathwohl, 1967). This sense of self—what a person is or is not—grows out of the reactions of significant others. Through the consensually shared personalities of the brands we purchase and consume, we tell others and ourselves who we are—what our core life values are, the reference groups we identify with, etc. A brand's personality tells consumers the kinds of people it is for (e.g., Pepsi is for aggressive, exciting people) and the kinds of emotions and feelings it supposedly creates and delivers when consumed ("you will feel energized and upbeat when you drink Pepsi").

These personality dimensions from social psychological research are certainly relevant to brand personality research, but they should not limit it. Consumers also buy brands, among other reasons, to define how old or young they are, how masculine or feminine they are, and how upscale or downscale they are. These basic brand personality dimensions are not captured in human personality measures. For this reason, our study attempts a fresh dimensionalization of brand (or product category) personality. The dimensions we report are not complete or exhaustive for the measurement of brand personality, and we suggest further work in this area, using projective techniques as well as adjective scales. After presenting the study, we return to some conceptual issues on the antecedents of brand personality.

BRAND NAME TRANSFERABILITY: A CONSEQUENCE OF BRAND PERSONALITY

Prior Literature

We have discussed the importance of brand extensions. A longstanding issue in marketing has been whether brand names should be used in several product categories or exclusively within a category. Although marketers desire to exploit the value of their brand names by extending them to new product categories, they also fear that inappropriate extensions might be failures, or worse, might weaken the existing value of the brand name. It is important to gauge the extent to which a brand name can be extended to other product categories and the importance of brand or category personality in such extensions.

Several researchers have examined the factors determining the success of brand extensions. Duncan and Nelson (1987) examined how meaning transfer occurs in a brand extension. They compared two models, using "extension beliefs'' as their dependent variable and ''parent beliefs'' and the logical consistency of the extension as independent variables. Aaker and Keller (1990) examined consumer responses to brand extensions and studied the transferability of brand goodwill (BG) across product categories, which is also an important objective in our study. Aaker and Keller used the attitude towards the extension (EXTATT)—the equivalent of BG transferability—as their dependent variable. To examine circumstances under which brand extensions are feasible, they looked at a number of independent variables, including: (a) quality of the original brand, (b) the credibility of the firm, (c) the complexity of the original product, (d) the extent to which the original and the extension are complements and substitutes, and (e) the number of common attributes they share. When we discuss the hypotheses, we show that the independent variables in our study are somewhat different. However, we use some of the Aaker and Keller measures, and their paper is a building block for the hypotheses in this chapter.

Hypotheses

The basic concept underlying the present study is that transfer is greatest for categories that are similar in both personality and specific objective attributes. Whereas previous research has examined only attribute similarity, we test whether personality similarity (which we refer to more broadly as *image similarity*) also impacts on brand name transferability.

Attribute similarity presumably impacts on a brand's transferability because a company's technological competencies are involved. A consumer might make the logical deduction that a company good at making one type of product (e.g., razors) will also be good at making a technically related product (e.g., blades). Image similarity refers to the relationship of categories in terms of the images of the brands in them. A consumer may again infer that a company good in developing one kind of image might also succeed in developing a similar image elsewhere in another category. For example, soda and T-shirts both share friendly, informal images, so a brand transfer across them might seem promising (even though the production technologies are quite different), whereas caskets and entertainment center furniture, even though technologically related, provoke decidedly different images and emotions. An attempt to transfer across these categories seems unlikely to succeed. The expected impact of these two determinants is summarized in the following hypotheses:

Hypothesis 1. BG transfers more readily between product categories that match on an image/personality dimension.

A theoretical basis for this first hypothesis might come from the favorable effect on attitudes of beliefs that are consistent with each other, rather than inconsistent (for a review of some related literature, see Mizerski, Golden, and Kernan, 1979). A brand name (BN1) in a given product category (PC1) evokes a certain image. When the same brand name is used in another product category (PC2), the image evoked by BN1 could be consistent or inconsistent with the image of PC2. In the former case, because there is consistency, there should be greater transferability of BG than there would be in the case where the two images are inconsistent.

Brand or Category Personality is measured through the use of trait adjectives, as we have already discussed. Anderson (1968) provided a rich source of trait terms by means of a likableness rating of 555 trait words. For our purposes, we draw from this source to determine a subset of trait words for measuring the personality of different brands/categories.

All of the image/personality literature reviewed deals with individual brands, not product categories. Here, we measure the images of specific brands and treat these as surrogates for the image of the category. This is done merely for simplicity in data collection; future research may investigate the homogeneity of brand imagery within product categories and segments.

Hypothesis 2.   BG transfers more readily between product categories that match on attributes.

This hypothesis is similar to the first hypotheses except that the match is on logical rather than emotional grounds. An interesting result of examining H1 and H2 is a comparison of the relative impact of image and attribute match on transferability of brand goodwill.

Hypothesis 3.   BG transfers more readily between hedonic product categories than between utilitarian product categories.

BG is the value of a product over the value derived from tangible attributes and it should logically be higher for hedonic products when the intangible value, by definition, dominates. Given that BG is higher and more meaningful in hedonic products, it is reasonable to expect it to transfer more easily between hedonic categories. Support for this notion is found in Sirgy (1982).

Hypotheses 4 through 6 were designed to see if some of the basic results of Aaker and Keller (1990) were replicated here.

Hypothesis 4.   Transferability is enhanced when the products are complements.

Hypothesis 5.   When the products are substitutes, there is no impact on transferability.

Hypothesis 6.   When a product category is difficult to make, the transferability of brands in that category is increased.

Method

This study used survey methods to collect rating scale data as the basis for analysis. The measures and sample are described in more detail here.

Product and Brands

Fourteen brands representing seven product categories were selected (Table 6.1). These brands are representative of a broad spectrum of product categories.

BG Transferability

To measure BG transferability, respondents were asked to evaluate each brand name in each product category. For example, in the cola category, respondents were presented with a list of brand names and asked how they viewed colas with each of the brand names (on a positive–negative scale). This is similar to the measure used by Aaker and Keller (1990) and is basically a measure of the attitude towards a proposed brand extension.

Brand Image (Personality) Similarity

For the purposes of this study, we develop a set of traits designed to be meaningful across a broad spectrum of products. As a starting point, Andersen's (1968) list of 555 trait words were used. This list contained a subcategory

TABLE 6.1
Brands Included in the Final Questionnaire

Product Categories	Brands
Cola-based sodas	Coca-Cola
	Pepsi
Personal stereos	Sony
	GE
Orange juice	Tropicana
	Minute Maid
Sneakers	Nike
	Reebok
Refrigerators	GE
	Whirlpool
35mm SLR cameras	Nikon
	Canon
Point & shoot cameras	Nikon
	Canon

TABLE 6.2
Bases for Attribute and Image Similarity Measures

Attributes	Image Dimensions
Flavor/taste	Reliable–Unreliable
Caffeine content	Old–Young
Price	Technical–Nontechnical
Packaging	Sensible–Rash
Size	Interesting–Boring
Calories	Creative–Noncreative
Brand name	Sentimental–Unsentimental
Sweetness	Impulsive–Deliberate
Weight	Trustworthy–Untrustworthy
Warranty	Conforming–Rebellious
Durability	Daring–Cautious
Convenience	Forceful–Submissive
Color	Bold–Timid
Style	Sociable–Unsociable
Comfort	
Freshness	
Construction material	
Availability	
Serviceability	
Compatibility	
Energy-efficiency	
Instructions	
Automation	
Ease of use	

of 200 words that were rated high in meaning by respondents in that study. Three additional words—old, young, and technical—were added to this list. The list was then circulated among 10 marketing faculty/doctoral students. They were asked to circle up to 30 traits from the list that they considered appropriate for measuring brand personality. A sublist of 35 words was generated from these responses. These words were then presented as 7-point bipolar scales to 15 respondents who were asked to rate nine brands on each of the scales. This resulted in a total of 135 data points which, after factor analysis, yielded seven factors that proved to be quite stable. Two trait scales were chosen from each of the seven factors. The 14 variables chosen for the main study appear in Table 6.2.

Attribute Similarity

Before finalizing the questionnaire, we asked a convenience sample of ten people to list all the attributes they evaluated when they considered a purchase in each of the product categories in this study. A list of 24 attributes, each relevant to more than one product category, was constructed from their responses (see Table 6.2).

In the final study, respondents were shown a table listing the 24 attributes across the vertical axis and the seven product categories across the horizontal axis. They were asked to rank the 5 (or more) most important attributes for each product category.

Hedonic and Utilitarian Measures

We employed the scales used by Batra and Ahtola (1991) to measure the hedonic/utilitarian character of brands and product categories. Specifically, we used three 7-point bipolar adjective scales. The anchors for the hedonic scales were: (a) *unpleasant–pleasant*, (b) *awful–nice*, and (c) *disagreeable–agreeable*. For the utilitarian scales, the anchors were: (a) *useless–useful*, (b) *harmful–beneficial*, and (c) *worthless–valuable*.

Other Measures

The following measures (on 7-point scales) were taken to replicate some of the work reported by Aaker and Keller (1990):

1. Difficulty in making a product in each product category (e.g., a rating of *extremely easy to make* to *extremely difficult to make* for cola-based sodas).
2. Degree of complementarity between categories (e.g., whether refrigerators were *not at all/extremely complementary* to cola-based sodas, with complementarity defined as "the extent to which products from the two categories might be used together").
3. Degree of substitutability between categories (e.g., whether refrigerators *cannot substitute at all* to *can substitute completely* for 35mm SLR cameras, where substitute means "the extent to which a product from one category can be used instead of a product from the other category").

The following additional measures (also on 7-point scales) were taken to examine their covariance with BG and other measures:

1. Perceived quality of each brand (*low quality* to *high quality* rating for GE personal stereo, for example).
2. Familiarity with each brand and with each product category (*extremely familiar* to *extremely unfamiliar* with Reebok sneakers, etc.)
3. Perceived reputation of each brand (e.g., *bad reputation* to *good reputation* of Reebok sneakers).

Sample

A total of 107 respondents were recruited from the campus of a university in the northeastern United States and given a monetary incentive. The cover page of the questionnaire told them that the objective of the study was to "determine some of the ways purchase choices are made." Subjects were run in groups of up to eight people.

Analysis and Results

Category Similarity

The hypotheses require measures of similarity between categories on both attributes and images. The image similarity measure was established as follows. The subjects rated two brands in each of the seven categories on the 14 traits in Table 6.2, using a 7-point scale. The category image was taken as the average of the two brands and distances between them were calculated using Euclidean distance. To establish the attribute similarity between categories, the respondents were asked to rank the five most important attributes for each product category from the list shown in Table 6.2. The attributes were then given values ranging from 9 (for the most important attribute) to 5 (for the fifth most important attribute), with 0 assigned to attributes which were not in the top five. Euclidean distances were then computed between the attribute values for each pair of categories.

Utilitarian/Hedonic Measures

The average ratings of the categories on the hedonic and utilitarian measures were calculated. To determine if there was a match between two categories, the scores of the two categories for the hedonic and utilitarian measures were multiplied together. This product was a large number only if both categories were high on either hedonic or utilitarian; otherwise, high scale values from one category would be multiplied by low scale values for the other category. The product score was then used to create a binary variable for the presence/absence of a match, using a cutoff determined judgmentally from the data.

Transferability

The relation of transferability to the variables discussed in the hypotheses was examined first by looking at the simple correlations between these variables, and then through multiple regression (Table 6.3). In order to remove any tendency to consistently rate transferability high or low across categories, a dummy variable was created for each subject and included in the analysis, treating the data as a repeated measures design (cf. Pedhazur, 1982). The use of a dummy variable should reduce the error variance in the data, providing a more powerful test of the hypotheses. Interestingly, these individual differences dummies account for about 28% of the total variance, the hypothesized variables 17%, and 55% of the variance is unaccounted for.

TABLE 6.3
Transferability Regression Results:
Predicting Attitudes Toward Proposed Extensions

Source	DF	Sum of Squares	F Values	R^2
Model	113	15653.54	63.83	.448
Error	8874	19258.10		

Source	DF	Sum of Squares	F Value
Within-person variance	106	9736.28	33.52

Variable	DF	Standardized Parameter Estimate	T Value*
Image distance	1	−.148	−15.62
Attribute distance	1	−.314	−33.51
Complement	1	.127	2.75
Substitute	1	.373	6.66
Difficulty	1	.333	9.98
Hedonic match	1	.000	0.01
Utilitarian match	1	.053	2.71

*All coefficients, except hedonic match, are significant at $p < .05$.

The results show that, with the exception of the hedonic match, all the factors hypothesized to have an effect significantly impact transferability. In addition, substitutability significantly enhances transferability. By comparing the standardized coefficients, the three largest effects are attribute distance, substitutability, and difficulty in manufacturing. This suggests that perceived technical competence in manufacturing has a major impact on transferability and that advice such as "stick to the knitting" may be well founded if customers perceive some technical synergies across categories. Crucially, for our purposes, the significance of the image match suggests that more than purely technical criteria may influence transferability. Personality similarity also has a significant impact. It is not clear why the hedonic match hypothesis failed to find support; perhaps the hedonic match is better conceptualized as a moderator of the other relationships, rather than as a directly contributing factor. Further research might pursue this possibility.

In summary, this study shows that brand goodwill transferability is strongly influenced by the perceived technological transferability from one category to another and, to a lesser extent, by the similarity in image of the two categories. Limitations, of course, are apparent in this study. It would be desirable to replicate this study using larger samples, more product categories, more brands within each category, and other measures of the variables and the distances between brands. Extension to the industrial area might show an even larger impact of technical product similarity.

Nonetheless, the results suggest that the transferability of brand goodwill is at least partly explainable on logical and theoretically appealing grounds. For managers, the study suggests quite strongly that any strategic planning regarding the extension of brand names to other categories ought to be based, at least in part, on the degree of image similarity between the present and proposed product categories. Furthermore, managements concerned with the development of extendable brand names should consider the image requirements of product categories to which the brand names might be extended in the future. We now consider research issues concerning the development of brand imagery through advertising.

RESEARCH ISSUES: ANTECEDENTS OF BRAND PERSONALITY

In this section we discuss the antecedents of a brand's personality—specifically, the role of advertising in creating a brand personality—and identify areas for future research.

It is reasonable to suggest that a brand's personality is created, over time, by the entire marketing mix of the brand—its price (high or low, odd or even), retail store locations (imagery associations), product formulation (ingredients, benefits), product form (solid/liquid, etc.), packaging details (color, size, materials, shape), symbols used in all phases of brand communication, sales promotions, and media advertising. Further, a brand's personality is stronger and clearer (a) if these elements of the brand's marketing mix are deliberately coordinated, (b) if the personality sought is competitively distinctive, and (c) if the sought-after personality is kept consistent over time and over media. Ogilvy (1966, p. 100) once said that every advertisement is an investment in the long-term image of a brand.

Within the advertising portion of this mix, it seems that every element of the ad (including the medium in which the ad appears) contributes to the brand personality. The verbal elements of the text copy clearly contribute by communicating both the benefits of the brand as well as its "tone" (friendly, serious, etc.). Yet the nonverbal elements might be even more important (Haley, Richardson, & Baldwin, 1984). In print ads, these include the illustrations, the typography, the colors, and the layout. In broadcast advertising, especially TV, important elements include the choice of music, camera techniques (including editing and segues), and, especially, the choice of endorsers and the casting of characters.

Clearly, this is nothing more than a "laundry list" of the elements of an ad execution, and it points to the major gap in the relevant literature. We have only a rudimentary understanding (and almost no academic literature) of how different levels or types of each of these nonverbal ad elements contribute to

the establishment or reinforcement of a particular type of brand personality. All that can be said with certainty is that the process by which advertisements give brands and product categories a personality, or cultural meaning,
involves associating the brand in an ad with other social and cultural symbols that contain that cultural meaning (see McCracken, 1988), with some
kind of "conditioning" process possibly involved as well (see Allen & Shimp,
1990).

McCracken's work gave us the broad outlines of how this transfer of cultural meaning occurs, but we have no body of systematic research on the
"microlanguage" of these nonverbal elements, with the possible exception of
color. For the most part, we rely only on the insight and wisdom involved in
the direction and creation of these ads. We simply need to know more about
the language of these nonverbal elements of advertising.

The way in which the nonverbal elements of an ad communicate is necessarily through inference. As we mention in the introduction, a brand personality implicates the consumer's social identity and, thus, the reactions of
significant others. An advertiser's message about the social usage context of
a brand, the kind of user the brand is for, and the kind of user personality
that the brand communicates, are likely to be symbolically and associatively
implied, rather than explicitly stated, through what Wells called "drama" advertising (Wells, 1988; see also Deighton, Romer, & McQueen, 1989). Perhaps
the process of forming beliefs through inferences rather than explicit claims
is especially powerful when the beliefs about the brand concern its social or
normative aspects (cf. Kardes, 1988).

If this is true, then more academic research is needed on the inferential
processes through which the nonverbal elements of an advertisement shape
a brand's perceived personality. Although there has been considerable research on inferential belief-formation processes in advertising (Ford & Smith,
1987; Huber & McCann, 1982; for a recent review, see Simmons & Lynch,
1991), this research has typically examined only the effects of an ad's verbal elements on functional attribute beliefs and overall attitudes about the
brand. Thus, most of the findings from this research—the information used
to make such inferences, why these inferences are discounted in evaluations,
the situations when such inferences are most likely to be made, and how
the existence of such inferential beliefs biases the assessed importance weights
of explicitly stated attributes—are not relevant to the issue of how an ad's
nonverbal elements shapes a brand's personality. Given this research vacu-
um, researchers should now conduct studies on inferential belief formation
that uses an expanded conception of what the important variables are, on
both the independent and the dependent sides, if we are to fully understand
the processes through which advertisements shape a brand's personality.

REFERENCES

Aaker, D. A., & Keller, K. L. (1990). Consumer evaluations of brand extensions. *Journal of Marketing, 54*(1), 27–41.

Allen, C. T., & Shimp, T. A. (1990). On using classical conditioning methods for researching the impact of ad-evoked feelings. In S. J. Agres, J. A. Edell, & T. M. Dubinsky (Eds.), *Emotion in advertising* (pp. 19–34). Westport, CT: Quorum.

Anderson, N. H. (1968). Likableness ratings of 555 personality-trait words. *Journal of Personality and Social Psychology, 9*(3), 272–279.

Batra, R., & Ahtola, O. (1991). Measuring the hedonic and utilitarian sources of consumer attitudes. *Marketing Letters, 2*(2), 159–170.

Belk, R. W. (1988). Possessions and the extended self. *Journal of Consumer Research, 15*(2), 139–168.

Birdwell, A. E. (1968). A study of the influence of image congruence on consumer choice. *Journal of Business, 41*(1), 76–88.

Deighton, J., Romer, D., & McQueen, J. (1989). Using drama to persuade. *Journal of Consumer Research, 16*(3), 335–343.

Digman, J. (1990). Personality structure: Emergence of the five-factor model. In M. Rosenzweig & L. W. Porter (Eds.), *Annual review of psychology* (pp. 417–440). Palo Alto, CA: Annual Reviews, Inc.

Duncan, C. P., & Nelson, J. E. (1987). *Meaning transfer in brand extension strategy* (working paper). University of Colorado, College of Business & Administration, Boulder.

Eysenck, H. J., & Rachman, S. (1973). Personality dimensions. In H. N. Mischel & W. Mischel (Eds.), *Readings in personality* (pp. 27–30). New York: Holt, Rinehart & Winston.

Ford, G. T., & Smith, R. A. (1987). Inferential beliefs in consumer evaluations: An assessment of alternative processing strategies. *Journal of Consumer Research, 14*(3), 363–371.

Gensch, D. H. (1978). Image-measurement segmentation. *Journal of Marketing Research, 15*(3), 384–394.

Grubb, E. L., & Grathwohl, H. L. (1967). Consumer self-concept, symbolism, and market behavior: A theoretical approach. *Journal of Marketing, 31*(4), 22–27.

Guilford, J. P. (1973). On personality. In H. N. Mischel & W. Mischel (Eds.), *Readings in personality* (pp. 22–23). New York: Holt, Rinehart & Winston.

Haley, R. L., Richardson, J., & Baldwin, B. M. (1984). The effects of nonverbal communications in television advertising. *Journal of Advertising Research, 24*, 11–18.

Huber, J., & McCann, J. (1982). The impact of inferential beliefs on product evaluations. *Journal of Marketing Research, 19*(3), 324–333.

Jacoby, J., & Olson, J. C. (Eds.). (1985). *Perceived quality: How consumers view stores and merchandise.* Lexington, MA: Lexington Books.

Kardes, F. (1988). Spontaneous inference processes in advertising: The effects of conclusion omission and involvement in persuasion. *Journal of Consumer Research, 15*(2), 225–233.

McCracken, G. (1988). *Culture and consumption.* Bloomington: Indiana University Press.

Mischel, W. (1986). *Introduction to personality* (4th ed.). New York: Holt, Rinehart & Winston.

Mizerski, R. W., Golden, L. L., & Kernan, J. B. (1979). The attribution process in consumer decision making. *Journal of Consumer Research, 6*(2), 123–140.

Ogilvy, D. (1966). *Confessions of an advertising man.* New York: Atheneum.

Pedhazur, E. J. (1982). *Multiple regression in behavioral research.* New York: Holt, Rinehart & Winston.

Plummer, J. T. (1985, February). *Brand personality: A strategic concept for multinational advertising.* Paper presented to the AMA Winter Marketing Educators Conference, Phoenix, AZ.

Reynolds, T. J., & Gutman, J. O. (1984). Advertising is image management. *Journal of Advertising Research, 24*(1), 27–37.

Reynolds, T. J., & Jamieson, L. F. (1985). Image representations: An analytic framework. In J. Jacoby & J. C. Olson (Eds.), *Perceived quality: How consumers view stores and merchandise.* Lexington, MA: Lexington Books.

Simmons, C. J., & Lynch, J. G., Jr. (1991, March). Inference effects without inference making? Effects of missing information and use of presented information. *Journal of Consumer Research, 17*(4), 477–491.

Sirgy, M. J. (1982, December). Self-concept in consumer behavior: A critical review. *Journal of Consumer Research, 9*(3), 287–300.

Wells, W. D. (1988). Lectures and dramas. In P. Cafferata & A. Tybout (Eds.), *Cognitive and affective responses to advertising.* Lexington, MA: D. C. Heath.

Chapter 7

Can Products and Brands Have Charisma?

Norman Smothers
California State University, Hayward

> These standard advertised wares—toothpastes, socks, tires, cameras, instantaneous hot water heaters—were his (George Babbitt's) symbols and proofs of excellence; at first the signs, then the substitutes, for joy and passion and wisdom.
>
> —Sinclair Lewis (1922)

INTRODUCTION

A popular analogy used in the marketing literature is that brands are like people. The analogy implies that brands, like people, can have an image or personality. Journal publications such as "Understanding Brand Personality" (Durgee, 1988), "Strategic Brand Concept-Image Management" (Park, Jaworski, & MacInnis, 1986), or "Brands, Like People, Have Personalities" (Duboff, 1986) are typical. This notion is not limited to the academic literature. For example, *Forbes* magazine asserts that "A Brand Is Like a Friend" (Flint, 1988) and *Advertising Age* discusses how "Brand Personalities Undergo Psychoanalysis" (Nathanson-Moog, 1984).

If we accept this analogy, then we must eventually ask, "What brand image or personality yields the greatest buyer motivation?" Many different approaches to this question can be taken. For my purpose, let us pursue the brand-personality analogy further.

If brands are like people, then perhaps we should determine the kinds of people that generate the highest levels of motivation. If we knew the answer

97

to this question, we could answer the same question for brands as well.

Fortunately, sociology literature includes a body of research that is directly relevant. People who generate the highest levels of motivation among large groups are called charismatic leaders. Is it not reasonable to propose the notion of a charismatic brand? This chapter is an exploration of this line of reasoning. We explore the brand-building process in the context of Weber's (1922/1966) framework of charismatic leadership and introduce the hypothesis that products and brands, as well as people, can have charisma.

Why, for example, did "Consumers Open Wallets For Brand Image in Athletic Footwear," as reported by Segal in the trade journal *Sporting Goods Business* (1989)? How did Nike create the mass perception that their athletic shoe was worth so much more than seemingly identical shoes offered by competitors? Products and brands that generate extremes of consumer attachment and purchase motivation, more so than average ones, should be of special research interest—especially to anyone focused on the study of marketing, brand building, or consumer psychology.

The juxtaposition of a compelling image onto a product helps to sell it, but why? Consider two famous cases.

Case 1: The Marlboro Cigarette Case

When Marlboro cigarettes were originally introduced, they were given a feminine image. Sales were slow. Then, the image of a cowboy with a tattoo on his wrist, smoking a Marlboro, was displayed with the product. Smokers were invited to try the "taste of Marlboro Country" (a fantasy land of horses and manly cowboys set in the mythical American West). Without changing the cigarette itself, the meaning of the brand was dramatically changed. Results? It was repositioned. Almost magically, sales and market share soared. Marlboro cigarettes now had something special!

Case 2: The Absolut Vodka Case

Objective differences between the leading brands of vodka are incredibly minor. Few people can tell any difference in blind taste tests. This creates a difficult marketing problem. How does one motivate buyers to prefer one brand over others? Absolut vodka found out when sales grew 1,750% in eight years. In 1979, Absolut "was a struggling new imported vodka selling about 54,000 cases annually. In 1987, it was the number one imported vodka selling 1.6 million cases annually" (Blount & Walker, 1988). Even more astoundingly, during this growth period Absolut was priced higher than the well-established American brands, such as Smirnoff. What accounts for Absolut's dramatic sales increases and market share gains against larger and stronger competitors? The explanation, according to Geoff Hayes and Graham Turner, who created the Absolut advertising campaign while at the TBWA, Inc. agency in New York, was to make "the bottle the hero of the campaign by depicting it with props to form a visual pun" (Blount & Walker, 1988). According to Michel Roux, president of Carillo Importers Ltd., USA, which imports Absolut, the solution was to give the message that "Absolut is a symbol. We are sending a message of smartness and sophistication. The consumer associates himself or herself with that symbol. In a subtle way, we tell consumers 'Absolut is something you need to be associated with if you are somebody in life.' . . . The image we project gives consumers self-confidence. . . . We are projecting an image that is stylish and fashionable" (Blount & Walker, 1988, pp. 20–31).

Here are two cases where an unsuccessful product was turned into a huge success, against stronger competitors, when the right symbolic personality was added. In the Marlboro case, the trappings of a cowboy myth were displayed in the product's advertising. What does a cowboy myth have to do with a cigarette's value? Why does a picture of a cowboy behind the product change the value of the product? In the Absolut case the bottle was made into a hero in a stylish and fashionable visual pun. How exactly does a pun increase the value of vodka and generate such extraordinary buyer motivation? Why does a visual pun make a brand of vodka into a powerful and successful market share challenger? What is happening here?

We know that anchoring a compelling image to a product or brand can increase its value to buyers. We know that associations of nonrational emotion, feelings, and other "substitutes for substance" (Starr & Ullmann, 1988), quite simply, sell products (Aaker & Stayman, 1987; Aaker, Stayman, & Hagerty, 1986; Batra & Ray, 1985; Edell & Burke, 1986; Holbrook, 1985b; Holbrook & Hirschman, 1982; Plummer, 1985). We know that a brand or product associated with the wrong image will not sell. Would the perfume "Obsession," which trades on a seductive sexual image, sell equally well if associated with a different name and image, say, the practical, wholesome, earthy image of "Iowa"? Neither image is more or less relevant in any objective sense, except in the way that consumers respond.

Hence, we know that the attribution of meaning to a brand through visual puns, images of cowboys, or sexy names can help, or hinder, product sales. However, we know much less about why this is so. The value of a seemingly irrelevant advertising image is not easily accounted for or explained. Why do customers want what they want? Why (and how) can we predict or explain cases such as the Absolut or Marlboro turnaround success stories?

One concept I find especially illuminating in this respect is that of *charisma*. I discuss here the hypothesis that brand building for certain extraordinarily successful brands may include aspects of a social process best described as charisma building. The aim is to understand extraordinarily successful brands through a better understanding of charisma. I first review my definition of charisma and then introduce into the marketing literature a new hypothesis: Brands and products, as well as people, can have charisma. The methodological approach is: (a) to provide proof by example and (b) to argue that such a construct is logically consistent.

CHARISMA: WHAT IS IT?

Charisma comes from two Greek roots: (a) *charizesthai*, which means "to favor or to gratify"; and (b) *charis*, meaning "gift." To the early Christians, it meant the "gift of prophecy or healing—a divine gift." Today it means:

• A widely perceived appeal which transcends ordinary conceptions of reality (Weber, 1922/1966).
• The ability to exercise diffuse and intensive influence over the normative or ideological orientations of others (Etzioni, 1961).
• The quality which is imputed to persons, actions, roles, institutions, symbols, and material objects because of their presumed connection with ultimate, fundamental, vital, or order-determining powers (Shils, 1968).

In the 1920s, Weber was the first theorist to apply the concept of charisma to secular social phenomena. According to Weber, the principle of charisma was a widely perceived "appeal which transcends ordinary conceptions of reality" (1922/1966). His use of the term was an adaptation from theology (likely borrowed from the work of Rudolf Sohn), with one significant change. Weber believed that charisma was bestowed on a leader by followers (i.e., socially constructed; see also Berger & Luckmann, 1967; Wildavsky, 1989) instead of by divine grace. To Weber, charisma was the devotion of followers "to the specific and exceptional; to the sanctity, heroism, or exemplary character of an individual person, and to the normative patterns or order revealed or ordained by him."

Charisma is a sociological construct associated with a leader who generates extremes of loyalty and motivation among followers. Current charisma research is used to explain how certain people, such as Martin Luther King, Mahatma Ghandi, or Hitler, capture the imagination of followers and, as a result, suddenly leap to influential leadership positions. These leaders not only inspire and generate extremes of motivation, they also engender nearly addictive levels of attachment. Because not all leaders ignite such responses in their followers, those who do are labeled charismatic leaders (e.g., Bass, 1985, 1988; Conger, 1988; House, Woycke, & Fodor, 1988; Trice & Beyer, 1986).

Research on charismatic leaders shows that they engender faith, hope, and trust in an inspiring metaphor or vision which the leader seems to embody; these charismatic individuals are more effective, motivate beyond expectations, and command extremes of attachment from their followers (Bass, 1985, 1988; Conger, 1988; House, Woycke, & Fodor, 1988; Trice & Beyer, 1986).

The definition of product charisma I choose, then, is as follows: That which is charismatic creates a response in its audience or followers that is characterized by extremes of motivation and attachment beyond expectation. By "expectation," I mean a level of motivation and attachment that would be engendered by an identical product, with comparable quality, functionality, and awareness, but without the trappings of myths, metaphors, images, personalities, and other forms of promotional hype designed to manipulate the meaning of the product.

RELEVANCE OF CHARISMA THEORY

How is charisma theory relevant to brand building and marketing? In his famous article "Marketing Myopia," Levitt argued, "No organization can achieve greatness without . . . a vision that can produce eager followers in vast numbers. In business, the followers are the customers" (1975).

If we agree with Levitt's assertion about the importance of producing eager followers among customers, the prospect of engendering motivation and attachment beyond expectation is especially noteworthy. Charisma building and brand building are, to some extent, parallel or analogous processes. Both are designed to build motivation and attachment among followers.

Can a Man-Made Artifact Have Charisma?

Normally, we think of charisma as something attributed to a person, a hero such as General George S. Patton, for example. Some people hold that only a person can have charisma. But what about a fantasy hero? The 1970s movie hero Luke Skywalker of *Star Wars*, a man-made creation, was clearly charismatic to millions of fans. Anyone around an ardent *Star Wars* fan knows just how influential the hero, Luke Skywalker, was. Although younger, these children had a special bond with their hero. The fictional character, Luke Skywalker, fulfilled Weber's definition of charisma. He had "a widely perceived appeal which transcends ordinary conceptions of reality" (Weber, 1922/1966). The bond between the children and their imaginary hero was built on a "devotion to the specific and exceptional; [on the] sanctity, heroism or exemplary character of an individual person; and [on the] normative patterns or order revealed or ordained by him" (Weber). Hence, at least a celluloid hero can have charisma.

Can other artifacts be charismatic as well? Yes—toys such as *Star Wars* Light Sabers, for instance. As you may remember, toys that had anything to do with the movie *Star Wars* were overnight, top-of-the-chart, best-selling "hit" products. Ordinary flashlights with long plastic cones, or "Light Sabers," were among the most popular items. They became the number one, best-selling, *Star Wars* product.

But why? After viewing the movie, many children engaged in pretend play, to re-enact and objectify deeply moving parts of the story. Owning a flashlight with a long plastic cone, a Light Saber, could make the *Star Wars* myth seem more real. *Star Wars* toys helped children identify with their hero, Luke Skywalker. The toy served:

- As a prop to help the child engage in the fantasy and experience the myth of being a *Star Wars* hero.
- As a badge of membership to help communicate the child's identification with the *Star Wars* theme to others.

Although the toy continued to look like just a flashlight with a long plastic cone, the meaning of the product was much more than that. It wasn't "just a flashlight." It was a Light Saber to be used in the fight against "the dark side of the force." Symbolism and fantasy were adroitly manipulated to imbue the product with a compelling image and personality. Value was thereby greatly increased. Despite being priced 5 to 10 times higher than ordinary flashlights, ardent fans of *Star Wars* were clearly motivated beyond expectation to get their genuine *Star Wars* Light Saber. As most parents will attest, their kids "had to have it" (i.e., a nearly addictive attachment). In short, the simple flashlight with a cone had been given charisma.

What about adults? Just as children's toys are transformed from ordinary to charismatic, artifacts for adults may be similarly transformed by encoding deep, compelling meanings into associations with the product. Let us begin by looking at everyday examples—jewelry, flags, and athletic shoes.

Consider metal molded into an artifact known as a "wedding band." Why do newlywed couples (and others) attach so much value to their wedding bands?

- Could it be that the ring reifies the metaphor of "two people joined as one," objectifies it, and makes it seem more real?
- Could it be that the ring helps the couple re-enact and re-experience deeply moving aspects of a vision they seek to embrace?
- Could it be that the ring's value stems not from its mundane physical attributes, but from the fact that it serves as a symbolic prop to help the couple more fully believe in and experience a hoped-for state of grace called "the commitment of marriage"?

To some degree, all of these are true. A wedding band is not just a metal ring. It can be said to have symbolic or sentimental value. Meaning is the basis of that value. Symbolic products, like a book or a highway sign, hold meaning in their symbols. Charismatic products are symbolic, but they also represent something deeply and emotionally significant, perhaps even sacred. Just as a flashlight with a long plastic cone serves as a prop to help children embrace their fantasies, a metal ring serves as a prop to help a newlywed couple embrace their dreams and is, thereby, imbued with deeply significant and metaphorical meaning.

As another example, consider why extremes of loyalty and motivation are often associated with the flag. Some patriotic Americans are so motivated by and loyal to the flag that they are literally willing to fight for and, if necessary, die to defend this piece of colorful cloth. Why? The flag has charisma. Clearly, it is not just an artifact, not just a colorful piece of cloth. The flag is an object which has been given compelling, perhaps sacred, meaning. It has value, not so much because of its mundane materials, but because of something "glorious" encoded onto those materials. This is key. The creation of charisma is not so much a function of underlying mundane substance as it is a function of the manipulation of meaning. The flag, like the Light Saber or wedding band, has charisma and, hence, value because of what it represents.

Can Ordinary Products or Brands Have Charisma?

The single hypothesis of this chapter is that brands and products, as well as people, can have charisma. But a Light Saber, a wedding band, and a flag are not ordinary consumer products. Can ordinary consumer products and brands become charismatic? As we shall soon see, the answer is "yes."

Unlike the flag, most products will not generate enough motivation or attachment so that followers are willing to fight for and, if necessary, "make the ultimate sacrifice" for ownership. However, such extreme and egregious situations do occasionally happen.

As we see in the next section, mundane products such as shoes can be imbued with charisma. Just as some followers of charismatic leaders are willing to do almost anything for a glorious cause, there are some followers of charismatic products who are extremely motivated by a particular product. These consumers are literally willing to do anything to get it or keep it. (I am not talking about addictive drugs here, although that raises an interesting parallel. . . .)

An Egregious Example of Product Charisma

Let us now consider branded athletic shoes and test the hypothesis that brands and products, as well as people, can have charisma. This case is cited not because it represents what I think marketers should do, but because it so vividly highlights the extremes of motivation and attachment consumers can associate with a particular brand.

How will we know if a product has charisma? From the brief review of charisma theory, we recall that charisma engenders extremes of motivation and attachment, beyond expectation. Using this, we ask if it is possible for consumers of an ordinary product to exhibit a degree of motivation and attachment that is far beyond any reasonable level of expectation. I think, for this case, you will agree that the answer is "yes." However, you be the judge. Here are excerpts from the case, as described in the *Los Angeles Times*, by staff writer Ron Harris:

> When 15-year-old Michael Thomas left home for school last May, he couldn't have been prouder. On his feet, thanks to his mother's hard work, were a pair of spanking new Air Jordans—$100 worth of leather, rubber, and status that to today's youth are the Mercedes-Benzes of athletic footwear. The next day it was James David Martin, 17, who was strolling down the street in Thomas' new sneakers, while Thomas lay dead in a field not far from his school. Martin was arrested for murder. For the Baltimore school system, Thomas' death was the last straw. He was the third youngster to have been killed over his clothes in five years. Scores of others had been robbed of name-brand sneakers, designer jogging suits, leather jackets, and jewelry. . . . "We've seen that to today's kids, the clothes and footwear are a sense of who they are," said Betty Richardson, vice president of marketing for Reebok. "They represent what they think to be special and what they think to be important to them." (Harris, 1989)

This is clearly outrageous, but it is not an isolated incident of random violence. It was the third killing. Furthermore, in the Michael Thomas case, the incident was not about ordinary shoes. It was about "important," expensive, designer-label, branded shoes.

Some consumers react to certain products in much the same way that ardent followers react to their beloved charismatic leader. Consumers become so motivated that they would do almost anything for the "right" shoes. Why? Because, to some degree, like patriots willing to die for the flag, the Air Jordan brand came to represent something worth fighting for.

Through judicious endorsements and repetitious advertising, glamorous metaphors of "high status" and "athletic stardom" were anchored to the Nike Air Jordan brand. Although continuing to look like an ordinary shoe to most people, the Air Jordan became much more than that to true believers. It was encoded with so much charisma that, to some, it had ceased being ordinary (i.e., profane). It had become sacred.

Several authors have made the case that certain consumer goods have gained "sacred status" and are "set apart" from ordinary objects (Belk, Wallendorf, & Sherry, 1989; Campbell, 1987; Mol, 1983). The transcending superiority of the Nike Air Jordan brand, to true believers, indeed led to the shoe's being treated as special and set it apart from ordinary shoes. To those willing to engage in physical combat over the right brand of shoes, the Air Jordan brand would seem to motivate far beyond any reasonable expectation.

OBSERVATIONS

Just as symbolic religious artifacts serve to help reify intangible constructs that are sacred in a religious sense, the Nike Air Jordan shoe served a similar symbolic function, but in a secular sense. The primary function of Nike Air Jordan shoes, in this sense, is to allow the owner to engage in a hoped-for dream of high status, that is:

- Transcendence of the desperate conditions of inner-city slums and association with a glamorous star athlete.
- Membership in an exclusive, elite, privileged "club" of those who own "the best"—something not just anybody can have.

To wear Nike Air Jordans was to reify a sacred experience. It was a vehicle to feeling as if one were the hero figure, Michael Jordan. To our benefit or detriment, it appears reasonable to say that products and brands, as well as people, can have charisma. To summarize:

1. A product or a brand can have charisma. Even something as ordinary as a shoe can have charisma. Functional utility was not the prime driving force behind the success of the Nike Air Jordan brand. Other shoes, costing much less, could deliver equal or superior functional performance. However, no other shoe in 1989 could deliver as much meaning (i.e., status).

2. Charismatic meaning appears to be socially constructed through anchoring (i.e., encoding, imbuing, juxtaposing) a product with associations to a compelling emotional metaphor of something transcendent or sacred. Nike, for example, used compelling metaphors of high status, athletic stardom, and "fly Air Jordan" (i.e., escape from the inner city). Other examples discussed herein include Marlboro Country, fighting the dark side, two joined as one (i.e., marriage), a glorious cause (i.e., the flag).

3. To gain charisma, products must not only be anchored to compelling emotional associations, but the very meaning of the product must become transformed. A cigarette becomes a ticket to Marlboro Country, a flashlight becomes a Light Saber, a piece of metal becomes the link between newlyweds, a piece of cloth becomes "my country," and shoes become the evidence and proof of one's high status.

4. The construction of charisma, if successful, results in extremes of loyalty and motivation. In the Air Jordan case, not just any shoe would do; it had

to be the one right (or sacred) brand. This additional buyer loyalty and motivation can be converted into market share gains, into a higher price ($115 for Air Jordans vs. $30–$60 for most other brands, circa 1989), or both. In other words, brand building and the construction of product charisma can lead to competitive advantage and/or profits.

5. The supposed function of athletic shoes is their use in sports, but "80% of sneakers purchased in this country are not used for sport" (Greenberg, 1990). In order to sell more Nike shoes, the brand had to be imbued with new meaning and, thereby, transformed.

All brands have imagery, symbolism, and prestige, to some degree. The difference is that brands with product charisma build on imagery, symbolism, and prestige (more so than objectifiable utility) to generate extraordinary levels of buyer attachment and motivation—levels beyond any reasonable expectation.

Because Nike Air Jordans were not "just a shoe," because they created such extremes of motivation and loyalty, it is reasonable to say that the Nike Air Jordan brand, in 1989, had product charisma.

Although we may question the ethics of "using" charisma, we cannot deny the real world extremes of demand generated for products like Nike Air Jordan shoes. In only a few years, Nike has grown from zero to over $1 billion/year in sales, overtaking much stronger competitors such as Adidas in the process. If we think about it, the implications are much broader.

For a product to have charisma, it is not necessary for a consumer to be willing to engage in physical combat over it. The brutal case of sneaker killings was chosen to bring the issues into high relief and highlight the phenomena. A willingness to fight for a product may be a rare example, but products with a lesser degree of charisma are not so rare. Charisma may be found in varying degrees in the marketing of almost every product or service. The social construction of product charisma is something that is happening, to a greater or lesser degree, with many other brands and products.

As we discussed earlier, Marlboro's sales gains were largely due to charisma borrowed from the cowboy myth. Absolut Vodka became charismatic by making the bottle "a symbol . . . something you need to be associated with if you are somebody in life" (Blount & Walker, 1988).

As another example, consider the television ads of the leading coffee companies. They no longer try to convince us that their brands taste better (a semiverifiable claim); instead they show heart-warming scenes of adults bonding with each other over a cup of coffee. Why? Because it works. They lend their brand charisma by positioning it as a prop necessary to support feelings of emotional bonding between adults. They position their brand as being sacred, imbued with deeply significant and metaphorical meaning. That is, they transform a simple cup of coffee into a sacrament of friendship, much more than just a cup of coffee.

Many brand managers try to lend charisma to their brands. For example, the leading beer manufacturer attempts to lend charisma to Budweiser by wrapping it in advertising featuring a "party animal" metaphor (symbolized by a dog dressed in human clothes). The implication is that "even a dog" (like you, the consumer) can attract beautiful women if you drink the right brand of beer. Several personal computer vendors attempt to lend charisma to their brands by wrapping their products in advertising featuring metaphors of order, efficiency, and the promise of high technology. IBM, the personal computer market leader, suggests that a complete novice (portrayed by a clone of Charlie Chaplin in IBM's ads) will become an effective executive if only he or she buys the right brand of high technology. A suitable "before" and "after" parable is presented to support the metaphor.

In each of these cases, the emphasis is on metaphors, not verifiable claims. In fact, verifiable product claims appear to be going out in favor, especially among television advertisers. According to Dave Adehra, president of Video Storyboard Tests, a company that measures the effectiveness of TV ads, "The reason product claims are vanishing is that we've reached the point where no one, including the manufacturers, thinks there is a bit of difference between advertised products" (Leerhsen, 1988). As Max Blackston, head of the Ogilvy & Mather's advertising agency research and planning department, recently observed: "In an age when most products do the same thing, the emotional relationship is the only thing that gets people to pay a premium for a particular brand" (Levine, 1989). The construction of product charisma is the manipulation of symbols, metaphors, and meaning to create such emotional relationships.

CONCLUSIONS

Differing brands, brand images, and brand personalities result in differing levels of buyer motivation. In this chapter, we look at a small subset of all brands—products which generate the very highest levels of buyer motivation and attachment. We ask, "Can products and brands have charisma?" The defining characteristics of charisma are occasionally exhibited by certain exceptional artifacts. Examples show that branded products can also exhibit such characteristics.

Being charismatic means being capable of generating motivation beyond expectation among followers. In order to establish the existence of at least one example of a charismatic artifact, we note that certain heroes have charisma, regardless of whether they are real (e.g., General George S. Patton) or an artifact (such as the man-made fantasy hero, Luke Skywalker, from the movie *Star Wars*). Other artifacts and special objects, such as wedding bands, flags, *Star Wars* toys, and Nike's Air Jordan shoes, may also have charisma. Just as some followers are willing to die for a charismatic leader who is associated with a glorious cause, some consumers exhibit extreme behaviors towards artifacts imbued with compelling meaning. It is possible for artifacts and products, as well as people, to generate extremes of motivation that are beyond expectation. It is possible for brands and products to have charisma.

Many unanswered questions about product charisma remain. For example, if we accept the hypothesis that products can have charisma, how do we operationalize it? How does one create charisma? How do we apply charisma theory in practice? A more complete conceptual framework needs to be built, more testable propositions advanced, and more evidence gathered. Perhaps the construct of product charisma can be scaled and measured. How much charisma does any given brand command? Case studies and statistical evidence need to be compiled. Perhaps, before these technical questions are flushed out, the ethical questions surrounding the use of charisma need to be thoroughly debated as well.

As interesting and tempting as they are, explorations such as these are beyond the scope of this chapter and remain for future research. However, future research should examine more closely how value and meaning are related and the process by which deeply significant emotions become embodied in an artifact or image.

The construct of product charisma, like any other construct, can never be proven the only true interpretation of the facts. It may frame a few key issues, stimulate thinking, and perhaps generate some genuine debate. To some extent, more questions may be raised than answered. This is valuable. Milton and Locke suggested that the best program for discovering truth was to let everyone state their beliefs and allow others to listen and form their own opinions; the ideas which would prevail in a free and open battle of wits would be as close an approximation to the truth as can be humanly achieved. Perhaps, in this sense, the true test of the construct presented here will be measured in terms of its role in the ongoing debates regarding our understanding of business strategy and buyer behavior.

So What?

Consumers are willing to pay more for a branded product than the identical product would command without promotional hype designed to imbue the product with emotional meaning. In situations where a product is associated to a emotionally compelling image or metaphor, charisma theory can help explain why consumers are willing to pay a premium for it.

The observation is that charisma building and brand building are, to some extent, parallel or analogous processes. Both change meaning and, thereby, change perceived value. Product charisma is related to notions such as brand image, symbolism, and prestige. All brands have imagery, symbolism, and prestige, to some degree. The difference is that brands with charisma build on imagery, symbolism, and prestige (more than objectifiable utility) to generate extraordinary levels of buyer attachment and motivation—levels beyond reasonable expectation.

Product charisma is not a rare phenomena. Charismatic products and brands generate extremes of consumer attachment and purchase motivation, such as Marlboro cigarettes in the 1960s, Calvin Klein's designer jeans in the 1970s, Absolut vodka in the early 1980s, Nike and Reebok's athletic shoes in the mid-1980s. Charismatic products are often part of popular culture, but they are certainly not a trivial part of our economy. The use of charisma in the marketing of cigarettes, soft drinks, and shoes can be, and is being, applied to other products. They represent the creation of billions of dollars of new value in our society each year.

There are, of course, limits to charisma theory and such a model cannot be pushed too far. However, the "lens" of charisma allows us to focus upon and "see" things we might otherwise miss. The introduction of the product charisma construct into the marketing literature is useful for at least four reasons:

1. It helps explain certain extraordinary levels of buyer attachment and motivation that, without such an hypothesis, are difficult to explain.
2. It allows us to draw on, leverage, and use sociological models of charisma in developing our understanding of brand building.
3. Exploring how charismatic leaders construct charisma may lead to useful managerial models for building charismatic brands.
4. As befits a fertile new conceptual framework, the hypothesis of product charisma raises interesting questions and opens up many new lines of inquiry and debate.

Ethical Questions

There are difficult ethical questions involved in the use of charisma. The egregious case of the sneaker killings, for example, highlights not only the potential motivational power inherent in the adroit use of charisma, but also what may arise when product charisma goes awry.

Is it ethical for marketers to use charisma to increase desire for their products? Is Nike responsible in any way for the sneaker killings? Is the use of charisma an unethical form of manipulation? Does the construction of product charisma induce addictive attachments? Questions such as these are vivid in the Nike case and are made more obvious by the line of analysis employed. These issues deserve more attention than the incomplete treatment here. Where, for instance, is the line between a charismatic metaphor and a lie? How does one, in any literal sense, "taste" Marlboro Country? Should metaphorical advertising claims, such as Nike's "fly Air Jordan," or Coca-Cola's "Coke adds life," or George Bush's "no new taxes!" be subject to truth in advertising laws? How, exactly, are we to verify that Coke really does add life? When are truth in advertising laws applicable? Is it not reasonable to ask for the empirical test of a producer's claim?

No, apparently not. These questions, in current practice, are seen as ridiculous. There can be no literal way to taste Marlboro Country or verify that Coke adds life. There is no empirical proof or disproof. It is not meant to be a verifiable claim. Why? The construction of product charisma is not about functional or instrumental utility; it is about manipulating emotional meaning, which is different from rational function.

Because the taste of Marlboro Country is not verifiable in experience, positivists of the Viennese school, such as Moritz Schlick and Rudolf Carnap, might have called the claim *metaphysical*. They would be right. In fact, Marlboro Country is not only metaphysical, but is, like all meanings, a "socially constructed reality" (Berger & Luckmann, 1967; Wildavsky, 1989). Marlboro Country, and the emotional charisma of Marlboro, exists only if people participate in its construction and maintenance. If such a metaphysical, but socially constructed, image is successfully anchored to a product, as in the case of Marlboro, it can have stunningly real impact. It can radically change the value of a brand or product. It can lend charisma.

REFERENCES

Aaker, D. A., & Stayman, D. M. (1987). What mediates the emotional response to advertising? The case of warmth. In P. Cafferata & A. Tybout (Eds.), *Cognitive and affective responses to advertising.* Lexington, MA: Lexington Books.

Aaker, D. A., Stayman, D. M., & Hagerty, M. R. (1986). Warmth in advertising: Measurement, impact, and sequence effects. *Journal of Consumer Research, 12*(4), 365–381.

Bass, B. M. (1985). *Leadership and performance beyond expectations.* New York: Free Press.

Bass, B. M. (1988). Evolving perspectives on charismatic leadership. In J. A. Conger, R. N. Kanungo, & Associates (Eds.), *Charismatic leadership.* San Francisco: Jossey-Bass.

Batra, R., & Ray, M. L. (1985). How advertising works at contact. In L. F. Alwitt & A. A. Mitchell (Eds.), *Psychological processes and advertising effects* (pp. 12–14). Hillsdale, NJ: Lawrence Erlbaum Associates.

Belk, R. W., Wallendorf, M., & Sherry, J. F., Jr. (1989, June). The sacred and the profane in consumer behavior: Theodicy on the Odyssey. *Journal of Consumer Research, 16,* 1–38.

Berger, P., & Luckmann, T. (1967). *The social construction of reality.* New York: Doubleday.

Blount, S., & Walker, L. (1988). *The best of ad campaigns.* Rockport, MA: Rockport.

Campbell, C. (1987). *The romantic ethic and the spirit of modern consumerism.* London: Basil Blackwell.

Conger, J. A. (1988). Theoretical foundations of charismatic leadership. In J. A. Conger, R. N. Kanungo, & Associates (Eds.), *Charismatic leadership.* San Francisco: Jossey-Bass.

Duboff, R. S. (1986). Brands, like people, have personalities. *Marketing News, 20*(1), 8.

Durgee, J. (1988). Understanding brand personality. *Journal of Consumer Marketing*, *5*(3), 21-25.

Edell, J. A., & Burke, M. C. (1986). The power of feelings in understanding advertising effects (working paper #86-11). Fuqua School of Business, Duke University, Durham, NC.

Etzioni, A. (1961). *A comparative analysis of complex organizations*. New York: Free Press.

Flint, J. (1988). A brand is like a friend. *Forbes*, *142*(11), 267.

Greenberg, A. (1990, May 22). How do we stop "sneaker killings"? *Los Angeles Times*, p. 1.

Harris, R. (1989, December 6). If looks could kill. *San Francisco Chronicle*, p. B3.

Holbrook, M. B. (1985). Emotion in the consumption experience: Toward a new model of the human consumer. In R. A. Peterson, W. D. Hoyer, & W. R. Wilson (Eds.), *The role of affect in consumer behavior: Emerging theories and applications*. Lexington, MA: D. C. Heath.

Holbrook, M. B., & Hirschman, E. C. (1982, September). The experiential aspects of consumption. *Journal of Consumer Research*, *9*, 132-40.

House, R. J., Woycke, J., & Fodor, E. M. (1988). Charismatic and noncharismatic leaders. In J. A. Conger, R. N. Kanungo, & Associates (Eds.), *Charismatic leadership*. San Francisco: Jossey-Bass.

Leerhsen, C. (1988, May 23). Pitches we love to catch. *Newsweek*, p. 77.

Levine, J. (1989, May 15). Desperately seeking "jeepness." *Forbes*, pp. 134-136.

Levitt, T. (1975, September/October). Marketing myopia. *Harvard Business Review*, pp. 26-48.

Lewis, H. S. (1922). *Babbitt*. New York: Harcourt, Brace & World.

Mol, H. (1983). *Meaning and place: An introduction to the social scientific study of religion*. New York: Pilgrim.

Nathanson-Moog, C. (1984). Brand personalities undergo psychoanalysis. *Advertising Age*, *55*(45), 18.

Park, C. W., Jaworski, B. J., & MacInnis, D. J. (1986). Strategic brand-image management. *Journal of Marketing*, *50*(4), 135-145.

Plummer, J. T. (1985, April). Advertising strategy. Presented at AMA Strategic Planning Conference. Chicago: AMA.

Segal, R. (1989). Consumers open wallets for brand image in athletic footwear. *Sporting Goods Business*, *22*, 81.

Shils, E. (1968). Charisma. In D. L. Sills (Ed.), *International encyclopedia of the social sciences: Vol. 2*. New York: Macmillan & Free Press.

Starr, M. K., & Ullmann, J. E. (1988). The myth of U.S. industrial supremacy. In M. K. Starr (Ed.), *Global competitiveness* (pp. 43-71). New York: Norton.

Trice, H. M., & Beyer, J. M. (1986). Charisma and its routinization in two social movement organizations. *Research In Organizational Behavior*, *8*, 113-64.

Weber, M. (1966). *The theory of social and economic organization*. In T. Parsons (Trans.), *Wirtschaft und Gesellschaft*. New York: Free Press. (Original work published 1922)

Wildavsky, A. (1989, November). On the social construction of distinctions. Paper presented at the APPAM Conference, Arlington, VA: APPAM.

Chapter 8

Beyond Brand Personality: Building Brand Relationships

Max Blackston
Research International

INTRODUCTION

In both the development of advertising and the measurement of its effects, a great deal of effort is spent on the content of a brand's messages—brand image and brand personality—and on the efficient transmission of those messages to the consumer. It is common, however, that neither brand image nor brand personality adequately represents the totality of a brand's relationship with the consumer.

It is argued that the problem does not just lie in inadequate means of measurement, but is rooted in the underlying constructs of brand image and brand personality, which only reflect the brand as the object of consumers' attitudes.

I postulate a communications model in which the brand and the consumer are considered as coequivalent parts of a single system, analogous to the relationship between two people. The relationship concept is defined as the interaction between consumers' attitudes toward the brand and the brand's ''attitudes'' toward the consumer. The development of a successful consumer-brand relationship depends crucially on the consumer's perceptions of the brand's attitudes, as it is these that create meaning out of the brand's messages. A research approach, designed to elicit and measure both components of the consumer-brand relationship, is outlined in this chapter.

I include examples illustrating the key role of brands' attitudes as differentiators, and argue the case for managing these across the spectrum of brand communications, with the same attention normally devoted just to brand images. The argument is extended from consumer product and service brands to corporate brands.

BACKGROUND

The genesis of the ideas presented in this chapter was an attempt to deal with the limitations of quantitative brand image measurement (Blackston & Holmes, 1983). Brand image studies have a notoriously limited ability to explain consumers' historic behavior—let alone provide any predictive power. Whether it is Usership and Attitude (U&A) studies or image tracking, brand images generally fail to give an adequate explanation for differences between brands or for changes in brands' franchises and shares over time.

The means to access the motivating factors in consumers' perceptions of brands do exist. Qualitative research—with its less structured elicitation techniques and analysis that takes into account the totality of respondents' reactions—can give really penetrating insights. The exploratory, "prescientific" (Calder, 1977) approach to qualitative research permits the generation of second-degree constructs, which reflect the underlying consumer consensus about a brand's image, from the variety of linguistic forms, and the different symbols and archetypes by which it is articulated. In fact, it is often the rich variety, or even the eccentricity of consumers' language, that informs us most.

The problem arises when we are forced to capture the essence of that language in formal measuring scales. In the transition to quantitative measurement, the idiosyncratic must be discarded because the context of the individual is no longer available to aid in interpretation. In the development of scales via Factor Analysis, for example, outlying statements are systematically eliminated; what remains are image statements which represent a sort of lowest common denominator. Using this type of process, we must often discard the very things that would allow us to see what makes a brand really different or unique.

The pressure of corporate decision making and the need to be accountable represent irresistible forces that militate against the small scale, the qualitative, the divergent, and the idiosyncratic. Inevitably, we are pushed towards being representative, quantitative, convergent, standardized. The dilemma was aptly described by Lannon and Cooper (1983), "Characteristically, qualitative data is only allowable at the very early stages; as things progress, the data needs somehow to be harder and so more people are asked fewer, more superficial, and less relevant questions."

The problem is not inherently quantification so much as the standardization that quantitative methods impose on us. The challenge is to find a way of preserving the divergence of qualitative data—even on a large, quantitative scale—in a convergent analytical framework.

The broad outlines of such a methodology are given later in the chapter. It is appropriate to consider first some theoretical underpinnings which, in a sense, are more important than the research methodology because they reflect fundamentally on the reality of consumers' perceptions of brands.

RELATIONSHIPS WITH BRANDS

We are all very comfortable with the idea of personifying brands. A lot of us spend a good proportion of our professional lives endeavoring to do just that. However, in treating brands as if they were people, we have rarely taken the analogy to its logical conclusion. If we had, we would have noted that people don't just "perceive" each other; a person does more than process information about the other's physical characteristics and personality. So, why do we treat brands in just this manner? People react and interact with other people; they have relationships with them.

The concept of a *brand relationship* is neither novel nor outrageous. It is readily understandable as an analogue—between brand and consumer—of that complex of cognitive, affective, and behavioral processes which constitute a relationship between two people.

Although the idea of a brand relationship may be acceptable, few attempts have been made to develop an operational definition or a system for identifying, measuring, and building brand relationships.

We can infer the nature of the relationship between two people by observing the attitudes and behaviors they display toward each other. Unless they are involved in an elaborate deceit, an experienced analyst can make some fairly accurate inferences.

Analogously, understanding the relationship between brand and consumer requires observation and analysis of:

- Consumers' attitudes and behaviors towards the brand.
- The brand's attitudes and behaviors towards the consumer.

Just as an example, let's look at a hypothetical relationship between a doctor and a patient (Fig. 8.1). If we let the doctor stand in for the brand, the characteristics on the left constitute the patient's attitude towards the doctor— the patient's perception of the doctor's "brand personality." He's highly skilled, caring, and funny. He sounds like a doctor we would all like to have, and we would expect the patient to like the doctor.

However, when we uncover the crucial bit of information about what the patient thinks the doctor thinks of him (a boring hypochondriac), our understanding of the nature of the relationship changes completely. It doesn't matter what the doctor really thinks because, for the patient, the relationship is based on what he thinks about the doctor's attitude (Fig. 8.2).

FIG. 8.1. The doctor–patient relationship.

Like a relationship with another person, everything we need to know about the brand relationship is going on inside the consumer's head. Thus, the real question we need to ask is, "What do the consumers think that the brand thinks of them?"

That's the difference between a one-dimensional brand image and a brand relationship. There are two independent sets of things going on that we must

FIG. 8.2. The doctor–patient relationship.

tap into in the consumer's mind: (a) the brand as the object of attitudes and (b) the subjective brand with its "own" set of attitudes. This means that, in designing and engineering our brands, we have to look beyond our traditional preoccupation with transmitting "objective" brand images.

In advertising, we are very skilled at crafting the images we want to project. Our advertising copy tests and tracking studies inform us that consumers "get the message." However, we need to spend just as much effort in creating and communicating the correct attitudes and behaviors of our brands, because it is these which create meaning out of the message.

Returning to the topic of brand image research, it seems that, in addition to the problems cited earlier, we have been concentrating all our efforts on understanding and measuring only one half of the relationship. The second half—the brand's attitudes—can often be the true brand discriminator and the link between attitudes and behavior.

RESEARCHING BRAND RELATIONSHIPS

The research approach developed for the study of brand relationships can be applied on either a small or large scale. In the former case, it consists essentially of a series of individual depth interviews, carried out by a skilled qualitative researcher using a specific interview protocol.

As discussed earlier, however, the challenge was to develop an approach that could be adapted equally well to those situations in which statistically projectable samples are required. In this case, the approach must be capable of collecting qualitative data on a large scale and analyzing each interview holistically to preserve the context of the data and permit the development of a qualitative analytical structure. This structure then forms the basis for quantification.

The research uses a questionnaire consisting mainly of open-end questions. This is administered in a one-on-one personal interview by standard interviewers—not qualitative specialists or experienced moderators. The data is collected in a standardized questionnaire format to facilitate the analysis of large volumes of open-end data, and to administer the various question stimuli in as pure and standardized a manner as possible, minimizing the influence of the individual interviewer. For example, interviewers are instructed not to paraphrase questions and to use only the specific probes written into the questionnaire.

The questionnaire varies slightly depending on the category but usually consists of two sections covering (a) generic relationships with the category, and (b) a specific brand. The general format of each section consists of a series of fairly standard projective tests and other qualitative questions:

- Word associations.
- Personification of the brand.

- Dialogue with the brand.
- Characteristics of the brand most liked.
- Characteristics of the brand least liked.

The analysis is carried out in three stages—the first two qualitative, and the third quantitative. The first qualitative stage of analysis consists of scanning the data and forming hypotheses about the nature and number of relationships and the criteria by which they can be identified. Clearly, prior qualitative insight is highly desirable because it is much easier to have some ingoing hypotheses.

The second stage consists of allocating respondents to relationship categories on the basis of the established criteria. Inevitably, this results in a series of modifications and redefinition of the original framework and criteria. It is an iterative process, analogous to the way in which a cluster analysis program proceeds.

As a practical issue, the qualitative analysis team consists of two or more researchers. At least one of these must be a practiced qualitative researcher and at least one must be knowledgeable about the category. Having agreed on a first classification hypothesis, team members work independently to classify a subset of the sample. They meet again to discuss and refine the classification scheme and then work separately on different subsamples.

Once the classification scheme stabilizes, it is formalized in a series of "pen portraits," with sufficient detail to ensure that each analyst uses the same criteria. The final classification is then relatively simple. In our experience, team members working independently can usually classify around 70% of the sample without difficulty—and agree on their classification. Classifying the remainder needs discussion and resolution.

Once a satisfactory and stable classification has been achieved, the analysis switches to quantitative mode. Respondents' relationship classification is coded and conventional tabulation is performed.

As in every research project, the sample size depends on the exact objectives, the investigation's scope, and the available time and resources. Because it is usually only practical to cover one specific brand per respondent, each brand requires a separate sample cell. We operate on a minimum cell size of 50, which allows a reasonably stable measure of the incidence of the more common relationships. Ideally, a sample of 100 or more per cell is used.

Consumers' Relationships with Credit Card Brands

One of our first studies in the United States involved the exploration of consumers' relationships with credit cards and brands of credit card. This was a quantitative study of 200 up-scale men.

We identified a variety of different relationships, reflecting the inherently complex consumer attitudes toward money and credit as well as the images and perceived attitudes of specific brands.

As described in the previous section, relationship segments were identified by what can best be described as qualitative cluster analysis. The segments thus reflect a holistic analysis of each respondent, in which specific answers and verbalizations are related to a higher order relationship construct. To illustrate the relationship between the data and its interpretation, two of the segments are exemplified in Figs. 8.3 and 8.4.

In each case, two of the most evocative types of verbalization are reported:

- Respondents' description of the brand as a person, its appearance, personality, and attitudes.
- The brand's side of the dialogue with respondents, in which the brand's attitudes are often most clearly articulated.

The first relationship was typical of many holders of this credit card—brand users. The credit card is respected by the card holder; it recognizes the worthiness of the card holder and offers to extend its status, authority, and power to the card holder. By association, the holder acquires feelings of power and authority from the card. The card functions as the classic status symbol; it gives evidence of his or her own worth to the card holder as well as to other people.

The second relationship was found frequently among non-users of the card.

CREDIT CARD AS A PERSON   *CREDIT CARD TO CUSTOMER*

- *Banker,dignified. Likes to be*   *" I can help you be the classy*
  treated fairly.   *person you really are."*

- *Distinguished. Someone I'd be*   *" My job is to help you get*
  proud to have with me.   *accepted."*

- *Sophisticated,educated,world*   *" You have good taste."*
  traveler.   *" I can open doors for you."*

- *Someone who would project in*   *" I can make normal people*
  a restaurant.   *think they are special."*

- *Very professional looking. I*   *" Don't forget you have to pay*
  would trust and respect him.   *me at the end of the month."*

- *Tall,female business person*
  in tailored suit,confident.

- *Male account exec.,tall,dark.*

FIG. 8.3. "Respect."

CREDIT CARD AS A PERSON	CREDIT CARD TO CUSTOMER
- *Sophisticated, very good looking, a bit snobbish.*	*" Are you ready for me ? I'm only saying it to protect you from spending more than you*
- *Aloof and condescending.*	*can afford. "*
- *Business person, very formal & proper. Not for me.*	*" You know what the conditions are. If you don't like them, go get a different card. "*
- *Celebrity, hard to approach.*	*" I'm so well known and well established that I can do as I want. "*
- *Very classy person. Would look down on me.*	*"I want your money like Uncle Sam wants you. "*
- *Old person with a lot of money to spend.*	*"I'd love to have dinner with you, but I have a prior arrangement. "*

FIG. 8.4.   "Intimidated."

This group also respects the credit card, attributing status and authority to it. Whereas the former segment felt their own worth and status to be enhanced by their association with the credit card, this group feels excluded, put down, and intimidated by it.

The remarkable thing is that it is only the way they perceive the credit card's attitude that distinguishes these two groups. In all other respects (except ownership and use of this card), they are virtually identical. They share the same demographic and socioeconomic profile and, in terms of conventional brand image, the two groups do not differ significantly.

Without this insight, we are left with no explanation for the difference between users and non-users—surely one of the most fundamental prerequisites for developing advertising strategy.

Extending the Concept of Brand Relationships to Corporate Brands

Many corporations are preoccupied with what they term their *relationship* with their customers. In the following section, we explore how corporate brands can give substance to this terminology via the brand relationships paradigm.

King (1991) argued that the corporate brand will be the only successful area of new brand-building in the future. According to King, as technology functions increasingly as the "great leveler," consumers' choices will depend much less on their evaluation of the single product or service and more on their assessment of the company with which they are dealing.

We have completed studies of consumers' relationships with corporate brands and have invariably found two components in successful, positive relationships: (a) trust in the brand and (b) customer satisfaction with the brand. These sound like two very familiar objectives for corporate brands, but new insights for achieving them emerge when they are dissected and analyzed in terms of our relationship paradigm—consumers' attitude towards the brand and the brand's attitude towards the consumer.

Trust in a relationship can be defined by this very elegant equation, formulated by Eric Baron of the Consultative Resources Corporation: TRUST = (1/RISK) × CREDIBILITY × INTIMACY. Many corporations act as if only one of these variables counts—credibility. They act as if producing good quality products and services, which give the corporation a good image for dependability and reliability, is sufficient to gain the consumer's trust.

However, this equation says that the greater the level of risk that consumers perceive, the less likely they are to place their trust in the brand. It also says that trust in a corporate brand is proportional to the level of credibility and reliability it has. Most crucially, it signifies that trust is dependent on intimacy. This is the brand's attitude, which locks trust into the relationship.

The degree of intimacy is a measure of the brand's success in creating a personal link with the individual consumer, of acknowledging that the individual is more than just a statistic or a client code. It means showing that the brand knows the consumer.

Lack of intimacy is illustrated by this comment made by one owner of a successful real estate business. Referring to his largest supplier, a local utility, he said, "I spend $5,000 a month with them and the only thing that even knows my name there is the billing computer." A corporate brand that doesn't act as if it knows who its customers are will not earn their trust—no matter how credible or reliable it is.

Customer satisfaction, the second recurrent relationship component, also lies at the intersection of two types of attitude—the consumer's and the brand's: PROACTIVE + SUPPORTIVE = SATISFACTION. Very few companies these days can count on customers beating a path to their door. Products and services must be taken to the consumer. People want to deal with companies they see as innovative, ambitious to succeed, ingenious in the development of new ideas, and hardworking. In image terms, this can be summarized in the term *proactive*. However, all this proactivity by itself comes down to aggressive salesmanship, which is not the same thing as creating customer satisfaction. There are many examples of this phenomenon.

In researching automotive brands five years ago, we were surprised at the jaundiced view many consumers held of some much-vaunted business success stories of the time:

1. Chrysler, which five years ago was considered a success story, is often viewed as having responded only to its own business needs—not the consumer's (e.g., "They fixed the company but not the cars").

2. Some midwestern "hold outs" against imported cars acknowledge the excellence of the Japanese or German product, but reject it as emanating only from the manufacturer's own national automotive culture (e.g., "They don't care about what the American consumer thinks").

In both cases, the brand's attitude towards the consumer was deficient. That attitude—crucial to securing customer satisfaction in the relationship—is what we have termed *supportiveness*.

Customer satisfaction results when customers perceive that their needs play a central role in all this activity. Customers want to see all the aggressive energy as a response to and support of their needs. They want some sign that the corporation has listened to them and responded appropriately. Otherwise, it's only high-pressure salesmanship.

The Influence of Brand Relationships on the Corporate Brand

With respect to classic brand-building skills, King (1991) pointed out some crucial differences between the classic brand and the new corporate brand.

One of the most important is the difference in the nature of the consumer for the corporate brand. When the company is the brand, there are far more critical points of contact with its consumers. Consumers range from the company's own employees, through its customers, to legislators, regulators, and the community at large.

These points of contact are not isolated from each other; they overlap and interact. Whereas we may find it convenient to divide up our brand's communications (e.g., corporate advertising, business-to-business advertising, consumer advertising), we should be aware that our various audiences will not accommodate us by partitioning their minds and tuning in only the appropriate set of messages.

This point is dramatically illustrated in one of our studies, in which customer groups of a large diversified corporation were segmented according to their relationships with the corporate brand.

Here are two of the types of relationship we identified, resulting from two very different perceptions of the brand's attitudes:

1. Identification (e.g., "You and I are very similar. We are hardworking, honest, and reliable. We can count on each other.") The brand here is perceived to be an intimate of its consumer. The resulting relationship, charac-

terized by a high degree of trust in the corporate brand, was found among both consumer goods customers and business-to-business customers.

2. Disrespect (e.g., "I don't need to listen to you. There are plenty of other people around who are happy to buy what I am selling.") The brand here is completely lacking in what we have defined as supportiveness and customer centeredness. This relationship (which, needless to say, was not characterized by a high degree of customer satisfaction) was found only among business-to-business customers.

Table 8.1 shows the influence of these relationships on consumers' purchases and use of the corporation's business and consumer products.

The disrespect relationship, created by the perceived indifference of the corporation to the views of its business customers, depresses their purchase of its business products and has a similar effect on their use of its consumer products (which we might have assumed are immune to such business-related attitudes).

Our research on corporate brands has demonstrated this point time and again: Consumers form a single, unitary relationship with a corporate brand; this relationship reaches into and influences every point of contact between the individual and the company.

Further, as illustrated by the case history quoted earlier, we have found that relationships are forged at the most critical point of contact—when the consumer's perception of risk is highest. This is why risk must be factored negatively into the equation defining consumers' trust in corporate brands.

Thus, the manager who has a negative business (higher risk) relationship is likely to avoid choosing that company's products or services at home—independently of their merits or those of the competition.

We have also found that a strong, positive relationship with a corporate brand, built on a solid basis and tested at critical points for the consumer, can survive the isolated bad product or unsatisfactory service experience. It acts as a cushion against the inevitable dictates of Murphy's Law, which can invade even the best corporate environments.

Hard as it may be to imagine, many of America's domestic automobile brands would be in even worse shape now if the relationships they had created over previous years had not helped them through the "bad" years of the late 1970s and early 1980s.

TABLE 8.1
Relationship Segment

Use Index of:	Identification	Disrespect
Consumer Products	120	75
Business Products	111	64

CONCLUSIONS

The concept of brand relationships has been applied mainly to the development of advertising. It has proved invaluable both in identifying the problem the advertising has to address and in providing specific direction for the attitude the brand should adopt. However, advertising is only one of the ways in which a brand communicates via attitudes and behaviors with consumers. Thus, brand relationships have a broad relevance for all areas of marketing communications.

The first and most obvious extension is to Direct ("Relationship") marketing, with its objective of marketing to consumers "one at a time." An articulation of the desired relationship with consumers can provide a guide to the appropriate behavior for the brand in its various transactions with the consumer. Similarly, brands' attitudes and behaviors, expressed through packaging, sales promotion, and public relations, should all be consistent with their relationships.

On a broader scale, as corporate brands become an increasingly important feature on the brandscape, the means of communicating brands' attitudes and behaviors will shift back to people themselves. The employees of a corporate brand represent both a means of communicating the brand's attitudes and an integral part of the brand. The wheel will have turned full circle; what started as an analogy for person-to-person relationships will return to its source.

REFERENCES

Blackston, M., & Holmes, M. (1983). *The use of transactional analysis in the development of a new brand's personality.* Paper presented at the European Society of Market Research (ESOMAR) seminar on new product development, Athens.

Calder, B. J. (1977). Focus groups and the nature of qualitative marketing research. *Journal of Marketing Research, 14*(3), 353–364.

King, S. (1991). Brand-building in the 1990's. *Journal of Marketing Management, 7*(3), 3–13.

Lannon, J., & Cooper, P. (1983). *Humanistic advertising: A holistic cultural perspective.* Paper presented at the European Society of Market Research (ESOMAR) seminar on effective advertising, Paris.

Chapter 9

The Value of the Brand:
An Anthropological Perspective

Grant McCracken
Royal Ontario Museum

The brand is an increasingly important concern for marketing researchers and practitioners. We are beginning to see the brand as a precious commodity, a resource to be managed. Suddenly, brands have value.

This new regard for the brand stems from our belated recognition of its power. Properly created and managed, brands can have extraordinary powers of influence. After all, it is the brand, not the product or the corporation, that wins the consumer's loyalty. Products change; they even disappear. Corporations are (especially at point of purchase) often vague, distant, changing things. What is constant and present in the consumer's life is the brand. Brands *have* value, it turns out, because they *add* value.

THE ANTHROPOLOGICAL APPROACH

The anthropological or cultural approach I use in this chapter defines the brand as a bundle or container of meanings. My argument is that brands have value because they add value, and that they add value because they add meanings to the consumer good (McCracken, 1988a).

The anthropological approach concentrates, then, on the meanings of the brand. It raises three key research questions:

1. What are the cultural meanings that exist in any particular brand?
2. How do these meanings get into the brand?

125

3. Why do consumers care about the meanings of the brand?

These are the questions we must understand to illuminate the value of the brand from an anthropological point of view.

I take each of the key questions in turn:

1. What are the cultural meanings that exist in any particular brand? A brand can stand for maleness or femaleness (the *gender* meaning), social standing (the *status* meaning), nationality (the *country* meaning), ethnicity (the *multicultural* meaning), and so on. The brand can also stand for notions of tradition, trustworthiness, excitement, love of country, authenticity, purity, family, nature, and so on. These are cultural meanings. All of these meanings can be invested in the brand. We do not yet have an exhaustive survey or a complete typography of all the possible meanings that exist in products and brands. However, certain key meanings have been relatively well canvassed (McCracken, 1988a, pp. 72–77).

For example, meanings of the Marlboro brand are relatively clear. The Marlboro brand is a powerful representation of certain cultural meanings of time, space, gender, and activity. The Marlboro brand can summon these meanings in the mind of the consumer, so that a red and white box of cigarettes signifies (a) a life of great challenge, freedom, and satisfaction, (b) a gender type of great resourcefulness, competence, and maleness, and (c) an activity of quintessentially American character. The meanings of the Marlboro brand are clear and compelling.

2. How do meanings get into the brand? Advertising and other parts of the marketing process put them there. Good advertising succeeds in capturing the meanings of the general culture and making them take up residence in the brand. The ad does this through a process of *meaning transfer*.

The creative team, following the objectives of the marketing team, chooses potent symbols from the general culture. It summons up the time, place, activity, and people for the ad. Each of these elements is chosen for the meaning it represents. The product is then inserted into this constellation. The ad is suggesting a kind of equivalence. It says, in effect, that the meanings that exist in the constellation of time, place, person, and activity also exist in the product and the brand. In this way, the product and the brand "soak up" meanings. Thus, cultural meaning is transferred from the culture to the product and the brand (McCracken, 1986, 1988a, pp. 77–79).

We know that in the Marlboro case several decades of advertising have helped develop the meanings of the product and the brand. Marlboro was originally introduced as a women's cigarette, but when this attempt failed, the brand was repositioned. The new motif for Marlboro advertising was established. The place was now the open plain; the time sometimes summer, sometimes winter. The person was always a rugged male cowboy on horseback, almost always alone. The activity was range work.

The meanings of this constellation were clear enough: (a) freedom, (b) the satisfaction of physical challenge, (c) the glory of the great outdoors, (d) release from urban strains and stresses, (c) freedom from industrial labor, (f) freedom from the confines of city life, and (g) the "true grit" of a real male activity. These were the new meanings of Marlboro. The advertising and marketing team had chosen their meanings carefully and the Marlboro brand was the beneficiary. The Marlboro brand now carries clear and compelling meanings. It does so because advertising put them there.

3. Why do consumers care about the meanings of the brand? Consumers possess social selves that are constantly under construction. Simple developmental changes force changes in the self. The change to high school or college forces change. Marriage forces change. Promotion, relocation, or retirement force change as well. But change does not come only from the developmental cycle. Shifts in style and outlook also make a difference. The hippie of the 1960s becomes the yuppie of the 1980s, and this too forces change. With all of these changes, the individual must redefine the self.

As a result, all of us are constantly constructing and reconstructing the self. This calls for new meanings or new ways of defining and presenting the self. There are several sources for these meanings, including consumer goods and brands.

Consumers, then, want the meanings to be contained in the brand. Part of the decision process for any particular purchase is the question "Does this product/brand contain cultural meanings that correspond to the person I am, or the person I want to become?" Consumers look to products and brands for the meanings they need to help construct, sustain, and reconstruct the social self.

The meanings that consumers take from the product and the brand do not come to them automatically. In fact, the meanings are lifted from the product and brand and transferred to the self. Consumers perform this act of transfer by using purchase and consumption rituals (McCracken, 1988a, pp. 83–88).

In the Marlboro case, consumers look to this particular brand because it supplies them with cultural meanings that appeal. The Marlboro brand, as we have seen, contains notions of time, place, person, and activity that have a very large market in America. It represents a version of maleness, outlook, aspiration, and work satisfaction that many Americans find powerfully attractive. These are meanings that help them build the person. Many Americans use Marlboro meanings to construct, sustain, and reconstruct the social self.

Summing up, the anthropological approach focuses on the cultural meanings of the brand. It concentrates on three key factors: (a) what the meanings are, (b) how they get into the product and the brand, and (c) what consumers do with these meanings. This approach may be called the meaning transfer or meaning movement process. According to this perspective, cultural meanings are constantly drawn from the general culture, transferred to products and brands by advertising, and then transferred to consumers. This model is summarized in Fig. 9.1.

Limits and Advantages of the Anthropological Approach

It must be noted that this meaning transfer model has not, traditionally, taken careful account of the brand. Instead, it has looked at products to the exclusion of brands. Too often, consumer products are seen as containers of meanings when indeed it is the brand, and not the product, that holds the meaning. Observers have treated products as the unit of analysis although the proper focus of attention is the brand itself. I attempt to help remedy the deficit.

The meaning transfer model has been slow to appreciate the significance of the brand. Nevertheless, it may be useful to the study of the brand. Indeed, the meaning transfer model can help us calculate the value of the brand. It can also help us to solve some of the marketing problems that surround the brand.

The meaning transfer model helps us to reconceptualize the brand. It encourages us to ask a new set of questions: (a) what are the meanings of the brand, (b) what are the meanings of the competitive brands, (c) what are the meanings now sought by consumers, and (d) what are the best vehicles for the delivery of the right meanings? In the case of Marlboro, we want to determine, exactly, the cultural meanings contained in the brand. Then we want to determine the extent to which Marlboro is the most powerful carrier of the meaning. Does Marlboro have competitors that contain this meaning or the alternate ones? How strong are the meanings carried by competitors? How do consumers use the Marlboro meanings? Are their uses of the meaning chang-

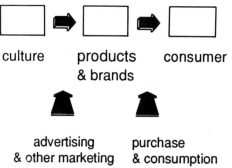

FIG. 9.1.   Meaning transfer model.

ing? Finally, is the cowboy on the open range creative theme still the best way to deliver the meanings consumers want?

In short, the anthropological perspective and the meaning transfer model let us determine the value of the brand according to the kind and the power of the meanings contained in the brand and its competitors. Meaning transfer tells us where to look in judging the "soft" value of the brand.

The meaning transfer model also lets us focus on why some brands succeed and others fail. Strong brands win loyalty because they contain appealing, useful, and powerful meanings. Consumers are loyal to the brands because they want these meanings, in this configuration, with this intensity. Strong brands are storehouses of the meanings consumers use to define their actual and their aspirational selves.

Weak brands, on the other hand, contain meanings that are uninteresting, conflicting or weak. These brands offer no storehouse of meanings that the consumer can use to define the self. In summary, the cultural approach to the brand defines the brand as a repository of meanings. It defines brand attractiveness as a match between the meanings of the brand and the needs of the consumer.

The cultural approach assumes, then, that the power of the brand is determined, in part at least, by the meanings that exist in the brand. The study of the brand from this point of view calls for an examination of several particular questions. We need to know more about the following: (a) the meanings consumers expect to find in a product category, (b) the meanings that exist in any particular brand, (c) the meanings that exist in the brands of its competitors, (d) how to identify the best meanings for the brand, (e) how to get these meanings into the brand, and (f) how to manage the meanings in the brand.

The anthropological half of this project begins with the assumption that brands are containers of meaning. It examines the product category, beer, to determine the meanings of the generic product and to decide which brands have succeeded in capturing this meaning. It looks at a single marketplace to see how beer brands compete with one another to capture cultural meanings and larger market share.

BEER BRANDS AND CULTURAL MEANING: AN EXPLORATORY RESEARCH PROJECT

I conducted a study of beer brands to determine the kinds of meanings consumers want in a beer and which of these meanings are present in the existing brands. I wanted to see: (a) how consumers get meanings out of the brand and into the self and (b) how brand bonding takes place between consumers and the brands in the market place.

The research project was qualitative in nature. I asked a series of open-ended questions to elicit the cultural meanings of consumer goods (McCracken,

1988b). The study was exploratory in nature and, therefore, small in size. I interviewed 11 respondents (9 men and 2 women) in six interviews, for a total of 14 hours of interview. All of the subjects were Canadian, between 22 and 26 years of age, and university educated.

To avoid any misunderstanding of my research results, I emphasize certain characteristics of the sample. At least five of the male respondents were from middle or upper-class homes; several were graduates of Ivy League American or equivalent Canadian universities. Most of the respondents were from professional families. Several participants were keen athletes, but none of them considered athletics the principal or major focus in life. This is not a sample of "jocks."

The questions I asked our respondents were general in nature and fell into two categories:

1. The first category concerned the respondents' college years. I asked respondents to describe their patterns of study, work, and leisure, the social groups to which they belonged, and especially their patterns of alcohol consumption. In this case, I was asking our respondents to look back to their college years.

2. The second category concerned the respondents' present life. I asked the same set of questions, but this time respondents were reporting their present patterns of study, work, sociality, and alcohol consumption.

I served as both interviewer and analyst for the interview data. All interviews were recorded with a Hi-8 video camera and analysis was performed from the videotape.

Cultural Meaning of Beer in the College Years

What is the cultural meaning that consumers seek from beer? I tried to go into the project with my eyes open. I knew any one of the many cultural categories and principals that make up North American culture might be contained in beer. It could be status, nationality, gender, or ethnicity, to name a few. I waited for the respondents to tell me. My first hint came when one of the respondents said, "[In college] you were more of a man if you could drink a lot." A second respondent said, "It's almost the measure of the man, how much beer you can drink."

There it was. Everywhere I looked, the connection between beer and masculinity was made. Indeed, it began to sound as if these young men could not talk about their maleness without talking about beer consumption, and vice versa. It looked as if you could not study one without studying the other. Beer had one overwhelming cultural meaning. This meaning was resolutely about maleness.

It turned out that beer is no mere incident of masculinity. The respondents told me that it was, in fact, essential. One of them said, "It's a male thing. They say women dress for women. Well, I think men drink for men." By this reckoning, beer is crucial to the way in which young men present themselves to other males. Beer is not just one of the things that happens to be invested with maleness in our culture; it is at the very heart of the way maleness is constructed and experienced.

This gave me a glimpse of the cultural meaning that resides in beer. I know that of all the meanings that reside in consumer goods and that could reside in beer, the gender meaning (specifically, the male gender meaning) is the crucial one.

The marketing implications of this are clear. Maleness is the meaning a brand has to control if it wants to make a real connection to the consumer. Maleness is the cultural meaning it must "own" if it wants to build real brand loyalty.

This was only my first glimpse of the cultural meaning of beer. The interviews offered more. Ironically, an important glimpse came from one of the female respondents. I asked her what would happen is she were to "drink like a man." She responded: "Ok, I'd drink beer; I'd drink lots of it, I'd act in a way I couldn't act unless I was drinking beer, which means less inhibited, more loud, more aggressive. These are all the characteristics I associated with beer consumption." The men in the sample confirmed this description of what it is to drink like a man.

Apparently, a transformation takes place around beer. When men drink, something happens to them. They seem to lose their sense of polite conduct. The rules of everyday life begin to slip away. They begin to conduct themselves in a more elemental manner.

Let's listen to one of the respondents as he describes the sensation of approaching a party on a Saturday night. He says, "It's a house just packed with people. You hear the loud music and you just get this feeling . . . that this is just the greatest moment on earth. Or something pretty close to it."

Why is this event so important, so appealing? A respondent explained: It's an evening to relax. You can just go and be yourself. You don't have to pretend to be intellectual like you do in classes. You don't have to pretend to be cultured. You're just yourself. Everyone there is loose. Everyone is pretty much just letting loose and going crazy. To this young man, drinking beer means letting loose. It means living without pretenses or controls, living authentically, without the management of appearances or the constraints of politesse.

Another respondent gave me a slightly different slant on beer consumption. He explained: "You increased your metal by being able to drink this stuff. You're sort of proud of this but you're not exactly thrilled by it. It's sort of something you have to do." When I asked him what he meant, he said beer "coarsens" you, that it makes you cruder.

These two comments come to the same conclusion. In the first case, we are told that beer helps you let loose. In the second, we are told beer makes you more coarse. In both cases, we hear that beer gets you out from under the niceties and constraints of everyday life. Letting loose and getting coarse have similar results. In both cases, beer enables young men to escape the rules of daily life.

As the interview unfolded and the connection between beer and maleness became evident, the interviewer began to probe for the kind of masculinity at issue here. I asked whether men drank "like John Wayne" (i.e., in an undemonstrative manner) on the assumption that Wayne is one of the exemplars of masculinity in North American culture. The answer to this probe was resolute: "No, no, no, you had to be wild, loud. That was the sign of drunkenness."

So strong is this notion of letting loose that it overwhelms even the conventional stereotypes of maleness. Drinking beer is not about every kind of maleness. It is certainly not about the taciturn "man of few words" or "shut-down" version of maleness. Beer consumption is about a much more extroverted, untrammeled version of maleness. As it turns out, the ritual of beer behavior even lets men throw off the constraints imposed upon them by gender stereotypes.

One of the techniques of the qualitative analyst is to take figurative language literally (McCracken, 1988b, p. 44). In this case, we might ask ourselves what this young man meant by saying, "You had to be wild." If we take this phrase literally, we are told that men who drink beer actually lose their domestication, that they become, in a sense, feral.

In summary, respondents said that they think of beer as a thoroughly male substance that has the effect of making men more masculine. They said they thought about this process in three ways: (a) they think about it as a process of letting loose, of abandonment; (b) they think about it as a coarsening substance, a way of adding metal to the self; and (c) they saw beer as a way of getting "wild." In all of these cases, young men described beer as a way of getting out from under the rules of everyday life. In all cases, they used the ritual of their beer behavior to get at the meanings contained in beer.

One of the respondents summed things up nicely with the following comment: "Partly [people think] it's manly to drink a lot, partly it's trying to live *Animal House* in their own lives. [People think] this is what we are supposed to be doing. We're in college, let's live this to the fullest. And part of it's just going further than we've gone before."

Two questions are raised by this analysis:

1. Why is escaping the rules of everyday life the best way of announcing one's masculinity? What, exactly, is the connection here?
2. How does escaping the rules of everyday life aid in the process of male bonding? Why should "going feral" bring men together?

These are vital questions but they cannot be addressed by the present study.

Beer and Competition

The picture the respondents have painted of beer and maleness is a happy one—guys drinking together, having a good time, living the good life. But, in fact, beer drinking is no tea party. It turns out that when men drink, they also compete. I asked young men what they talked about when they drink. One of them said: "A lot of the comments would be directed at the way people drink. If you are a slow drinker . . . you'd be ridiculed. If you couldn't hold your liquor, like if you took a drink and spit it out. That would be pretty funny." Apparently, there is a competitive element here. Men use beer consumption to test themselves, to prove themselves.

I asked this same man to tell me something more about competitive drinking. He said: "Somebody would take a drink and they would sort of start to gag, and somebody would say, 'Oh, ya, buddy, you're a big drinker, there, buddy. Big drinker there, buddy, big drinker.' And the guy would probably fire back, 'Oh, yeh? I could drink you under the table any day.' And the first guy would say, 'Yeh, right, look at you now.' And that would be the end of it."

The lesson here is that if a man makes a mistake while he is drinking, he pays a penalty. If he fails to drink competitively, he does the opposite of proving his manhood. He makes himself appear to be unmanly. Worse than that, the opposite of male bonding takes place and connection to the group is put at risk. If you lose control, you forfeit your claim to being a man and your claim to a place in the group.

In fact, this kind of thing can get nasty. The respondent told us, "If you knew [drinking partners] were starting to feel a little sick, and they really didn't want to play this [drinking] game anymore, then it would be fun to make them play . . . maybe make them puke, I guess." Proving one's manhood is a serious business. Young men do not suffer failures gladly. The stakes are high, the risks are great.

Beer is a way out of one set of rules and a way into another set. A man may give up the rules of everyday life but a new set of competitive rules descends on him. Men are entitled to make demands of him, and he is obliged to respond successfully. People are watching. If he shows weakness or reserve, he can forfeit claims to maleness and group membership.

The Female Reaction

Needless to say, the cult of beer and maleness does not impress everyone. As one woman put it, "[My fellow students at McGill University] were completely respectable by day, and completely abusive and sleazy by night. Definitely, it was associated with drinking, heavy drinking, and losing that respectable . . . [breaks off sentence]. The rugby team was famous for taking off its clothes at parties.'' As it turns out, the behavior that men use to impress one another impresses women not at all.

Many women are, in fact, repelled by the rituals of beery maleness. They dislike the abandon, the coarseness, the wildness, and the competition. These women generally avoid the company of men who are in their ''beer cult'' mode. In fact, respondents told me they insist that a ''date'' must repudiate beer in order to demonstrate that they are out of beer cult mode. I asked one of the female respondents to tell me how a woman feels when a man orders a beer on a big date. She explained: ''I think she would feel she is not special enough. He [i.e., the date] would not be willing to perpetuate the romantic myth. He will be keeping it at a common level. When you order that wine, the male is trying to participate the myth of the romantic evening.'' On special occasions, men are obliged to show women that they have put the beer cult behind them.[1]

The logic of this repudiation is clear. On a big date, a man has to show that he is a civilized creature who believes in the rules and regulations of polite society. He must demonstrate that he is giving up the abandon and the wildness of his usual behavior. Not surprisingly, the best way of repudiating this behavior is by repudiating the substance that is so intimately connected to it. By giving up beer, a man is showing that he is, in fact, prepared to return to polite society and the good manners required of him.

Beer and Cultural Meaning: The Postcollege Years

The ethnographic data showed a clear developmental cycle in the male consumption of beer. Young men adopt a pattern of beer consumption in their college years; some of them move on to very different patterns in the postcollege period (Fig. 9.2).

For many men, however, the beer cult lasts forever. Even into adulthood and family life, these men will continue to drink for other men and to look to beer for looseness, coarseness, wildness, and competition. These men are, in a sense, ''stuck'' in the college years stage and they will never move on. The meanings supplied by beer in this first stage are sufficient and these consumers seek no others (Fig. 9.3).

---

[1]I mentioned this ''no beer on a big date'' rule to a friend in industry. He told me that some beer customers solve it not by moving to something ''civilized,'' like wine or a mixed drink. They solve the point of etiquette by forsaking their usual brand of beer and moving to a brand like Heineken. The assumption here is that because Heineken is a ''classier'' brand of beer it sends the signal that the male is putting aside the beery cult of maleness to honor his companion.

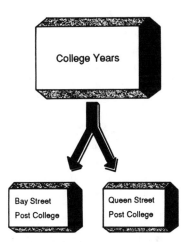

FIG. 9.2. Cultural meanings of beer: The developmental view.

For other men, the beer cult does come to an end. As they leave college and enter professional school and life, a change takes place. They begin to adopt new patterns of masculinity, new ways to express their masculinity, and new brands of beer. This group continues to look to beer to supply certain gender meanings, but the meanings they are now looking for are quite different.

This group is much less interested in abandon, coarse wildness, or competition. These are no longer the key qualities these men seek for the self. Therefore, these are no longer qualities they look for in their beer consumption. This group is now more settled. Drinking is less riotous. People drink more slowly; they drink less beer and they drink with greater calm. These young men drink less often in large groups, parties, and crowded pubs. They are more inclined to drink with a couple of friends in tranquil bars. Beer consumption has begun to lose its "blow-out" quality. These young men are no longer looking for *Animal House*.

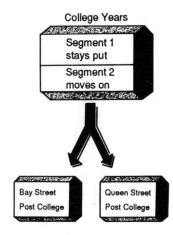

FIG. 9.3. Cultural meanings of beer: The developmental view.

There are, in fact, two distinct groups at this second stage (Fig. 9.2). The first might be called the "Queen Street" group, after the neighborhood in which these men are found in Toronto. (I might also have called this the "Greenwich Village" group.) The second group is called the "Bay Street" group (and here I could have used "Wall Street").

The Queen Street and Bay Street groups are very different. The Queen Street group is creative, artistic, hip, and stylish. These young men have graduated to a much more expressive, more vivid, more style-conscious version of their masculinity. They are not "gay," but they do give close attention to matters of style and self-presentation.

I talked to one young man from the Queen Street group, who told me about the ads and the beers he now takes seriously:

> It all has to do . . . with style. You know, Black Label [i.e., a brand of Canadian beer] came out with these very fashionable, Vogue-looking, commercials. Molson Dry [i.e., another brand of Canadian beer] did something similar. They had these fabulous looking women. When you see a Budweiser commercial, it's just water spraying on women and guys in cowboy boots, and big cowboy hats, and beards . . . you know, that very tough football image. The other commercials are just beautiful women and clothes.

For the Queen Street group, style is now more important than toughness. This man has left the traditional pattern of beer consumption and the traditional definition of himself as a man. What's striking is that this young man is still looking to beer to help define his new version of masculinity. He may have changed his notion of who he is as a man. He has not changed the idea that beer is an important way to establish the private and public realities of this gender definition. When he graduates from the college brands, he moves on to the new concepts of masculinity, new brands of beer, and new rituals of beer consumption (Fig. 9.4).

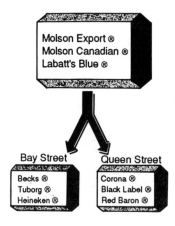

FIG. 9.4. Cultural meanings of beer: How brands line up to capture them.

The Bay Street group is much more conservative. This group consists of young lawyers, accountants, and managers. They are fashionable, but a little conservative. They avoid anything that appears to be too stylish or flamboyant.

I talked to one member of the Bay Street group—a young man who is about to graduate from law school—and asked him how his drinking patterns have changed. He answered, "Now it's enough already. You're 25 years old, you just don't do this [i.e., drink to excess] any more." The entire male cult of beer drinking has come undone. As this young man put it, "We used to [drink a lot] to look cool and now that you're grown up [it turns out] people don't do that, so we were wrong all along [laughs]."

The Bay Street group has changed its objectives. As one respondent put it, "People are into careers." What matters is not whether you belong to the group, but how you succeed in your upward drive for success as an individual. This group now cares about a more managed, more managing social self. Gone is the feeling for abandon, the wildness. Competition remains, but it is now transformed into career aspiration. Promotions have taken the place of drinking contests.

Like the Queen Street group, the Bay Street group looks to new brands of beer. Their preferences are the European brands, like Becks or Tuborg. European brands are considered more polished, more sophisticated than the college brands. That is to say, they carry new cultural meanings that are essential to this new cultivation of the male self. The Bay Street boys have moved on to new kinds of masculinity and new brands of beer (Fig. 9.5).

CONCLUSION

An anthropological approach suggests that brands have value because they add value and they add value by adding meaning. The present study shows the cultural meanings that exist in beer brands. On the basis of exploratory research, it suggests that the chief cultural meaning carried by beer is masculinity.

Using the meaning transfer model, we have seen that masculinity and beer are intimately tied with one another. Among the most compelling cultural mean-

FIG. 9.5.   Meaning transfer model (applied to beer brands).

ings are gender meanings in general and masculinity in particular. We have shown how this meaning is contained in Canadian beer brands through the efforts of advertising and other marketing tools. We have shown how young men seek out these meanings. The rituals of beer consumption help young men take possession of the cultural meanings contained in the brands.

This study observes that the gender meanings of masculinity contained in our culture have a developmental character. Some young men adopt certain masculine meanings in their college years and then move on to new masculine meanings. In a sense, these young men "graduate" from their college gender identities to new and rather different ones. Now that they have moved to new concepts of the self, they seek out products that contain the new meanings they need to construct the self. In the Canadian case, young men move on to Bay Street and Queen Street gender identities, and this takes them to a new set of brands. We observe that the present Canadian beer brands have captured all three of these cultural meanings. This relationship is summarized in Fig. 9.6.

In summary, the present study shows how beer brands stand between culture and consumers. In the Canadian case, these brands have been invested with cultural meanings of masculinity through advertising and marketing. Brands help deliver these meanings into the lives of the young men who use them to define themselves as males in both early and later stages of life. In this study, the value of the brand is the meaning of the brand.

IMPLICATIONS

This study has two striking implications for brands.

1. The study tells us that a substantial amount of the soft part of the brand's value consists of the cultural meanings of the brand. If we wish to assess the value of the brand properly, we must inventory the meanings it contains, the

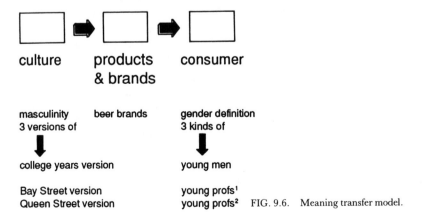

FIG. 9.6.   Meaning transfer model.

power of these meanings, and how well these meanings compete against those meanings carried by competitive brands.

2. This perspective tells us that, from a marketing point of view, we augment and manage the value of the brand when we attend to the cultural meanings it contains. Our objective is to determine the meanings of the brand and then to manage these meanings through better marketing. We want to augment the meanings that give us competitive advantage and jettison those that do not. A determination of these meanings enables us to design better advertising and other marketing instruments to capture and maintain the cultural meanings that give us brand loyalty.

In summary, the value of the brand is, to some extent, the meaning of the brand. I have suggested that the anthropological perspective can capture and manage this critical piece of the marketing package.

REFERENCES

McCracken, G. (1986). Advertising: Meaning or information? *Advances in Consumer Research, 14,* 121–124.

McCracken, G. (1988a). *Culture and consumption.* Bloomington, IN: University Press.

McCracken, G. (1988b). *The long interview.* Newbury Park: Sage Publications.

Part III

The Role of Advertising in Creating Brand Equity

Advertising, Perceived Quality, and Brand Image

Amna Kirmani
Valarie Zeithaml
Fuqua School of Business, Duke University

In the past few years, marketing managers and academics have shown increasing interest in what constitutes and affects brand equity (Aaker, 1991). This interest has highlighted a number of unresolved issues or questions:

1. A fundamental issue involves the meaning of brand equity and its similarity to related concepts, such as brand name and brand image.
2. Another issue is the relationship between brand equity or image and perceived quality, which is sometimes used as a measure of these brand concepts.
3. As managers try to influence brand image, the issue of how advertising can affect such images becomes important (Park, Jaworski, & MacInnis, 1986).

We distinguish brand equity from brand image in terms of perspective. *Brand equity* is a managerial concept: Managers engage in strategies (e.g., advertising, pricing) designed to build positive brand equity for their products. On the other hand, *brand image* is the perceptual concept of a brand that is held by the consumer (e.g., Dobni & Zinkhan, 1990). Biel (1991) made a similar distinction elsewhere in this book. He distinguished brand equity (a financial variable) from brand image (a customer or marketing variable), and he showed that brand image affects brand equity. Brand equity and brand image are highly related terms because in building brand equity, managers attempt to influence consumer perceptions of a product (i.e., develop a positive brand image).

Aaker (1991) identified five dimensions of brand equity: (a) name awareness, (b) perceived quality, (c) brand associations other than quality, (d) customer base, and (e) other proprietary brand assets. To the extent that these variables affect consumers' brand perceptions, they are likely to influence brand equity through brand image. Thus, it is important to consider how these dimensions affect brand image.

This chapter focuses on one of these dimensions—perceived quality—and its role in influencing brand image. Perceived quality as a concept is relevant to academics, who have examined its antecedents (e.g., Olson, 1977; Zeithaml, 1988), and to advertisers, who have attempted to affect quality perceptions through cues that signal quality. We develop a model that depicts the antecedents and consequences of perceived quality as it relates to brand image. Antecedents of quality include concrete-level intrinsic and extrinsic attributes, as well as more abstract dimensions of quality. Consequences of quality include: (a) brand attitude, (b) perceived value, and (c) brand image. Further, by reviewing prior literature and offering examples from ad campaigns, we examine the effects of advertising on quality perceptions. Along the way, we offer propositions about advertising's effects on perceived quality and brand image. These propositions deal with characteristics of the product, consumer, and ad, which can be manipulated to create advertising that more effectively conveys quality and, thus, promotes a positive brand image.

In the next section, we introduce our conceptual model and discuss the effect of perceived quality on brand image. We then conduct a detailed examination of the antecedents of perceived quality, followed by consideration of how advertising can affect quality perceptions. Finally, we offer implications for future research and management on the topics of advertising, perceived quality, and brand image.

THE EFFECT OF PERCEIVED QUALITY ON BRAND IMAGE

There are multiple inputs to brand image: (a) perceived quality, (b) brand attitudes, (c) perceived value, (d) feelings, (e) brand associations, and (f) attitude toward the ad. Because our intention is to specify the role of perceived quality in the development of brand image, we concentrate on those variables that are related to quality. For this reason, the model omits the role of feelings and attitude toward the ad, which affect brand attitude independently from perceived quality (cf. Holbrook & Batra, 1987). Similarly, we exclude brand associations and direct effects of advertising on brand image because these are not mediated by perceived quality.

Perceived quality can be defined as the consumer's judgment about a product's overall excellence or superiority. As described elsewhere (Zeithaml, 1988), per-

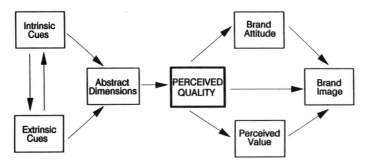

FIG 10.1.   The perceived quality model.

ceived quality is a higher level perceptual abstraction, rather than a concrete attribute. Although some multiattribute models have included perceived quality as a lower level attribute, this practice has been criticized (see Ahtola, 1984, and Myers & Shocker, 1981).

As shown in Fig. 10.1, perceived quality can affect brand image directly or indirectly through the constructs of perceived value or brand attitude. Perceived quality is one of the beliefs that determines *brand attitude*, but the two concepts frequently become blurred because they are measured similarly. Researchers often measure brand attitude on a set of scales (e.g., *good/bad, inferior/superior, high quality/low quality*) that relate more to quality than affect (e.g., *pleasant/unpleasant, appealing/unappealing, like/dislike*). We conceptualize brand attitude as a more complex construct than perceived quality. Brand attitude contains both affective and cognitive elements. For instance, feelings generated from an ad may affect brand attitude (e.g., AT&T's emotional "Reach out and touch someone" campaign for long-distance telephoning), but are unlikely to affect perceived quality (e.g., customer perceptions of sound quality and reliability).

We define *perceived value* as the consumer's overall assessment of the utility of a product, based on perceptions of what is received (e.g., quality, satisfaction) and what is given (price, nonmonetary costs).[1] Value differs from quality in two ways: (a) Value is more individualistic and personal than quality, making it a higher level abstraction (Zeithaml, 1988); (b) value involves a tradeoff of "give" and "get" components (e.g., the money, time, and effort the consumer exchanges for the features, benefits, and returns from the product). Although many conceptualizations of value have specified quality as the only get component in the value equation, the consumer may implicitly include other factors, such as convenience.

---

[1]We realize, of course, that there should be other arrows leading into perceived value in Fig. 10.1 (e.g., from price, which is an extrinsic cue). Because the focus of this paper is on perceived quality, these arrows have been omitted for reasons of simplicity.

Perceived value can be the basis for a product's brand image or positioning. For example, Suave shampoo's slogan claims the low-priced product "makes you look like you spent a fortune on your hair." Similarly, L'Oreal hair coloring admits it costs more, but justifies the high price by the color, shine, and feel delivered by the product (hence, the slogan "I'm worth it"). Alternatively, a brand image can lead to perceptions of value, particularly when the image conveys multiple get components provided by the brand. For example, the Ritz Carleton Hotel emphasizes the added value of its extra services that make it well worth its high price tag.

The notion that the information about products that consumers hold in memory does not always (or even usually) coincide with actual physical profiles is well documented (Herzog, 1963; Newman, 1957). Brand image is the concept often used to express consumers' interpretations (cognitions, feelings) of the actual intrinsic and extrinsic characteristics of a product. Researchers have defined brand image in various ways which capture the perceptual recasting of concrete, specific attributes. Examples of these definitions include "sum of the total impressions" (Herzog, 1963) and "everything the people associate with the brand" (Newman, 1957).

In summarizing interpretations of the brand image concept in the history of the marketing literature, Dobni and Zinkhan (1990, p. 118) concluded that "brand image is largely a subjective and perceptual phenomenon that is formed through consumer interpretation, whether reasoned or emotional." In addition, brand image "is not inherent in the technical, functional, or physical concerns of the product." We view perceived quality as a different construct from brand image, although it is sometimes used as a proxy for brand image. Because brand image includes conceptions of quality, value, and attitude—as well as brand associations and feelings—it is more multidimensional than perceived quality and, therefore, at a higher level of abstraction.

THE ANTECEDENTS OF PERCEIVED QUALITY

To fully understand how advertising affects perceived quality, we must determine how quality perceptions are formed. The antecedents of quality are shown in Fig. 10.1. At the most concrete level, these antecedents include intrinsic and extrinsic cues. These concrete cues are summarized by the consumer in midlevel perceptual abstractions, such as style and performance, which can be considered dimensions of perceived quality. Moving from left to right, the figure shows an increase in abstraction and dimensionality and a decrease in measurability. This increasing level of abstraction is consistent with other conceptualizations of product attributes (e.g., Geistfeld, Sproles, & Badenhop, 1977; Olson & Reynolds, 1984) known as means–end chains.

Lower level attributes that signal quality have been dichotomized into intrinsic and extrinsic cues (Olson, 1977; Olson & Jacoby, 1972). Intrinsic cues refer to concrete, physical properties of the product (i.e., lower level specific brand beliefs). These intrinsic attributes cannot be changed without altering the nature of the product itself and are consumed as the product is consumed (Olson; Olson & Jacoby). Examples include color, texture, miles per gallon, and horsepower. Extrinsic cues are product related, but not part of the physical product itself. By definition, they are external to the product, and changing them does not change the physical product. Price, brand name, level of advertising, and warranty are examples of extrinsic cues to quality (Zeithaml, 1988).

In the conceptualization proposed in this chapter, we view *brand name* as a lower level, extrinsic attribute. A company's brand name contains specific information about the product. Many researchers have examined the role of brand name as an extrinsic cue to perceived quality (Andrews & Valenzi, 1970; Dodds & Monroe, 1985; Gardner, 1970, 1971; Jacoby, Olson, & Haddock, 1971; Jacoby, Szybillo, & Busato-Schach, 1977; Mazursky & Jacoby, 1985; Peterson & Jolibert, 1976; Raju, 1977; Rao & Monroe, 1987; Wheatly & Chiu, 1977). These studies consistently show that brand name is selected more frequently than any other intrinsic or extrinsic cue, including price. The primary explanation researchers provide for the dominance of brand name is that it provides a chunk of information to consumers (e.g., Jacoby, Olson, & Haddock, 1971; Jacoby, Speller, & Kohn-Berning, 1974; Jacoby, Szybillo, & Busato-Schach, 1977; Mazursky & Jacoby, 1985). We extend this line of reasoning to propose that brand name serves as an extrinsic signal for a chunk of intrinsic cues. For example, the brand name of Ivory signals the following intrinsic cues: white, floats, pure. The brand name Federal Express connotes fast, on time, reliable.

Generalizing about quality across products has been difficult for managers and researchers. Specific and concrete intrinsic attributes differ widely across products, as do the attributes consumers use to infer quality. Obviously, the attributes that signal quality in fruit juice (color, presence of pulp) are not the same as those indicating quality in washing machines or automobiles. Even within a product class, specific attributes may provide different signals about quality.

Whereas the concrete attributes that signal quality differ across products, higher level abstract dimensions of quality can be generalized to categories of products (Zeithaml, 1988). Garvin (1987), for instance, proposed that product quality can be captured in eight dimensions: performance, features, reliability, conformance, durability, serviceability, aesthetics, and perceived quality (i.e., image). In describing the way consumers compare noncomparable alternatives, Johnson (1984) posited that consumers represent the attributes in memory at abstract levels. Similarly, Olson (1978) discussed ''descriptive beliefs,'' which involve a restatement of the original information into more abstract terms (e.g., ''accelerates from 0 to 60 mph in 5 seconds'' generates the belief ''high performance''). Olson suggested that consumers may use informational cues (e.g., intrinsic and extrinsic cues) to develop descriptive beliefs about products. These beliefs, in turn, could affect evaluation and choice.

Brucks and Zeithaml (1991) contended on the basis of exploratory research that six abstract dimensions could be generalized across categories of durable goods: (a) ease of use, (b) functionality, (c) performance, (d) durability, (e) serviceability, and (f) prestige. Parasuraman, Zeithaml, and Berry (1985) found consistent dimensions of perceived quality across seven service industries. These dimensions included: (a) reliability, (b) responsiveness, (c) assurance, (d) empathy, and (e) tangibles.

In summary, the antecedents of perceived quality range from concrete and specific attributes that are either intrinsic or extrinsic through abstract dimensions that capture key perceptual facets of quality.

The Effect of Concrete Attributes on Perceived Quality

There is a large body of literature that shows the impact of intrinsic and extrinsic cues on perceived quality. These studies often measure overall quality without measuring the dimensions of quality. For instance, in the product category of beer, Jacoby, Olson, and Haddock (1971) found that both brand name and actual composition characteristics were more important determinants of product quality perceptions than price. Pincus and Waters (1975) varied intrinsic cues as well as price of ballpoint pens and found that intrinsic cues accounted for most of the variance in product quality ratings.

In some studies, abstract dimensions of quality are also measured. Valenzie and Andrews (1971), for example, found that actually tasting margarine samples had a stronger influence on taste perceptions (a quality dimension) than did the price of the margarine. Etgar and Malhotra (1981) varied both intrinsic (sole, color, upper) and extrinsic (place of purchase, price) attributes of running shoes and revealed that both types of cues were important in determining product quality. Respondents in their study used different extrinsic and intrinsic cues for different dimensions of quality (e.g., comfort, durability, and style). For example, price was important in judging the dimension of durability, whereas color was more important in judging the style dimension.

Extrinsic cues other than price also affect quality perceptions. As mentioned earlier, brand name is considered a signal of quality. The importance of other extrinsic cues, such as product warranties (Bearden & Shimp, 1982; Boulding & Kirmani, 1991) and advertising costs (Kirmani, 1990; Kirmani & Wright, 1989), has also been documented. According to Kirmani, ad size affected perceptions of ad costs, which in turn affected perceived comfort and quality of an athletic shoe.

Intrinsic and extrinsic attributes can affect each other. Intrinsic cues (such as size of a stereo speaker) can lead to an inference about price (an extrinsic attribute) of the speakers. Conversely, the price of a product can lead the consumer to a lower level belief about the concrete aspects of the product. A $3 price for a candy bar, for instance, would likely signal "large size." As described earlier, brand name can represent a cluster of intrinsic attributes.

Extrinsic cues can affect each other as well. For instance, ad expenditures can affect perceived price of the product (Kirmani, 1990). A high warranty on a product is likely to lead to the inference that the product carries a high price. Despite the importance of extrinsic cues in forming quality perceptions, not much is known about how different extrinsic cues affect each other. Similarly, the effect of intrinsic cues on extrinsic attributes is also underresearched. Inferences drawn from cues at the same level of abstraction are thus a fruitful avenue for future research.

Both intrinsic and extrinsic attributes are important in quality perceptions; their relative weight may differ across consumers, products, or situations. Zeithaml (1988) identified conditions under which extrinsic or intrinsic cues would predominate. Intrinsic attributes are more important at the point of consumption because they can generally be gauged easily at that time. Prior to actually trying a new cereal, for instance, the consumer cannot determine its sweetness or crunchiness; however, consuming the cereal provides the needed information about these intrinsic cues. In prepurchase situations, intrinsic attributes are important when they are search attributes (i.e., when they can be assessed prior to purchase) rather than experience attributes, which can only be assessed at consumption. Extrinsic attributes are critical in initial purchase situations when intrinsic attributes are unavailable or not diagnostic (e.g., many purchases made by direct mail), when the evaluation of intrinsic attributes requires too much time or effort (e.g., low-involvement products), and when quality is difficult to evaluate (e.g., experience goods). Consistent with these conditions, Kirmani (1990) showed that when ad content was uninformative about a particular attribute (i.e., comfort or durability of an athletic shoe), subjects relied on advertising expenditures as a quality cue. However, when ad content was informative (i.e., showed a photo of a shoe) about a quality dimension (style), subjects did not rely on advertising expenditures as a quality cue. Boulding and Kirmani (1991) found that an extrinsic cue in an ad (i.e., information about product warranty) affected durability perceptions although the ad was informative about intrinsic product cues.

THE EFFECT OF ADVERTISING
ON PERCEIVED QUALITY

In order to influence quality perceptions, advertising or advertising campaigns can be targeted at the antecedents of quality or at perceived quality itself. Advertising can affect perceived quality directly by explicitly mentioning quality in the ad; it can influence perceived quality indirectly through inferences drawn about overall quality from intrinsic cues, extrinsic cues, or abstract dimensions. In this section, we consider both of these paths and develop propositions about how ads may be designed to effectively convey high quality.

Advertising components can be described in various ways. Mitchell (1986) divided ads into verbal and visual components. Another, perhaps more specific, compartmentalization involves copy (claims, appeals, headline) and executional elements (e.g., media vehicle, celebrities or other spokespeople, bleed color, layout, photos, size, frequency, music, camera techniques). Advertisers use these copy and executional elements to maximize impact on consumer response variables such as attention, brand beliefs, and brand attitudes. (For summaries of the effects of such variables on consumer responses to advertising, see Stewart & Furse, 1986, and Percy, 1983.) Ads may contain explicit information about product attributes, or these attributes may be inferred from ad copy and elements.

Prior literature has considered the role of advertising directed at providing information about intrinsic and extrinsic cues. For instance, Mitchell (1986) proposed a structural model in which the visual and verbal components of an ad affect product (i.e., brand) attribute beliefs. These cues may be stated explicitly in ad claims (e.g., Crest fights cavities, or Chrysler comes with a 7 year/70,000 mile warranty), or they may be inferred from ad elements. For instance, a photo of a cat may suggest that a facial tissue is soft (Mitchell & Olson, 1981) or a multipage ad may signal high ad expenditures (Kirmani, 1990).

The Indirect Effect of Advertising

There are two streams of literature relevant to determining advertising effects on perceived quality:

1. The more extensive body of research examines the impact of advertising components on brand beliefs and attitudes. The major dependent variable is generally brand attitude; beliefs are measured not for their own sake, but as an input to expectancy-value attitudes. These studies examine the effect of ad content and elements on intrinsic attributes and abstract dimensions of quality. Perceived quality is seldom mentioned explicitly; however, the brand beliefs measured are often abstract dimensions of quality. Among the advertising elements documented to influence brand beliefs about intrinsic attributes are the factualness (Holbrook, 1978), concreteness (MacKenzie, 1986), and attribute prominence (Gardner, 1983) of advertising copy. For instance, Holbrook varied the degree of factualness/evaluativeness of intrinsic cues in a car ad and measured consumers' beliefs about the brand's appearance, handling, safety,

comfort, service, and economy. In our model, these attributes are considered abstract dimensions of quality. Other elements investigated in research include the photograph (e.g., Mitchell & Olson, 1981) and picture size and color (Percy & Rossiter, 1983).

2. The second stream of research, which investigates the impact of ads on extrinsic cues, is less extensive; however, its focus is on quality rather than on brand attitude. Most studies that examine the effect of extrinsic cues on perceived quality (e.g., price–quality studies) manipulate the extrinsic cue through nonadvertising stimuli. However, some studies have directly examined the effect of advertising stimuli on perceptions of extrinsic attributes. For instance, Freiden (1982) found that the presence of a celebrity endorser affected perceptions of the price of the product. Aaker and Brown (1972) discovered that an ad in a prestigious magazine affected perceived product price and perceived quality under some conditions. Anderson and Jolson (1980) found that the use of technical wording in an ad for a computer affected perceptions of price, durability, and ease of operation. Kirmani (1990) showed that ad size affected consumers' perceptions of advertising expenditures, as well as perceptions of the comfort, durability, and overall quality of a hypothetical brand of athletic shoes. The focus of these studies has been on the impact of extrinsic cues on perceived quality rather than on the effect of ad content and elements on these cues.

Although these two streams of literature ask fundamentally different questions, both provide insight into how advertising may impact quality perceptions. They also highlight possibilities for future research. For instance, earlier we described studies that explored the link between concrete attributes and abstract dimensions of quality. It would be useful to extend this research to the advertising area by explicitly examining the effect of intrinsic cues on perceived quality in an advertising context. Conversely, researchers could examine the effect of extrinsic cues on brand attitudes. Both these questions/issues are relevant to understanding brand image. In addition, they might help to point out the differences between perceived quality and brand attitude.

Another result of the focus on either intrinsic or extrinsic cues is that there is little research on the combined influence of intrinsic and extrinsic cues in an ad on quality perceptions. Earlier, we pointed out that intrinsic and extrinsic cues are related to each other, and consumers may draw inferences about one cue from another. Although some studies deal with the relative influence of intrinsic and extrinsic cues (e.g., price) on quality, few of these use advertising stimuli, despite the fact that advertising is often the means of conveying these cues to consumers. Moreover, few ads exclusively feature one type of cue; most ads contain both extrinsic and intrinsic cues, implying that we need to determine how the cues should "fit" together. This leads to the following proposition:

Proposition 1. Ads in which intrinsic and extrinsic cues are consistent with each other (i.e., point to the same abstract dimension) are more effective than ads in which these cues are inconsistent.

If an ad's intrinsic attributes signal high quality (e.g., when the copy makes a high quality claim), then extrinsic attributes should also signal high quality. Extrinsic attributes, such as ad expenditures, can convey high quality because expensive advertising is a signal of high quality. A poorly executed ad which makes high product quality claims is not likely to be believed. Consumers may doubt that the manufacturer of such low quality advertising could produce a high quality product (Kirmani & Wright, 1989). Alternately, an ad that claims that the brand has a lot of features but also promises a low price may lead consumers to wonder whether there's a catch.

The Direct Effect of Advertising

The foregoing studies deal with advertising effects on intrinsic cues, extrinsic cues, and abstract dimensions of quality. There is less documentation of ads that try to directly manipulate overall quality perceptions. However, there is evidence of this in actual ad campaigns. For example, Ford's slogan, "Quality is Job 1," explicitly states that the company makes high-quality products.

A question raised by this analysis is whether explicit claims of overall quality are more effective than ads in which quality must be inferred from more concrete attributes. Because the term *quality* is used so frequently in advertising and marketing and has multiple meanings, direct claims that a product possesses quality may be less effective than those that provide more specific information at a lower level of abstraction. Part of the effectiveness of the lower levels derives from the specific evidence contained in information about features. Part of the effectiveness comes from more precisely targeting consumers' needs in the advertisement. Moreover, any company can claim high quality without documentation. This may contribute to increased skepticism with advertising of experience versus search attributes (Ford, Smith, & Swasy, 1990). Claims about search attributes can be verified prior to purchase, whereas claims about experience attributes cannot be verified until the product is consumed. Similarly, concrete claims are likely to be more verifiable than abstract quality claims.

However, consumer characteristics, such as product familiarity and involvement, may moderate this process. Some consumers may lack the motivation or ability to process concrete information and, therefore, respond better to a more general quality claim. This leads to the following proposition:

Proposition 2. The higher the consumer's familiarity with the product class, the more likely that advertising focusing on specific product attributes will be effective.

When consumers are familiar with the product class, they have the knowledge required to interpret concrete product attributes (Alba & Hutchinson, 1987). For instance, consumers familiar with cars can understand horsepower information and evaluate the concrete information to form their own quality assessments. Consumers with low familiarity with cars, on the other hand, may find the horsepower information meaningless; for these consumers, quality information at a more abstract level (perhaps at the abstract dimension level discussing performance or economy) may be more effective. Moreover, the familiar consumer probably wants specific information that can distinguish this brand from others or from product class norms.

Proposition 3. The higher the consumer's level of involvement (with the product class or the situation), the more likely that advertising which discusses specific product attributes will be effective.

Highly involved consumers require more concrete information because they are either more knowledgeable or more motivated to seek information. They may want to evaluate the information on their own, rather than have it summarized for them by the advertiser. Consumers with low involvement are uninterested in buying the brand and, therefore, do not seek specific information. An overall quality statement may be all that is necessary for them to process. As shown in the elaboration likelihood model (Petty & Cacioppo, 1981), high involvement increases the motivation to process an ad; low involvement decreases this motivation.

A related question is whether overall quality claims are more effective than attribute-oriented claims in affecting brand image. Nakomoto, MacInnis, and Jung (1991) address this issue elsewhere in this book.

THE LINKS AMONG ADVERTISING, PERCEIVED QUALITY, AND BRAND IMAGE

Thus far, we have proposed a model which delineates the role of perceived quality in the formation of brand image. We have also reviewed literature dealing with advertising's effect on quality perceptions and offered some propositions about how ads may best convey quality. In this section, we use all three concepts—advertising, perceived quality, and brand image—to generate propositions about how to design ads to best convey brand image.

Park, Jaworski, and MacInnis (1986) described three types of brand concepts:

1. *Functional brand concepts* emphasize the brand's functional performance in solving consumption-related problems. Product classes such as microwaves and power tools are likely to have functional brand concepts because they emphasize features of products that solve consumer problems or satisfy consumer needs.

2. *Symbolic brand concepts* emphasize the brand's relationship with group members or self. Product classes such as cars and perfume often have symbolic concepts.

3. *Experiential brand concepts* emphasize the brand's effect on sensory satisfaction or cognitive stimulation, highlighting the brand's experiential or fantasy aspects. Product classes such as vacations and movies tend to have brands with largely experiential concepts.[2]

This classification scheme has implications with respect to the perceived quality model presented in this chapter.

Proposition 4.   To best communicate functional brand concepts, advertising should be aimed at intrinsic attributes that signal the desired abstract dimension (e.g., performance, functionality, durability).

Because consumers of functional brands are most interested in how the brand performs, advertising should focus on conveying these aspects. Thus, ads for computers, microwaves, stereos, and industrial products would describe intrinsic attributes or product features that convey performance. For instance, an ad for IBM's PS/1 personal computer describes specific intrinsic attributes (such as high-resolution photographic display, keyboard and built-in modem, and use of software) to convey ease of use, power, and value. Similarly, an ad for Panasonic word processors discusses features such as simple menus, a 45,000-word thesaurus, spell check, and a built-in spreadsheet program, all intended to convey power and ease of use.

The manner in which this strategy is implemented can, of course, differ.

---

[2]There are two words of caution here. First, although the examples have been of product classes that are largely functional, symbolic, or experiential, PJM's classification scheme (and our implications for advertising) applies to brands rather than to product classes. Within a product class such as cars, for instance, some brands may be more functional, some more symbolic, and some more experiential. Moreover, not all brands can be easily classified into one of these groups; some brands may be mixtures. The advertising strategy in that case would also be mixed.

Some ad styles or components may be more powerful than others. Thus, a magazine ad could use descriptive content or a photograph which highlights the features. A television ad could employ demonstration or a problem–solution format. Regardless of the technique, the basic idea of this strategy is to emphasize intrinsic attributes that convey functionality and performance.

Proposition 5.   To best communicate symbolic brand concepts, advertising should be aimed at extrinsic attributes which signal the desired abstract dimension (e.g., style, prestige).

Because symbolic concepts imply concern with self-identification or group membership, advertising should convey a prestigious image, identify users of the product, or convey a lifestyle. This generally implies using celebrities or other spokespersons the audience can relate to, respect, or admire. Alternately, the ad may convey quality using extrinsic cues, such as ad expenditures and price, cues that have been shown to signal prestige. In particular, the use of expensive production or media elements in advertising would portray the desired image. For instance, an ad for Paloma Picasso jewelry at Tiffany and Company may use extrinsic cues, such as the celebrity (Paloma Picasso), the media vehicle (runs in Vogue), and the type of store (Tiffany), all of which convey prestige. Of course, the ad may also show the jewelry, which conveys intrinsic attributes of gold and shininess, and hence style. The main point is that the extrinsic cues are probably more important in this situation than are intrinsic cues.

Similarly, many ads for luxury items, such as liquor (e.g., the Dewar's profile), pens (e.g., Waterman), or perfume (e.g., Liz Claiborne), use extrinsic cues to portray a certain type of user and to convey prestige. Moreover, some ads (e.g., Calvin Klein) don't even show the product, but just create an image. Others (e.g., Levi's 501 jeans) show the product, but are largely intended to create an image of the user. The visual component of the ad becomes fairly important in this strategy.

Proposition 6.   To best communicate experiential brand concepts, advertising should be aimed at a level of abstraction higher than perceived quality.

With experiential brand concepts, consumers are interested in fun and fantasy. Thus, advertising should convey the fun, fantasy, or pleasure potential of the product, perhaps by showing people enjoying themselves. Often, this is done through advertising that emphasizes feelings or evokes personal memories, implying a nonquality route (i.e., alternate route through brand attitudes and associations). For instance, an ad for Royal Caribbean Cruise Lines could show the different ways of having fun aboard a cruiser, the mouth-watering variety of food to eat, and the beautiful scenery. Some food or restaurant ads show appetizing food arranged beautifully to appeal to the senses.

Many ads targeted at children (e.g., candy, toys, games) emphasize the fun aspect of the product; children are more likely to respond to this type of appeal than to a more rational exposition of product features. Jell-O ads show kids having fun making shapes that jiggle. Barbie Doll ads show young girls playing together with their dolls.

In summary, advertising intended to convey different brand concepts needs to emphasize different quality or nonquality aspects. With functional brand concepts, advertising should emphasize intrinsic attributes; with symbolic brand concepts, extrinsic attributes; and with experiential brand concepts, nonquality variables.

RESEARCH AND MANAGERIAL IMPLICATIONS

Our model has implications for research on the topics of advertising, perceived quality, and brand image. Because generating brand equity is such an important managerial objective, research on each of the areas discussed in this section would have important practical implications as well.

Other Relationships in the Model

The focus in this chapter has been on the role of perceived quality in the development of brand image; the impact of other variables on brand image remains to be researched. For example, two variables shown in the model—brand attitudes and perceived value—are likely to contribute strongly to brand image. Comparing the relative impact of these variables to the impact of perceived quality is one avenue for future studies. For example, one line of inquiry could be whether perceived quality or perceived value has greater impact on brand image perceptions. Under some conditions (e.g., strong value positioning for the brand) perceived value may be more important. Thus, for a brand such as Suave shampoo, value rather than quality is likely to be more important in influencing brand image. The critical question is whether this is brand-specific or generalizable across product classes. No research as yet examines the amount of variance explained by each antecedent on brand image.

Other variables, omitted in the model for the sake of parsimony, may also be useful. Feelings, brand associations, and attitude toward the ad may affect brand image either directly or indirectly through brand attitude. Researchers could investigate how a cognitive route differs from an affective route to brand image. For example, is one longer lasting than the other? Under what circumstances?

We also acknowledge that the direction of relationships proposed in the model may not represent all possible influences. It is likely that many links could be multidirectional; for example, knowledge of abstract dimensions may lead consumers to infer concrete level attributes. In some cases, brand image could lead to perceptions of the presence of lower level intrinsic attributes or midlevel abstract dimensions. In fact, this process may represent what happens in successful brand extensions: Consumers ascribe to new versions of the product the same abstract dimensions that earlier product versions contained. In other words, marketers may design brand extension campaigns to begin with brand image (e.g., another product from Vaseline) that signals the brand's intrinsic attributes or abstract dimensions (softening, gentle, effective).

Effectiveness of the Alternate Advertising Strategies

We have proposed that advertising can enter the model in several different ways to influence brand image. A worthwhile research question, particularly for managers, would involve testing the relative effectiveness of the proposed advertising strategies in creating desired brand image. Of course, one necessity in such research is that measures of effectiveness be specified or operationalized. A multiplicity of measures, occurring at different levels of abstraction, could serve this end. For example, traditional advertising effectiveness measures of recall could occur at (a) the concrete level (recall of specific brand attributes or specific price), (b) the abstract level (unaided recall of brands that possess, for example, high performance in automobiles), and (c) the perceived quality level (what brand in this product category has advertised quality?). Identifying the advertising elements that create or contribute to strong brand image is a complex issue that requires researchers to consider the multiple levels and variables presented in the model.

Distinction Between Extrinsic–Intrinsic Attributes and Central–Peripheral Processing

A degree of similarity exists between the extrinsic–intrinsic dichotomy and Petty and Cacioppo's (1981) distinction between central and peripheral processing. To the extent that extrinsic cues are external to the product and intrinsic cues are inherent in the physical product, the former appear to be peripheral cues whereas the latter are central cues. The two dichotomies are different, however, in that the extrinsic–intrinsic distinction is a description of product attributes and the central–peripheral distinction describes alternate routes to persuasion in responding to ads. According to Petty and Cacioppo, individuals who engage in central processing cognitively elaborate on information conveyed by ad copy and claims; individuals who engage in peripheral processing attend to noncopy cues, such as the number of arguments or the presence of a celebrity.
   As discussed earlier, both intrinsic and extrinsic cues can be conveyed

through either ad copy or ad elements. Thus, an intrinsic cue (e.g., variety of colors of facial tissues), can be conveyed through the photograph of a sunset or through a direct statement in ad copy. The photograph would make it a peripheral cue; the direct statement would make it a central cue. An extrinsic cue such as warranty is often conveyed through ad claims, making it a central cue. One cue that is probably both extrinsic and peripheral is advertising expenditures, because this is typically conveyed via ad elements rather than ad copy.

Implications for Brand Extensions

The model presented in this chapter has implications for research done on brand extensions. Many studies of brand extensions measure the transfer of quality perceptions from the original brand to the extension (e.g., Aaker & Keller, 1990). Our analysis shows that a measure of overall quality may not adequately capture the nature of the transfer in an extension context. Some dimensions of perceived quality may transfer, but others may not. An overall quality measure may hide this. Hence, in brand extension research, it may be better to measure the abstract dimensions of quality rather than overall quality. Measuring abstract dimensions will also help determine which aspects of the brand image are fundamental to the brand and which are changeable.

Another implication derives from the notion that brand name is an extrinsic cue which signals a chunk of other attributes. One of the issues in extensions is that the original brand and the extension must fit together in order for the extension to be successful. However, researchers have found it difficult to specify what is meant by fit. One form of fit may be whether the abstract dimensions signaled by the brand name are consistent with the abstract dimensions signaled by intrinsic attributes of the extension. When both are consistent, there will be a fit between the original brand and the extension. Inconsistency may indicate the potential failure of the extension. It is probable that fit is at the abstract dimension level, rather than at the concrete attribute level, because intrinsic attributes can differ across brands, whereas abstract dimensions are more generalizable. Testing these ideas would provide valuable insight to marketing managers.

CONCLUSION

Of the five dimensions of brand equity identified by Aaker (1991)—(a) name awareness, (b) perceived quality, (c) brand associations other than quality, (d) customer base, and (e) other proprietary brand assets—perceived quality was the focus of this chapter because of its importance to both academics and managers. We developed a model that depicts the antecedents and consequences of perceived quality as it relates to brand image. This perceptual concept of a brand held by the consumer (Dobni & Zinkhan, 1990) strongly affects brand equity, which we see as a managerial concept. In addition to reviewing prior literature and offering examples from advertising campaigns, we developed propositions about the way advertising may affect quality perceptions and, in turn, brand image. Finally, we discussed implications for future research and management on the topics of advertising, perceived quality, and brand image.

REFERENCES

Aaker, D. A. (1991). *Managing brand equity*. New York: The Free Press.

Aaker, D. A., & Brown, P. K. (1972). Evaluating vehicle source effects. *Journal of Advertising Research*, *12*, 11–16.

Aaker, D. A., & Keller, K. L. (1990). Consumer evaluations of brand extensions. *Journal of Marketing*, *54*, 27–41.

Ahtola, O. T. (1984). Price as a "give" component in an exchange theoretic multicomponent model. In T. Kinnear (Ed.), *Advances in consumer research* (Vol. 11, pp. 623–626). Ann Arbor, MI: Association for Consumer Research.

Alba, J. W., & Hutchinson, W. W. (1987). Dimensions of consumer expertise. *Journal of Consumer Research*, *13*(4), 411–454.

Anderson, R. E., & Jolson, M. A. (1980). Technical working in advertising: Implications for market segmentation. *Journal of Marketing*, *44*(1), 57–66.

Andrews, I. R., & Valenzi, E. R. (1970). The relationship between product purchase price and blind rated quality: Margarines and butters. *Journal of Marketing Research*, *7*, 393–395.

Bearden, W. O., & Shimp, T. A. (1982). The use of extrinsic cues to facilitate product adoption. *Journal of Marketing Research*, *19*(2), 229–239.

Biel, A. (1991, May). *Turning brand image into brand equity*. Paper presented at 10th Annual Advertising and Consumer Psychology Conference, San Francisco, CA.

Boulding, W., & Kirmani, A. (1991). *An experimental examination of signalling theory: Do consumers perceive warranties as signals of quality?* (working paper). Fuqua School of Business, Duke University, Durham, NC.

Brucks, M., & Zeithaml, V. A. (1991). *Price and brand name as indicators of quality dimensions* (working paper). Duke University, Durham, NC.

Dobni, D., & Zinkhan, G. M. (1990). In search of brand image: A foundation analysis. In M. E. Goldberg, G. Gorn, & R. Pollay (Eds.), *Advances in consumer research* (Vol. 17, pp. 110–119). Provo, UT: Association for Consumer Research.

Dodds, W. B., & Monroe, K. B. (1985). The effect of brand and price information on subjective product evaluations. In E. Hirschman & M. Holbrook, (Eds.), *Advances in Consumer Research*, (Vol. 12, pp. 85–90). Provo, UT: Association for Consumer Research.

Etgar, M., & Malhotra, N. K. (1981). Determinants of price dependency: personal and perceptual factors. *Journal of Consumer Research*, *8*(2), 217–222.

Ford, G. T., Smith, D. B., & Swasy, J. L. (1990). Consumer skepticism of advertising claims: Testing hypotheses from economics of information. *Journal of Consumer Research*, *16*(4), 433–441.

Freiden, J. B. (1982). An evaluation of spokesperson and vehicle source effects in advertising. In J. H. Leigh & C. R. Martin (Eds.), *Current issues and research in advertising* (pp. 77–88). Ann Arbor: University of Michigan.

Gardner, D. M. (1970). An experimental investigation of the price–quality relationship. *Journal of Retailing*, *46*(3), 25–41.

Gardner, D. M. (1971). Is there a generalized price–quality relationship? *Journal of Marketing Research*, 8(2), 241–243.

Gardner, M. P. (1983). Advertising effects on attributes recalled and criteria used for brand evaluations. *Journal of Consumer Research*, 10(3), 310–318.

Garvin, D. A. (1987). Competing on the eight dimensions of quality. *Harvard Business Review*, 65(6), 101–109.

Geistfeld, L. V., Sproles, G. B., & Badenhop, S. B. (1977). The concept and measurement of a hierarchy of product characteristics. In K. Hunt (Ed.), *Advances in consumer research* (Vol. 4, pp. 302–307). Ann Arbor, MI: Association for Consumer Research.

Herzog, H. (1963). Behavioral science concepts for analyzing the consumer. In P. Bliss (Ed.), *Marketing and the behavioral sciences* (pp. 76–86). Boston: Allyn & Bacon.

Holbrook, M. B. (1978). Beyond attitude structure: Toward the informational determinants of attitude. *Journal of Marketing Research*, 15(4), 545–556.

Holbrook, M. B., & Batra, R. (1987). Assessing the role of emotions as mediators of consumer responses to advertising. *Journal of Consumer Research*, 14(3), 404–420.

Jacoby, J., Olson, J. C., & Haddock, R. A. (1971). Price, brand name, and product composition characteristics as determinants of perceived quality. *Journal of Applied Psychology*, 55, 570–579.

Jacoby, J., Speller, D. E., & Kohn-Berning, C. A. (1974). Brand choice behavior as a function of information load: Replication and extension. *Journal of Consumer Research*, 1, 33–42.

Jacoby, J., Szybillo, G. J., & Busato-Schach, J. (1977). Information acquisition behavior in brand choice situations. *Journal of Consumer Research*, 3, 209–215.

Johnson, M. D. (1984). Consumer choice strategies for comparing noncomparable alternatives. *Journal of Consumer Research*, 11(3), 741–753.

Kirmani, A. (1990). The effect of perceived advertising costs on brand perceptions. *Journal of Consumer Research*, 17(2) 160–171.

Kirmani, A., & Wright, P. (1989). Money talks: Perceived advertising expense and expected product quality. *Journal of Consumer Research*, 16(3), 344–353.

MacKenzie, S. B. (1986). The role of attention in mediating the effect of advertising on attribute importance. *Journal of Consumer Research*, 12(2), 174–195.

Mazursky, D., & Jacoby, J. (1985). Forming impressions of merchandise and service quality. In J. Jacoby & J. Olson (Eds.), *Perceived quality* (pp. 139–154). Lexington, MA: Lexington Books.

Mitchell, A. A. (1986). The effect of verbal and visual components of advertisements on brand attitudes and attitude toward the advertisement. *Journal of Consumer Research*, 13(1), 12–24.

Mitchell, A. A., & Olson, J. C. (1981). Are product attribute beliefs the only mediator of advertising effects on brand attitudes? *Journal of Marketing Research*, 18(3), 318–332.

Myers, J. H., & Shocker, A. D. (1981). The nature of product-related attributes. *Research in Marketing*, 5, 211–236.

Nakamoto, K., MacInnis, D. L., & Jung, H. (1991, May). *Advertising claims and evidence as bases for brand equity and consumer evaluation of brand extension*. Paper presented at 10th Annual Advertising and Consumer Psychology Conference, San Francisco, CA.

Newman, J. W. (1957). New insight, new progress, for marketing. *Harvard Business Review*, 35(6), 95–102.

Olson, J. G. (1977). Price as an informational cue: Effects in product evaluation. In A. G. Woodside, J. N. Sheth, & P. D. Bennet (Eds.), *Consumer and industrial buying behavior* (pp. 267–286). New York: North Holland.

Olson, J. G. (1978). Inferential belief formation in the cue utilization process. In H. K. Hunt (Ed.), *Advances in consumer research* (Vol. 5, pp. 706–713). Ann Arbor, MI: Association for Consumer Research.

Olson, J. G., & Jacoby, J. (1972). Cue utilization in the quality perception process. In M. Venkatesan (Ed.), *Proceedings of the Third Annual Conference of the Association for Consumer Research* (pp. 167–179). Iowa City: Association for Consumer Research.

Olson, J. G., & Reynolds, T. J. (1983). Understanding consumers' cognitive structures: Implications for advertising strategy. In L. Percy & A. Woodside (Eds.), *Advertising and consumer psychology*. Lexington, MA: Lexington Books.

Parasuraman, A., Zeithaml, V. A., & Berry, L. (1985). A conceptual model of service quality and its implication for future research. In L. Percy & A. Woodside (Eds.), *Advertising and consumer psychology*. Lexington, MA: Lexington Books.

Park, C. W., Jaworski, B. J., & MacInnis, D. J. (1986). Strategic brand concept-image management. *Journal of Marketing, 50*(3), 135–145.

Percy, L. (1983). A review of the effect of specific advertising elements upon overall communication response. In T. Leigh & C. Martin (Eds.), *Current issues and research in advertising* (Vol. 2, pp. 77–118). Ann Arbor: University of Michigan.

Percy, L., & Rossiter, J. R. (1983). Effects of picture size and color on brand attitude responses in print advertising. In R. Bagozzi & A. Tybout (Eds.), *Advances in consumer research* (Vol. 10, pp. 17–20). San Francisco: Association for Consumer Research.

Peterson, R., & Jolibert, A. (1976). A cross-national investigation of price brand determinants of perceived product quality. *Journal of Applied Psychology, 61*(3), 533–536.

Petty, R. E., & Cacioppo, J. T. (1981). *Attitudes and persuasion: Classic and contemporary approaches*. Dubuque, IA: William C. Brown.

Pincus, S., & Waters, L. K. (1975). Product quality ratings as a function of availability of intrinsic product cues and price information. *Journal of Applied Psychology, 60*, 280–282.

Raju, P. S. (1977). Product familiarity, brand name, and price influences on product evaluation. In W. Perrault (Ed.), *Advances in consumer research* (Vol. 4, pp. 64–71). Ann Arbor, MI: Association for Consumer Research.

Rao, A. R., & Monroe, K. B. (1987). The effect of price, brand name, and store name on buyer's perceptions of product quality: An integrative review. *Journal of Marketing Research, 26*(3), 351–357.

Stewart, D. W., & Furse, D. H. (1986). *Effective television advertising*. Lexington, MA: D. C. Heath & Co.

Valenzi, E. R., & Andrews, I. R. (1971). Effect of price information on product quality ratings. *Journal of Applied Psychology, 55*(1), 87–91.

Wheatley, J. J., & Chiu, J. S. (1977). The effects of price, store image, and product and respondent characteristics on perceptions of quality. *Journal of Marketing Research, 14*, 181–186.

Zeithaml, V. A. (1988). Consumer perception of price, quality, and value: A means–end model and synthesis of evidence. *Journal of Marketing, 52*(3), 2–22.

Chapter 11

Asking the Right Questions:
What Do People Do with Advertising?

Judie Lannon
Marketing and Communications Consultant

THE COMPETITIVE ENVIRONMENT OF THE 1990S

Package goods marketers in the 1990s in the United States and Europe face a particularly competitive environment, stemming from reasons much deeper than the current slight recession and the temporary fluctuations of the business cycle. A long look backwards and a summary of the key trends in each aspect of the marketing environment paints a picture of increasing limits for marketing maneuver and greater reliance on building consumer brand franchises (Table 11.1).

The recent past has been characterized, particularly in the United States, by stagnation in above-the-line advertising and a growth in the use of promotions. In the *Harvard Business Review*, Jones (1990) lucidly analyzed the suicidal rush to discount; Biel (1991) described, from a longitudinal data base, the effects of a decline in advertising expenditure on brand share.

These very worrying signs of a retreat from aggressive brand building activities form the background for this chapter, which addresses the communication dimension of brand advertising and the constructive or destructive contribution of research.

My argument develops as follows:

1. That strong brands are valuable to manufacturers is taken as given. We develop the view that strong brands are valuable to the consumer and

TABLE 11.1
Markets Controlled by Consumers and Trade

	1950s		1990s
Technology	A few leaders with a big R&D advantage over a lot of followers.	→	Speed of technology transfer shortens lead time and narrows gap. Many companies share same technology.
Markets	Mass markets with moderate competition fueled growth.	→	Mass markets are stagnant with aggressive competition.
Products	Simple single runs. Production stable and relatively simple.	→	Segmentation and customization require more complex, flexible manufacturing capabilities.
Trade	Fragmented, weak, dependent on manufacturer.	→	Concentrated, powerful control of manufacturer. Retail brands.
Media	Simple structures and concentrated usage. Beginning of long period of television dominance.	→	Explosion in all forms. Individual media use fragmented.
People	Mass tastes, stable traditional values, predictable lifestyles.	→	Individualistic tastes, discovered values, eclectic lifestyles.
Communication	Inform and persuade of Product benefits. Rational argument.	→	Emotional expression of Brand benefits. Metaphor, symbols.

that value stems from the utility of brand imagery in the individual's wider communication system.

2. Therefore, if brand imagery has utility for consumers, what is the nature of this utility and how does it vary by product category?

3. The advertising research process, from the development research to pretesting, fails to follow the logic of the philosophy of strong brand development and unwittingly contributes to weaker rather than stronger advertising. How and why do practitioners and marketers switch models in midstream?

4. It is necessary to consciously detach the language of advertising from the military imperative language of marketing through new and fresh metaphors more appropriate to the way consumers choose.

HOW DO PEOPLE CHOOSE?

Brands are bought for who they are as much as for what they are; the equity is the sum total of the what and the who. Hence, it is critical that the function is competitive and that the who (the personality) is distinctive, robust, desirable, and constant.

Because people use the term *personality* in different ways, it is worth describing what we mean by it, how to develop it, and how to maintain it.

Personality is a Discriminator, Not a Motivator

Personality is not a laundry list of desirable generic adjectives (e.g., good quality, liked by the family, well-known). Phrases like these refer to category motivators; personality is the discriminator.

Form Follows Function

Personality must stem directly from what the product does—a variation of the *form follows function* dictum. The inseparability of form and function is regularly illustrated via blind versus named-product tests. The example in Table 11.2 is extreme, but it illustrates the extraordinary motivating power of a strong personality in a competitive situation.

Furthermore, brand personalities serve different purposes in different product categories—a very important subtlety.

Brand Personalities are not User Personalities

This is an area of considerable confusion. Researchers often labor under two major misconceptions: (a) that user personalities and brand personalities will be/should be the same; and (b) that the task of consumer research is to match the two. The model inherent in all psychographic segmentation analyses uses this as its basic assumption.

TABLE 11.2
Impact of Branding on Product Testing

	Blind (%)	Branded (%)
Prefer Diet Pepsi	51	23
Prefer Diet Coke	44	65
Equal/DK	5	12

Note. From "How an Appreciation of Consumer Behaviour Can Help in Product Testing" by L. de Chernatony and S. Knox, 1990, *Journal of the Market Research Society, 32*(3), p. 333. Copyright 1990 by Market Research Society. Adapted by permission.

User and brand personalities match if brand choice is the direct manifestation of a set of personal values or lifestyles (e.g., newspapers or cars) but will seldom hold up for the majority of package goods. This is the crux of the problem of segmentations and lifestyles for packaged goods.

There are several reasons why user personalities and brand personalities for fast moving consumer goods (fmcg) brands won't match:

1. In most categories of ordinary frequently purchased supermarket goods, people tend to buy a repertoire of brands. Thus, the role of advertising is to move the brand up a mental shortlist. In other words, the same people are buying the main brands. Solus usage is very rare. Most people buy most brands at some time or other. This has been well documented by analysis of panel data.

2. The obvious reason is that people buy different categories in different modes. Thus, whereas value-laden choices may match up comfortably with psychographic types, brands of coffee, tea, cereal, toilet paper, or paper towels are of a different, more trivial order.

3. A more complex reason for this mismatch is that the utility of the brand personality to consumers will differ by product category, and this will depend on the reasons for which consumers use brand imagery.

HOW PEOPLE USE BRAND PERSONALITIES

Self-expressive categories, such as alcoholic drinks, perfumes, cigarettes, certain clothing, and some toiletries, are "badges" for displaying an aspect of personality (e.g., "I choose this under these circumstances to say this about myself or how I wish you to see me" or "I choose this because it expresses the way I feel even though others may not know"). They are essentially personal display items and, as such, the nature of the message will be image and style based.

Other brands act as reassurance. The personality of After Eight Mints, for instance, is elegant, sophisticated, upper class, secure. The users are far from that; it is a mass-market brand with imagery providing reassurance to the socially insecure or unimaginative.

A somewhat different use of the brand personality is the way it can metaphorically stand for the brand's function. The girl and boy situation featured in the advertising for Timotei shampoo, for instance, is not a direct representation of the user personality but rather an emotional representation of the brand's functional characteristics—natural, herbal, gentle, pure.

For many categories of household products, the brand personality performs an additional function, acting as a familiar and constant authority to help consumers make choices and simplify complex shopping. Furthermore, many commentators on the U.S. consumer scene observe that there can be real limits on the amount of choice that consumers can handle. The thousands of new products reaching the market every year can produce a kind of paralysis, the net effect of which is that consumers stick with brands they know and trust. Choice beyond a certain point reduces risk taking and induces conservatism. In the United Kingdom, names like Persil, Oxo, and Andrex are not self-expressive in the same individualistic self-expressive sense as toiletries, perfumes, or drinks; they are valued because they are trustworthy and safe, standing as they do for different core authority values. This is the area in which brand equity can be leveraged most successfully.

The most enduring packaged goods personalities—whether they use an actual device such as the Andrex puppy or the Lux film stars, a consumption-related device such as the Kit Kat "break," or an archetype such as the After Eight dinner party—express who the brand is through a unique and appropriate blend of functional and emotional components.

Consequently, psychological segmentations may be more directly helpful in describing brand personalities than in defining user personalities. For instance, Table 11.3 shows a segmentation for the brand personalities of the major brands of shavers in France.

How to Measure Personality

The strength of personality and its contribution to brand equity was illustrated earlier in the example of the Diet Pepsi/Diet Coke blind-named product test.

This strikes me as a simple and unarguable measure of the strength of a brand's equity vis-à-vis main competitors with similar product formulations

TABLE 11.3
Brand Personalities of Shavers Sold in France

Wilkinson: The Squire Traditional nobility. English colonizers. The Knights of the Round Table. Experience, long-term know-how. Feeling of belonging to a special caste.	**Schick: The Sleeping Brand** Lethargy. Vanished civilization. Lost planet. Faceless inhabitants. No soul, no culture.
Bic: The "Charlatan" Anarchy. A shapeless world. No ideas, no know-how. No figure-head and no order.	**Gillette: The Champion of Civilization** Authority and social order. Dictatorship, tough regime. Clean, controlled world. Official Gillette TV propaganda. Little room for individual differences.

or, as is increasingly the case, vis-à-vis own-label versions. Furthermore, the logic of tracking, which is characteristically complicated by a host of attitude measures, most of which tell us nothing about the strength of brand equity and provide little insight into the personality of the brand, tells us we should be substituting regular blind/name tests combined with regular qualitative studies for the conventional cumbersome and expensive brand-tracking studies.

Diagnosing the character of the personality requires imaginative and projective approaches. Whether the research uses small samples or large samples is irrelevant; the point is the nature of the questions and the interpretive framework. The most commonly used techniques are outlined in Table 11.4.

Very few marketing people would dispute the general thesis so far:

- That brand building is the prime function of their job.
- That brand equity is comprised of competitive performance combined with a distinctive and "wantable" personality.
- That the major contributing factor to the character of the brand's personality and thereby an important contributor to the total equity is the communication.
- That the communication is composed of everything that impinges on the consumer. They may be *above-the-line* or *below-the-line*. A more useful distinction is between brand-building activities and messages and brand-exploiting activities and messages. After all, conventional media advertising can damage brands and, with the exception of discounting, below-the-line activities can build them.

ASKING QUESTIONS THE WRONG WAY ROUND

If, as I've described, the major contributor to the brand's reputation and character is the communication, then it follows that the same techniques (or, if not the same techniques, at least the same philosophical model) should be used at all stages of the advertising development process. Of course, this is not at all what happens.

The research and marketing world is schizophrenic about its decision-making research. This schizophrenia leads, at best, to confusion and a vast wastage of money, and at worst, to wrong or misguided decisions.

The reason is that part of the research world is interested in one set of questions and the other part of the research world is interested in another set of questions. Put succinctly, the difference is between asking

- What does advertising do to people? and
- What do people do with advertising?

TABLE 11.4
Diagnostic Techniques

Role playing:	"Imagine you are the maker of this brand."
Personal analogies:	"Describe yourself as a cornflake, a can of Ajax," etc. Direct and symbolic analogies: "Imagine the brand as a kind of flower, cat, animal," etc.
Fantasy solutions and future scenarios:	"Describe the ideal solution to cleaning clothes."
Psychodrawings:	"Draw brown bread compared to white bread."
Adjectivization:	"What would a Lux kind of day be? A Kodak sort of car be?" etc.
Personifications:	"If Listerine came to life as a person, who would it be?"
Obituaries/story completions/ cartoon captions:	"Write an obituary for Close-Up toothpaste," etc.

What Advertising Does to People

It is important to identify the model that underlies these different philosophical approaches and to ensure that the methodologies are consistent with that model. The model and the accompanying measurements that address the question "What does advertising do to people?" make the assumption that advertising is acting in a more or less active way on more or less passive people.

The model derives from the *hierarchy of effects* concept of some 30 years ago and has a number of variations. Most basic is the simple hammer-and-nail notion—advertising is there to hammer messages into people's heads, hence the emphasis on repetition. The rational argument, whereby a series of facts and evidence of a product's superiority are assembled, is more sophisticated.

However, most significant are the assumptions about the process whereby advertising progresses people from one stage to another. I would call these *linear sequential models* or, more simply, *transportation models*. This is a very convenient conceptualization. It allows us to attach measurements to each stage and it makes the whole process more logical and rational. We have measurements of advertising working on people conceptualized in Fig. 11.1.

I needn't belabor these models and their measurements, as they are very familiar. Let me just say a few words about what is wrong with them.

Inappropriate Theories. Perhaps most importantly, they are based on inappropriate psychological theories—behaviorism, learning theory, and decision theory. At a perceptual level, they don't account for the participation of the receiver; at a behavioral level, they don't account for unconscious motivation or self-expressive choice.

Yet, most of psychological literature and one's own experience, suggest exactly the opposite. People are active and participating receivers of communication. Gestalt psychology emphasizes perception of totalities rather than a

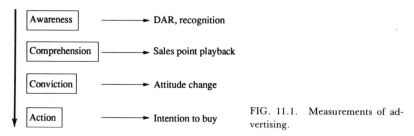

FIG. 11.1. Measurements of advertising.

cataloguing of individual elements; cognitive theorists stress resistance to change and fragmentation; mass communication theories contribute *uses and gratification* theories. The everyday experience of interviewers talking to people about advertising regularly demonstrates how people select, distort, and create messages according to personal perceptions. Because these models assume rational and considered choice, they do not reflect the widely different ways in which people choose and buy.

Organizational Utility.   If these models aren't relevant, why do they continue to dictate thought? The greatest strength and appeal of the linear sequential models come precisely because they lend themselves so neatly to hard measurement and a methodological businesslike working process. Characteristically, qualitative data is allowable only at the very early stages. As things progress, the data needs somehow to be harder, so more people are asked fewer, more superficial, and less relevant questions.

Procedures like this are useful in the maintenance of organizational systems, despite the fact that they reflect a reality that few would recognize. Numbers have a comforting universality to brand managers needing to justify decisions up the organizational hierarchy or across countries. It is a little like the man looking for his keys in the dark under a lamppost, not because he dropped them there but because that's where the light is.

Perhaps the simplest reason for the continuance of research of this sort is that the mechanistic metaphors of the transportation models are close to the imperative language of symbolic war that characterizes marketing; moving into markets, mapping out strategies, devising tactics—competitive, purposive, logical, military. It is natural that advertising as a tool of marketing should use the same set of phrases and metaphors.

BETTER THEORIES ON HOW PEOPLE CHOOSE

I suggest that it is necessary to consciously detach the language of advertising from the language of marketing. To do this requires more appropriate theories which carry with them new and fresh metaphors—language and concepts

TABLE 11.5
Underlying Theories/Models of Thought ("-isms" and "-ologies")

United States	Europe
Positivism	Humanism
Empiricism	Subjectivism
Behaviorism	Phenomenology
Pragmatism	Eclectism
Data-based	Feeling-based

Note. Parts of this table are from "Differing roles of qualitative research: Europe and the USA," by P. Cooper, 1989, *Journal of the Market Research Society*, *31*(4). Copyright 1989 by The Market Research Society.

more in tune with the intuitive and mystical creative process rather than the rational logical organizational process. If we think of research that primarily serves the needs of creative people and consumers, we will produce different sorts of research and, more significantly, different sorts of advertising that, I propose, are not merely more appealing and more rewarding but satisfy the commercial requirement of being more effective. (Further discussion of advertising models may be found in Lannon & Cooper, 1983.)

United States versus Europe

Cooper (1989) described differences in styles of research between the United States and Europe. He illustrated these differences in three broad areas (Tables 11.5, 11.6, and 11.7).

In my experience, this goes a long way toward explaining why person-centered research philosophies and models guide European research more than U.S. research. John Philip Jones, a Welshman by birth but currently professor of communication at Syracuse and author of a number of books and articles about advertising, adds another, common sense explanation (1989). He described the situation in the United States where large brands occupy smaller

TABLE 11.6
How Respondents Are Treated

United States	Europe
Object	Subject
Watched	Participant
Standardized	Variable
Representative	Individual

Note. Parts of this table are from "Differing roles of qualitative research: Europe and the USA," by P. Cooper, 1989, *Journal of the Market Research Society*, *31*(4). Copyright 1989 by The Market Research Society.

TABLE 11.7
Models of the Way Advertising Works

United States	Europe
Linear	Holistic
Measurable	Symbolic
Assertive	Complex
Control	Rapport

Note. Parts of this table are from "Differing roles of qualitative research: Europe and the USA," by P. Cooper, 1989, *Journal of the Market Research Society, 31*(4). Copyright 1989 by The Market Research Society.

shares than larger brands in other countries. This means that there are many brands of equal size crowded together. He contended, "It therefore becomes an important advertising task to distinguish between them. This leads to the use of rational, factual, competitive, discriminating arguments." This strikes me as a perfectly plausible rationale for why manufacturers run the advertising they do. However, it should not necessarily be considered a defense of the effectiveness of such an approach with consumers because it confuses what is transmitted with what is received. "Hard" information, single mindedly conceived, can be conveyed, after all, in very "soft" ways. The real difference is between cluttered, unfocused, complex stimuli versus clear and single-minded stimuli, not, as is often described, between hard rational information and soft emotional images. Both, after all, are messages carrying meaning.

How Consumers Describe Advertising

Hard sell versus soft sell are phrases commonly used by practitioners to describe the presence or absence of a logical rational "reason why" argument employed in the construction of a commercial or campaign.

Leaving aside the issue of which is more effective in selling goods (the wrong question, anyway), there is an implicit assumption that consumers see ads in these terms. The picture is more complex. Recent research in five European countries, conducted by Young and Rubicam (Y&R) and reported by Bonnal (1990) in *Admap*, describes the differing ways that advertising (as a cultural phenomenon) is perceived and described by different nationalities.

There appear to be two basic dimensions on which people describe their expectation of ads. The first dimension relates to executional form: Is the execution literal and straightforward, with the implication of honesty, or is it stylish or stylized? The second dimension could be described as *tone of voice*: Is the tone of voice of the advertisement serious or does it set out deliberately to entertain?

The findings of the study tend to support the conclusions that a regular attender of Cannes film festivals might come to. There are differences in the way different nationalities describe the characteristics of their ideal advertisements. Germans feel they should be honest, straightforward, and down to earth; Italians want their ads to be, above all, stylish; the French include both wit and style; the English combine honesty with wit; and the Danes eschew wit and style and feel that advertisements should be serious, thoughtful, and literal.

This study and many others attest to the very sophisticated decoding skills that modern consumers, especially the young and, it would appear from this study, Southern Europeans, bring to advertising. This is not surprising, given the influence of films and television, as well as editing techniques and other production skills contributed by the advertising industry itself. Because form and content of communication are inseparable, a range of different analyses has proved very insightful in describing advertising styles.

One such categorization of advertising is semiological in origin and derivation. It categorizes styles of advertising, not in the way creative advertising people typically describe advertising conventions (e.g., talking head, slice of life, montage, etc.) but rather in terms of how much complicity is required by the viewer. In other words, what assumptions does the advertisement make about what the viewer knows or understands and, thus, what assumptions are implied about how the communication is intended to work?

Figure 11.2 charts the five broad categories of advertising style and illustrates how advertising communications have evolved over time as consumers have become more visually literate and more adept at the decoding.

Category One: The Manufacturer Speaks. The simplest and arguably the most primitive form of advertisement is the salesman in the living room. The assumption is: (a) that the receiver believes manufacturers know best, (b) that manufacturers tell the truth, and (c) that claims will be accepted if they come from the source of ultimate authority, the manufacturer.

Category Two: Target Groups Consume with Pleasure. The assumption here is that viewers will identify literally or aspirationally with the people portrayed and that they will believe in the value of the product because they see people like themselves consuming/praising it.

Both of these categories are the staple fare of advertising in less industrialized countries. They make very few assumptions about the viewer beyond a

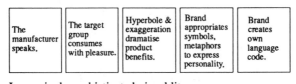

Increasingly sophisticated visual literacy ⎯⎯⎯⎯⎯➤

FIG. 11.2.   Evolution of advertising conventions over time.

basic credulousness. There is no complicity, no understanding of a shared project, no invitation to the viewer to participate, no seduction, and no rewards for the viewer's having taken the time to watch.

As consumers have developed an understanding of the game of consumption, however, advertisements have taken more liberties and make more assumptions.

Category Three: Hyperbole and Exaggeration. Commercials in this category flatter the viewer by assuming he or she will understand the hyperbole, will recognize and enjoy the exaggeration as an advertising convention. Usage of the brand of, say, soft-soled shoes, will not literally make you float on clouds or walk above the pavement; viewers are expected to work this out for themselves and, as a consequence, be suitably impressed with the brand's performance. The rewards are in the satisfying fit between the exaggeration and the reality and, at another level, in the fantasy/play world created by the commercial in which magical things happen.

Category Four: Brand Expresses Who It Is Through Metaphor, Myth, and Symbol. The difference between this category and the previous one is a difference in degree and complexity. Commercials for long-established brands with evolved and complex visual codes fit into this category. International brands such as Marlboro (cowboy), Lux (film stars), Rolex (high achievers), Pepsi (pop music heroes) are typical examples of brands that use archetypes. Other brands such as Bacardi (the myth of the Caribbean) have appropriated country-of-origin myths. More complex brand metaphors are seen in advertising for Apple computers, Perrier, Levis, Schweppes, Chivas Regal, and Nike.

The use of brand metaphor is obviously not restricted to international brands. Most long-established brands have developed a visual language that is unique to them. The viewers' rewards are a rich mixture of sensual, emotional, and rational pleasures. The ultimate test is the viewers' agreement that the commercial could be for no other brand. Irrespective of product claim, the language code, tone of voice, and visual construction identify it as a communication for a specific brand. The viewer knows that the manufacturer recognizes the complicity and is flattered by it.

Category Five: The Brand Invents Its Own Language. This form of communication embodies the most extreme form of flattery and assumed knowledge. In effect, the advertiser is saying, "You know me well, so I don't have to explain myself; I can concentrate on stretching and engaging your imagination." The complicity and involvement are total.

Cigarette advertising is forced by prohibiting legislation into this elliptical category. In Europe, Benson & Hedges has demonstrated that engaging executions work over time by teaching viewers the code. By excising all product references and concentrating solely on brand language, however, communications run serious risks and few examples truly come off. By giving insufficient information and offering inadequate clues, they assume too much and are merely insulting and irritating.

An example here is Benetton. The advertising has evolved from the richly metaphorical "United Colors of Benetton" (in which the product promise of a color range was always prominent as an excellent example of the previous stage on the continuum) to advertising that abandons colors entirely and appears to exploit an unconnected variety of moral issues. In the company's attempt to develop a morally provocative stance, the clothes made by Benetton have been completely abandoned.

This conceptualization is extremely useful in understanding how modern consumers relate to persuasive communication. If the old transport and transmit models were concerned with what advertising does to people by measuring recall, sales point playback, attitude change, and intention to buy, the new model looks at what people do with advertising. What rewards and satisfactions do consumers gain from advertisements?

Following this logic, the significance of the Advertising Research Foundation study on "liking" and the subsequent study by the Center for Research on what liking means to consumers, described by Biel (1990), is clear. Liking turns out to be a kind of proxy for a range of reactions.

Biel (1990) put forward five reasons why *likability* should, from the consumer's standpoint, be such an effective measure:

1. Commercials that are liked get better exposure. People don't consciously avoid it, nor do they subconsciously "tune out." Indeed, for some, they actively look forward and pay attention.

2. Commercials as brand personality attributes. In categories where products are identical, or certainly similar, the advertising itself becomes part of the brand. Certainly in "icon" brands (Marlboro, Levi's, Coke), the advertising is essential to the brand's status and desirability.

3. Liking as a surrogate for cognitive processing. This is the most compelling of all the reasons; indeed, it is the basis for the J. Walter Thompson philosophy of advertising. The notion that people are not passive receivers but active participants in the communication process leads, certainly, to a search for collusion between sender and receiver (Categories 3, 4, and 5). Many psychological theories support this; cognitive response theory is perhaps the most relevant.

4. Positive affect is transferred from commercial to brand. This could be ascribed to simple conditioning or affect transfer, where proximity to a well-liked communication rubs off on the brand.

5. Liking evokes a gratitude response. This seems to be an extension of the foregoing and can be explained by studies of source effects—the reverse of the "shoot the messenger" phenomenon.

I agree with Biel that the last two reasons lead dangerously towards advertising that is merely entertaining; relevance and meaningfulness are the essential ingredients.

This forms a philosophical standpoint and begins to link the development and diagnostic phases of advertising to the evaluative phase, because the common strand running through the entire process starts from the same basis—what people do with advertising, how they use it, and what they use it for.

REFERENCES

Biel, A. (1990). Love the ad. Buy the product? *Admap*, *26*(9), 21–25.

Biel, A. (1991). The cost of cutbacks. *Admap*, *27*(5), 28–31.

Bonnal, F. (1990). Attitudes to advertising in six European countries. *Admap*, *26*(12), 19–23.

Cooper, P. (1989, October). Differing roles of qualitative research: Europe and the USA. *Journal of the Market Research Society, 31*(4), 509–520.

de Chernatony, L., & Knox, S. (1990). How an appreciation of consumer behaviour can help in product testing. *Journal of the Market Research Society, 32*(3), 329–347.

Jones, J. (1989). *Does it pay to advertise?* New York: Macmillan.

Lannon, J., & Cooper, P. (1983). Humanistic advertising. *International Journal of Advertising, 2*, 195–213.

Chapter 12

Expansion Advertising and Brand Equity

Brian Wansink
Amos Tuck School of Business Administration,
Dartmouth College

Michael L. Ray
Graduate School of Business,
Stanford University

What causes certain products—such as Campbell's Soup or Coca-Cola—to have high brand equity whereas others don't? Not surprisingly, such brand equity is highly related to the set of mental associations one has with a brand (Aaker & Keller, 1990). In this chapter, we propose that a brand's equity can be influenced by a consumer's perception of a product's versatility and also by the specific attitude a customer has about using or consuming the product in a new way or in a different situation. In effect, a company can increase a brand's equity by increasing the number of different consumption situations that consumers associate with a product.

This chapter shows how advertising can make these associations between brands and situations most effectively. Furthermore, it suggests the types of ads that will be most desirable, given the specific product and the particular consumption situation under examination. In a general sense, the overall intent of this research is to determine how this form of advertising can increase a brand-loyal user's consumption rate of that brand.

LEVERAGING BRAND EQUITY THROUGH EXPANSION ADVERTISING

Brand equity is important to managers because it enables advertising to leverage this equity by stimulating the frequency with which the brand is consumed by its loyal consumers. For such brands, spending advertising dollars to try and capture an incremental share point may be less cost effective than trying to raise total category consumption (Marketing Science Institute, 1988; Rossiter & Percy, 1987). One approach to stimulating such usage or consumption involves encouraging these loyal consumers to expand their use of a product by consuming it in new situations in which it is not frequently considered (see Table 12.1). We refer to advertising which encourages this new or different use of a brand as *expansion advertising*. This is defined with respect to a particular segment of brand-loyal consumers who did not use the brand in a previously identified situation (e.g., drinking Coca-Cola in the morning) or who do so infrequently as a secondary use of the brand.

Expansion advertising plays a potentially important role in increasing brand equity because it broadens the appeal or perceived utility of the brand. The more uses one has for a product, the more favorable one should feel toward it (Hirschman, 1980; Zaichkowsky, 1985) and the more frequently it will be used. For example, Clorox can increase its brand equity by advertising its bleach as a sink cleaner; Ocean Spray can increase its brand equity by advertising its cranberry sauce as a complement to an everyday chicken dinner.

Expansion advertising, however, is not without its risks. If this new use of a product is perceived as offensive or manipulative, such advertising might backfire and actually erode brand equity. Indeed, when Coca-Cola was decid-

TABLE 12.1
Expansion Advertising Opportunities for Products
and Services with High Brand Equity

Product or Service	*Possible Expansion Advertisements*
Campbell's Soup	• Eat with a special family dinner. • Eat for breakfast.
Clorox Bleach	• Clean counters and sinks.
Heinz Vinegar	• Clean windows.
Jell-O Brand Gelatin	• Use in recipes. • Eat after exercising. • Consume (in liquid form) as a cold drink.
Pepsi-Cola or Coca-Cola	• Drink in the morning.
Burger King	• Celebrate ''small'' events (e.g., good report cards). • Carry-out for picnics. • ''Take home'' food.
Kodak Film	• Take photos of dinner parties and guests. • Take photos of ''minor'' holidays (e.g., Father's Day). • Take photos of pets.
AT&T	• Use business calls as ''personal'' calls. • Use calls to ''relive'' good memories.
American Express	• Use for small purchases. • Consider as short-term (10-day) loans.

ing how to position itself as a morning beverage alternative, the concern was that the wrong ad would "be disastrous for the brand's image" (Winters, 1989, p. 3). Thus, the potential of using expansion advertising to build total brand consumption is counterbalanced by the risks of eroding the equity of a brand. This trade-off stimulates the following questions:

- When will expansion ads help (or harm) A_{brand}?
- When will increasing A_{brand} lead to the greatest increases in usage?

A powerful mediator of any ad's effectiveness are the thoughts one generates when viewing such an ad (Wright, 1973). The impact of an expansion ad on a person's attitude toward a brand (A_{brand}) and on one's attitude toward an expansion is similarly mediated by these thoughts one generates. After reviewing relevant literature, we present a model which contends that there is a distinction between the types of thoughts that will influence $A_{new\ use}$ and those that will instead influence A_{brand}. We argue that $A_{new\ use}$, in turn, indirectly influences A_{brand} by altering one's perception of the brand's versatility.

BACKGROUND

By first examining what types of thoughts (or beliefs) an expansion ad might stimulate, we can determine if these thoughts have any possibility of affecting A_{brand}.

Situation-Specific and Product-Specific Beliefs

Thoughts stimulated by expansion ads can affect not only $A_{new\ use}$ but also A_{brand}. Such thoughts—in the form of cognitive responses—are frequently analyzed in persuasion research (see Fiske & Taylor, 1984; Wright, 1973). These cognitive responses are collected by having subjects write down the thoughts they had while viewing an ad. These thoughts, or cognitive responses, are then typically categorized or coded as being directed either toward the message (counter/support arguments), toward the source (source enhancing, source derogation), or toward the advertisement itself (execution-related thoughts).

When examining expansion advertising, however, it is important for us to distinguish between thoughts specific to the brand and thoughts that are more specific to the expansion situation. That is, a brand-loyal consumer may have positive thoughts about the brand (e.g., "I love Campbell's Soup") but may have very negative thoughts about consuming it in the extended situation (e.g., "I would hate it in the morning") because it may be considered inappropriate (Belk, 1974, 1975).

Brand-loyal consumers have certain beliefs about the brand that exist long before they see an expansion ad. Although these beliefs need not always be well formed or even salient, they are general beliefs which define the brand in all general situations (Lutz, 1975). Barsalou (1982a, 1982b) called these beliefs "independent" because they are context free and stable across all situations (e.g., too salty, too expensive, great flavor, etc.). Along with these general (product-specific) beliefs, however, consumers also have beliefs about a brand that are important in defining it with respect to very specific situations (e.g., too salty for breakfast, too expensive for everyday dinners, great flavor with ice cream, etc.). Barsalou called these situationally "dependent" beliefs because they are context dependent. For simplicity, independent beliefs will be referred to as *product-specific* beliefs (because they exist independently of a particularly situation), and dependent beliefs will be referred to as *situation-specific* beliefs.

We argue that the type of thoughts a consumer generates upon seeing an expansion ad (i.e., product-related thoughts versus situation-related thoughts) are related to the attributions he or she will make as to why such an expansion is either appropriate or inappropriate. The next section outlines the implications of these attributions.

Attributions and Expansion Advertising

In the context of this chapter, an attribution is defined as an inference one makes as to why a person behaves (or responds) to a stimulus or situation in a particular way (Jones & Davis, 1965). A common conclusion of attributional research is that this inferred cause (i.e., *why* a person thinks he or she behaved in a particular way) can often explain attitude change (Fiske & Taylor, 1984). Consider a scenario where a man sees an ad that encourages people to drink Coca-Cola in the morning. Assume that he finds drinking Coke in the morning to be unappetizing. If asked to articulate why he finds this unappetizing, he can attribute or "blame" this lack of fit on the unique characteristics of the situation (e.g., a morning drink should not be bitter), or he can blame it on the shortcomings of the brand (e.g., Coke is too bitter). Although he may essentially be making the same argument, in the first case the emphasis is on the needs of the situation (situation attribution) and in the second case the emphasis is on the attributes of the product (product attribution).

A major finding in attribution theory is that when a type of behavior has a number of plausible causes, the viability of any single cause is weakened or discounted (Kelley, 1973). This perception of alternative causes essentially reduces the impact of any one of them. Going back to our scenario, if the perceived lack of fit between a brand and a situation (e.g., Coke in the morning) can be attributed to idiosyncratic needs of the situation, it should affect one's attitude differently than if this lack of fit were also tangled up in the general shortcomings of the brand.

Our theory states that brand-related attributions encourage product-specific thoughts and will be more highly related to changes in A_{brand} than situation-related attributions, which are instead more likely to encourage situation-specific thoughts and help form $A_{new\ use}$.

THEORETICAL FRAMEWORK

Impact of Cognitive Responses on A_{brand}

Consider two thoughts a viewer might have upon seeing an expansion ad which encourages him to drink Coca-Cola in the morning: (a) "It's too bitter," or (b) "It's too bitter to drink in the morning." These two thoughts may have very different impacts on $A_{new\ use}$ and on A_{brand}. The first is a general statement about the product and is product-specific (PS). The second is specific to a particular situation (morning) and is situation-specific (SS).

Distinguishing between these two different categories of thought is crucial. These thoughts indicate the types of attributions that have been made about the expansion and will—in turn—determine whether an expansion ad will help or harm A_{brand}.

Let us continue to consider the case when an expansion ad inadvertently stimulates negative thoughts about consuming the brand in that particular situation. This inability of the brand to be a satisfying alternative in that situation can either be attributed or blamed on the shortcomings of the brand, or it can be attributed to the unique or idiosyncratic demands of the situation (Jones & Davis, 1965). These two different attributions should be evident in the types of thoughts one generates and the way in which he or she articulates these thoughts. Attributions toward a brand are likely to be stated in a way that is specific to the brand and not related to any particular situation (e.g., "Coke's too bitter."). In contrast, attributions toward a situation should be conditioned on the situation (e.g., Coke's too bitter to drink in the morning). These attributions (and the subsequent PS and SS thoughts they generate) are the driving force behind whether an expansion ad will have its primary impact on $A_{new\ use}$ or on A_{brand}.

An expansion ad which stimulates a situation-related attribution is likely to stimulate SS thoughts in a consumer. In this way, the consumer can discount any negative thoughts by thinking of them in isolation from the brand itself. Even though these negative SS thoughts will have a negative impact on $A_{new\ use}$, the fact that they are seen as specific to the situation (and are *not* specific to the brand itself) lessens the probability that they will adversely affect A_{brand}.

In contrast, an expansion ad which stimulates brand-related attributions is likely to generate PS thoughts that can be interpreted as specific beliefs about the brand across all situations. Figure 12.1 shows how these beliefs can influence A_{brand} when consumers are already brand-loyal to a product. Insofar as such beliefs are general to the brand in all situations, they should be strongly related to A_{brand}. To the degree, however, that they are perceived as specific to the expansion (SS), they should have little impact on A_{brand}, for they would be attributed to specific needs of the situation, and not to the general utility of the brand. Therefore:

- H_1: Situation-specific (SS) thoughts will have a greater influence on $A_{new\ use}$ than product-specific (PS) thoughts.

- H_2: Product-specific (PS) thoughts will have a greater influence on A_{brand} than situation-specific (SS) thoughts.

Impact of $A_{new\ use}$ on A_{brand}

In general, A_{brand} is an overall measure of one's utility for a brand, and it is highly related to one's familiarity with a brand, one's involvement with it, and one's knowledge of it (Zaichkowsky, 1985; Richins & Bloch, 1986). Any ad that increases the perceived versatility of a brand also increases that brand's utility and increases A_{brand}. In effect, an expansion ad that succeeds in enhancing $A_{new\ use}$ should also increase A_{brand} if it succeeds in raising one's perception of the versatility or flexibility of the brand (Ram & Jung, 1989). One exception to this positive relationship would be expansion advertising that encourages a use that is inconsistent or contradictory to the typical use of the brand (using Coca-Cola to clean acid off a car battery). Under such circumstances, one is better off not advertising such an expansion. However, returning to a more reasonable context, if no significantly negative PS thoughts are generated, any positive changes in $A_{new\ use}$ will be directly related to changes in A_{brand} because of its impact on one's perception of the brand's versatility. In general:

- H_3: One's perceived versatility of a brand will be correlated with A_{brand}.

A_{brand} and Brand Consumption

A basic premise of expansion advertising is that the majority of food products can be consumed in a much wider range of situations than most brand-loyal consumers generally consider. Any increase in $A_{new\ use}$ is also likely to make certain brand attributes more salient, thereby influencing one's attitude (A_{brand}) to the brand. Any improvement in A_{brand} should also increase the likelihood that the brand will be consumed more frequently, perhaps through substitution with another product category. In short:

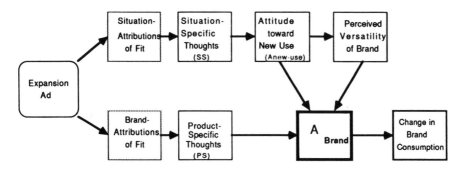

FIG. 12.1.   Hypothesized impact of expansion advertising on A_{brand}.

- H_4: A_{brand} should be correlated with one's consumption rate of a brand.

Although increasing A_{brand} should have an impact on one's consumption of a product, such increases are most likely to occur with light users of a brand than with heavy users. In effect, it is assumed that the A_{brand} (and the usage frequency) of heavy users is closer to a "ceiling" and that expansion advertising will be more effective when targeted at consumers who are loyal to the brand but who use it relatively less frequently.

- H_5: Light users of a brand should be more likely to increase their consumption rate of a brand than heavy users.

METHODOLOGY

The basic premise of this theory is that expansion advertising can affect A_{brand} directly by stimulating PS thoughts and indirectly by influencing $A_{new\ use}$ (through SS thoughts). It is assumed that this occurs regardless of the brand under investigation or how appropriate or inappropriate the expansion. To emphasize the generalizability of the model, three different brands were examined, each at two different levels of appropriateness. For analysis, however, this data has been combined.

Prestudies were conducted to select the brands, the expansions (situations), and the claims that would be used in developing the stimuli for the main study.

Prestudies

After conducting a series of focus groups, a structured questionnaire was developed and presented to 44 Parent Teacher Association (PTA) members of a local school district. They were recruited as part of a fundraiser whereby $6 was donated to the PTA for each member who participated. These subjects were asked questions about 17 common brands, and were asked to indicate on a semantic differential scale ranging from 1 to 7 how appropriate (i.e., *inappropriate-appropriate, unappealing-appealing, unreasonable-reasonable, bad-good*) it would be to consume the brands in a number of different situations. The Cronbach alpha for these four measures was .81. This factor is referred to as the "appropriateness" of an expansion situation although it is actually the average of all four measures.

Three brands with which people were highly familiar were then chosen, and a relatively appropriate (mean value = 5.3; 1 = *inappropriate* and 7 = *appropriate*) and inappropriate (mean value = 2.1) expansion situation was selected for each of the three brands. The three brands and their appropriate (inappropriate) expansions included Campbell's Soup for dinner (breakfast), Ocean Spray Cranberry Sauce for an informal family dinner (a snack), and Jell-O Brand Gelatin for a snack (breakfast).

Main Study

The goals of the main study were to determine how the thoughts stimulated by expansion ads affect A_{brand}, and to determine if such an effect will have a subsequent impact on total consumption.

Subjects and Design

Again, subjects were recruited through four northern California PTA groups. For each member who participated in the study, $6 was donated to the organization. A total of 219 subjects participated. Eighty percent of the subjects were between the ages of 30 and 45 and were not employed outside the home. Their educational background was heterogeneous.

In order to emphasize the generalizability of this model, the basic design of the experiment was a correlational one using three brands to increase the generalizability of the findings and two expansions for each brand (an appropriate one and a less appropriate one) to increase the variance in responses.

Procedure and Stimuli

Subjects were seated in groups of 15 to 30 at the school where their PTA met. They were asked to take alternate seats, and were given a closed packet of materials by the experimenter which contained a cover sheet of instructions and a number of consecutively labeled booklets. The subjects were told they were going to compare whether transcripts of commercials are as comprehensible as storyboards of commercials. They were asked to read through the target ad and answer the questions which followed it, and then to read an unrelated storyboard and answer the questions following it.

Each subject saw a transcript of a hypothetical television commercial for one of the three brands. There were six basic transcripts: three brands (Campbell's Soup, Jell-O Brand Gelatin, and Ocean Spray Cranberry Sauce) by two levels of expansion appropriateness (*appropriate–inappropriate*). The initial drafts were professionally edited by a copywriter who had significant experience with consumer products. They were then re-edited to eliminate any irrelevant variation.

Measures

Subjects were asked to write down the thoughts and feelings they had while reading the transcripts. Following that, a measure of $A_{\text{new use}}$ was obtained by asking subjects to indicate (on a 7-point scale) whether a particular expansion was *bad–good*, *unappealing–appealing*, *inappropriate–appropriate*, and *unreasonable–reasonable*. Because of the high Cronbach alpha (.92), $A_{\text{new use}}$ was analyzed as the average of the four items (Nunnally, 1967). Next, a measure of the flexibility of a brand was obtained by asking subjects to indicate (on a 7-point scale) whether a particular brand was *not flexible* or *flexible*. Throughout this chapter, this variable will be referred to as a brand's *versatility*.

A measure of A_{brand} was taken, which consisted of the average of four different items using a similar 7-point scale as $A_{\text{new use}}$ (Ajzen & Fishbein, 1980). The variables were *very bad–very good*, *dislikable–likable*, *low quality–high quality*, *unappetizing–appetizing* (Cronbach alpha = .94). Last, subjects were asked how many times in the past year they consumed the target brands (Campbell's Soup, Jell-O Brand Gelatin, and Ocean Spray Cranberry Sauce) and how many times they consumed these product categories (canned soup, gelatin, cranberry sauce). They were then asked their age, sex, education, English-speaking ability, and the number of children they had living at home.

To determine the actual consumption of these brands, subjects were telephoned 12 weeks after they were involved in the experiment. Among other questions, they were asked how many times (in total) they had consumed the target brand since participating in the experiment.

Coding of Cognitive Responses

Upon viewing a commercial or reading an ad, one generates various thoughts; some are relevant to the brand, others are relevant to the ad itself, still others are irrelevant to both. In an experimental situation, when one is asked to write down these thoughts, they are referred to as *cognitive responses*. These responses are believed to reflect the mediating forces behind any resulting change in $A_{\text{new use}}$ or in one's attitude toward the brand (A_{brand}). Of particular interest are those responses that are expansion related (dealing with $A_{\text{new use}}$ and expanded consumption) and those that are more brand related (dealing with A_{brand} and conventional consumption). These responses were initially coded into a number of different categories which indicated whether a response referred to product attributes or to the consumption of the product. Within each category, each response was additionally coded as positive or negative in valence.

The cognitive responses that each subject generated after reading the ads were photocopied and coded independently by three coders (including one author). During the process, the coders noted the valence of each response and whether the response was a general thought about the brand (PS thought) or was specific to the given expansion situation (SS thought). Cognitive responses were recoded to account for whether a subject's mention of an attribute appeared to be a general comment about that product (PS thought) or specific to the given expansion situation (SS thought). The specific guidelines used by the coders were as follows:

- PS Thoughts—Did the subject refer to the attribute in a way that indicated that he or she thought it was general to the brand in all situations?
- SS Thoughts—Did he or she refer to the attribute in a way that indicated that it was specific to, or conditioned on, the expanded situation under examination?

The three coders agreed on 85.8% of the cognitions. The remaining cognitions were discussed, and a consensus determined how they would be coded. On average, subjects had approximately 3.4 cognitions for each ad they saw. Approximately 1.6 of these were product specific, 1.1 were situation specific, and the remainder were unrelated to either the product or the situation (e.g., ad related, unrelated memories, etc.). In addition, 2.0 of these were positive or favorable comments and 1.4 were negative or unfavorable.

RESULTS

Overview

Recall that the focus of this study was to explore how advertising can most effectively make associations between brands and situations, and, eventually, to suggest the types of ads that will be most desirable, with a particular product and a particular consumption situation. In a larger sense, the overall intent of this research is to determine how this form of advertising can increase the A_{brand} and consumption of brand-loyal consumers.

For the purposes of this study, a *brand-loyal consumer* was liberally defined as someone who had consumed the target brand at least half the time he or she consumed a brand from that product category (Jacoby & Chestnut, 1978).

In general, the typical individual in the study consumed the target brand 84% of the time he or she consumed a product from the category. We assume this model can be generalized across various brands. In order to emphasize the generalizability of this model, three different brands were examined, each at two different levels of appropriateness. To examine whether this assumption is valid, a two-way ANOVA (Product × Appropriateness) was conducted on key dependent variables (i.e., $A_{\text{new use}}$, A_{brand}, flexibility). As expected, results indicated that there were significant mean-level differences between the brands, but that there were no interactions. Because the basic interaction patterns of these three different brands were similar and it was primarily their means that differed, the analyses for these three brands were combined. Each brand was represented by a dummy variable to account for the mean-level differences in response.

Impact of Cognitive Responses on A_{brand}

Recall from H_1 and H_2 that SS thoughts should be highly associated with $A_{\text{new use}}$ whereas PS thoughts should be highly related to A_{brand}. To examine this, a regression of the number of SS and PS thoughts (along with product category dummy variables and prior usage volume) was conducted on $A_{\text{new use}}$ and A_{brand}.

As suggested in H_1 and shown in Table 12.2, the number of SS thoughts were significantly related to $A_{\text{new use}}$ but not to A_{brand}. This was true of both positive thoughts ($t = 2.88$; $p < .01$) and negative thoughts ($t = -1.92$; $p < .06$). In examining H_2, we found that PS thoughts were highly related to A_{brand}, both when positive ($t = 2.38$; $p < .05$) and when negative ($t = -3.60$; $p < .001$). Although it was believed that PS thoughts would have no impact on $A_{\text{new use}}$, it appears that any negative PS thoughts stimulated by an expansion ad had a negative impact on A_{brand} ($t = -2.03$; $p < .05$). Nonetheless,

TABLE 12.2
Regression Coefficients of Cognitive Responses on A_{brand} and $A_{\text{new use}}$

	Situationally Dependent		Situationally Independent		Prior Consumption Rate	R^2
	Positive Responses	Negative Responses	Positive Responses	Negative Responses		
A_{brand}	.248 (.242)	.210 (.162)	.258** (.108)	−.478** (.133)	.016** (.004)	.332
$A_{\text{new use}}$	.883** (.306)	−.392* (.204)	.211 (.137)	−.344** (.169)	.013** (.005)	.343

Note. (Standard Errors in Parentheses)
*$p < .10$. **$p < .05$.

this result is consistent with the basic premise that SS thoughts are isolated enough from the brand that they will not reflect poorly on the brand itself.

Impact of $A_{new\ use}$ and Versatility on A_{brand}

It was suggested (H_3) that although an expansion ad may have no direct impact on A_{brand}, if such an ad positively affects $A_{new\ use}$, it can have an indirect impact on A_{brand} because it will be perceived as being versatile or "flexible to consume." Indeed, a regression on A_{brand} (which included measures of perceived versatility, $A_{new\ use}$, prior consumption rate, and product category dummy variables; R^2 = .515) indicated that versatility was highly related to A_{brand} ($p <$ .001). However, the fact that $A_{new\ use}$ was also included in the model and was moderately significant ($p <$ .10) provides further support that the perceived versatility of a brand is important on its own and not simply as a surrogate for $A_{new\ use}$.

Comparing the impact of perceived versatility on A_{brand} with the impact of $A_{new\ use}$ on A_{brand}, the standardized beta value for $A_{new\ use}$ was .098 (se = .053). The standardized beta value for versatility was .236 (se = .051), indicating that one's perception of the brand's versatility was much more strongly related to A_{brand} than was $A_{new\ use}$. (The correlation between $A_{new\ use}$ and versatility is .412.) Evidently, the impact that an expansion ad has on A_{brand} has less to do with its impact on $A_{new\ use}$ than with its impact on one's perception of a brand's versatility.

It is important to understand that an expansion ad might not appear to be effective (with respect to changing $A_{new\ use}$), but it can still be successful in encouraging consumers to view a brand as being more versatile. In this way, even an "unsuccessful" expansion ad might have a positive (indirect) impact on A_{brand} as long as it did not generate too many negative PS thoughts. This analysis underscores how one's thinking about an expansion ad can produce thoughts which can influence A_{brand} and thoughts which can influence $A_{new\ use}$. Furthermore, because these thoughts need not be related, it is possible for expansion ads to be tailored to maximize their opportunity to positively change $A_{new\ use}$, while minimizing the risk of adversely affecting A_{brand}.

A_{brand} and Changes in Consumption Volume

Recall that during the experiment, subjects were asked to estimate their consumption of the target brand over the past year. This number was then divided by 12, and this measure of average monthly consumption was subtracted from the reported monthly consumption that was obtained during the callback 11 to 12 weeks later. The difference represents a measure of one's change in brand consumption per month.

Consistent with H_4, one's attitude toward the brand (A_{brand}) was highly related to one's total consumption of the brand following the experiment. A regression of A_{brand}, prior consumption, and $A_{new use}$ on one's total brand consumption (following the experiment) generated an R^2 of .471. Measures of A_{brand} and prior consumption were both significant ($p < .05$); $A_{new use}$ was not. The fact that both of these were significant is important because it shows that A_{brand} is an important predictor of total consumption in and of itself and not simply as a surrogate for one's prior consumption of the brand. In other words, although one's prior consumption of a brand helps predict one's future consumption (after seeing an expansion ad), a measure of A_{brand} will help make such a prediction even more accurate.

The statistical significance of prior consumption is important because it emphasizes that the more frequently a person has consumed a product in the past, the greater the probability of that person consuming it even more frequently in the future. This was in contrast to H_5, which argued that light users would be more likely to increase their consumption than heavy users. As we will discuss later, this indicates that expansion ads may be most effective if aimed at getting heavy users to use more of the product than in trying to get light users to use more.

DISCUSSION

As mentioned earlier, this analysis of PS and SS thoughts shows how expansion ads can promote thoughts which can influence both A_{brand} and $A_{new use}$. Furthermore, these thoughts can exist independently of each other and it may be possible for expansion ads to be tailored to maximize the probability of positively changing $A_{new use}$, while minimizing the risk of adversely affecting A_{brand}. For instance, an ad which focuses on attributes that are isolated to the situation would have the greatest chance of influencing $A_{new use}$ while minimizing the negative impact on A_{brand}.

If an expansion ad has a positive influence on $A_{new use}$, it is almost certain to have a positive impact on A_{brand} because it also changes one's perception of that brand's versatility. The more versatile a brand is perceived to be, the more its value is enhanced. However, because expansion advertising can effectively promote a brand's versatility, such ads can enhance A_{brand} even if they do not affect $A_{new use}$. In effect, even if a consumer rejects an expansion ad (e.g., "There's no way I'll drink Coke in the morning"), his or her thoughts about the brand's versatility can still have a positive impact on A_{brand}. Although it is uncertain whether A_{brand} can be an effective measure of a brand's equity to a given consumer, it seems clear that A_{brand} is related to one's total consumption of a product (even after taking prior brand consumption into account).

Although we expected to find a positive relationship between A_{brand} and actual consumption (H_4), it is important to note that heavy users seem to be even more sensitive to increasing their consumption of a product than light users. The argument (H_5) that heavy users might be up against a usage ceiling seems invalid; this research suggests that heavy users are most prone to changing their usage patterns of the product by using it even more frequently. What seems plausible is that heavy usage of a product increases one's predisposition to an expansion ad. Indeed, those consumers who had consumed more than the median amount of the brand in the prior year were also those consumers who were most favorable toward the advertising expansion [$F(1,217)$ = 4.55; $p < .01$]. Although light users may be more sensitive to potentially increasing consumption (H_5), they seem less affected by the expansion ad than heavy users.

LIMITATIONS

The propositions suggested here were examined using correlational methods. Because of the difficulties in drawing irrefutable conclusions of causality from such data, our principal contribution lies in proposing a model and presenting data that are not inconsistent with it. Confirmation of this model needs to be done in a more controlled experimental context.

In addition, future research will need to define, measure, and manipulate the flexibility or versatility of a product more carefully. This was attempted with an earlier pilot study, but too much realism was sacrificed for not enough control (other confounds still existed). Whereas the methodology used in this study seemed sufficient to examine the basic results of one's perceived versatility and A_{brand}, future studies could try to manipulate this variable in the context of a hypothetical brand.

Although measures of brand consumption were taken, they are not without the typical flaws and biases associated with self-report measures. Despite prior knowledge of such flaws and biases, these measures of reported consumption were taken to add richness to the study and a degree of credibility to the results.

MANAGERIAL IMPLICATIONS

Recall that the objectives of this chapter were to answer two questions:

1. *When will expansion ads help (or harm)* A_{brand}? It appears that expansion ads harm A_{brand} when any resulting increases in $A_{new\ use}$ and in the perceived versatility of the product do not offset any negative PS thoughts that might be generated. In contrast, these ads help A_{brand} when they increase $A_{new\ use}$,

when they increase perceived versatility or, when they generate positive PS thoughts. The flowchart in Fig. 12.2 provides a framework to help a manager decide whether to use a particular expansion campaign, based upon intuition about the types of thoughts such a campaign is most likely to stimulate.

2. *When will increasing A_{brand} lead to the greatest increases in usage?* Although increasing A_{brand} leads to direct increases in consumption, this is most effective when it occurs along with an increased perception in the brand's versatility. In addition, it appears that heavy users of the brand are more likely to increase their usage of a brand than are light users.

How exactly can expansion ads be designed to elicit SS thoughts versus PS thoughts? The bottom of Fig. 12.2 provides some suggestions. One recent study showed that the way in which the expansion ad "framed" the consumption of a product would influence whether one generates SS thoughts or PS thoughts (Wansink, 1990). For instance, an expansion ad can compare or frame the consumption of this product with a product that is more frequently consumed in this situation (e.g., drinking Coke for breakfast vs. drinking coffee for breakfast). Similarly, an expansion ad can compare or frame consuming this product in this situation with consuming this same product in a more common situation (e.g., drinking Coke for breakfast vs. drinking Coke later in the afternoon). The first approach is referred to as a *product frame* and the second is referred to as a *situation frame*. Even if the identical claims are used in both

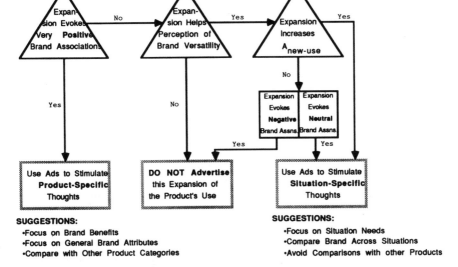

FIG. 12.2.   Suggested advertising objectives for alternative expansion ads.

types of frames, it appears that product frames are more likely to generate PS thoughts and situation frames are more likely to generate SS thoughts.

As a result, it appears that a manager who has any doubt as to how an advertising expansion will be received should execute such an expansion using a situation frame. On the other hand, if there is no doubt that the advertising expansion will be well received, a situation frame will be most effective at increasing $A_{\text{new use}}$ whereas a product frame will be most effective at increasing A_{brand}.

Future Research

The major issue addressed by this stream of research is how a manager can leverage the brand equity of a consumer package good or service. One option is to increase the frequency with which a brand-loyal consumer consumes the product or uses the service. To this end, numerous questions can be raised about how one might best advertise these new uses. (Although the words *product* or *brand* are used here, it is important to realize that these insights are also relevant for many *services*.)

There are a number of different advertising executions that can expand the use of a product into a particular situation (Wansink, 1990). For example, an advertisement can position or associate the target brand with another product from another category that is currently eaten or used in this target situation. In such comparative contexts, a host of questions can be asked about what types of comparisons (similar vs. dissimilar product categories) would generate the desired responses and whether such comparisons focus on commonalities or differences between the target brand and these "replaced" products (Wansink, 1993).

Because most academic and copy-testing research has not spent much effort studying or measuring usage variables yet, there is a need for research to determine various measures of consumer processing (such as cognitive responses) that can distinguish between relative differences in experimental treatments or in campaigns (Wansink, Ray, & Batra, 1992). It is also important to know what type of questioning procedures will provide the most valid indicators of consumption and whether the measures that result from these procedures will vary by product or by heavy versus light usage. It has been suggested (Wansink & Ray, 1992) that volume estimates best approximate the actual consumption of heavy users (or of frequently consumed brands) and that likelihood estimates are best used with light users (or with infrequently consumed brands). More studies need to be done on this topic.

There are also issues of importance that are outside the scope of advertising. If brand equity can be highly associated with brand loyalty, it would be useful to know if encouraging a person to stockpile the product (through promotions) actually increases usage beyond what routine purchase would encourage (Wansink & Deshpande, 1992). The answer to this could help determine whether such equity would be best leveraged by increasing inventory or by encouraging steady purchases that mirror steady usage. An even more basic level of inquiry would study those noneconomic and nonseasonal factors which cause variations in how frequently one consumes a specific product. A better understanding of the factors that encourage sonenone to binge will provide an understanding of how marketer-controlled factors can best influence these consumption behaviors (Wansink, 1992).

SUMMARY

There are a number of components which comprise a product or service's brand equity. We argue that one's perception of the product's versatility and one's attitude toward using the product in new or different situations can be a strong part of this, as evidenced by its impact on A_{brand} and on actual consumption. In general, this research shows that when a consumer sees an expansion ad for a product, the ad will affect A_{brand} if it causes the consumer to generate product-specific (PS) thoughts, *or* if it changes perceptions of the $A_{new\ use}$ brand's versatility. As long as the PS thoughts are nonnegative (positive or neutral), the net impact of the expansion ad on $A_{new\ use}$ will be positive.

Lastly, it has been shown that these expansion ads can increase consumption and that heavy users of a product are most greatly affected by the ad. That is, after seeing these ads, they are more prone to increase their consumption frequency than light users. Examples of possible expansion advertising campaigns for various products and services are provided in Table 12.1.

REFERENCES

Aaker, D. A., & Keller, K. L. (1990). Consumer evaluations of brand extension. *Journal of Marketing, 54,* 27–41.

Ajzen, I., & Fishbein, M. (1980). *Understanding attitudes and predicting social behavior.* Englewood Cliffs, NJ: Prentice-Hall.

Barsalou, L. W. (1982a). Ad hoc categories. *Memory and Cognition, 11,* 211–227.

Barsalou, L. W. (1982b). Context-independent and context-dependent information in concepts. *Memory and Cognition, 10,* 82–93.

Belk, R. W. (1974). An exploratory assessment of situational effects in buyer behavior. *Journal of Marketing Research, 11,* 156–163.

Belk, R. W. (1975). Situational variables and consumer behavior. *Journal of Consumer Research, 2,* 157–164.

Fiske, S. T., & Taylor, S. E. (1984). *Social cognition.* New York: Random House.

Hirschman, E. C. (1980). Innovativeness, novelty seeking, and consumer creativity. *Journal of Consumer Research, 7,* 283–295.

Jacoby, J., & Chestnut, R. W. (1978). *Brand loyalty: Measurement and management.* New York: Wiley.

Jones, E. E., & Davis, K. E. (1965). From acts to dispositions: The attribution process in person perception. In L. Berkowitz (Ed.), *Advances in experimental social psychology* (Vol. 2, pp. 220–226). New York: Academic Press.

Kelley, H. H. (1973). The processes of causal attribution. *American Psychologist, 29*(3), 107–128.

Lutz, R. J. (1975). Changing brand attitudes through modification of cognitive structure. *Journal of Consumer Research, 2,* 49–59.

Marketing Science Institute. (1988). *Research priorities 1988-1990.* Cambridge, MA: Author.

Ram, S., & Jung, H. (1989). The link between involvement, use innovativeness and product usage. In T. Srull (Ed.), *Advances in consumer research* (Vol. 16, pp. 160–166). Provo, UT: Association for Consumer Research.

Richins, M. L., & Bloch, P. H. (1986). After the new wears off: The temporal context of product involvement. *Journal of Consumer Research, 13,* 280–285.

Rossiter, J. R., & Percy, L. (1987). *Advertising and promotion management.* New York: McGraw-Hill.

Wansink, B. (1990). *Consumption framing and extension advertising.* Unpublished doctoral dissertation, Stanford University, Stanford, CA.

Wansink, B., (1992). *You can't eat just one: Salience and food consumption* (working paper). Amos Tuck School of Business, Dartmouth College, Hanover, NH.

Wansink, B. (in press). Advertising's impact on category substitution. *Journal of Marketing Research.*

Wansink, B., & Deshpande, R. (1992, February). *Inventory stockpiling and consumption rate.* Paper presented at the AMA Winter Educator's Conference, San Antonio, TX.

Wansink, B., & Ray, M. L. (1992). Estimating an advertisement's impact on one's consumption of a brand. *Journal of Advertising Research, 32*(3), 9–16.

Wansink, B., Ray, M. L., & Batra, R. (1992). *Increasing the sensitivity of cognitive response elicitation procedures* (working paper). Amos Tuck School of Business, Dartmouth College, Hanover, NH.

Wright, P. (1973). The cognitive processes mediating acceptance of advertising. *Journal of Marketing Research, 16,* 53–62.

Zaichkowsky, J. L. (1985). Familiarity: Product use, involvement or expertise? In E. Hirschman & M. Holbrook (Eds.), *Advances in consumer research* (Vol. 12, pp. 296–299). Provo, UT: Association for Consumer Research.

Chapter 13

The Impact and Memorability of Ad-Induced Feelings: Implications for Brand Equity

Julie A. Edell
Marian Chapman Moore
Fuqua School of Business, Duke University

The feelings experienced by consumers while they view an ad can have powerful effects on the way they respond to the ad. Feelings can influence attitude toward the ad, attitude toward the brand, brand beliefs, brand recall, change in brand attitude, and so forth (Batra & Ray, 1986; Burke & Edell, 1989; Edell & Burke, 1987; Russo & Stephens, 1990; Stayman & Aaker, 1988). In almost every study, however, the effects of feelings were evaluated right after the subjects viewed the ad. In reality, the ad is usually not present when consumers make their purchase decisions and may not be present when they evaluate the ad or the brand. This inconsistency may have serious implications regarding the practical application of the findings from the stream of research related to the effects of ad-induced emotions. This is especially true with respect to the effects on brand equity, which develops over time.

In this chapter, we investigate (a) whether ad-induced feelings are stored in memory, (b) whether those feelings have a different effect when they are retrieved from memory three days after the initial exposure to the ad. These assessments are important first steps in determining the robustness of the effects of feelings that consumers experience while viewing an ad, with important implications for both understanding the development of brand equity and designing the consumer's information environment. Reactions to an ad for a new brand can create the memory structure that will influence subsequent reactions to the brand (Deighton, 1984; Edell & Keller, 1989). These reactions can be based on repeated exposure to the original ad, subsequent ads, point-of-purchase displays, coupons, package design, and so forth. If early reactions include feelings that are stored in memory and can be retrieved, then ad-induced feelings may actually structure the associations that consumers link to the brand and become part of the context for responses to any subsequent marketing communication about the brand.

BACKGROUND

Advertising and Brand Equity

Brand equity is ". . . the 'added value' with which a given brand endows a product" (Farquhar, 1989, p. 24). For example, consumers expect that any product with the brand name Ivory is pure; consumers know that Betty Crocker, not Duncan Hines, dessert mixes are the ones that help them "Bake someone happy." These associations are valuable. In fact, Aaker (1991) stated that brand equity is so valuable that it should be treated as "the most important asset of any company" (p. 14). Judging from the plethora of brand name extensions in the last few years, companies are at least acting as if they agree.

Advertising can influence brand equity in two ways (Edell, 1992). First, advertising can influence brand attitude, an important component of brand equity. Second, and more important, advertising can influence brand equity by influencing the consumer's memory structure for a brand. Herr and Fazio (1992) stated that the key to the value of brand equity is highly accessible associations that can be instantly evoked with positive results.

Quite often, exposure to an advertisement may result in no change in the consumer's attitude toward the brand. It is not necessarily correct, however, to conclude that advertising had no effect. Advertising may have influenced the nature of the memory structure or strengthened particular associations in the memory structure even though the consumer's attitude toward the brand did not change. For instance, one of the authors likes Diet Pepsi's current "You've got the right one, baby. Uh-huh" campaign featuring Ray Charles. Her attitude toward Diet Pepsi is so positive that exposure to an "Uh-huh" ad affects her attitude toward Diet Pepsi imperceptibly. What could be affected, however, is the strength of the associations that form the basis for the equity in the brand Diet Pepsi.

Advertising and Feelings and Brand Equity

Similarly, ad-induced feelings may influence brand equity through their effect on attitude toward the ad and brand, which has been demonstrated repeatedly, or by influencing the memory structure associated with a brand. That is, ad-induced feelings may, over repeated experiences with a brand's advertising, becomes strongly associated with the brand and highly accessible. These emotional associations in brand memory may be one basis for the brand's equity. For instance, Calder and Gruder claimed, "Emotional ads influence attitude only to the extent that the emotion becomes part of the relevant cognitive framework and is associated with other concepts" (1989, p. 285). In the Diet Pepsi example, the positive, upbeat feelings that are induced by the ad become associated with Diet Pepsi.

Researchers in other areas have shown that feelings, in general, are stored in memory (Brewer, 1988; Frijda, 1988). Page, Thorson, and Heide (1990) found some support for their proposal that emotion strengthens the memory trace for an ad, which enhances the likelihood that the brand name will be recalled. Whether ad-induced feelings are stored in memory as part of the memory trace for the brand has not been unequivocally demonstrated. This is an important issue. For instance, American Express ads have very similar executional styles and all carry the tag line "Don't leave home without it." It is generally accepted that the memory trace for American Express probably includes the executional elements of the ad. This makes an American Express ad instantly identifiable and triggers other elements of the memory trace, such as knowledge about and attitude toward American Express.

We wonder, however, if the feelings generated by the ads are also part of the trace. Further, if the emotional reactions are stored, will they be triggered in the same way that cognitions about the brand are? How will these stored feelings influence subsequent communication and, eventually, brand equity? Englis (1990) suggested that product cues may become associated with emotions experienced while viewing a commercial. Then, when the consumer is reexposed to the product cue, say at the point of purchase, the emotional associations may influence choice. We extend this notion to include the whole range of experiences with the brand as outcomes that the emotional associations may influence.

Purpose of the Study

In order to build the links between feelings and brand equity, we must first show that feelings are: (a) stored in memory, (b) can be retrieved, and (c) have an effect once retrieved. This chapter reports the results of a demonstration study designed to address those issues. We consider four propositions that, if supported empirically, help build the foundation for considering feelings as an important part of brand equity:

Proposition 1 (Feelings Recall): Ad-Induced Feelings and Brand Claims can be Recalled Equally Well. Previous research has shown that emotional commercials are more likely to be recalled than neutral ones (Goldberg & Gorn, 1987; Thorson & Friestad, 1989) and that brand claims can be recalled. We expect that subjects can recall ad-induced feelings as well as they can recall brand claims. This is an important phenomenon to document if we are eventually going to link feelings with brand equity.

Proposition 2 (Cue Effect): A Cue will Facilitate the Recall of Feelings Experienced During the Initial Exposure to the Ad. Keller (1987) explored the role of cues in recall of brand information, but the relationship between cues and feelings was not investigated. In this study, three different cues are used to help the subject retrieve the feelings experienced during the first exposure to the ad: (a) the actual feelings scales that were used after the initial exposure, (b) a still shot from the ad (i.e., a scene from the ad similar to one that might be used in a print ad, on a package, or on a coupon), and (c) the entire ad. The ads we investigate are for unfamiliar products and the memory trace is accessed only three days after initial exposure. Therefore, we have no reason to expect that one cue will lead to better recall of feelings than any other cue for the situation investigated here. Under less tightly controlled situations, when consumers have more experiences with the brand than just an ad exposure, the type of cue may influence the retrievability of the feelings.

Proposition 3 (Robust to Delay Effect): There will be No Difference in the Effects of Ad-Induced Feelings on Attitude Toward the Ad (A_{Ad}) and Attitude Toward the Brand (A_B), Based on Whether the Effects are Measured Immediately After Exposure to the Ad or Following a 3-day Delay. In all of our studies (and most of the other studies that appear in the literature), subjects' reactions to ads are measured immediately after ad exposure. Even if the subject was in a delayed measurement condition, providing reactions up to a month after the initial exposure to the ad, the subject saw the ad again during the measurement session. Under those conditions, we found that the effects of feelings on A_{Ad} and A_B were robust to the delay. It is now important to test that finding when the entire ad is not available as a cue. Since television material (the context here and in our earlier studies) is especially good at eliciting emotions (Wells, Burnett, & Moriarty, 1989), we expect that ad-induced feelings will have the same effect on A_{Ad} and A_B, regardless of whether the ad is evaluated immediately or after a 3-day delay between exposure and measurement.

Proposition 4 (Robust to Cue Effects): The Nature of the Memory Cue Used to Retrieve the Feelings Experienced During the Initial Exposure to the Ad will not Influence the Effects of Ad-Induced Feelings on Delayed Measures of A_{Ad} and A_B. This proposition represents the interaction of Propositions 2 and 3. For the reasons already stated, we expect that retrieved feelings will influence A_{Ad} and A_B and that the specific nature of the cue will not affect that relationship, even when ad measures are delayed.

METHOD

Overview

Data for this study were collected in a theater setting. Subjects were assigned to one of five groups—a control group and four memory conditions. The control group differed from the memory groups on the length of time between exposure to the ads and the measurement of attitudes. The four memory conditions varied on the nature of the cue used to access the memory trace prior to measuring A_{Ad} and A_B. The variations are described in detail in the Procedure section.

Subjects

Subjects included 41 people recruited by announcements distributed on a university campus. Subjects were compensated for their participation in the study.

Stimuli

The stimuli for the study were ten 30-second television commercials (one practice ad and nine test ads). The test commercials had not aired in the area previously and were for products and services not available in the area, including potato chips, a bank, a photo-processing service, salad dressing, a volunteer program, mayonnaise, bottled water, a soft drink, and a charity.

Measures

The measures collected in this study were the feelings inventory, claims recall, attitude toward the ad, and attitude toward the brand.

Feelings Inventory. The feelings inventory included 65 items: the 56 items used by Burke and Edell (1989) and the 9 items added by Goodstein, Edell, and Moore (1990). The subscales (i.e., the feelings scales used in the analysis) are *upbeat feelings, warm feelings, negative feelings,* and *uneasy feelings.* The items and the scales they formed are presented in Table 13.1. The instructions for completing the feelings inventory were:

> We would like you to tell us how the commercial for (the advertised product or service) made you *feel.* Here we are interested in *your reactions* to the ad *not* how you would describe it. Please tell us how well you think each of the words listed

TABLE 13.1
Feelings Scales

Upbeat Feelings	Warm Feelings	Uneasy Feelings	Negative Feelings
Active	Affectionate	Afraid	Bored
Alive	Calm	Anxious	Critical
Amused	Emotional	Concerned	Defiant
Attentive	Hopeful	Contemplative	Disinterested
Attractive	Kind	Depressed	Dubious
Carefree	Moved	Edgy	Dull
Cheerful	Peaceful	Lonely	Skeptical
Creative	Sentimental	Pensive	Suspicious
Delighted	Warmhearted	Regretful	
Elated		Sad	
Energetic		Tense	
Happy		Troubled	
Humorous		Uncomfortable	
Independent		Uneasy	
Industrious		Worried	
Inspired			
Interested			
Joyous			
Lighthearted			
Playful			
Pleased			
Proud			
Satisfied			
Stimulated			
Strong			

Note. Confident, convinced, lazy, patriotic, silly, and surprised were items measured that did not load greater than .5 on any factor.

below describes your feelings in response to the ad you just saw. If the word describes the way you felt . . . *Extremely well* . . . put a 5; *Very well* . . . put a 4; *Fairly well* . . . put a 3; *Not very well* . . . put a 2; *Not well at all* . . . put a 1.

Claims Recall. Subjects completed a structured claims recall task. The measure consisted of six feasible claims for each product or organization. Between two and four of the six statements were actually made in the ad. Subjects were told, "Some of the claims were mentioned in the ad; some of them were not mentioned." They were asked to indicate on a 7-point scale, "How certain are you that each of the claims was made in the ad you saw?" The scale was anchored by − 3 (*very certain the ad did not mention the claim*) and 3 (*very certain the ad mentioned the claim*), with 0 indicating uncertainty. The scores on this scale ranged from − 18 to + 18.

Attitude Toward the Ad. Attitude toward each of the ads was measured as the average of three 7-point scales (*very unfavorable–very favorable*, *dislike very much–like very much*, and *very bad–very good*).

Attitude Toward the Brand.   Attitude toward each of the brands or organizations was measured as the average of three 7-point scales (*very unfavorable–very favorable, very bad–very good, dislike very much–like very much*).

Procedure

Table 13.2 is a flowchart that represents the experimental procedure, which is described in this section.

On the first day of the study, all subjects came to a theater on campus to view the commercials. Subjects were told that the producers of these products and services were interested in their reaction to the commercials. After the first commercial aired, respondents completed the feelings inventory for that commercial. (The first commercial shown was not a test commercial. It was included to allow subjects to become familiar with the questions and procedures before the test ads were shown.) Then the second commercial was shown and subjects completed the feelings inventory. This procedure was repeated for all of the commercials. Subjects were then asked to indicate how certain they were that each of six feasible claims had or had not been made in each of the commercials they saw. Subjects in the control group completed the attitude toward the ad and attitude toward the brand measures immediately following the exposure session.

Subjects assigned to the memory conditions were dismissed and asked to return three days later to complete the study. During the second session, subjects were asked to think back to the commercials they had seen during the initial session and to recall how they had felt while watching the ad, as well as to recall claims from the ad. All subjects completed the feelings inventory, the claims recall instrument, and A_{Ad} and A_B measures at some point during the session. The feelings and claims recall had been measured in the initial session as well. The same instruments were used in this session.

The memory conditions varied with respect to the cue that was used to facilitate recall of feelings and claims and the order in which particular activities took place, as described here and in Table 13.2.

No Cue Condition.   After A_{Ad} and A_B for all of the brands or organizations were measured, subjects thought back to the first commercial (brand or organization name provided) from the initial session and indicated how they felt while watching that commercial. Then they completed the claims recall again. Next, subjects thought back to the second ad and completed the feelings inventory and the claims recall. This procedure was followed for the remaining ads. Note that the A_{Ad} and A_B measure for each brand came before the feelings and claims measures. Hence, the only "cue" to the ad when A_{Ad} and A_B were measured was the name of the brand or organization.

TABLE 13.2
Procedure

Memory Conditions

	Control Group	No Cue	Scales as Cue	Scene as Cue	Ad as Cue
DAY 1	Ad Exposure → Feelings$_1$ → Brand Claims$_1$ A_{Ad} → A_B	Ad Exposure → Feelings$_1$ → Brand Claims$_1$	Ad Exposure → Feelings$_1$ → Brand Claims$_1$	Ad Exposure → Feelings$_1$ → Brand Claims$_1$	Ad Exposure → Feelings$_1$ → Brand Claims$_1$
DAY 3		A_{Ad} → A_B → Feelings$_2$ → Brand Claims$_2$	Feelings$_2$ → Brand Claims$_2$ → A_{Ad} → A_B	5-second exposure to a scene from the ad → A_{Ad} → A_B → Feelings$_2$ → Brand Claims$_2$	Ad exposure → A_{Ad} → A_B → Feelings Scales$_2$ → Brand Claims$_2$

202

Scale Cue Condition. Subjects in this group completed the A_{Ad} and A_{B} measures after completing the feelings and claims measures, which served as cues for the ad memory. Subjects thought back to the first commercial they had seen during the session three days earlier (brand or organization name provided), recalled how they felt while watching that commercial, and completed the feelings inventory and the claims recall measure for that ad. Then they indicated their A_{Ad} and A_{B}. Subjects completed all of measures in this order for each of the remaining ads.

Scene Cue Condition. This group completed the A_{Ad} and A_{B} measures before the feelings and claims measures. These subjects, however, saw a scene from the commercial prior to indicating their A_{Ad} and A_{B}. (The scene was picked at random from the ad, other than the first and last five seconds of the ad, and projected on a screen for five seconds.) This procedure was repeated for each commercial. Then subjects completed the feelings inventory and the structured claims recall task for each commercial.

Ad Cue Condition. The procedure for subjects in ad cue memory condition was the same as that for subjects in the scene cue memory condition, except that those in the former group saw the entire 30-second commercial again rather than just a scene from the ad.

RESULTS

The propositions were tested using analysis of variance (ANOVA). Memory condition is a between-subjects factor. Ad (a dummy variable indicating the particular ad), the four feelings scales, and the claims recall scale are within-subject factors. Many of the propositions in this study were tested by contrasting effects between particular conditions. The conditions used in the analysis will be specified under the test of each proposition.

Proposition One: Feelings Recall

The Feelings Recall Proposition states that ad-induced feelings will be recalled as well as brand claims will be recalled. To test this proposition, we examined whether the subjects in the four memory conditions could recall the feelings they experienced while watching the ad with the same accuracy as they could recall the claims they thought were made in the commercials they had seen three days earlier.

In this analysis, the dependent variable ($Score_2$) is composed of subjects' responses to the commercials three days after exposure to the commercial. The responses were the claims recall score, the upbeat feelings score, the warm feelings score, the uneasy feelings score, and the negative feelings score. $Score_1$, an independent variable, is composed of the corresponding responses to the commercials as measured during the initial exposure session.

The effect of $Score_1$ on $Score_2$ is positive and significant (coefficient = 0.69, $F_{(1,700)}$ = 123.18, $p < 0.0001$), which indicates that the feelings and claims are remembered from the time of exposure to the time of the measurement session three days later. The $Score_1$ × Type of Response interaction was not significant ($F_{(4,700)}$ = 0.45), indicating that the effect of $Score_1$ on $Score_2$ is the same regardless of whether the response is any one of the four feelings scores or the claims recall score. Together these results show that both feelings and claims can be recalled quite well three days after a single exposure to the commercial, supporting the Feelings Recall Proposition.

Proposition Two: Cue Effect

The second proposition examines whether the retrievability of the feelings experienced on Day 1 is affected by the type of memory cue used three days later. The test of the Cue Effect Proposition was similar to that used for the Feelings Recall Proposition. The four memory conditions were included in the analysis and the dependent variable was $Score_2$. In this analysis, however, $Score_2$ was limited to just the subjects' feelings responses; therefore, $Score_1$ was the corresponding feelings responses as measured during the initial exposure session.

The results indicate that three days after exposure all of the memory cues were equally successful in helping subjects retrieve the feelings induced by the ad. The $Score_1$ × Memory Cue Condition interaction term was not significant ($F_{(3,556)}$ = 1.86), indicating that the relationship between $Score_1$ and $Score_2$ was the same for each of the memory cue groups (the coefficient on $Score_1$ was 0.69). The 3-way interaction, $Score_1$ × Memory Cue Condition × Type of Feeling, was also insignificant ($F_{(9,556)}$ = 0.89). The cues were equally effective at retrieving each type of feeling, supporting the Cue Effect Proposition.

Proposition Three: Robust to Delay Effect

This proposition states that feelings will have a significant effect on A_{Ad} and A_B (a) when the attitude measures are taken shortly after exposure to the ad and (b) when the attitude measures are taken three days after exposure. To test the Robust to Delay Effect Proposition, the control group was contrasted with the no cue memory condition. The other memory conditions were not included in the test of this proposition because, in these conditions, the feelings were cued either directly or indirectly before the measurement of the attitudes. Thus, using only the no cue memory condition and the control group provides a conservative test of the Robust to Delay Effect Proposition.

Separate analyses were conducted using A_{Ad} or A_B as the dependent variable. If the effect of each of the feelings scales on A_{Ad} or A_B is significant and each Feelings Scale × Memory Cue Condition interaction term is insignificant, Proposition 3 would be supported. This would indicate that feelings have a significant effect on A_{Ad} and A_B and that the effect of the feelings scales is the same for the no cue memory condition and for the control group.

A_{Ad} *Results.*   The Robust to Delay Effect Proposition is partially supported for attitude toward the ad. As proposed, the main effects of upbeat feelings, warm feelings, and uneasy feelings are positive (coefficients are 0.08, 0.05, and 0.03, respectively) and significant ($F_{(1,40)}$ = 43.16, p < 0.0001; $F_{(1,40)}$ = 54.19, p < 0.0001; $F_{(1,40)}$ = 14.24, p < 0.005, respectively). The negative feelings have a significant effect on A_{Ad} ($F_{(1,40)}$ = 40.20, p < 0.0001), but the effect is negative; the coefficient is -0.12. The Feelings × Condition interaction is insignificant for upbeat feelings ($F_{(1,40)}$ = 0.12), uneasy feelings ($F_{(1,40)}$ = 0.06), and negative feelings ($F_{(1,40)}$ = 0.00). These findings support the Robust to Delay Effect Proposition of no difference in the effect of feelings on A_{Ad} between the no cue memory condition and the control group. The Warm Feelings × Condition interaction is significant ($F_{(1,40)}$ = 5.25, p < 0.08), however. Warm feelings have less impact on A_{Ad} when the attitude is measured three days after exposure rather than immediately (the coefficients are 0.04 and 0.11, respectively).

A_B *Results.*   A similar analysis was conducted for attitude toward the brand and the results are similar to those obtained for A_{Ad}, although the effects of the feelings on A_B are less strong. The effect of upbeat feelings on A_B is marginally significant and positive ($F_{(1,40)}$ = 4.07, p < 0.10, coefficient = 0.02). Warm feelings have a significant, positive effect on A_B ($F_{(1,40)}$ = 18.15, p < 0.001; coefficient = .05); negative feelings have a significant negative effect on A_B ($F_{(1,40)}$ = 12.68, p < 0.005; coefficient = -0.04). Uneasy feelings do not influence A_B ($F_{(1,40)}$ = 0.69). The differences between the effects of upbeat, uneasy, and negative feelings on A_B for subjects in the control group and the no cue condition are not significant (the F-statistics, each with 1 and 40 degrees of freedom, for the Feelings × Condition interactions are 1.01, 0.06, and 2.94, respectively). However, as with A_{Ad}, the effect of warm feelings does vary by condition; the Warm Feelings × Condition interaction is significant ($F_{(1,40)}$ = 10.67, p < 0.005). Warm feelings have less impact on A_B when A_B is measured three days after exposure rather than immediately (the coefficients are 0.002 and 0.09, respectively).

Proposition Four: Robust to Cue Effects

The Robust to Cue Effects Proposition states that feelings will have a significant effect on A_{Ad} and A_B regardless of the type of cue (i.e., the scales alone,
a scene from the commercial, or the entire commercial) used to retrieve the
feelings. To test this proposition data from subjects in the scales only memory
condition, the scene cue, and the ad cue memory conditions were included
in the analyses. Separate analyses were conducted using A_{Ad} or A_B as the dependent variable.

A_{Ad} *Results.*   The Robust to Cue Effects Proposition is only partially supported with respect to A_{Ad}. Whereas each of the retrieved feelings has a significant main effect on A_{Ad} (upbeat feelings: $F_{(1,100)} = 29.34$, $p < 0.001$; warm
feelings: $F_{(1,100)} = 20.63$, $p < 0.001$; uneasy feelings: $F_{(1,100)} = 15.39$, $p <
0.005$; negative feelings: $F_{(1,100)} = 34.20$, $p < 0.001$), only the effect of nega-
tive feelings on A_{Ad} is the same for the three cue conditions as proposed ($F_{(2,100)}
= 1.90$ for the Negative Feelings × Memory Cue Condition interaction; the
coefficient on the main effect is -0.10).

   The magnitude of the effects for upbeat, warm, and uneasy feelings on A_{Ad}
depends on the nature of the cue used to facilitate retrieval of the feelings, which
is the opposite of the prediction. (The two-way interactions, Upbeat, Warm,
and Uneasy Feelings × Memory Cue Condition, are significant; $F_{(2,100)} =
3.13$, $p < 0.05$; $F_{(2,100)} = 3.27$, $p < 0.05$; $F_{(2,100)} = 15.39$, $p < 0.005$, respec-
tively.) Upbeat feelings have a greater impact on A_{Ad} when they are cued with
a scene from the ad (coefficient $= 0.19$) or with the entire ad (coefficient $=
0.18$) than when they are cued only with the scales (coefficient $= 0.02$). The
effect of warm feelings on A_{Ad} is less if the warm feelings are cued with the
scales (coefficient $= -0.01$) than with the entire ad (coefficient $= 0.08$) or
an ad scene (coefficient $= 0.08$). The impact of uneasy feelings on A_{Ad} is less
negative when uneasy feelings are cued with the scales alone (coefficient $=
-0.08$) or with the scene from ad (coefficient $= -0.06$) than when the entire
ad is seen again (coefficient $= -0.19$).

A_B *Results.*   The Robust to Cue Effects Proposition receives somewhat
better support for A_B. The retrieved upbeat, warm, and negative feelings have
significant main effects on A_B ($F_{(1,100)} = 2.91$, $p < 0.10$; $F_{(1,100)} = 7.43$, $p <
0.05$; $F_{(1,100)} = 4.93$, $p < 0.05$, respectively). The effect is positive for upbeat
and warm feelings; it is negative for negative feelings. Interestingly, and counter
to our proposition, the effect of uneasy feelings on A_B is insignificant ($F =
0.23$).

   In the A_B analysis, three of the four Feelings × Memory Cue Condition
interactions are insignificant. As proposed, the nature of the cue used to retrieve
the feelings does not affect the impact of upbeat feelings, warm feelings, or

uneasy feelings on A_B (the F-statistics, each with 2 and 100 degrees of freedom, for the two-way interactions are 0.93, 0.72, and 0.23, respectively). The impact of negative feelings on A_B, however, does vary by cue condition, as the Negative Feelings × Memory Cue Condition is significant ($F_{(2,100)}$ = 4.93, $p < 0.05$). The coefficient for negative feelings is -0.07 when the negative feelings are cued by the feelings scale or a scene from the ad. When cued by the entire ad, the coefficient for negative feelings is -0.13.

Summary of Results

All four propositions are supported, at least partially, by the empirical results. Importantly, the Feelings Recall Proposition received strong support. Feelings Recall is a legitimate construct and may become as useful an advertising effectiveness measure as Claims Recall. The second proposition, Cue Effect, was also supported. Not only can feelings be retrieved, but each of the three types of cues was effective at facilitating feelings recall. A consumer does not have to reexperience the ad in order to recall the feelings induced by the ad.

Propositions 3 and 4 address the robustness of the effect of the retrieved feelings on A_{Ad} and A_B, with respect to delay and type of cue, respectively. Each proposition was partially supported. The results are summarized in Table 13.3. For both A_{Ad} and A_B, the Robust to Delay Proposition is supported, except for warm feelings. Warm feelings have a weaker effect when the feelings are retrieved and measured three days later; the measurement effects of upbeat, uneasy, and negative feelings on A_{Ad} and A_B do not vary based on delay.

The pattern of results for the Robust to Cue Effect Proposition for A_{Ad} is opposite the pattern for A_B. The proposition receives stronger support for A_B as only the effect of negative feelings on A_B varies by cue type. Using the feelings scale or a scene from the ad to facilitate recall of negative feelings results in a less negative effect on A_B than when the feelings are cued by re-exposure to the ad. For A_{Ad}, however, negative feelings are the only feelings whose effect does not vary based on cue type (per the proposition). The effect of retrieved upbeat and warm feelings on A_{Ad} is greater when the retrieval cue is the entire ad or a scene from the ad than when the scales serve as the cue. The effect of uneasy feelings on A_{Ad} is less negative when the scales or an ad scene is used than when the entire ad is used to cue the feelings.

DISCUSSION AND FUTURE RESEARCH DIRECTIONS

The results of this study provide the basis for future research examining the role of feelings in building and maintaining brand equity. We demonstrated that:

TABLE 13.3
The Differential Effects of Feelings on A_{Ad} and A_B
by Time of Measurement and Type of Cue*

| | Attitude Toward the Ad | |
	Immediate versus Delayed A_{Ad} Measure	Type of Memory Cue
Upbeat Feelings	N.S. ~	Scene, Ad > Scales**
Warm Feelings	Immediate > Delayed	Scene, Ad > Scales
Uneasy Feelings	N.S.	Scales, Scene > Ad
Negative Feelings	N.S.	N.S.
	Attitude Toward the Brand	
	Immediate versus Delayed A_B Measure	Type of Memory Cue
Upbeat Feelings	N.S.	N.S.
Warm Feelings	Immediate > Delayed	N.S.
Uneasy Feelings	N.S.	N.S.
Negative Feelings	N.S.	Scales, Scene > Ad

*The main effects of Upbeat, Warm, and Negative Feelings on A_{Ad} and A_B are significant at the $p < 0.10$ level or better. The main effect of Uneasy Feelings is significant for A_{Ad} but not for A_B.

**This row should be read as follows: The effect of Upbeat Feelings on A_{Ad} does not vary based on when A_{Ad} is measured. The effect of Upbeat Feelings on A_{Ad} does vary based on the cue used to facilitate the retrieval of the feelings. Upbeat Feelings have a more positive effect on A_{Ad} when a scene from the ad or the entire ad is used as a cue than when the feelings scale serves as the cue for Upbeat Feelings experienced during the first session.

1. Ad-induced feelings are stored in memory.
2. Ad-induced feelings can be retrieved as well as brand claims can be retrieved.
3. Retrieved ad-induced feelings influence A_{Ad} and A_B three days after the initial exposure to the ad.
4. The retrievability and the effects of retrieved feelings on A_{Ad} and A_B occur independently of the particular type of memory cue that is used to facilitate retrieval.

There is, however, some variation in the effects of particular types of feelings on A_{Ad} and A_B based on delay and cue type. Some implications of these variations is discussed in the following sections. The results are summarized in Table 13.3.

The Effect of Delay

There is no difference in the main effects of all four retrieved feelings on A_{Ad} and A_B based on whether A_{Ad} and A_B were measured right after the ad is seen or three days after the ad is seen. Upbeat, warm, and negative feelings have significant effects on both A_{Ad} and A_B, whereas the effect of uneasy feelings is significant only for A_B. The only significant differences in the coefficients are for warm feelings. The effect of warm feelings on A_{Ad} and A_B, although still significant, is less powerful after a delay between ad exposure and measurement.

It is important to note that the only cue provided to subjects in the delay condition in this analysis (i.e., the no cue condition) prior to measuring A_{Ad} and A_B was the brand/organization name. The feelings experienced on Day 1 of the study were significant predictors of A_{Ad} and A_B even when there was no explicit cue. This suggests that even if the evaluation of an ad or brand/organization is not made at ad exposure, it is quite likely that ad-induced feelings will be retrieved from memory and will influence the evaluation when it is made. However, as the time interval between exposure and evaluation increases, and the viewer has other experiences with the brand or organization, a more specific cue may be necessary to facilitate the retrieval of the ad memory trace.

It is essential not only that the ad memory trace is retrieved, but that the correct link is made between ad-induced feelings and the brand/organization. Ad specific cues may encourage the correct associations. Continuing our earlier example, retrieval of the positive feelings induced by the Ray Charles Diet Pepsi TV commercial may be facilitated if there is an ad cue available in the purchase or use environment. We expect that PepsiCo's recent move to put "Uh-huh" boldly across the Diet Pepsi can will work in exactly this way. Note that by providing the ad cue on the package, the ad memory trace may be tapped at purchase and during use. Thus, the opportunity is created for making brand–ad associations in memory and strengthening those associations.

The Effect of Cues

Interestingly, all of the memory cues used in this study—the feelings scales, a scene from the ad, and the entire ad—facilitated the retrieval of some ad-induced feelings. This suggests that one does not have to reexperience the ad in order for feelings to have an effect on A_{Ad} or A_B. A picture from the ad on the package, or even the package itself, may be as effective an in-store cue as having the ad shown on a videocart.

Although all the cues resulted in significant effects of feelings on A_{Ad} and A_B (except for the effect of uneasy feelings on A_B), there are some interesting differences based on cue type. When the positive valence feelings, upbeat and warm, were retrieved by either the scene or the entire ad, the effect of those feelings on A_{Ad} was stronger than when the feelings were cued using the feelings scales. There were no differences, however, in the effect of the positive valence feelings on A_B based on cue type. We expect that differences may emerge when we study these relationships in a more realistic environment. In this study, the ad was the subjects' only source of information about the brand. The associations among ad-induced feelings, the ad, and the brand are only beginning to be formed. It is important for advertisers to know that ad-induced feelings do not rely solely on exposure to the ad for their effects.

The pattern for the negative valence feelings, uneasy and negative, indicates that where significant differences exist, the scales and the scene produce less negative effects than the ad itself. This is true for the effect of uneasy feelings on A_{Ad} and the effect of negative feelings on A_B. Subsequent exposures to an ad that generated predominantly uneasy or negative feelings may not only facilitate retrieval of those feelings, but may intensify their effect, countering attempts to build brand equity for a new brand. This effect may be especially serious in the case of an existing brand. If a new ad generates negative or uneasy feelings that are not offset by positive feelings or experiences, the brand's equity may be destroyed.

There is more work to be done on the role of cues in facilitating linkages and associations between feelings and brand equity using particular types of cues. For instance, the scene from each ad in this study was selected at random. That was important here because our goal was to determine whether any scene from the ad would facilitate retrieval of the ad memory trace. The effect of retrieved feelings may be stronger if the scene selected as a cue is one that facilitates the retrieval of positive feelings by most viewers. For instance, it might be possible to design a cue that would trigger the recall of warm feelings rather than uneasy feelings, mitigating some of the concerns expressed above.

Implications for Future Research on Brand Equity

These findings provide a basis for future research—they should not be interpreted as definitive. We limited the study to one exposure to an ad for products with which the subjects were unfamiliar. The setting is typical of a new brand (i.e., the brand name is just beginning to take on meaning and brand equity is just beginning to build). This is a particularly important time to study the associations that are made because future encounters with the brand will be shaped by these early associations. Our results demonstrate that ad-induced feelings can be influential in the developmental stages of brand equity. Future research will focus on exploring how feelings influence the accessibility of associations that are important to building and maintaining brand equity.

REFERENCES

Aaker, D. A. (1991). *Managing brand equity: Capitalizing on the value of a brand name.* New York: Free Press.

Batra, R., & Ray, M. L. (1986). Affective responses mediating acceptance of advertising. *Journal of Consumer Research, 13*(2), 234–249.

Brewer, W. F. (1988). Memory for randomly sampled autobiographical events. In U. Neisser & E. Winograd (Eds.), *Remembering reconsidered: Ecological and traditional approaches to the study of memory* (pp. 21–90). Cambridge: Cambridge University Press.

Burke, M. C., & Edell, J. A. (1989). The impact of feelings on ad-based affect and cognition. *Journal of Marketing Research, 26*(1), 69–83.

Calder, B. J., & Gruder, C. L. (1989). Emotional advertising appeals. In P. Cafferata & A. M. Tybout (Eds.), *Cognitive and affective responses to advertising* (pp. 277–285). Lexington, MA: Lexington Books.

Deighton, J. (1984). The interaction of advertising and evidence. *Journal of Consumer Research, 11*(3), 763–770.

Edell, J. A. (1992). Advertising interactions: A route to understanding brand equity. In A. A. Mitchell (Ed.), *Advertising exposure, memory, and choice.* Hillsdale, NJ: Lawrence Erlbaum Associates.

Edell, J. A., & Burke, M. C. (1987). The power of feelings in understanding advertising effects. *Journal of Consumer Research, 14*(3), 421–433.

Edell, J. A., & Keller, K. L. (1989). The information processing of coordinated media campaigns. *Journal of Marketing Research, 26*(2), 149–163.

Englis, B. G. (1990). Consumer emotional reactions to television advertising and their effects on message recall. In S. J. Agres, J. A. Edell, & T. M. Dubitsky (Eds.), *Emotion in advertising: Theoretical and practical explorations* (pp. 231–253). Westport, CT: Quorum Books.

Farhquhar, P. H. (1989, September). Managing brand equity. *Marketing Research.*

Frijda, N. H. (1988). The laws of emotion. *American Psychologist, 43*(5), 349–358.

Goldberg, M. E., & Gorn, G. J. (1987). Happy and sad TV programs: How they affect reactions to commercials. *Journal of Consumer Research, 14*(3), 387–403.

Goodstein, R. C., Edell, J. A., & Moore, M. C. (1990). When are feelings generated? Assessing the presence and reliability of feelings based on storyboards and animatics. In S. J. Agres, J. A. Edell, & T. M. Dubitsky (Eds.), *Emotion in advertising: Theoretical and practical explorations* (pp. 255–268). Westport, CT: Quorum Books.

Herr, P. M., & Fazio, R. H. (1992). The attitude-to-behavior process: Implications for consumer behavior. In A. A. Mitchell (Ed.), *Advertising exposure, memory, and choice.* Hillsdale, NJ: Lawrence Erlbaum Associates.

Keller, K. L. (1987). Memory factors in advertising: The effect of advertising retrieval cues on brand evaluation. *Journal of Consumer Research, 14*(3), 316–333.

Page, T. J., Jr., Thorson, E., & Heide, M. P. (1990). The memory impact of commercials varying in emotional appeal and product involvement. In S. J. Agres, J. A. Edell, & T. M. Dubitsky (Eds.), *Emotion in advertising: Theoretical and practical explorations* (pp. 255–268). Westport, CT: Quorum Books.

Russo, J. E., & Stephens, D. L. (1990). Ad-specific emotional responses to advertising. In S. J. Agres, J. A. Edell, & T. M. Dubitsky (Eds.), *Emotion in advertising: Theoretical and practical explorations* (pp. 113–123). Westport, CT: Quorum Books.

Stayman, D. M., & Aaker, D. A. (1988). Are all the effects of ad-induced feelings mediated by A_{Ad}? *Journal of Consumer Research, 15*(3), 368–373.

Thorson, E., & Friestad, M. (1989). The effects of emotion on episodic memory for television commercials. In P. Cafferata & A. M. Tybout (Eds.), *Cognitive and affective responses to advertising* (pp. 305–325). Lexington, MA: Lexington Books.

Wells, W., Burnett, J., & Moriarty, S. (1989). *Advertising: Principles and practice.* Englewood Cliffs, NJ: Prentice-Hall.

Chapter 14

Varieties of Brand Memory Induced by Advertising: Determinants, Measures, and Relationships

H. Shanker Krishnan
Indiana University

Dipankar Chakravarti
University of Arizona

If one took a time machine back to the grocery and drug stores of 1923 and asked for the leading brands of soap, canned fruit, and chewing gum, the answers would be the same as they are today—Ivory, Del Monte, and Wrigley's. The Campbell and Nabisco names would hold sway in soup and crackers; Kodak and Gillette would still be the most popular cameras and razors; and, of course, the leading soft-drink brand would be no surprise—Coca-Cola!

The Boston Consulting Group study (1991), on which the above is based, also reported that of over 6,000 new products placed on the shelves in the first five months of 1991, only 5% had new brand names. The rest, presumably, were extended brand names through which firms were attempting to capitalize on an existing consumer franchise. Consistent with research findings showing that brand extensions have higher sales growth rates and lower advertising costs (Smith, 1991), firms recognize that durable brand names are a tangible part of their equity base. There is interest in brand valuation methods (Barwise, Higson, Likierman, & Marsh, 1989) and discussion of moving beyond historical cost to using a brand's future benefits as formal, supplemental data in valuation (Farquhar, Han, & Ijiri, 1991).

Researchers have recognized and extensively discussed the priorities in brand equity research (Leuthesser, 1988; Marketing Science Institute, 1990). Many new empirical research programs are now under way. Brand extension issues have received the most attention (e.g., Aaker & Keller, 1990, Boush et al., 1987; Chakravarti, MacInnis, & Nakamoto, 1990; Herr, Farquhar, & Fazio, 1990; Keller & Aaker, 1992; Park, Milberg, & Lawson, 1991). The findings show that brand and product category associations in consumer memory play an important role in extension and meaning transfer. Yet, to date, few bridges have been built to the literature on how such memory associations develop via advertising exposure and/or other experiences with the brand.

Awareness and visibility of a brand's name and symbols are an important component of brand equity (Aaker, 1991). Advertising helps develop such brand equity in many different ways. It creates awareness and enhances a brand's likelihood of inclusion in consumers' consideration sets. Familiar brands benefit (a) from assumptions that consumers make about product performance, (b) from inertial barriers to information search, and (c) from the affective consequences of familiarity. In addition, advertising exposure may create memories that translate into nonconscious, but reliable, behavioral predispositions toward a brand. These conscious and nonconscious consumer memories induced by advertising contribute to a brand's equity.

This chapter describes the role that advertising plays in the development of brand equity. The first section overviews the process by which advertising creates enduring brand memories that influence brand-related behaviors. The second section develops a framework that distinguishes between varieties of brand memory (explicit and implicit) induced by advertising exposure and shows how these memories may be measured by direct and indirect tests. The third section discusses and empirically illustrates how memory effects of selected ad and viewer characteristics and of selected encoding and retrieval factors may be detected in such a framework. Finally, we discuss the implications of this research for understanding how advertising develops, sustains, and enhances a brand's equity pool.

ADVERTISING AND THE DEVELOPMENT OF BRAND EQUITY

Current perspectives on brand equity stress a need to go beyond what consumers know about a brand's tangible features and capabilities (see Aaker, 1991) and to tap behavioral predispositions toward the brand and what consumers will assume and associate naturally with it. Consumer brand memory is an important repository of these predispositions and associations. Although many aspects of brand memory are enduring consequences of favorable usage and other experiences with the brand, other memories that underlie brand-name awareness and the quality perceptions and associations that determine positioning derive from the brand's advertising and communication campaigns. In other words, advertising plays a significant role in initiating the impressions that gel into customer-level brand equity.

Although advertisers may design messages for holistic processing by viewers, it is useful to keep the message components in mind when assessing their impact on viewers. The *brand name* and the *brand claim(s)* are two key message components; most ads have a minimal objective of impressing and associating these two elements in the consumer's mind. An ad usually also contains *executional elements*, designed to cut through clutter and enhance its effectiveness. For example, an ad may use a celebrity endorser (e.g., Michael Jordan for Nike) or a humorous appeal (e.g., Wendy's' "Where's the beef?'') to convey the brand name and the brand claim.

Building brand equity through advertising programs involves a consistent message or theme that differentiates the brand. The ad must facilitate (a) the encoding and retrieval of the brand name, (b) its claims to quality, and (c) the key positioning associations. It must also create a predisposition to purchase. Moreover, the interaction between the message elements must be kept in mind. Some ads are well remembered but poorly associated with the brand. For example, an execution element (e.g., strong humor) may attract attention to the ad but distract consumers from processing the brand name and claim (Krishnan & Chakravarti, 1990). In other situations, an ad claim may be vivid and salient (e.g., the battery that "keeps on going and going . . .'') but become associated with a competing brand (Duracell) rather than with the sponsor (Eveready Energizer). Such ads, in effect, build the competitor's equity. Hence, an ad must not only cue the brand claim but also associate it clearly with the brand name, sustaining it against other brands' messages.

Advertisements are often designed to create positive viewer affect. For example, the baby in a Michelin tire ad presumably communicates positive feelings and care associations. However, the affect must ultimately be associated with the advertised brand if the ad is to build brand equity. Thus, the brand name should be associated in memory with (a) the affect inducing ad concept (the baby), (b) the idea (care and safety), or (c) an elaborated interpretation of the message (Cohen & Areni, 1991).

This suggests that advertising builds brand equity by developing brand memories. Some memory traces induced by advertising may be accessible to the cognitive conscious and are seen as a precondition for a brand's inclusion in a consumer's consideration set (Nedungadi, 1990). Such memory traces may also be affective or have affect intertwined with brand cognitions (Isen, 1989; Cohen & Areni, 1991). They may be captured by traditional name recognition and recall tests (Singh, Rothschild, & Churchill, 1988). A key feature of such direct tests is a contextual cue that explicitly links the memory trace to the corresponding encoding episode.

Other memory traces that also stem from advertising exposure may not be consciously linked to the encoding (viewing) episode. Such implicit memory traces may also have affective response potential. They may not surface in recognition and recall tests but may be detected by enhanced performance on indirect tests that do not cue the encoding episode (Schacter, 1987). Even without direct and conscious access to brand knowledge, implicit memory may predispose and influence behavior toward the brand. If consumers exposed to a brand's advertising develop reliable (but nonconscious) predispositions toward the brand, implicit memory may also contribute to a brand's equity pool.

Thus, exploring customer-based brand equity requires: (a) an understanding of the conceptual underpinnings of the forms (varieties) of brand memory that may be induced by advertising exposure and (b) knowledge of how these may be measured by indirect and direct tests. One must anticipate how they are affected by ad and viewer characteristics and by encoding and retrieval factors. One must also develop a diagnostic logic for detecting the influences by using the patterns or relationships between performance on memory tests.

BRAND MEMORIES INDUCED
BY ADVERTISING EXPOSURE

The complexities of memory measurement in the advertising context have led some authors to term it an "industry dilemma" (Krugman, 1985). Marketing academics have their own share of controversies. Some view dissociations between recall and recognition measures (e.g., Bagozzi & Silk, 1983) as evidence of the "multidimensional" structure of memory. Others contend that little can be said about memory structure in the absence of a theory-based construal of the dissociation/association patterns observed on memory tests (Howard & Sawyer, 1988). For memory measurement to gain status in brand equity valuation, the advertising community must become more familiar with the theoretical principles that underlie the detection and measurement of memory traces. This section provides a brief overview of the issues.

Varieties of Memory

Recent reviews of the human learning and memory literature in psychology distinguish between various varieties (forms) of memory. One distinction uses the label *procedural* (semantic) to designate a memory system that supports gradual or incremental learning of habits and skills, and the label *declarative* (episodic) for a system supporting rapid learning from single trials about specific situations and episodes (Sherry & Schacter, 1987). An important distinction is now being drawn between implicit and explicit memory forms (Richardson-Klavehn & Bjork, 1988; Roediger, Weldon, & Challis, 1989). These two forms are seen not as memory "stores" per se, but as varieties of memory inferred through examination of the patterns of associations and dissociations between various memory tests (Schacter, 1987).

Explicit Memory

Knowledge of a prior event or episode may be expressed with or without explicit awareness or remembering. For example, before a trip to the grocery store, a consumer may try to free recall a brand name or claimed brand benefit from a previously seen ad to include on the shopping list. Alternatively, an attempt to recall elements of a previously seen ad may be cued in the store when the consumer walks past the product category shelf. Finally, the ad elements (e.g., brand name and brand claims) may be recognized on the product package in the store (Alba, Hutchinson, & Lynch, 1991). In each case, the accessed memory is termed *explicit memory* because the consumer consciously remembers the ad-viewing episode.

The literature (see Richardson-Klavehn & Bjork, 1988; Schacter, 1989) also distinguishes between whether the previous encoding episode is experienced by conscious effort (*explicit intentional memory*) or without it (*explicit involuntary memory*). For instance, there may be situations where brand name and advertisement-related information "pop" into a person's mind without the person consciously trying to remember the ad. There is explicit remembering that the information has come from the ad, but without the strategic and effortful processes usually associated with retrieval. The phenomenological quality of this recollective experience suggests a distinct type of retrieval process.

Implicit Memory

In some cases, exposure to an advertisement may subsequently enable a consumer to (a) identify better, (b) have a positive attitude toward, or (c) even choose the brand more often from among those displayed on a crowded store shelf. However, the consumer may be unaware of the ad's facilitating effect and may not attribute it to the prior exposure. The memory form accessed here is termed *implicit memory* (Schacter, 1987) because traces of the ad-viewing episode are revealed by the consumer without consciously remembering it. Thus, in an advertising context, the distinction between explicit and implicit memory rests on whether or not the consumer is aware of prior ad exposure as the basis for expressions of brand related behavior.

Theoretical Accounts

The literature provides alternative theoretical accounts of explicit and implicit memory (Richardson-Klavehn & Bjork, 1988; Schacter, 1987):

1. The *activation view* suggests that, in some cases, temporarily activated prior representations drive performance without explicit reference to a prior episode. This view is consistent with the finding that elaborative processing does not influence implicit memory for preexisting representations (Graf & Mandler, 1984; Jacoby & Dallas, 1981). However, it does not adequately explain priming effects

due to newly acquired information in both amnesics and normal subjects (Graf & Schacter, 1985, 1987) or the extended persistence of such facilitation.

2. In *processing views*, dissociations between performance on direct versus indirect tests are explained by the idea that the former draw primarily on subject-initiated, conceptually driven elaboration processes, whereas indirect tests use information or data provided in test materials (Roediger & Blaxton, 1987; Roediger, Weldon, & Challis, 1989). Because research in this area has typically confounded the type of processing required on the tests (data driven and conceptually driven) with the theoretical memory form that the tests access (implicit/explicit), it is difficult to untangle the effects. Preliminary studies comparing multiple indirect and direct tests with different processing requirements find that conceptually driven indirect tests show patterns similar to direct tests (Srinivas & Roediger, 1990). Other findings (e.g., short-lived activations and elaborative dependence of implicit memory for new associations) are not explained (Schacter & Graf, 1986).

3. The *multiple memory view* attributes explicit and implicit memory to different hypothesized memory systems. Conscious recollection is thought to be a property of declarative (Squire & Cohen, 1984) systems, whereas implicit memory effects are attributed to procedural systems. Once again, these distinctions provide some insights into the differences between implicit and explicit memory, but are unable to explain all the findings.

In summary, advertising exposure may create brand equity by developing both explicit and implicit memory. Although explicit memory (as revealed by recall and recognition tests) has been studied, less is known in marketing about implicit memory (cf. Krishnan & Chakravarti, 1990). Nevertheless, it is clear that implicit memory traces produce some behavioral change (e.g., brand identification, facilitation of brand learning, or a predisposition to brand purchase) without conscious awareness of it. The effects are robust across domains, tasks, and subject populations, and, if also representative of ad exposure effects, may be an important manifestation of brand equity. Because the specific memory form accessed is related to the nature and demands of the memory tests, we now turn to a description of various memory measures.

MEASURING ADVERTISING-INDUCED BRAND MEMORY

Direct and Indirect Tests

Traditional tests of ad memory focus on direct measures where the consumer is cued to the ad-viewing episode to retrieve relevant information. For instance, in a recall test, the subject is asked to recollect everything they remember from the ad they viewed before. The subject is cued by the reference to the ad-viewing episode and this context cue is used to sample images sequentially from memory (Gillund & Shiffrin, 1984). These images are then identified by the subject as being components of the ad they saw earlier. Other recall tests may provide cues beyond the encoding context to aid or focus retrieval (recall the brand name from an ad they saw before).

In a recognition (brand name) test, a person is provided with a list of "old" (seen before) and "new" (not seen before) brand names. The subject is asked to identify the brand names that they remember seeing in the ads. Thus, in addition to the context cue, the target item is also provided as a cue. Recognition involves matching of the test items with images in memory (Mandler, 1980). The response is based on whether the familiarity activated for the item exceeds an individual-generated cutoff point. Because individuals may have different cutoffs, ad-recognition scores are often reported as A' scores (Singh & Rothschild, 1983; Taschian, White, & Pak, 1988) after correcting for individual response propensities.

The common element in the two direct tests (recall and recognition) is that the instructions focus the subjects on the ad-viewing episode. Thus, the encoding context (the ad) is provided as a retrieval cue. In indirect tests, the instructions focus on the task without requiring the individual to think back to the ad. For instance, a word-completion task for the brand name NAVY may instruct subjects to complete several word stems, including the target (e.g., NAV__), as quickly as possible. Completions of these word stems are compared with baseline completion scores of individuals not exposed to the ads. If the incidence of "NAVY" completions is higher for subjects exposed to the ad, this is viewed as evidence of memory priming due to exposure to the ad. Presumably, ad exposure affected task behavior without conscious awareness of the ad-viewing episode.

One may also investigate distinctions between various indirect tests of memory. Recent research has focused on conceptually driven versus data-driven tasks (e.g., Hamman, 1990; Srinivas & Roediger, 1990). Conceptually driven tasks involve top–down associative processes, which rely on encoded meanings of concepts. Data-driven tasks rely on whether task cues lead to a match of perceptual features between encoding and testing episodes. Preliminary results suggest that performance on conceptually driven indirect tests is similar to performance on direct tests (Hamman, 1990). This is consistent with the notion that direct tests operate through associative processes (Gillund & Shiffrin, 1984).

Operational Issues in Inferring Implicit Memory

The claim that a specific memory test is indirect rests on the fact that the ad-viewing episode was not explicitly cued in the test. Inferring access of implicit memory from such a test assumes that the subject was not aware or conscious of the viewing episode at the time of the test. However, even if the ad-viewing episode is not explicitly cued, subjects may: (a) attempt to remember the relevant information by retrieving the ad from memory or (b) be involuntarily reminded that one or more of the test items pertained to the ads seen earlier. Procedures must therefore be implemented to ensure that implicit memory is accessed. In particular, self-reports of test awareness (Bowers & Schacter, 1990) and comparisons with cued recall (Merikle & Reingold, 1991) may be used to ascertain whether the test indeed accessed implicit memory.

The self-report measure involves a series of posttest questions that investigate whether subjects were aware of the relationship between the indirect task and the ad. Subjects are then classified as *aware* or *unaware* and their results are reported separately. A problem with this procedure is that the questions may create demand effects that distort the level of reported test awareness. Alternatively, one may compare indirect test performance with that on a cued recall test, using identical cues but different instructions (Schacter, Bowers, & Booker, 1989). Such a test provides NAV— as a cue, with instructions to think back to the ad and complete the word with a brand name. Differential performance on the cued recall and indirect tests are attributed to different memory processes. Absence of performance differences suggests that subjects may have treated the indirect test as a direct test. Moreover, since elaboration affects these two tests differentially, one may use this to diagnose the form (variety) of memory accessed in the indirect test condition.

It is often assumed that direct tests access explicit memory whereas indirect tests access implicit memory. Yet, as some researchers (Schacter, 1987; Tulving, 1985) have noted, the correspondence between test type and memory form is not always clear cut. We highlight the key distinctions in Table 14.1. The examples provided are intended to help advertisers recognize the nature of the memory impressions that are made by an ad. Next, we show how the measures may help detect and diagnose the effects of ad and viewer characteristics, as well as encoding and retrieval factors, on brand memory. We also show how advertisers may use this approach to design and evaluate messages that build brand equity.

DETERMINANTS AND RELATIONSHIPS

Following Jenkins (1979) and Keller (1986), we group the determinants of brand memory in four categories:

1. *Individual* viewer characteristics include prior brand knowledge and viewer descriptors, such as age, which are related to ad-processing ability.
2. *Stimulus* characteristics, such as the prominence of the brand name in an ad or its relationship to executional elements, may also influence brand memory.

TABLE 14.1
Taxonomy of Forms and Tests of Memory

Forms of Memory	*Tests of Memory*		
	Recognition	*Recall*	*Indirect*
	Instructions refer to encoding episode; target item present at retrieval.	Instructions refer to encoding episode; target item not present at retrieval.	Instructions do not refer to encoding episode; target may/may not be present.
Explicit Reexperiencing of encoding episode*	Market researcher calls consumer at home and asks if particular brand name and claim was advertised on TV the previous night. Consumer remembers ad and the brand name/claim.	Market researcher calls consumer at home and asks what brand names and claims were advertised on TV the previous night. Consumer remembers ad and the brand name/claim.	Shopper in mall asked about attitude toward a particular brand. She tries to remember brand name and claim from an earlier seen ad.
Implicit No reexperiencing of encoding episode; focus is on performing current task.	Because direct tests make an explicit reference to the encoding episode, they do not access implicit memory.		Shopper in mall asked about attitude toward a set of brands; one brand seems familiar but there is no recollection of the previously seen ad. Shopper sees brand and can identify having seen it; he or she does not know/remember where it was previously encountered.

Note. Adapted to the advertising context from Richardson-Klavehn and Bjork (1988).
*These examples involve cases where the ad-viewing episode is reexperienced with conscious effort (explicit intentional memory). The ad-viewing episode may also be experienced with no conscious effort (explicit involuntary memory).

3. Instructed or naturally occurring *encoding* operations during ad exposure may also impact upon brand memory. For instance, elaboration of the ad for its meaning may form stronger encoding traces, thereby enhancing future retrieval.

4. The *retrieval* task and the surrounding cues in the retrieval environment may affect brand memory. Ad-related cues will usually facilitate retrieval whereas distractors may interfere with retrieval of ad information.

In the next section, we present a concise discussion of these factors to illustrate how advertisers may use previously discussed memory concepts and measurement procedures to generate and monitor brand equity.

Individual Viewer Characteristics

Advertisers are often interested in monitoring the development of their brand's equity in specific demographic segments. For instance, communicating effectively to the elderly is a tricky proposition due to processing ability and/or motivational deficiencies. In Table 14.2, we present excerpts from Cole and Houston's (1987) data on memory performance of their younger adult and elderly subject groups following exposure to seven target print ads.

We see that the elderly scored lower on both recall and recognition tests. Younger adults had relatively higher recall and recognition. Based on these results and a similar pattern of data for TV ads, the authors concluded that the elderly suffered from encoding deficits. In other words, relative to younger adults, the elderly subjects did not encode the brand when originally exposed to the ads. These direct memory test results raise questions about the ads' effectiveness in this target segment. Thus, the nature of processing deficits is inferred from the test outcomes.

Although recognition may not be the ultimate measure of encoding (see Watkins, 1990), it is usually viewed as closer to detecting encoded information than other explicit memory measures. Because there is some evidence that the elderly show preserved priming effects on indirect tests even when their performance on direct tests is impaired (Light & Singh, 1987), there is a need to perform a more comprehensive analysis. We illustrate such an analysis by adding hypothetical indirect test data to the test battery in Table 14.2 for two scenarios.

In Scenario 1, indirect test performance parallels the direct test results, with the elderly showing performance deficits on all three tests. This supports the original conjecture (Cole & Houston, 1987) of an encoding deficit. In Scenario 2, however, the data show that the elderly perform well on indirect tests despite weak direct test performance. This not only suggests that the brand stimulus was encoded, but also reveals that the direct test results may be attributed to

TABLE 14.2
Memory Performance

Test Type	Elderly	Younger Adults
Brand recall	0.09	0.87
Brand recognition	0.81	3.36
Indirect test (Scenario 1)	0.50	0.75
Indirect test (Scenario 2)	2.25	2.75

a retrieval deficit for the elderly, stemming from difficulty with tests requiring conscious access to memory. The results suggest different approaches to both designing messages and measuring brand memory for the elderly.

Stimulus (Advertisement) Characteristics

Two factors of interest in a brand equity context are the memorability of the brand name itself and its associations with other ad components. A brand name's association set size is known to affect memory. Thus, the number of concepts associated with the brand name may either: (a) facilitate brand name memory by providing multiple retrieval paths, or (b) inhibit brand name memory through retrieval interference. One finding (Meyers-Levy, 1989), that encoding distinctiveness offsets interference from multiple associations, implies that brand names conveying a distinctive meaning will be easier to remember.

Strong associations between various ad components may enhance memory through viewer elaboration of the component relationships. Such effects are known for execution elements like music (MacInnis & Park, 1991) and pictures (Edell & Staelin, 1983; Houston, Childers, & Heckler, 1986). Similarly, multiple associations between the brand name and other ad components can help recall by providing additional retrieval cues. For instance, the Ivory brand name may be cued by: (a) a reference to the soap product category, (b) a claim (99% pure), or (c) a picture of the soap in the ad. Conversely, failure to establish strong associations between the ad components and the brand name may render the ad relatively ineffective.

Well-associated ad components should also facilitate recognition through increased familiarity, although the incremental benefit may be smaller. The additional retrieval cues are not as essential in recognition because the brand name is present for identification. Stronger associations may overcome interference from other distractors in the environment. Conceptually driven indirect tests would also be affected by increased ad-associations that would prime the brand name during a memory search. In contrast, data-driven indirect tests would not be influenced by such associations because attention focuses on the task and not on search of a preexisting memory.

From a brand equity standpoint, this signals the degree of advertiser success in endowing brands with a set of associations that facilitate brand name retrieval. In product categories where choices are mainly memory based, strong associations between ad components are advantageous for brand name retrieval. When choices are typically made in-store, the brand name must be distinctive to facilitate recognition from among competing brands. For low involvement situations where conscious recollection may be less relevant, a brand name prominent on the package may prompt consumers to act on a predisposition and purchase the brand.

Encoding Factors

Information processing during the encoding of an ad is generally under the viewer's control. The viewer chooses the aspect(s) of the ad on which to focus (e.g., brand name, pictures, music) and the manner in which information is processed (e.g., focus on sensory cues vs. meanings of the concepts). Differential elaboration influences subsequent memory. Thus, relative to nondirected processing, semantic elaboration facilitates performance on direct tests of memory (Craik & Tulving, 1975; Jacoby & Craik, 1979). By providing a rich encoding that integrates prior knowledge with stimulus information and contextual cues, elaboration facilitates both recall and recognition (direct test) performance.

In contrast, indirect tests do not refer to the encoding episode. Yet, exposed subjects show a reliable increment in task performance relative to those not exposed. Unlike its facilitative effect on direct tests, semantic elaboration does not have a parallel impact on indirect tests (Jacoby & Dallas, 1981; Schacter, 1987, 1989). Meaning-based encoding processes appear unnecessary for these priming effects, representing a marked dissociation between direct and indirect tests of memory.

We replicate this dissociation in a study examining memory for brand names following exposure to print advertisements. We recruited 96 undergraduates from a marketing subject pool at the University of Arizona. Fifteen color print ads were chosen from various consumer magazines, with an equal mix of products targeted to males and females. Each ad depicted a single brand name. Each brand name (Appendix, Table 1) consisted of at least four letters (one of the indirect tests was a word stem completion task) of which each three-letter stem had multiple completions. Each brand name was a common noun (or a derivative) and was chosen because it was not too distinctive.

Each ad was projected on an overhead screen for 10 seconds. Subjects in the elaboration condition were asked to evaluate the effectiveness of each ad and brand name. In the no elaboration condition, subjects were only exposed to the ads and did not evaluate them. After an unrelated filler task, subjects' memories for the brand names were examined, using recall, recognition, and indirect tests. Subjects taking the indirect test answered a test-awareness questionnaire to ascertain implicit memory access. See Appendix, Table 2, for the indirect and cued recall tests used.

The key dependent variable used in the study was the mean number of brands remembered (out of 15) in each test. These data are reported by elaboration condition in Table 14.3.

The data in Table 14.3 show:

1. Compared to the baseline level of performance (2.00) in the no exposure condition, indirect test performance was significantly ($p < 0.05$) facili-

TABLE 14.3
Number of Brands Remembered

Test Type	Type of Elaboration	
	None	Semantic
Free recall	5.56	6.95
Recognition	11.50	12.89
Cued recall	4.38	7.30
Indirect test (exposed to ads)	3.58	3.73
Indirect test (no exposure baseline)	2.00	

tated following ad exposure, both with and without elaboration. Because subjects were screened for test awareness, this result provides evidence of implicit memory for brand names following a single exposure to an ad.

2. Elaboration had a positive effect on all three direct tests. For cued and free recall, the difference was significant ($p < 0.05$), whereas for recognition it approached significance.

3. The indirect tests were unaffected by semantic elaboration.

Perhaps the most telling comparison is between the cued recall and the indirect tests. The cues were identical; the only difference was whether or not a reference was made to the viewing episode. Consistent with the theory underlying memory tests, elaborative processing at encoding had the strongest effect on recall, a mild facilitative effect on recognition, and no effect on indirect memory tests.

Retrieval Factors

The presence of a cue referring to the encoding context defines a direct memory test. Free recall tests usually provide no additional cues beyond a reference to the encoding context. Other recall tests may use more specific cues. Some cues (e.g., product, pictures, or claims) are facilitators, aiding retrieval via encoding specificity (i.e., by producing a better match between the encoding and retrieval contexts; Keller, 1987; Tulving & Thomson, 1973). Other cues act as inhibitors and lower memory performance by interfering with the target trace. When the target brand name is itself a retrieval cue (with or without other distractors), we have a recognition test. A retrieval test that omits the context cue is effectively an indirect memory test.

In addition to elaboration, our study also manipulated the retrieval cues that were provided. Two additional tasks, picture-aided recall and recognition, were used. The cues were identical to the ad pictures but with all references to the brand name deleted. Subjects were asked to identify the pictures

TABLE 14.4
Mean Number of Brand Names Remembered

Test Type	Cues Provided	
	No Picture	Picture
Recall	5.56	8.90
Recognition	11.50	12.62

that they remembered seeing during the ad-viewing episode and to write down the relevant brand name (recall) or identify the brand name from a list of potential brand names (recognition). The mean number of brand names remembered is shown in Table 14.4.

The picture cues had a significant effect on recall ($p < 0.001$), whereas the improvement was not significant in recognition. It appears that the ad picture was a strong memory cue for recall. However, in the recognition test, the picture cue did not increment performance on the brand name even with distractors present.

The four sets of factors discussed here may also interact to influence brand memory. We illustrate this in Table 14.5, by describing the interactive effect of elaboration (an encoding factor) and picture cues (a retrieval factor) on brand name memory.

The data show that, for recall, elaboration accentuates the effect of the picture cue ($p < 0.01$). Moreover, taken together, elaboration and the picture cue enhance brand recognition ($p < 0.05$). In this situation, the picture cue at retrieval had a weaker effect than elaboration at encoding. Interestingly, the picture cue had a stronger effect on recall. Also, the recall scores suggest that, taken together, elaboration and the picture cue enhanced brand memory to the levels observed in recognition (where the target brand name is provided as a cue). This powerful cuing effect of the brand name suggests that advertisers may gain from designing ads that attract attention to the brand name and from making the brand name a significant presence in the in-store environment.

TABLE 14.5
Effects of Factors on Brand Name Memory

Test Type	Elaboration	
	None	Semantic
Free recall	5.56	6.95
Picture-aided recall	8.90	11.50
Recognition	11.50	12.89
Picture-aided recognition	12.62	14.12

DISCUSSION

Advertising plays a major role in creating the awareness, perceived quality, and other associations that make up a brand's equity pool. Effective management of this resource can create powerful and durable brands. The point is that, because consumer memory is a significant repository of a firm's equity, it is critical to understand how consumer memory is influenced by exposure to a brand's advertising. To this end, we review the varieties of memory that may stem from ad exposure and how such memories may be measured. We also develop and empirically illustrate a conceptual framework which shows how viewer and stimulus factors, as well as the nature of encoding processes and retrieval cues, influence memory.

To review the key issues, recall is significantly facilitated by elaborative processing of the stimulus. Hence, an ad with well-integrated components that produces a consistent set of positioning associations creates an accessible impression in consumer memory. Meaningful elaboration at encoding can enhance accessibility and overcome retrieval interference. Dissociations between recognition and recall permit assessment of whether the brand advertising is being effectively encoded and retrieved. Managerial actions based on such diagnostics can help enhance advertising effectiveness.

We argue that nonconscious predispositions toward a brand may also be a significant equity-building consequence of ad exposure. In a competitive shopping environment, implicit memory may underlie identification of a brand on a crowded grocery store shelf and also stimulate brand-related behaviors. Indirect tests of brand memory offer insights into (a) brand-related behavioral predispositions, (b) memory representations that are unaffected by elaboration and distraction, and, finally, (c) into the stable, long-lasting priming effects observed. This information is useful in designing ads and monitoring ad effectiveness toward the goal of building powerful brands.

Detection and diagnosis of such memory effects is important to advertisers (Cohen & Chakravarti, 1990). Theory-driven interpretation of performance on direct and indirect tests of brand memory provides the basis for such diagnoses. We hope that the framework provided here will aid in understanding how ad exposure affects brand name memory and contributes to brand equity.

APPENDIX

TABLE 1
Brand Names and Product Categories in Target Ads

Brand Names	Products
Vivid	Laundry detergent
Finesse	Shampoo
Cambridge	Cigarette
Black & Decker	Electric iron
Eclipse	Automobile
Safari	Perfume
Wild Turkey	Bourbon whiskey
Clinique	Skin lotion (for men)
Singer	Sewing machine
Regal	Coffeemaker
Guess	Jeans
Fairgate	Measuring tools
Revere	Cookware
Hunter	Ceiling fan
Navy	Perfume

TABLE 2
Indirect and Cued Recall Tests for Brand Names

Word-Completion Task and Cued Recall Task

Indirect Test Instructions
Please complete the following word beginnings with the *first word* that you can think of which fits. Do not use proper nouns (names) for the fragments. For instance, if TOD__ were given to you, you may add AY to it to make it TOD<u>AY</u>.

Cued Recall Instructions
We have provided several word-beginnings below, some of which may be completed with brand names from the ads that you saw earlier. *Think back to the ads* and try to remember *all* the brand names that you saw using these word-beginnings. For instance, if TOD__ were given to you, and you remembered seeing a brand name TODAY, you would write down <u>AY</u> to make it TOD<u>AY</u>.

Examples of Test Cues:	Target Brand Name:
1. VIV__	VIVID
2. FIN__	FINESSE

Word-Association Task and Cued Recall Task

Indirect Test Instructions
On this page, your task is to free associate with each word listed below. For each word below, write down the *first word* that comes to mind. For instance, if BOY were one of the words, you could write down GIRL.

(Continued)

TABLE 2
(Continued)

Cued Recall Instructions
We have provided several words below, some of which may be closely associated with brand names from the ads that you saw earlier. *Think back to the ads* and try to remember *all* the brand names that you saw using these words to help your memory. For instance, if BOY were one of the clues, this may help you remember GIRL as one of the brand names that you saw earlier.

Examples of Test Cues:	Target Brand Name:
1. SOLAR-	ECLIPSE
2. ARMY-	NAVY

REFERENCES

Aaker, D. A. (1991). *Managing brand equity*. New York, NY: The Free Press.

Aaker, D. A., & Keller, K. L. (1990). Consumer evaluations of brand extensions. *Journal of Marketing, 54*(1), 27–41.

Alba, J. W., Hutchinson, J. W., & Lynch, J. G. (1991). Memory and decision making. In T. S. Robertson & H. H. Kassarjian (Eds.), *Handbook of consumer behavior* (pp. 1–49). Englewood Cliffs, NJ: Prentice-Hall.

Bagozzi, R. P., & Silk, A. J. (1983). Recall, recognition, and the measurement of memory for print advertisements. *Marketing Science, 2*(2), 95–134.

Barwise, P., Higson, C., Likierman, C., & Marsh, P. (1989). *Accounting for brands*. London: London Business School & the Institute for Chartered Accountants in England and Wales.

Boush, D. M., Shipp, S., Loken, B., Gencturk, E., Crockett, S., Kennedy, E., Minshall, B., Misurell, D., Rochford, L., & Strobel, J. (1987). Affect generalization to similar and dissimilar brand extensions. *Psychology and Marketing, 4*(3), 225–237.

Bowers, J. S., & Schacter, D. L. (1990). Implicit memory and test awareness. *Journal of Experimental Psychology: Learning, Memory, and Cognition, 16*(3), 404–416.

Chakravarti, D., MacInnis, D. J., & Nakamoto, K. (1990). Product category perceptions, elaborative processing, and brand name extension strategies. In M. E. Goldberg, G. Gorn, & R. W. Pollay (Eds.), *Advances in consumer research* (Vol. 17, pp. 910–916). Provo, UT: Association for Consumer Research.

Cohen, J., & Areni, C. S. (1991). Affect and consumer behavior. In T. S. Robertson and H. H. Kassarjian (Eds.), *Handbook of consumer behavior* (pp. 188–240). Englewood Cliffs, NJ: Prentice-Hall.

Cohen, J. B., & Chakravarti, D. (1990). Consumer psychology. *Annual Review of Psychology, 41*, 243–288.

Cole, C. A., & Houston, M. (1987). Encoding and media effects on consumer learning deficiencies in the elderly. *Journal of Marketing Research, 24*, 55–64.

Craik, F. I. M., & Tulving, E. (1975). Depth of processing and the retention of words in episodic memory. *Journal of Experimental Psychology, 104*, 268–294.

Edell, J. A., & Staelin, R. (1983). The information processing of pictures in print advertisements. *Journal of Consumer Research, 10*(1), 45–61.

Farquhar, P. H., Han, J. Y, & Ijiri, Y. (1991). *Recognizing and measuring brand assets* (working paper). Graduate School of Industrial Administration, Carnegie-Mellon University, Pittsburgh.

Gillund, G., & Shiffrin, R. M. (1984). A retrieval model for both recognition and recall. *Psychological Review, 91*(1), 1–67.

Graf, P., & Mandler, G. (1984). Activation makes words more accessible, but not necessarily more retrievable. *Journal of Verbal Learning and Verbal Behavior, 23*, 553-568.

Graf, P., & Schacter, D. L. (1985). Implicit and explicit memory for new associations in normal and amnesic subjects. *Journal of Experimental Psychology: Learning, Memory, and Cognition, 11*, 501-518.

Graf, P., & Schacter, D. L. (1987). Selective effects of interference on implicit and explicit memory for new associations. *Journal of Experimental Psychology: Learning, Memory, and Cognition, 13*, 45-53.

Hamman, S. B. (1990). Level-of-processing effects in conceptually driven implicit tasks. *Journal of Experimental Psychology: Learning, Memory, and Cognition, 16*, 970-977.

Herr, P. M., Farquhar, P. H., & Fazio, R. (1990). *Extending brand equity to new categories* (working paper). Graduate School of Business, Indiana University, Bloomington.

Houston, M. J., Childers, T. L., & Heckler, S. E. (1986). Picture-word consistency and the elaborative processing of advertisements. *Journal of Marketing Research, 24*, 359-370.

Howard, D. J., & Sawyer, A. G. (1988). Recall, recognition, and the dimensionality of memory for print advertisements: An interpretive reappraisal. *Marketing Science, 7*(1), 94-98.

Isen, A. M. (1989). Some ways in which affect influences cognitive processes: Implications for advertising and consumer behavior. In A. M. Tybout & P. Cafferata (Eds.), *Advertising and consumer psychology* (pp. 91-117). New York: Lexington Books.

Jacoby, L. L., & Dallas, M. (1981). On the relationship between autobiographical memory and perceptual learning. *Journal of Experimental Psychology: General, 3*, 306-340.

Jacoby, L. L., & Craik, F. I. M. (1979). Effects of elaboration of processing at encoding and retrieval. In L. S. Cermak & F. I. M. Craik (Eds.), *Levels of processing in human memory* (pp. 119-139). Hillsdale, NJ: Lawrence Erlbaum Associates.

Jenkins, J. J. (1979). Four points to remember: A tetrahedral model of memory experiments. In L. S. Cermak & F. I. M. Craik (Eds.), *Levels of processing in human memory*. Hillsdale, NJ: Lawrence Erlbaum Associates.

Keller, K. L. (1986). *Memory factors in advertising: The effects of advertising memory cues on brand evaluations*. Unpublished doctoral dissertation, Duke University, Durham, NC.

Keller, K. L. (1987). Memory factors in advertising: The effect of advertising retrieval cues on brand evaluations. *Journal of Consumer Research, 14*(2), 316-333.

Keller, K. L., & Aaker, D. A. (1992). The effects of sequential introduction of brand extensions. *Journal of Marketing Research, 28*(1), 35-50.

Krishnan, H. S., & Chakravarti, D. (1990). Humor in advertising: Testing effects on brand name and message claim memory. In W. Bearden & A. Parasuraman (Eds.), *Enhancing knowledge development in marketing* (pp. 10-16). Proceedings of the AMA Summer Educators' Conference, Washington, DC.

Krugman, H. E. (1985). Point of view: Measuring memory—an industry dilemma. *Journal of Advertising Research, 25*(4), 49-51.

Landler, M., Schiller, Z., & Therrien, L. (1991, July 8). What's in a name? Less and less. *Business Week*, pp. 66-67.

Leuthesser, L. (1988). *Defining, measuring, and managing brand equity: A conference summary* (Report No. 88-104). Cambridge, MA: Marketing Science Institute.

Light, L. L., & Singh, A. (1987). Implicit and explicit memory in young and older adults. *Journal of Experimental Psychology: Learning, Memory, and Cognition, 13*(4), 531-541.

MacInnis, D. J., & Park, C. W. (1991). The differential role of characteristics of music on high- and low-involvement consumers' processing of ads. *Journal of Consumer Research, 18*(2), 161-173.

Mandler, G. (1980). Recognizing: The judgment of previous occurrence. *Psychological Review, 87*, 252-271.

Marketing Science Institute. (1990). *Research priorities 1990-1992*. Cambridge, MA: Author.

Merikle, P. M., & Reingold, E. M. (1991). Comparing direct (explicit) and indirect (implicit) measures to study unconscious memory. *Journal of Experimental Psychology: Learning, Memory, and Cognition, 17*(2), 224-233.

Meyers-Levy, J. (1989). The influence of a brand name's association set size and word-frequency on brand memory. *Journal of Consumer Research, 16*(2), 197-207.

Nedungadi, P. (1990). Recall and consumer consideration sets: Influencing choice without altering brand evaluations. *Journal of Consumer Research, 17*(3), 263-276.

Park, C. W., Milberg, S., & Lawson, R. (1991). Evaluation of brand extensions: The role of product feature similarity and brand concept consistency. *Journal of Consumer Research, 18*(2), 185-193.

Richardson-Klavehn, A., & Bjork, R. A. (1988). Measures of memory. *Annual Review of Psychology, 36*, 475-543.

Roediger, H. L., & Blaxton, T. A. (1987). Retrieval modes produce dissociations in memory for surface information. In D. S. Gorfein & R. R. Hoffman (Eds.), *Memory and cognitive processes: The Ebbinghaus Centennial Conference* (pp. 349-379). Hillsdale, NJ: Lawrence Erlbaum Associates.

Roediger, H. L., Weldon, M. S., & Challis, B. H. (1989). On the relation between implicit and explicit measures of retention: A processing account. In H. L. Roediger & F. I. M. Craik (Eds.), *Varieties of memory and consciousness: Essays in honor of Endel Tulving* (pp. 3-41). Hillsdale, NJ: Lawrence Erlbaum Associates.

Schacter, D. L. (1987). Implicit memory: History and current status. *Journal of Experimental Psychology: Learning, Memory, and Cognition, 13*(3), 501-518.

Schacter, D. L. (1989). On the relation between memory and consciousness: Dissociable interactions and conscious experience. In H. L. Roediger & F. I. M. Craik (Eds.), *Varieties of memory and consciousness: Essays in honor of Endel Tulving* (pp. 355-389). Hillsdale, NJ: Lawrence Erlbaum Associates.

Schacter, D. L., Bowers, J., & Booker, J. (1989). Intention awareness and implicit memory: The retrieval intentionality criterion. In S. Lewandowsky, J. Dunn, & K. Kirsner (Eds.), *Implicit memory: Theoretical issues*. Hillsdale, NJ: Lawrence Erlbaum Associates.

Schacter, D. L., & Graf, P. (1986). Effects of elaborative processing on implicit and explicit memory for new associations. *Journal of Experimental Psychology: Learning, Memory, and Cognition, 12*, 432-444.

Sherry, D. F., & Schacter, D. L. (1987). The evolution of multiple memory systems. *Psychological Review, 94*, 439-454.

Singh, S. N., & Rothschild, M. L. (1983). Recognition as a measure of learning from television commercials. *Journal of Marketing Research, 20*, 235-248.

Singh, S. N., Rothschild, M., & Churchill, G. A. (1988). Recognition versus recall as measures of television commercial forgetting. *Journal of Marketing Research, 25*, 72-80.

Smith, D. C. (1991). *An examination of product and market characteristics that affect the financial outcomes of brand extensions* (Report No. 91-103). Cambridge, MA: Marketing Science Institute.

Squire, L. R., & Cohen, M. J. (1984). Human memory and amnesia. In J. McGaugh, G. Lynch, & N. Weinberger (Eds.), *Proceedings of the Conference on the Neurobiology of Learning and Memory* (pp. 3-64). New York: Guilford Press.

Srinivas, K., & Roediger, H. L. (1990). Classifying implicit memory tests: Category association and anagram solution. *Journal of Memory and Language, 29*, 389-412.

Taschian, A., White, J. D., & Pak, S. (1988). Signal detection analysis and advertising recognition: An introduction to measurement and interpretation issues. *Journal of Marketing Research, 25*(4), 397-404.

Tulving, E. (1985). On the classification problem in learning and memory. In L. G. Nilsson & T. Archer (Eds.), *Perspectives in learning and memory* (pp. 67-94). Hillsdale, NJ: Lawrence Erlbaum Associates.

Tulving, E., & Thomson, D. M. (1973). Retrieval processes in recognition memory: Effects of associative context. *Journal of Experimental Psychology, 87*, 175-184.

Watkins, M. J. (1990). Mediationism and the obfuscation of memory. *American Psychologist, 45*(3), 328-335.

Part IV

Perspectives on Brand Equity

Decomposing a Brand's Consumer Franchise into Buyer Types

Josh McQueen
Leo Burnett Company, Inc.

Carol Foley
Leo Burnett Company, Inc.

John Deighton
University of Chicago

Some kinds of consumers are much more important to a brand's health than others. For example, if a brand's sales are concentrated among consumers (a) who buy it frequently, (b) who buy competitors' brands less frequently, and (c) who buy less on deal, the franchise may be more valuable than if the same level of sales comes from consumers who also buy competitors' brands and buy brands on deal more often.

This chapter describes an approach to valuing the consumer franchise of a brand, based on the study of this kind of consumer buying pattern. Aaker (1991) argued that brand equity is the sum of five asset dimensions, one of which is the value of the brand's consumer base. Our goal, then, is to develop a method to value a brand's consumer franchise as a component of brand equity.

A consumer franchise is the sum of the discounted present values of the firm's relationships with many consumers. Some buy regularly and in large amounts, and the net present value of those relationships is high. For many others, the brand is only one of a number of brands bought, perhaps regularly or perhaps for trial, and consumer value is lower or less predictable. We try to classify these relationships into types, each making a different contribution to the strength of the franchise.

STRUCTURE OF CONSUMER FRANCHISE

Ours is not the first work on this topic. Much previous research has considered how a brand's consumer base may be structured. One distinction is between buyers and new triers (Aaker, 1973). Among the buyers, the distinction is often made between loyal and nonloyal consumers. Jacoby and Chestnut (1978) reviewed a substantial body of work on the brand loyal consumer. Among nonloyal consumers, a distinction can be drawn between those who are deal prone and those whose multibrand buying has other causes. Webster (1965) developed a measure of purchasing on deal relative to all purchasing; Blattberg, Buesing, Peacock, and Sen (1978) found that a similar measure correlated with measures of a household's inventory holding costs. Blattberg and Neslin (1989) reviewed 18 studies of the behavioral and psychographic correlates of deal proneness. McAlister (1986) combined the concepts of loyal, deal prone, and stockpiler types to form a seven category nonexhaustive typology and computed the profitability of each type from scanner data.

An inadequately considered question in this literature is whether these buyer types are a phenomenon of brands or consumers. Are brand loyal consumers, to take one example, loyal because the particular set of brands offered to a market happens to contain some brands they find really attractive, or because this group is innately disposed to form loyal bonds? Is there high loyalty in the toothpaste category because Crest is a fine toothpaste, or because the toothpaste category does not reward much experimentation? Is deal-proneness a function of the number of deals offered to a category, or is the number of deals a competitively derived optimum response to consumers' preexisting deal propensity?

Our in-going assumption was that although brand characteristics are important, enduring consumer characteristics also play a pivotal role. Within a category, external attributes of the buyers would help to explain patterns of brand buying and, therefore, these patterns would be stable and enduring, not transitory, evolutionary, or easily disrupted by marketing expenditures. We speculate that although marketing actions could cause consumers to switch brands, they would not normally or routinely cause them to switch from one pattern of brand buying to another.

What set of consumer characteristics could cause a household to adhere for a long time to a particular pattern of brand buying? We speculate that one group of causes has to do with aspects of the consumer's living arrangements, such as dual career families with marginal value for time, the presence of children in the household, and the number and variety of different problems to be solved by the products which might demand the purchase of multiple brands. Because these causes are slow to change, the household's pattern of multibrand buying tends to persist for years or decades. Another group of reasons has to do with variation in price sensitivity. Consumers who are sensitive to small differences in price will usually purchase more brands than those who are not. The price sensitivity of a household is also a cause which tends to persist over years.

Product differences, clearly an important determinant of choices among brands, are hypothesized to be a minor factor in changing patterns of multibrand use. Except for a few significant and infrequent changes, such as the introduction of oat bran cereals or liquid detergents, we do not expect product introductions to disrupt the number of brands a household buys or the overall purchase pattern to which they conform.

If this is so, a brand's consumer franchise could be decomposed into a relatively small number of stable cohorts. Within a cohort, consumers would adhere to the same pattern of interbrand buying and would exhibit the same strength of bond to the brand, but across cohorts there would be material differences and some cohorts would be much more valuable to a franchise than others. The revenues attributable to the brand's consumer franchise could be expressed as the sum of the revenues due to each cohort. We could assess the overall strength of a particular brand's franchise by asking whether the most valuable kinds of consumer group are well represented.

The Approach

The consumer characteristics identified in previous research—frequency of buying one brand, frequency of multibrand buying, and frequency of purchase on deal—seemed plausible dimensions to explore in the search for the structure of buyer types, but the general approach was more heuristic. We would study purchase sequences to look for recurring patterns of multibrand buying, and then to try to interpret them.

The method, in overview, was: (a) to look for stable brand buying patterns in scanner panel diaries across a number of product classes, (b) to form groups that conformed to these patterns, and (c) to find attitudinal correlates that would explain why the groups behaved differently.

At the start, then, the process was simply a hunt for patterns (Fig. 15.1).

Buyer #1	Buyer #2	Buyer #3
Folgers	Folgers	Hills Brothers ($)
Folgers	Folgers	Folgers ($)
Folgers	Brim	Sanka ($)
Folgers	Folgers	Folgers ($)
Folgers	Brim	Maxwell House ($)
Folgers	Folgers	Sanka ($)
Folgers	Brim	G.F. Intern. ($)
Folgers	Brim	Hills Bros. ($)
Folgers	Folgers	Brim ($)
Folgers	Brim	Folgers ($)
Folgers	Folgers	Hills Bros. ($)

FIG. 15.1. Three coffee purchase records.

Hundreds of diaries from one product category were scanned and hand-sorted into groups of households which seemed to be doing the same thing with respect to the number of brands bought and the pattern of switching among brands. No attention was paid to the particular brands bought, and there were no preconceptions of what should constitute a group. Over time a consensus began to emerge that seven buyer groups accounted for most of the variance, with an eighth small group to hold the nonconforming cases.

This process was repeated for four other product categories. The impressionistic judgment process used in the hand-sorts was then reduced to a set of formal rules. The rules were implemented as a computer program and were later used to classify purchase diaries from other product categories.

The buyer types that emerged were labeled and could be described as follows:

• Long Loyals	Buy one brand almost exclusively.
• Short Loyals	Buy more than one brand, but buy each in moderately long runs.
• Rotators	Buy several different brands one after the other or in short runs, seldom on deal.
• Deal Selectives	Buy generally on deal, choosing from among a limited set of brands.
• Name Brand Price Driven	Buy many different brands, generally on deal.
• Store Brand Price Driven	Buy mainly generics or private label brands.
• Light Users	Make so few purchases that no pattern can be reliably discerned.
• Transitionals	All others.

Table 15.1 is an illustration of how these rules were applied to four product categories, with cutoff points selected judgmentally for each category. Light users accounted for about 10% of category volume and 45% of consumers across

TABLE 15.1
Product Category Volumes by Consumer Type

	Detergent	*Coffee*	*Ketchup*	*Tissue*
Long Loyals	37	22	39	32
Short Loyals	7	11	5	4
Rotators	34	52	50	49
Deal Selective and Price Driven	13	1	1	12
Transitionals	9	14	6	3
	100%	100%	100%	100%

all categories. The other groups varied quite considerably from one category to another, as the distribution shows.

The proportion of unclassified cases (Transitionals) was respectably low for all product categories. The memberships of the groups appeared to be stable over the 2½ years of data used to construct them, suggesting that the categorization stemmed more from characteristics of the shoppers than the patterns of learning which might change over time.

Attitudinal Correlates

Are these patterns of buying merely artifactual or are they the result of stable dispositions toward the product category? A survey was undertaken to explore the attitudinal correlates of the behavioral regularities in several product categories. Information on past buying behavior was collected from a sample of supermarket shoppers and used to categorize them into approximately the buyer types observed in the scanner panel analyses. Their responses to a series of attitude questions were then gathered. The items included: (a) category practices, (b) category attitudes, (c) buying motives, (d) lifestyle battery, (e) demographics, (f) emotions, and (g) buying practices.

Having placed each respondent into one of the buyer type groups based on reasonably consistent responses to reported behavior questions, we then analyzed responses to factors constructed from the batteries of individual items by groups. Only four groups were sufficiently large to look at: (a) Long Loyals, (b) Rotators, (c) Deal Selectives, and (d) Name Brand Price Drivens. For these groups, however, pronounced differences in attitude and behavior were seen. The following discussion summarizes the important differences.

Long Loyals. The brand purchase behavior of Long Loyals is driven by three motives:

1. Many believe their brand is superior to other brands in a way that is meaningful to them (e.g., it is more convenient to use, performs better, and so on).
2. There is an element of habit and simplification to their loyalty. Many claim that they have fallen into the routine of just picking up the same brand each time, and shopping goes faster.
3. They have often developed strong emotional ties to their brands.

For these reasons, Long Loyals tend to express high involvement with their brands. They want them to be readily available and are unhappy to make substitutions. Some will forgo purchasing in the category altogether or make a special trip to another store.

Despite high brand involvement, they are not involved in the category. They tend to be both less aware of, and less likely to have tried, many of the other available brands. They display the least interest of any group in learning about new category innovations or new brands.

They are also the least price sensitive of any group. They often do not have a clear sense of what any of the brands in the category cost and are unwilling to go to the trouble of finding out. They usually only take advantage of coupons or deals for their own brands. They are less likely ever to use store brands or generics and have more negative perceptions of these brands. They have generally low awareness, trial, and preference for new brands.

Rotators.   The behavior of this group is driven predominantly by co-use (use of different brands for different tasks) or variety seeking. They indicate that they purchase multiple brands, shelve them all at home simultaneously, and rotate use across the entire inventory in response to need for variety or the demands of particular applications, occasions, or family members.

Like Long Loyals, Rotators have strong positive feelings about their brands. They seek high quality and associate it with particular brands, but their involvement is with a repertoire of brands. Like Long Loyals, they have a tendency to make brand decisions out of the store and to find this a boon to shopping simplification.

They are, however, more involved with the product category and are quite knowledgeable about the brands in the market. They are aware of and willing to try new brands. They are not price sensitive. They will take advantage of coupons and deals on their regular brands, but seldom use incentives to buy outside of their repertoire. They have relatively unfavorable opinions of store brands, generics, and other low-priced brands.

Deal Selectives.   This group has more of a price orientation than the previous two groups. They have a generally adequate knowledge of the prices of brands in the category, they check prices as they shop, and they are alert to deals and use coupons as much as possible. They will buy for inventory when one of their brands is on sale. They confine purchases, however, to a group of preferred brands drawn from category leaders, well-known name brands, and other brands of accepted quality.

This group is willing, when necessary, to pay full price for one of the brands in the preferred group. They have relatively strong positive feelings about these brands and think of themselves as brand loyal. Within the set of acceptable brands, however, they perceive minimal brand differences.

They know before they get to the store what brand they are going to buy, usually because they have a coupon available. Although they will change this selection if they find a good deal in the store, they have, in general, below-average interest in experimenting outside of their brand group and they tend not to buy impulsively.

Name Brand Price Driven.   This group has a strong price orientation. Their household income is no lower than that of other groups, and they do not perceive themselves to be financially deprived. Their motives to economize seem to be twofold:

1. Deals appeal to them. They do not like to appear to waste money. They want to be smart shoppers.
2. Most important, they perceive few differences among brands in the category. All name brands are of acceptable quality (although generally store brands and generics are not so regarded) so that brand choice is driven almost entirely by price and deal across most of the name brands in the category.

The lack of perceived brand differentiation is associated with little involvement in the category. Although they are often heavy users of the product category, they have little interest in the process of using the product and no emotional attachments to brands. Their involvement is with cost-saving strategies. In addition to monitoring the price environment, they will trade coupons with other shoppers. They indicate willingness to try a new brand simply because they have a coupon for it.

Application to Brands

The focus so far is on patterns within diaries of shoppers, and the result is a classification of shoppers. Our interest, however, is in a classification of the consumer franchise of a particular brand. Clearly, a brand can have different roles in the diaries of different members of the same buyer type, and some roles are more desirable than others. It is common, for example, for some of a brand's consumers to be Long Loyals without those consumers being loyal to the brand in question. They may, for example, be Long Loyal to another brand but have tried the focal brand just once. Therefore, we need to classify brands as well as consumers.

In our hand-sorting procedure we observed that a brand tends to be used in five different ways:

1. Dominant: Bought on an ongoing basis; much larger than any other brand in the diary.
2. Rotated: Bought on an ongoing basis; roughly equal in size to one or more other brands in the diary.
3. Occasional: Bought on an ongoing basis, but less often than other brands in the diary.
4. Short-termed: Bought for a brief period of time, then dropped.
5. Experimental: Bought once, not repeated.

Therefore, the franchise of a brand is specified by a matrix of 8 buyer types by 5 buying types. When the matrix for one brand within a category is compared to another, the results are often strikingly different. We have observed brands whose shares are roughly equal but whose franchises are constructed of very different buyer types. One brand might draw a disproportionate volume from Long Loyals, another might be skewed toward Rotators, and another from price prone groups.

Implications for the Management of Brands

It is clearly a good idea to have a large proportion of Long Loyal consumers in a brand's consumer franchise for two reasons: (a) they count for more revenue per consumer than any other group, and (b) they seem to be well insulated against competition. It may be (although this work cannot yet show it) that they require less marketing investment to keep. However, this research suggests that it is difficult to move consumers from one group to another. It suggests that group membership is the result of enduring characteristics of the shopper and is not a transitional condition. Consequently, there is no reason to think that the best use of marketing resources is to get consumers to join a profitable group. Rather, we should try to shift consumers within a group to a brand. It might be easier, for example, to shift the allegiance of Long Loyals from one brand to another than to persuade other consumers to be loyal. It may be even easier, and as useful, to increase a brand's frequency of use in a rotation pattern. Rotators are numerically the largest group in the categories we studied and the heaviest users. In the coffee category, Rotators bought 16% more coffee than the mean, whereas Long Loyals bought 5% more.

When each consumer in a data set is classified into one of the eight buyer groups and every brand purchase is classified into one of the five buying types, there is considerable diagnostic value in profiling a brand's sources of volume. Compare these three brand profiles (Figs. 15.2, 15.3, and 15.4).

	Dom.	Rot.	Occ.	S.T.	Exper.
Loyal	43	-	1	-	-
Rotator	4	25	2	-	1
Deal Selective	-	5	3	1	2
Price Driven	-	-	2	-	1
Transitional	-	-	1	2	3
Light User	3 (any purchase type)				

FIG. 15.2.   Percent of Brand *A* volume.

	Dom.	Rot.	Occ.	S.T.	Exper.
Loyal	14	-	1	-	1
Rotator	3	30	12	-	-
Deal Selective	-	21	5	-	1
Price Driven	-	1	3	1	1
Transitional	-	-	1	1	1
Light User	5 (any purchase type)				

FIG. 15.3.   Percent of Brand B volume.

In Fig. 15.2, Brand A draws nearly half its volume from Loyals for whom A is the chosen brand. In addition, it draws 29% of its volume from Rotators. Given what is known of the motivating of these two groups, the consumer franchise of this brand is a valuable asset.

In Fig. 15.3, Brand B exhibits a different pattern. It lacks a solid core of Loyals and makes up ¾ of its volume from Rotators and Deal Selectives. A significant amount of its volume comes in the form of occasional purchases. In these instances, the brand is bought by households which buy other brands more often. This franchise is clearly less attractive than that of Brand A.

In Fig. 15.4, Brand C derives most of its volume from price-sensitive consumers—Deal Selectives or Price Drivens. It generates most of its volume from occasional sequences or sequences which have already terminated. Thus, although the current share commanded by Brand C is essentially the same as Brand A, the lifetime value of this franchise must be computed on the assumption of a decline in its future share and on the expectation that the price of achieving even those sales will be paid in coupons and consumer price promotions.

	Dom.	Rot.	Occ.	S.T.	Exper.
Loyal	6	1	-	-	1
Rotator	2	12	4	-	-
Deal Selective	-	22	8	-	-
Price Driven	-	-	17	14	4
Transitional	-	-	-	4	3
Light User	2 (any purchase type)				

FIG. 15.4.   Percent of Brand C volume.

FUTURE RESEARCH PRIORITIES

As we see it, the most provocative research question posed by this work is the effect of marketing variables on brand switching within each buyer type. Common sense suggests that elasticity of response to advertising, for example, should be lower for loyal consumers than rotators. Our speculation is, however, that switching a loyal type from one brand to another may not be as difficult as, say, converting a rotator to a loyal. With a long data series, it should be possible to classify consumers according to their buyer types in a calibration period and then estimate the parameters of marketing variables in a choice model in a subsequent estimation period.

Another important question deals with the extent to which a buyer type is a stable characteristic of the buyer. Our data sample is too short to have tested for group membership stability using a calibration period approach. As longer data series become available, this issue can be revisited.

When we understand the cost of converting customers from one buyer type to another and the cost of inducing brand switching within a type, it may be possible to develop a lifetime valuation method for a brand's consumer franchise. Marketing expenditures can be decomposed into acquisition costs and consumer retention costs and set against the asset value generated by these investments.

CONCLUSION

The valuation of a brand's consumer franchise is a desirable objective for managers who want to understand the effects of marketing expenditures on the assets of the firm and not simply on the current year's income. Sales data tell how consumers have responded over a fixed interval of time. The lifetime value of the consumer base, by contrast, is an asset measure. It allows marketing expenditures to be judged by the criterion of efficiency in producing assets.

A consumer's lifetime value can be computed through (a) the development of historical consumer retention statistics, (b) marginal costs of the products sold, (c) promotional expenditures, and (d) pricing to the consumer. If consumers can be clustered into groups with similar retention rates and marginal promotion costs, the computation of lifetime value is likely to be more reliable.

This chapter suggests that groups with these properties can be formed by inspection of scanner data and that the attitudinal profiles of groups formed in this way are consistent with relatively enduring differences in motives and buying styles.

REFERENCES

Aaker, D. A. (1973). Toward a normative model of promotional decision making. *Management Science, 19*(6), 593–603.

Aaker, D. A. (1991). *Managing brand equity.* New York: The Free Press.

Blattberg, R. C., Buesing, T., Peacock, P., & Sen, S. (1978). Identifying the deal prone segment. *Journal of Marketing Research, 15*(3), 369–377.

Blattberg, R. C., & Neslin, S. A. (1990). *Sales promotion: Concepts, methods, and strategies.* Englewood Cliffs, NJ: Prentice-Hall.

Jacoby, J., & Chestnut, R. W. (1978). *Brand loyalty: Measurement, management.* New York: Wiley.

McAlister, L. (1986). *The impact of price promotions on a brand's market share, sales pattern, and profitability* (Report No. 86-110). Cambridge, MA: Marketing Science Institute.

Webster, F. E. (1965). The "deal-prone" consumer. *Journal of Marketing Research, 2*(2), 186–189.

Chapter 16

Cognitive Strength of Established Brands: Memory, Attitudinal, and Structural Approaches

Curtis P. Haugtvedt
Clark Leavitt
Wendy L. Schneier
Ohio State University

INTRODUCTION

The goal of advertising strategies, in many cases, is to create reactions to a brand that are relatively more favorable after exposure to the advertising message. Depending on the objective of a specific campaign, these reactions can range from increases in simple awareness to increases in attitude favorability and purchase intention. Advertising for brands is sometimes considered successful by managers when typical survey measures reveal that a brand is held in high positive regard by consumers and commands a loyal consumer following.

In this chapter, we suggest that in addition to continuous monitoring of typical performance measures, brand managers might also benefit from a careful analysis of factors that comprise the overall cognitive strength of a brand. That is, even though a brand may be successful on some basic dimensions, managers may be better able to maintain and enhance the strength of a brand by gaining an understanding of the cognitive factors underlying its strength. In addition, information regarding the overall strength of a brand may be useful in determining the overall value of a brand when businesses consider the purchase of a brand franchise.

Examination of academic journals and trade publications suggests that academicians and managers share a view that advertising needs to have some readily observable change in memory for a brand name, in memory for brand attributes, or in the extremity of attitudes in order to be considered effective. However, a unique challenge for advertisers and marketers of established and

247

well-known brands[1] is that advertising for such brands is unlikely to result in the same kinds of changes observed when advertising for unknown or new brands. That is, it may be unrealistic to expect additional advertising to significantly increase awareness or the extremity of existing positive attitudes toward established brands.[2] Thus, it is often unclear how to assess what continued advertising does or does not accomplish.

In the sections that follow, we argue that an important goal for continued advertising should be the creation of what we will characterize a *strong brand image*. Specifically, we suggest that managers of established brands need to examine the extent to which advertising and other promotions contribute in the development of brand memories and attitudes that: (a) remain highly salient and accessible, (b) persist over time without continued advertising exposure, (c) are more resistant to interference or competitive challenge, and (d) are more likely to guide purchase behavior. In our view, the relative rating of a brand in the aforementioned dimensions provides information about the overall strength of a brand. That is, performance on each of the dimensions can be considered indicators or correlates of an overall brand strength construct.

ADDITUDINAL CORRELATES OF STRENGTH

In many situations (e.g., grocery shopping), consumers make choices between a variety of brands where many brand names are physically present. In such situations, one of the most important variables influencing a consumer's choice may be the attitudes held for the different purchase alternatives. That is, when all else is equal, consumers will choose the brand for which they possess the most favorable attitude. Indeed, attitudes are seen as important guides to behavior by many theoretical frameworks (Fazio, 1986; Lutz, 1991; Petty & Cacioppo, 1986).

Interestingly, although the concept of attitude is easily defined as a positive or negative feeling about some person, object, or issue, the concept of attitude strength is much less frequently discussed and much less clearly defined by social psychologists and marketers. Yet, the strength of a consumer's brand attitude may be one of the most significant components of overall brand strength.

Although the ideal situation many marketers hope for is one in which consumer attitudes toward their own brand is significantly more positive than those

---

[1]By established brands, we mean those brands that, within a given consumer segment, are held in positive regard by consumers and command a high level of awareness. Such a designation is, of course, relative rather than absolute.

[2]Although the focus of our discussion is on positive brand images and attitudes, much of our discussion is also relevant to situations where individuals may possess negative attitudes toward a brand, service, issue, person, or object.

toward other brands, in many situations consumers possess very similar attitudes toward competing brands. That is, the same individual may possess and express equally positive attitudes toward two or more competing brands. In the same manner, two consumer segments may possess what appear to be equally positive attitudes toward the same brand (e.g., a score of 6 on a 7-point attitude scale). It is our contention, however, that these attitudes may differ in important ways with regard to dimensions related to strength and that these dimensions will also be important factors in determining behavior. These dimensions include:

1. The number and kind of cognitions supporting the attitude.
2. The persistence (relative lack of decay) of a positive brand attitude over time without continued advertising exposure.
3. The resistance of a brand attitude to changes in the face of counterpersuasive appeals (e.g., competing brands, negative brand evaluation information from other consumers or publications, etc.).
4. The speed with which an individual's positive feelings toward a brand come to mind when exposed to product displays or advertisements.

Early approaches to understanding attitude change emphasized that the learning and memory of persuasive arguments were critical determinants of initial attitude changes, as well as the maintenance of attitudes over time (Hovland, Janis, & Kelly, 1953). Research, however, failed to demonstrate that a significant correlation existed between amount of learning and persuasion (Greenwald, 1968). The cognitive response approach—which emphasized the importance of an individual's idiosyncratic cognitive reactions to a message as a basis for persuasion—was offered as an alternative to the message learning approach (e.g., Greenwald, 1968; Petty, Ostrom, & Brock, 1981). From the perspective of the cognitive response approach, attitudes that are supported by a large number of positive or bolstering thoughts would be considered stronger than equally positive attitudes supported by few or no positive thoughts.

Related to this point is the idea that two attitudes may be equal at one point in time but one of the attitudes will decay less over time in the absence of continued advertising. That is, a stronger attitude may show more persistence than a weaker attitude. One possible explanation for such greater persistence is that the existence of a larger number of supportive thoughts might prevent an individual from "forgetting" why they held a positive attitude toward the brand. Even if one or two reasons were "lost," others would remain. Importantly, the self-generated and elaborated nature of the thoughts may also make such information more memorable and salient than externally provided advertising information (Cialdini, Petty, & Cacioppo, 1981).

An often correlated but conceptually distinct aspect of attitudes that may most clearly represent attitude strength is the ability of an attitude to stay positive in the face of relatively stronger counterpersuasive attacks (Haugtvedt, 1989; Haugtvedt & Petty, 1992; Haugtvedt, Schumann, Schneier, & Warren, 1992). That is, a stronger brand attitude should be relatively more resistant to change in the face of higher levels of competitive challenge or counterpersuasive attacks than an equally positive though weaker brand attitude. Similar to their role in attitude persistence, the availability of self-generated supportive thoughts is also hypothesized to play an important role in mediating resistance to many kinds of attacks (Haugtvedt & Petty, 1992).

A final dimension of attitudes that is likely to be related to their strength is the speed with which the attitudes come to mind upon mere presentation of the attitude object. Fazio and his colleagues (Fazio, Powell, & Herr, 1983; Fazio, Powell, & Williams, 1989) suggested that the strength of an object-evaluation association is captured by the speed with which individuals are able to access their evaluation of an object from memory. That is, an individual may hold similar positive attitudes toward two attitude objects (e.g., brands), but the speed with which they are able to access the evaluations may be faster for one object (brand) than the other. Importantly, research suggests that attitudes which are more accessible (i.e., easily accessed from memory) are more likely to guide actual behavior, such as choice (e.g., Fazio, Powell, & Williams, 1989). Further, it appears that like attitude persistence and resistance, greater attitude accessibility may be conferred by greater elaboration or thought about an attitude object (Haugtvedt & Warren, 1992).

THE ROLE OF STRENGTH IN STIMULUS AND MEMORY-BASED CHOICE

As discussed, the relative strength of brand attitudes can play an important role in the choice process. Situations exist, however, where attitudes are either inaccessible or nondiagnostic for a particular choice task (Lynch, Marmorstein, & Weigold, 1988). In such situations, brand strength dimensions related to memory for brand-related information may be of critical importance. For instance, choice in real world settings is unlikely to be entirely stimulus based. That is, consumers may rarely encounter situations where all the choice alternatives are presented or all of the relevant information for a decision is at hand (Alba, Hutchinson, & Lynch, 1991).[3] When choice is memory based, in whole or in part, anything which influences the ease with which information is retrieved from memory has important implications for subsequent decision outcomes (Cf. Lynch & Srull, 1982).

---

[3]For an excellent review of existing research and suggestions for future research on how consumer memory may influence consumer choice, the interested reader is referred to the Alba, Hutchinson, & Lynch (1991) chapter in the *Handbook of Consumer Behavior*.

Existing theory and research offers some guidelines as to the processes by which brand memory strength may be increased. A consistent theme in such research is that greater elaboration of stimulus material at encoding and over repeated exposures is likely to increase memory strength. The general idea is that the more a consumer is able to associate new material or brand information with existing complex knowledge structures, the greater the likelihood that such material will not be easily lost in memory. That is, theoretical notions suggest that the primary cause of forgetting is not the "decay" of memory traces (Crowder, 1976), but rather the interference caused by competing associations, which reduces a consumer's ability to correctly recall information. Thus, it follows that the existence of a greater number of associations for a particular memory trace decreases the likelihood that the memory will be lost. These associations can include a large number of factors, including a wide variety of usage situations.

Memory correlates of brand strength may therefore include:

1. The likelihood of a consumer recalling a brand name when questioned about brands belonging to a particular category.
2. The ability of brand to be less susceptible to competitive interference effects (Alba & Chattopadhyay, 1985; Burke & Srull, 1988).
3. The likelihood of a brand being evoked in a wide range of situations in which the product might be used (Leavitt & Herren, 1992).

At a more general level, the concept of *image* is one way to characterize overall memories and attitudes toward brands. Like most psychological constructs, individuals have images because they are useful. Related to brands, the availability of particular images may facilitate the choice process. Images of brands can be activated either by external aids present in the situation—package displays, labels, lists, catalogs, and directories—or they can be activated from memory by means of cues that associate the brand with the situation.

The memorial function of images is clearest when thought of in terms of a two-stage model of choice:

1. At the time a choice is made, the initial stage of the process is the formation of a set of alternatives to choose from. This consideration or evoked set limits the probability of choosing any particular brand at the outset.
2. Choice probabilities are then based on the evaluation of the brands in the consideration set—evaluations that may also be memory based (Feldman & Lynch, 1988).[4]

---

[4]For a detailed discussion of how alternative cognitions in memory are used as inputs in memory-based or mixed judgments, the interested reader is referred to Feldman and Lynch (1988). For empirical evidence supportive of Feldman and Lynch's propositions, see Lynch, Marmorstein, and Wiegold (1988) and Biehal and Chakravarti (1983).

The role of memory in making a brand part of the consideration set is often overlooked in research on consumer choice. Most academic studies of choice begin by providing the subjects with the alternatives to be evaluated, as well as the attributes on which the evaluation is made. This kind of choice situation seems to be quite different from the kind of choice situation in which consumers often find themselves. In such memory-based situations, the ability to recall the alternatives is an important determinant of choice probabilities. For instance, Nedungadi (1990) demonstrated that the probability of choosing a brand can be changed without changing its evaluation, simply by changing its likelihood of entering the consideration set.

Brand and product images, then, may be part of a larger structure whose function is to prepare the consumer to deal with life situations. Components of the image serve to link the brand name and features of the brand with choice situations where memory plays a part. Memory research emphasizes how matches between cues present at the time of information encoding and the cues present at the time of information recall can enhance the role of memory in judgment and choice. This appears to be a promising direction for future research (Keller, 1987; Tulving & Thomson, 1973).

In the case of memory-based choice, brands with images with a wider array of associations may be more effective from both the advertiser's and the consumer's point of view. Cues that call up the brand in any particular situation—point of purchase, point of use, point of recommendation—require an image with greater associations. As the strength of memory for a brand image increases, the likelihood of memory-based choice of the brand also increases.

We suggested earlier that attitude accessibility and attitude resistance may also be ways in which to gauge the strength of a brand image. The notion that accessibility of evaluation can be greater for one brand than another has important implications for consumer choice, especially when one considers that more accessible attitudes may automatically guide behavior in some situations (Fazio, 1986; Fazio, Powell, & Williams, 1989). On the other hand, in situations where a consumer is likely to deliberate and think about options when making a choice, the ability of a brand attitude to resist change when attacked by claims of other brands or discussed with salespeople becomes important.

The challenge of strengthening memory and attitudes for well-established brands is unique because of multiple exposures to advertisements and products in consumer's lives. Typical laboratory studies on attitudes have focused on issues of change rather than strength. In addition, exposure to stimulus materials in a laboratory setting has little relation to the amount of exposure to such materials in consumer settings. In the following section, we examine some theoretical possibilities for the impact of multiple exposures.

STRUCTURAL APPROACHES TO STRENGTH

The discussions of brand memory strength and brand attitude strength suggest that cognitive structure may play an important role in determining the overall cognitive strength of a brand. This is not surprising, given that a consumer's image of a brand includes all the components associated with a brand, including memories, attitudes, beliefs, schemas, scripts, and expectations. The structural dimensions that we consider in the following sections are based on an analogy to theoretical notions from personality and stereotyping research. We believe the idea that individuals can have rather simple or complex cognitive structures with regard to a particular object, class of objects, persons, or ideas, may have important implications for assessing, maintaining, and enhancing the strength of a brand in the consumer's mind.

One of the unique aspects of established brands is the fact that consumers have been exposed to them over a long period of time—via advertising and sometimes via product experience. Consequences of such exposure may vary from the development of a simplified brand-image structure to a more complex, varied, and enriched image structure. Advertising factors and/or the nature of the product may influence the kind of cognitive structure individuals form. That is, only a very narrow range of factors may underlie the positive attitudes toward a brand in some cases, whereas a larger set of more diverse factors may underlie liking for a brand in other cases. Understanding the kind and extent of structures underlying an image may have important implications regarding the maintenance and development of brand strength.

Researchers in psychology have attempted to examine how underlying structural factors relate to individual's attitudes. In this kind of work, the extent of belief differentiation and/or evaluative consistency are examined for their relationship to the individual's overall attitude. Differentiation is assessed by the number of belief dimensions used by an individual in thinking about an object or class of objects. The extent to which evaluative implications of different beliefs are consistent with each other serves as an assessment of evaluative consistency (Azjen, 1989).

In general, research in psychology has shown that the greater the differentiation of the belief system, the less the evaluative consistency (Scott, 1969). Related to this observation are findings, from research on group stereotypes, that the more complex one's beliefs, the less extreme one's evaluation (Linville, 1982). Extrapolating from such research to the marketing situation, one might be tempted to conclude that a more complex structure underlying a consumer's perception of a brand might be associated with a less extreme (i.e., less positive) attitude. Although such a relationship may be observed with existing brands, it is important to point out a critical difference between existing psychology research and the case in marketing. That is, the psychology research has typically examined cases where there is likely to be a mixture of both positive and negative beliefs about an object or group. Marketers and advertisers, on the other hand, may often be able to control the kind of beliefs (or at least the salience of certain beliefs) that come to mind when thinking about a brand. The ideal marketing situation, we suggest, may be the creation of a brand image that is complex and differentiated but evaluatively consistent. In such a case, individuals may develop and possess what we consider extreme positive strong attitudes.

DEVELOPMENT OF STRUCTURE

In the following discussion, we characterize more complex image structures as *multiplex* and less complex image structures as *simplex*. The terms multiplexity and simplexity were used by Krech, Crutchfield, & Ballachey (1962) to refer to structural states resulting from encounters with an object over time. From this perspective, the structure of the image consumers possess for a brand arises from repeated experiences on the various occasions in which the brand has been used, seen, or mentioned. High in importance among these events are the advertising messages about the brand to which they have been exposed. At least two variables related to advertising strategy may influence the development of relatively simplex or multiplex brand images: (a) the nature of the repetition itself, and (b) the way that the audience responds to each of the advertising messages.

Development of Simplexity

Simple forgetting offers insight into one course of development of image structure over time. When an object is encountered, the mental image created on the original occasion shows systematic changes in the absence of further exposure to the object, if memory is tested at varying time intervals. The less important parts of a structure drop out and the overall organization changes by leveling, sharpening, or assimilation (e.g., Wulf, 1922). Leveling refers to the simplification of the figure as a whole, sharpening to the emphasis on one central feature, and assimilation to the tendency to make the figure more like some standard or norm.

Memory for an event may show a simplification of the structure of the original impression for two reasons: (a) the basic gestalt forces of organization, and (b) the tendency to relate the image to some preexisting schema. Repeated exposure of the original object can reinforce the tendency to assimilate each exposure to the preestablished image. Both direct experience with the product itself and experience through advertising may produce a more simplex image by emphasizing the same features at each encounter.

Development of Multiplexity

Repeated exposure also might move the brand image in the opposite direction, toward multiplexity, if explicitly designed for this purpose. Learning has been construed by some (e.g., Gibson, 1949) as a process of progressive differentiation. Each encounter with an object may be seen as an opportunity to distinguish different aspects or features of the object or different types of objects. One implication of this perspective is that simply repeating a message without variation will produce simplexity, whereas systematically varying a message may facilitate multiplex-like associations. Consistent with ideas presented in recent research on advertising repetition (Schumann, Petty, & Clemons, 1990), the same advertisements may be repeated or varied on mainly cosmetic (product endorsers or ad execution factors) or substantive (the kind of information presented about a brand) dimensions. In such a framework, it is possible to think about multiplex images based mainly on cues associated with a brand as well as multiplex images based on more differentiated arguments for liking the brand. Similarly, one can think of simplex images based mainly on a brand associated with a limited range of cues or presented with only the same small number of brand attributes. Initial research on the influence that simplex and multiplex structures may have on attitude persistence and attitude resistance suggests that such distinctions may be important in understanding the construct of brand strength (Haugtvedt, Schumann, Schneier, & Warren, 1992).

AN EXISTING POSITIVE ATTITUDE AS AN ASSET AND A LIABILITY

In the last decade, approaches to understanding processes underlying attitude formation and change have been usefully guided by Petty and Cacioppo's (1986) Elaboration Likelihood Model (ELM). In brief, the ELM characterizes attitude change as the result of the relative operation of one of two routes to persuasion. In some situations, or for certain kinds of persons,[5] attitude change may be based on careful evaluation of product relevant attributes. Attitude change, in such cases, would be based on the kinds of the thoughts stimulated by such evaluations. In other situations, or for other certain kinds of persons, attitude change may be based more on simple inferences or positive cue associations and less or no evaluation of product-relevant attributes. The former case is characterized as the *central route to persuasion*, the latter case the *peripheral route to persuasion*. Importantly, as suggested by our earlier discussions, following either route could result in the development of attitudes that appear iden-

---

[5]See Haugtvedt, Petty, & Cacioppo (1992) for an example of an individual-difference approach to understanding consumer attitude change processes.

tical with only surface-level examination. However, initial research on persistence and resistance of attitudes has shown that new attitudes created via central route processes tend to be stronger than new attitudes created via peripheral route processes (Haugtvedt, 1989; Haugtvedt & Petty, 1992; Haugtvedt, Schumann, Schneier, & Warren, 1992).

Earlier in the chapter we suggested that an important goal of advertising for well-established brands should be the maintenance and enhancement of brand strength. This leads to an interesting consideration. One of the common factors in virtually all existing persuasion research has been the use of counterattitudinal appeals. That is, the goal of past persuasion research has typically been to examine the roles different variables played in changing attitudes from negative to positive. In the case of existing well-established brands, however, consumers typically approach the persuasive appeals with preexisting positive attitudes.

Throughout the chapter, a common theme has been the role of greater elaboration in enhancing strength. Interestingly, however, the fact that an individual approaches a persuasive appeal with a positive attitude may actually make it more difficult to obtain greater elaboration of product relevant attributes via typical advertising strategies. Even if an individual engaged in effortful elaboration during initial encounters with advertising for a brand, once such positive attitudes are formed, individuals may be unlikely to engage in such effortful processing or to think about the basis for their positive attitude in later encounters with advertising or promotional stimuli for the same brand. That is, the existence of a positive attitude may actually reduce or bias the elaborative processing of additional advertising for the brand. A consumer is aware that he or she already likes the brand and, therefore, will avoid investing cognitive resources in elaboration. Indeed, this is one of the reasons theorists have suggested that individuals come to hold attitudes—they free us from constant evaluative effort.

CREATING AND MAINTAINING STRONG IMAGES

Greenwald and Leavitt (1985) suggested that even if messages are processed at an elaborative level initially, repetition leads to regression of control. That is, even if an advertisement or product experience induced the development of a multiplex structure, repetition and future exposures to the brand may be processed at a more automatic level. Structure, we suggest, may drift toward simplexity unless executional or other factors occasionally push processing toward more elaboration.

An avenue worthy of exploration in future research may be the determination of the kinds of advertising strategies that encourage the *reactivation* and *reinvigoration* of the cognitive structures underlying positive brand images. Such strategies might include the influence of how advertisements are framed—that is, getting persons to think that an ad will be contrary to their preexisting attitude (thereby increasing processing motivation) and then presenting supportive brand information. Alternatively, research might explore the influence of "mild challenges"—promotions that encourage individuals to access and use their own cognitive responses to defend their positive attitudes. Importantly, neither kind of approach need reduce the extremity of individuals' positive attitudes toward a brand.[6] Instead, by increasing the accessibility and salience of why individuals hold positive brand attitudes, they should increase brand strength.

Advertising objectives for well-established brands, in our view, should focus on an analysis of the cognitive structures underlying the favorable perceptions and high levels of awareness. Advertising strategies for such brands should aim for changes in the dimensions discussed. Depending on the goal of the advertiser and the manager, strength can be achieved and maintained via either a simplex or multiplex approach. However, as with any strategic suggestion, there are tradeoffs to consider.

For example, a unidimensional or simplex structure may be easier to achieve, and it is commonly stated as an advertising goal (Martin, 1989). Frequent repetition of single-theme campaigns and brand use in a limited range of situations may contribute to the development of simplex structures. The cost of developing or maintaining a simplex brand structure may be less because of lower advertising development costs. It is important to keep in mind, however, that simplex images may be more vulnerable to flanking attack or gradual tidal changes in the way the product is likely to be used. A simplex structure may be strong when only a few aspects of a product are important and where choice is stimulus based.

Multiplex structures are more differentiated, and there may be more elements associated with the brand. Such a differentiated and elaborated structure may stem from more varied experience with the brand by the consumer—including experience guided by advertising (Deighton, 1984; Hoch & Ha, 1986; Puto & Wells, 1984). Because of the multiple associations, the brand name is more likely to come to mind in a variety of situations. In addition, because of multiple cognitive links and personal elaborations regarding attributes, such a brand may be less susceptible to competitive attack—that is, a multiplex-based structure may be more resistant to change.

A consideration for managers and advertisers, therefore, is the kind of strategy

---

[6]The former example is consistent with research on inoculation theory by McGuire (1964), in which he examined ways in which attitudes could be made more resistant to attack by training persons how to respond to an attack. The latter example draws on the ELM notion that individuals whose attitudes are formed or changed via the central route will naturally marshall their own cognitive responses to defend their attitudes. For further discussion on the relationship between McGuire's work and the ELM, see Haugtvedt (1989) and Haugtvedt & Petty (1992).

best suited for a particular brand. Why would one choose to create simplex rather than multiplex structures? One consideration may be the breadth of attributes available for the brand or product category. If only a narrow range of uses or attributes is available, a simplex approach may suffice. In addition, there is some suggestion that extreme performance on the few considered attributes leads to a more extreme evaluation. On the other hand, a multiplex approach may be desirable when a product possesses a wide array of important features and when the possibility of doing well on many of the commonly considered features is high.

Determining whether a multiplex or simplex structure may be more cost effective or beneficial for a given brand may require research into the behavior surrounding the brand, especially with regard to the conditions under which choice occurs. Brands for which the choice occasion is supported by stimulus-based information may have less need for an image that requires "built-in" cues to call the brand and its attributes to mind. Choosing from a vending machine, for example, requires only the evaluation of clearly presented alternatives. Moreover, if the evaluation is based purely on a single evaluative dimension, such as taste, a strong simplex structure will be effective. On the other hand, when the product is capable of being used in a variety of situations, a different set of situationally specific cues may be needed to evoke the brand in each situation. Following the implications of the encoding specificity hypotheses, situationally specific attributes will need to be part of the image if the evaluation is memory based.

SUMMARY

We began the chapter with a discussion of how advertising objectives for well-known and established brands may be quite different than those for new or less well-known brands. It was suggested that traditional measures of advertising effectiveness, such as changes in awareness or changes in evaluation (e.g., from negative or neutral to positive), are of little diagnostic value in understanding the effectiveness of advertising for such brands. Instead of traditional measures, we suggested that advertisers and managers of existing brands might benefit by examining the cognitive strength of the brands. As a starting point for a discussion of the concept of strength, we suggested that existing brands could be analyzed for the strength of memory and strength of evaluation. After briefly exploring the importance of attitude and memory strength in consumer choice and competitive environments, we suggested that the structures underlying memory and attitude may be critical in determining their performance on the measures of strength outlined. The concepts of simplex and multiplex structure were introduced to illustrate alternative structural dimensions underlying memory and evaluation. In addition, we hypothesized that homogeneous and invariant advertising and/or product experience may contribute to the development of a simplex structure, whereas varied advertising and multiple use settings may lead to the development of a multiplex structure.

In summary, in today's competitive marketplace, careful monitoring of brand performance is necessary for competitive survival and continued profitability. In addition to traditional measures of brand strength and performance, businesses might benefit from an examination of the cognitive strength of brands they already own or brand franchises they might consider purchasing. Information gained from such examinations may result in more complete information regarding the influence of promotional strategies and more insight as to why a brand may be successful. In addition, such information may enable a manager to discern weaknesses in the cognitive strength of a brand before a brand franchise loses strength in other dimensions.

ACKNOWLEDGMENTS

Preparation of this chapter was facilitated by summer research support provided to Curtis P. Haugtvedt from the Ohio State University Department of Marketing. The authors thank Alex Biel, David Boush, Larry Lockshin, Jeff Kasmer, David W. Schumann, and Deepak Sirdeshmukh for comments on an earlier draft.

REFERENCES

Alba, J. W., & Chattopadhyay, A. (1985). The effects of context and part-category cues on the recall of competing brands. *Journal of Marketing Research, 22,* 340–349.
Alba, J. W., Hutchinson, J. W., & Lynch, J. G. (1991). Memory and decision making. In T. S. Robertson & H. H. Kassarjian (Eds.), *Handbook of consumer behavior* (pp. 1–49). Englewood Cliffs, NJ: Prentice-Hall.
Azjen, I. (1989). Attitude structure and behavior. In A. J. Pratkanis, S. J. Breckler, & A. G. Greenwald (Eds.), *Attitude structure and function* (pp. 241–274). Hillsdale, NJ: Lawrence Erlbaum Associates.
Biehal, G., & Chakravarti, D. (1983). Information accessibility as a moderator of consumer choice. *Journal of Consumer Research, 10,* 1–14.
Burke, R. R., & Srull, T. K. (1988). Competitive interference and consumer memory for advertising. *Journal of Consumer Research, 15,* 55–68.
Cialdini, R. B., Petty, R. E., & Cacioppo, J. T. (1981). Attitude and attitude change. *Annual Review of Psychology, 32,* 357–404.
Crowder, R. G. (1976). *Principles of learning and memory.* Hillsdale, NJ: Lawrence Erlbaum Associates.
Deighton, J. (1984). The interaction of advertising and evidence. *Journal of Consumer Research, 11,* 763–770.
Fazio, R. H. (1986). How do attitudes guide behavior? In R. M. Sorrentino & E. T. Higgins (Eds.), *Handbook of motivation and cognition* (Vol. 1, pp. 204–243). New York: Guilford Press.
Fazio, R. H., Powell, M. C., & Herr, P. M. (1983). Toward a process model of attitude-behavior relation: Accessing one's attitude upon mere observation of the attitude object. *Journal of Personality and Social Psychology, 44,* 723–735.

Fazio, R. H., Powell, M. C., & Williams, C. J. (1989). The role of attitude accessibility in the attitude-to-behavior process. *Journal of Consumer Research, 16*, 280–288.

Feldman, J. M., & Lynch, J. G. (1988). Self-generated validity and other effects of measurement on belief, attitude, intention, and behavior. *Journal of Applied Psychology, 73*, 421–435.

Gibson, E. J. (1949). A systematic application of the concepts of generalization and differentiation to verbal learning. *Psychological Review, 47*, 196–229.

Greenwald, A. G. (1968). Cognitive learning, cognitive response in persuasion, and attitude change. In A. G. Greenwald, T. C. Brock, & T. M. Ostrom (Eds.), *Psychological foundations of attitudes* (pp. 147–170). New York: Academic Press.

Greenwald, A. G., & Leavitt, C. (1985). Cognitive theory and audience involvement. In L. F. Alwitt & A. Mitchell (Eds.), *Psychological processes and advertising effects* (pp. 221–240). Hillsdale, NJ: Lawrence Erlbaum Associates.

Haugtvedt, C. P. (1989). Persistence and resistance of communication-induced attitude changes. In D. W. Schumann (Ed.), *Proceedings of the Society for Consumer Psychology* (pp. 111–113). Knoxville, TN: The University of Tennessee.

Haugtvedt, C. P., & Petty, R. E. (1992). Personality and persuasion: Need for cognition moderates the persistence and resistance of attitude changes. *Journal of Personality and Social Psychology, 62*, 308–319.

Haugtvedt, C. P., Petty, R. E., & Cacioppo, J. T. (1992). Need for cognition and advertising: Understanding the role of personality variables in consumer behavior. *Journal of Consumer Psychology, 3*, 239–260.

Haugtvedt, C. P., Schumann, D. W., Schneier, W. L., & Warren, W. L. (1992). *Advertising repetition and variation strategies: Implications for Attitude Strength* (working paper). College of Business, Ohio State University, Columbus, OH.

Haugtvedt, C. P., & Warren, W. L. (1992). *Attitude change processes and attitude accessibility: Implications for persistence, resistance, and behavior guide roles of attitudes in consumer choice settings* (working paper). College of Business, Ohio State University, Columbus.

Hoch, S. J., & Ha, Y. (1986). Consumer learning: Advertising and the ambiguity of product experience. *Journal of Consumer Research, 13*, 221–233.

Hovland, C. I., Janis, I., & Kelly, H. H. (1953). *Communication and persuasion*. New Haven, CT: Yale University Press.

Keller, K. L. (1987). Memory factors in advertising: The effect of advertising retrieval cues on brand evaluations. *Journal of Consumer Research, 14*, 316–333.

Krech, D., Crutchfield, R. S., & Ballachey, E. L. (1962). *Individual in society*. New York: McGraw-Hill.

Leavitt, C., & Herren, T. (1992). *Brand image and brand awareness* (working paper.) College of Business, Ohio State University, Columbus, OH.

Linville, P. W. (1982). The complexity-extremity effect and age-based stereotyping. *Journal of Personality and Social Psychology, 42*, 193–211.

Lynch, J. G., Marmorstein, H., & Weigold, M. F. (1988). Choices from sets including remembered brands: Use of recalled attributes and prior overall evaluations. *Journal of Consumer Research, 15*, 225–233.

Lynch, J. G., & Srull, T. K. (1982). Memory and attentional factors in consumer choice: Concepts and research methods. *Journal of Consumer Research, 9*, 18–37.

Lutz, R. J. (1991). The role of attitude theory in marketing. In H. H. Kassarjian & T. S. Robertson (Eds.), *Perspectives in consumer behavior* (pp. 317–339). Englewood Cliffs, NJ: Prentice-Hall.

Martin, D. N. (1989). *Romancing the brand*. New York: AMACOM.

McGuire, W. J. (1964). Inducing resistance to persuasion: Some contemporary approaches. In L. Berkowitz (Eds.), *Advances in experimental social psychology* (Vol. 1, pp. 191–229). New York: Academic Press.

Nedungadi, P. (1990). Recall and consumer consideration sets: Influencing choice without altering brand evaluations. *Journal of Consumer Research, 17*, 263–276.

Petty, R. E., & Cacioppo, J. T. (1986). *Communication and persuasion: Central and peripheral routes to attitude change*. New York: Springer-Verlag.

Petty, R. E., Ostrom, T. M., & Brock, T. C. (1981). Historical foundations of the cognitive response approach to attitudes and persuasion. In R. E. Petty, T. M. Ostrom, & T. C. Brock (Eds.), *Cognitive responses in persuasion* (pp. 1–29). Hillsdale, NJ: Lawrence Erlbaum Associates.

Puto, C. P., & Wells, W. D. (1984). Informational and transformational advertising: The differential effects in time. In T. C. Kinnear (Ed.), *Advances in consumer research* (pp. 638–648). Ann Arbor: Association for Consumer Research.

Scott, W. A. (1969). Structure of natural cognitions. *Journal of Personality and Social Psychology, 12*, 261–278.

Schumann, D. W., Petty, R. E., & Clemons, D. S. (1990). Predicting the effectiveness of different strategies of advertising variation: A test of the repetition variation hypotheses. *Journal of Consumer Research, 17*, 192–202.

Tulving, E., & Thomson, D. M. (1973). Encoding specificity and retrieval processes in episodic memory. *Psychological Review, 80*, 352–373.

Wulf, F. (1922). Uber die Veranderung von Vorstellungen [About the change of ideas]. (Gedachtnis und Gestalt [Memory and Form].) *Psychol. Forsch., 1*, 333–373.

Chapter 17

The Dual Structure of Brand Associations

Peter H. Farquhar
The Claremont Graduate School

Paul M. Herr
University of Colorado, Boulder

INTRODUCTION

A well-known brand can enhance the perceived value of a product. For example, a brand can assure customers of consistent product quality, differentiate the product from competitive offerings, or facilitate customers' purchase decisions. In many cases, the principal source of a brand's added value is the set of associations customers hold in memory.

Most brands evoke several types of associations. For instance, a brand may be associated with the product categories bearing its name, as well as the usage situations for which it is appropriate. Likewise, a brand may be associated with specific product attributes, related customer benefits, and various summary evaluations. Figure 17.1 illustrates different types of brand associations (cf. Aaker, 1991).

The Dove brand illustrates the associations in Fig. 17.1. Dove is associated with several product categories, including soap, ice cream, and others. Its specific positioning in the soap category is as a "beauty bar." The associated product attribute of "one-quarter moisturizing cream" supports the customer benefit "doesn't dry your skin." This benefit is important for the usage situation "facial cleansing." Together, these core associations position the Dove brand relative to competing soap products and enhance its perceived value with customers.

Brand management involves two complementary activities:

1. *Brand building* focuses on creating a brand image that is easy for customers to remember and on fostering the brand's core associations consistently over

FIG. 17.1.   Types of brand associations.

time (Aaker, 1991; Farquhar, 1989). Such core associations also affect a brand's ability to stretch beyond its initial use to other products in the same line or in related categories (Aaker & Keller, 1990; Tauber, 1981, 1988).

2. *Brand leveraging* is also an important marketing activity, because many brands are explicitly developed as platforms for later extensions. No longer do marketing managers ask whether or not to extend a brand. The relevant question is often, "How far can we reasonably stretch the brand?"

The recent emphasis on brand leveraging is motivated by several considerations: (a) the relatively high costs of launching and building a new brand, (b) the unavailability of satisfactory trademarks in some markets, and (c) strong competition for distribution within the trade. Leveraging an established brand helps to overcome many of these difficulties. Moreover, stretching the brand to other products can reinforce the core associations, strengthen and expand the customer franchise, and build the overall business.[1]

A key factor in deciding how far to stretch a brand is to determine the boundaries of a brand's core associations (Aaker & Keller, 1990; Farquhar, Han, Herr, and Ijiri, 1992). In this chapter, we distinguish the orientation of brand associations (i.e., either the associate-to-brand direction or the brand-to-associate direction). We show that this dual nature of brand associations is an essential part of determining the limits of a brand's stretch. Unfortunately, many research studies neglect the directionality of brand associations or confuse one direction with another.

---

[1]On the other hand, brands stretched too far (even if successful) risk diluting the core associations and eroding the customer base (John & Loken, 1990; Keller & Aaker, 1992; Ries & Trout, 1986).

BRAND ASSOCIATIONS

Associative Networks

An *associative network* provides a convenient representation of brand information in semantic memory.[2] Such networks consist of "nodes," corresponding to brands and their associates, and "links" that connect pairs of nodes associated in some way. Activating one node in memory presumably leads to the activation of a linked node, with a likelihood reflecting the strength of association between the two nodes. Thus association strength reflects the "semantic relatedness" between two nodes in a network. Alba, Hutchinson, and Lynch (1990) and Collins and Loftus (1975) further described aspects of associative network models of consumer memory.

Brand building activities focus on establishing favorable attitudes and strengthening the relationship from the brand to a particular category, product attribute, customer benefit, or usage situation. Herr and Fazio (in press) noted that favorable attitudes for a brand are not sufficient to guide customer perceptions and purchase behavior—attitudes must be readily accessible from memory.[3]

Brand leveraging activities, on the other hand, must consider the strength of existing associations directed towards the brand (Farquhar, Herr, & Fazio, 1990; Herr, Farquhar, & Fazio, 1992). For example, the product category "greeting cards" is strongly associated with the Hallmark brand; the usage situation "washing windows" likely evokes the Windex brand; the product attribute "baking soda" is at the core of the Arm & Hammer brand; the customer benefit "mildness" belongs to Ivory. In trying to create new associations for brand extensions, the strengths of these existing directional associations limit the stretchability of the brands.

Directional Associations

The semantic relatedness between two nodes in an associative network might be represented by either a nondirectional relation or a pair of directional rela-

---

[2]Associative models offer quite general representations of semantic memory. For example, Collins and Loftus (1975) noted, "Any process that can be represented in a feature model is representable in a network model" (p. 410). Estes (1991) showed that a trace model of memory is homologous with networks of associative models. Further research on associative models is found in Collins and Quillian (1969), Raaijmakers and Shiffrin (1981), and Smith and Medin (1981).

[3]Meyer and Schvaneveldt (1971) and Posner and Snyder (1975) observed that if associations are particularly strong, the activation of one node automatically activates its associate. Fazio, Sanbonmatsu, Powell, and Kardes (1986) demonstrated that an attitude can be activated automatically upon mere observation of an object and that the resulting process culminates in behavior consistent with the stored evaluations. Fazio, Powell, and Williams (1989) further examined the effects of *attitude accessibility* on consumer choice behavior.

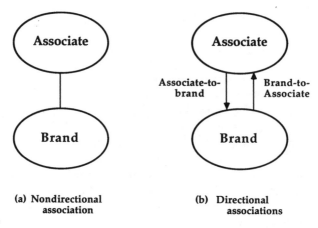

**(a) Nondirectional   (b) Directional
        association   associations**

FIG. 17.2.   Nondirectional and directional associations.

tions. Figure 17.2 illustrates both cases for a brand and some associate, such as a category, situation, attribute, or benefit. If the strengths of these directional relations are not equal, the network must distinguish the orientation of the links.[4] Even small asymmetries in association strength can make a large difference in the managerial recommendations drawn from these models.

Moreover, both directional associations can be important even when only one appears to be so. In categorization studies, a subject might be asked to classify an instance A as belonging or not belonging to category B (e.g., True or false: A robin is a bird.). Collins and Loftus criticized the assumption that "memory search to make a categorization judgment proceeds from the instance to the category" (1975, p. 410). They added that "the search proceeds from both the instance and the category in parallel. However, if one or the other is presented first, this gives the search from that node a head start, which is the notion of priming" (p. 410). Thus, in searching memory, the spreading activation of nodes requires specific orientations for the associations that link nodes.

Heading in the Right Direction

Brand managers need to distinguish between: (a) those directional associations that start from the brand and spread outward (*brand-to-associate relations*), and (b)

---

[4]For example, Tversky and Gati (1978) showed that similarity is not a symmetric measure of semantic relatedness. Most consumers regard Dr. Pepper as more similar to Coca-Cola than Coke is to Dr. Pepper. Likewise, the brand Dove is regarded as more similar to the product category "soap," than "soap" is to Dove.

the reciprocal associations that start at some outside node and move inward to the brand (*associate-to-brand relations*). It is easy to confuse the two.[5]

Both directions are important in brand leveraging. For instance, Tauber (1981) described a brand extension search process that (a) starts with the brand, (b) generates its various associations, and then (c) identifies related product categories for possible extensions. This process helps to find target categories that fit with the brand—that is, categories of products that consumers would likely expect from the brand.

This brand-to-associate relation is also found in consumer research studies on typicality. *Typicality* is defined as the degree to which an instance represents a category. Representativeness is often measured by asking subjects to judge "how good an example" an instance is of its category (Rosch & Mervis, 1975).[6] Collins and Loftus (1975) explained how such measures of typicality can obscure the orientation of brand associations. Such measures can lead to mistaken inferences about consumer behavior. For example, Loken and Ward explained, ". . . If a consumer decides to buy a product from a particular category (e.g., 'white table wine') but is not sufficiently motivated to compare specific brands, the consumer might tend to choose whatever brand is typical because it is easier to recall" (1990, p. 111).

This particular choice prediction depends little on a brand's typicality or the brand-to-category association because the purchase goal is already decided. Therefore, the category "white table wine" is activated first, and an asymmetry is thus created between the directional associations. In such cases, the category-to-brand association is more predictive of brand recall than the reciprocal association (see Ashcraft, 1978; Barsalou, 1983; Loftus, 1973).

Another problem is misinterpreting the orientation of a brand association. By way of informal definition, Tauber said, "*Leverage* is when the consumer,

---

[5]More serious problems can occur when the directionality of the brand associations is not even considered. For example, Rangaswamy, Burke, and Oliva (1992) modeled a consumer's utility for a given product i as

$$U(\text{Product } i) = U(A_i) + U(B_i) + U(A_i \cdot B_i),$$

where (a) $U(A_i)$ represents the part-utility of product i's tangible attributes, (b) $U(B_i)$ represents the part-utility from the brand name on product i, and (c) $U(A_i \cdot B_i)$ "represents the value consumers attach to the links between the brand name and its category dependent attributes" (p. 7). Use of a nondirectional interaction term $U(A_i \cdot B_i)$ ignores the possible asymmetry of directional brand associations. A properly specified model might require two interaction terms—one for each directional link in Fig. 17.2(b).

With their nondirectional model, Rangaswamy, Burke, and Oliva reported the results of several previous studies on typicality and associative strength as exactly the opposite of the effects observed. Their model also gives contradictory recommendations for brand managers (see Herr & Farquhar, 1992).

[6]On the other hand, Barsalou (1983, 1985) pointed out that product categories exist to achieve customers' goals. *Graded structure* is defined as the degree to which an instance satisfies the goal of a category. The "ideal" in the category is the instance that best serves the goal.

by simply knowing the brand, can think of important ways that they perceive the new brand extension would be better than competing products in the category'' (1988, p. 28). Aaker (1991, p. 232) operationalized this definition by asking consumers "to provide an overall evaluation of the brand extension on the basis of just the name." Although the brand-to-associate relation is appropriate for measuring the fit of a brand with an extended category, this directional relation is the opposite of what is needed for measuring leverage.

Later in the same article, Tauber clarified that leverage is determined by what the brand "owns." An associate is owned by a brand if, in mentioning the associate, the brand immediately comes to mind. Thus "photography" is owned by the Kodak brand, and "bleach" is owned by the Clorox brand. Therefore, it is the strength of the associate-to-brand relationship that determines what a brand owns.

These examples emphasize to both consumer researchers and brand managers the importance of recognizing the dual structure of brand associations. One must be careful to distinguish the proper orientation of brand associations in assessing prospective brand extensions.

MEASURING ASSOCIATIVE STRENGTH

Dominance refers to the strength of the directional association between a brand and an associate (cf. Ashcraft, 1978; Barsalou, 1983; Farquhar, Herr, & Fazio, 1990; Loftus, 1973; Mervis & Rosch, 1981). This chapter examines dominance measures for the category-to-brand association and its reciprocal relation.[7]

Category-Dominance Measures

Category dominance is defined as the strength of the directional association from a product category to a brand. For example, the brands Crest and Close-Up are both instances of the product category "toothpaste." Category dominance is measured by the degree to which the label of the product category (toothpaste) evokes the subordinate brand (Crest or Close-Up). Fazio (1987, 1990) described three classes of methods that have been used to measure the strength of this category-to-brand association:

1. Naming Methods. Subjects are presented with the category label (e.g., "toothpaste") and instructed to recall brands that are instances of the product category. To reduce the effects of brands named earlier on the recall of subse-

---

[7]It is straightforward to extend the discussion presented here to the other brand associates in Fig. 17.1. The reader should not view the measurement of associative strength as limited to just product categories.

quent brands, subjects are given either a maximum number of items to list (the first four) or a short time to respond (20 or 30 seconds). Category dominance is measured by: (a) the order in which a brand is listed or (b) the frequency with which the brand is mentioned. Adjustments for the size of the category are often made to normalize these measures.

2. Latency Methods. The category label ("toothpaste") is flashed on a screen for a period of about 750 milliseconds. Then a brand name (Crest or Samsung), which may or may not belong to the category, is shown on the screen. Subjects are asked to classify the brand as a member or nonmember of the category as quickly as possible by responding "yes" or "no." Subjects' reaction times are recorded automatically by a computer or other device. Category dominance is measured by the speed of a correct classification that a brand belongs to a category.

3. Facilitation Methods. The category label ("toothpaste") appears briefly on a computer screen and is then replaced by a brand name initially obscured by dots. The dots are randomly removed by a computer until the brand name (Close-Up) is eventually revealed. The subjects' task is to identify the brand as rapidly as possible without making a mistake. (The category label is used only as a "memory word" that subjects are asked to repeat after identifying the brand name.) Category dominance is measured by the speed of correct recognition of the brand.

Naming and latency methods have been used successfully in consumer research for years (Collins & Quillian, 1969; Fazio, 1990; Luce, 1986; Mervis & Rosch, 1981). Both methods determine how easily a brand comes to mind when a subject is directly told to consider the product category. Facilitation methods use a priming-recognition task that differs from these other methods: subjects are asked only to recognize the brand, not to decide its membership in the product category that is primed. The facilitation measure is more difficult to use, although it provides an arguably better measure of the category-to-brand association.

Fazio (1987) showed that these methods converge for measuring the strength of the category-to-brand association. A strong category-to-brand association results in a brand being named earlier, recalled more frequently, classified faster, and recognized sooner. In comparing brands of toothpaste, for example, Fazio (1987) found Crest was more strongly category dominant than Close-Up on all measures of associative strength.

Instance-Dominance Measures

Instance dominance is defined as the strength of the directional association from a brand to a product category. Instance dominance is measured by the degree to which the brand name evokes the superordinate product category. Although the naming, latency, and facilitation methods can be adapted to measure the strength of brand-to-category associations by simply interchanging category and brand, further changes are sometimes necessary.

For instance dominance, the naming method presents a brand name (Close-Up) to a subject and asks for a list of product categories sold with that brand (e.g., "toothpaste" or "mouthwash"). The number of existing product categories, however, is likely to be quite small for brands other than corporate names (General Electric) and umbrella brands (Panasonic). On the other hand, a common brand name (e.g., United) may be used by several unrelated companies and therefore evoke diverse product categories (such as "airlines," "gasoline," "food," "security," or "household moving").

In searching for potential category extensions, Tauber (1981) asked subjects to name product categories they might expect from given brand. Instance dominance is thus measured by: (a) the order in which a category is listed, or (b) the frequency with which the category is mentioned. This variation of the naming method has apparently proven helpful in many studies for measuring the "perceptual fit" of potential brand extensions to new categories (Tauber, 1988).

The latency method for measuring instance dominance is straightforward to use. The brand name is flashed on a screen, followed by a category label. The category may or may not include products sold with that brand. As above, subjects are asked to classify the brand as a member or nonmember of the category as quickly as possible, without making errors, by responding "yes" or "no." Instance dominance is thus measured by the speed of a correct classification that a category contains the brand.

Likewise, use of the facilitation method for measuring instance dominance is analogous to its use for measuring category dominance. The roles of brand and category are simply switched; the brand name is presented first, followed by the category label initially obscured with dots. Instance dominance is then measured by the speed of correct recognition of the category.

Although typicality and graded structure are related to instance dominance, the concepts are not equivalent. In particular, the latter does not require: (a) an underlying feature or goal structure for the instances of a category, or (b) any comparison with a prototype or ideal of the category. Collins and Loftus (1975) and Murphy and Medin (1985) described inherent problems with feature structures and similarity comparisons. Instance dominance is a simpler concept—the degree to which an instance evokes the superordinate category. It is measured by naming, latency, or facilitation.

ASYMMETRIES IN ASSOCIATIVE STRENGTH

Directional brand associations would not be of much interest if the strengths of the two relations were equal. Yet, Loftus (1973) demonstrated asymmetries in associations between an instance and a category. Her study provides compelling evidence for directional relations in associative network models of memory.

For any category/instance pair, there are two directions of dominance. Loftus (1973) measured category dominance by the frequency with which the instance is named in response to the category label.[8] Instance dominance is measured by the frequency with which the category is named in response to the instance. By splitting the frequencies into "high" or "low," there are four possible combinations of category dominance and instance dominance. Loftus (p. 71) observed,

1. Tree-oak has both high category and high instance dominance (HH). When asked to name trees, 89% of the subjects said "oak." When asked for the superordinates of oak, 74% said "tree."

2. Insect-butterfly has low category dominance and high instance dominance (LH). When asked to name insects, 11% said "butterfly." When asked for the supersets of butterfly, 80% said "insect."

3. Seafood-shrimp has high category dominance and low instance dominance (HL). When asked to name seafood, 70% said "shrimp." When asked for the superordinates of shrimp, 26% said "seafood."

4. Cloth-orlon has both low category dominance and low instance dominance (LL). When asked to name cloths, 17% said "orlon." When asked for the superordinates of orlon, 7% said "cloth."

Loftus independently varied the levels of category dominance and instance dominance according to norms established previously with frequency data. The dependent measures in her experiments were response latencies for correct classification of: (a) category-to-instance pairs, and (b) instance-to-category pairs. Table 17.1 summarizes the main results (Loftus, 1973, p. 71).

In Experiment 1 (where the category was presented first, followed by the instance), note that the reaction times for High-High and High-Low are much faster than for Low-High and Low-Low. Category dominance accounted for 41% of the variance, whereas instance dominance accounted for only 12%. Both main effects were significant, and there was no interaction.

In Experiment 2 (where the instance was presented first, followed by the category), note that the reaction times for High-High and Low-High are much faster than for High-Low and Low-Low. Category dominance accounted for none of the variance, while instance dominance explained 43%. Only the main effect of instance dominance was significant.

These results cannot be explained by models of semantic memory that presume (a) all instances of a category are stored under the category label, or

---

[8]Loftus' terminology and results are translated to conform with the definitions of instance and category dominance given here.

TABLE 17.1
Mean Reaction Times for Categorizing the Four Types of Critical Stimuli

| | Reaction Time (in s) | |
| | Experiment 1 | Experiment 2 |
Stimulus Pair	Category Instance	Instance Category
High–High	.71	.72
Low–High	.77	.73
High–Low	.72	.84
Low–Low	.87	.90

Note. Adapted from Loftus (1973).

(b) each instance has associated with it all the categories to which it belongs. Although the results could be explained by the order of presentation of the category and instance, a simpler explanation is given by an associative network model of semantic memory (Collins & Loftus, 1975; Collins & Quillian, 1969).

Loftus (1973) used a spreading activation model of memory search to interpret these results. The node corresponding to the first member of a pair is accessed directly in memory. The directional link to the second member of the pair is then activated, and the node is scanned. The matching process likely ends if this directional link is highly dominant. On the other hand, if a match does not occur, the process continues. The directional link from the second node to the first node is then activated, and the process is repeated. The matching process ends if this directional link is highly dominant. Otherwise, the process will end with some judgment that may be prone to error.

IMPLICATIONS FOR BRAND MANAGEMENT

Brand Building

The Loftus (1973) experiment provided important insights for brand building. For example, Alba and Hutchinson observed, "In some cases evaluative processes determine the category but not the specific brand. In such situations, brand selection is a simple matter of finding a category member" (1987, p. 416). The likelihood of choosing a particular brand thus depends mostly on its category dominance. If the category-to-brand association is highly dominant, then the brand will be evoked automatically and will likely be chosen over others. Fazio, Herr, and Powell (1992) described how to strengthen category-to-brand associations.

Herr, Farquhar, and Fazio (1992) examined the category and instance dominance of several well-known brands. Table 17.2 illustrates brands in each of the four combinations of high and low levels of category and instance dominance.

TABLE 17.2
Category Dominance and Instance Dominance for Several Brands

	Instance Dominance	
Category Dominance	High	Low
High	Crest toothpaste Schwinn bicycles Folgers coffee	Skippy peanut butter Listerine mouthwash White Cloud bath tissue
Low	Peter Pan peanut butter Scope mouthwash Charmin bath tissue	Close-Up toothpaste Huffy bicycles Hill's Bros. coffee

Note. Adapted from Herr, Farquhar, and Fazio (1990).

Often the product category is activated first in a consumer purchase situation, as in the formation of consideration sets (Nedungadi, 1990). In such cases, instance dominance has little effect on brand choice. The search process ends if category dominance is high enough that the brand is automatically activated. Therefore, with other factors held constant, brands with high category dominance are more likely to be chosen regardless of whether they have high instance dominance (like Crest toothpaste) or low instance dominance (like Listerine mouthwash).

On the other hand, if the directional association from the category to the brand is not sufficiently strong, then other brands will be accessed in searching the category for a choice. In the second stage of the search process, a brand with high instance dominance gains the advantage. For example, if consumers do not find any brands of bath tissue sufficiently high on category dominance, then Charmin wins over White Cloud because the former has higher instance-dominance than the latter in Table 17.2.

Thus, a brand with a strong association toward the product category is likely to be the choice only if no other brand owns the association from the category. If no brand automatically comes to mind when the product category is mentioned, then a strong brand-to-category association will guide the brand choice.

Brand managers also find instance dominance useful in another way. It provides coherence that "pulls" a category of branded products together (Murphy & Medin, 1985). Thus, a narrower product line results in greater instance dominance for a given brand (Boush & Loken, 1991; Collins & Quillian, 1969; Rosch & Mervis, 1975).

Brand Leveraging

Herr, Farquhar, and Fazio (1992) also explored the implications of category dominance for stretching a brand from an existing product category to a new one. They find that category dominance facilitates recall of a brand in its parent category and affects the "push" the brand extends to a new product in a related category.

It is generally easier to extend brands to closely related categories than to distantly related categories. However, the affect associated with strongly category-dominant brands appears to transfer to an extension only when the target category is closely related to the parent category. Thus, highly category-dominant brands have sharper boundaries than less dominant brands.

These results have important implications for assessing potential brand extensions. Herr, Farquhar, and Fazio's (1992) results show how learning and liking of prospective brand extensions are influenced by two factors: (a) the category dominance of the brand in its parent category, and (b) the relatedness of the parent category to the target category of the extension. Whereas the individual effects of these factors are plain to see, the joint effect of category dominance and intercategory relatedness is news.

SUMMARY AND CONCLUSIONS

Brands are associated in consumer memory with product categories, usage situations, product attributes, customer benefits, and other elements. We emphasize the need for distinguishing the orientation of such brand associations: the associate-to-brand direction, or the brand-to-associate direction. This distinction is not well appreciated because many researchers either treat associations as nondirectional or employ the wrong directional association in studying brands.

The orientation of an association becomes apparent when certain methods are used to measure association strength. We examine three approaches to measuring association strength: (a) naming methods, (b) latency methods, and (c) facilitation methods. Indeed, the dual structure of brand associations becomes critically important when the strengths of the directional associations differ. Earlier research by Loftus (1973) and others demonstrated the existence of asymmetries in association strength between a given category and an instance of that category. These results are easily generalized to other types of brand associates.

We define the strength of the category-to-brand association as category dominance and the strength of the brand-to-category association as instance dominance. Prior research by Herr, Farquhar, and Fazio (1992) and others showed that brands with high category dominance often enjoy a substantial market share of the parent category but have substantial inertia in extending very far to other categories. The reason is that the affect associated with a highly category-dominant brand transfers to an extension only when the target category is closely related to the parent category.

Recognizing the directionality of associations and using a spreading activation model of consumer memory yields several insights for brand management. In those purchase situations where the product category is likely to be activated first in consumer memory (e.g., as in goal-directed search or with consideration sets), a brand manager is advised to measure both category dominance and instance dominance.

One of three conditions applies for the brand: (a) It is highly category dominant. (b) It is not highly category dominant, but it is highly instance dominant. (c) It is neither highly category dominant nor highly instance dominant. Table 17.2 illustrates these conditions in (a) the two cells in the top row, (b) the left cell in the bottom row, and (c) the right cell in the bottom row.

In the first condition, the brand should "stay close to home" and harvest its strong position in the parent category. Direct extensions of a highly category-dominant brand are not likely to succeed, unless the target category is closely related to the parent category.[9]

In the second condition, the brand will only have a strong position in the parent category by default, that is, when no brand is highly category dominant. There are two possible strategies for managing the brand: (a) Foster category dominance and thus preempt competing brands. (b) Exploit the high instance dominance that already exists and stretch to new product categories that appropriately fit the brand.

In the third condition, the brand associations are too weak to leverage, so the brand needs to be strengthened first. Middle brands are likely to be lost among consumers in those purchase situations where the product category is activated first in memory. Such brands rarely enter a consumer's consideration set or emerge from a search process.

ACKNOWLEDGMENTS

The authors gratefully acknowledge financial support for this research from the Marketing Science Institute and Claremont's Product Strategy Institute. An earlier version of this paper was presented at the Tenth Annual Advertising and Consumer Psychology Conference in San Francisco on May 17, 1991. The authors appreciate David Aaker's and Arvind Rangaswamy's helpful comments on an earlier paper and Dennis Epple's assessment of the direction and impact of this research.

---

[9]Farquhar, Han, Herr, and Ijiri (1992) described several strategies for leveraging highly category-dominant (or more generally, highly associate-dominant) brands. They refer to these as "master brands" and show how to extend such brands indirectly to new categories.

REFERENCES

Aaker, D. A. (1991). *Managing brand equity.* New York: The Free Press.

Aaker, D. A., & Keller, K. A. (1990). Consumer evaluations of brand extensions. *Journal of Marketing, 54,* 27–41.

Alba, J. W., & Hutchinson, J. W. (1987). Dimensions of consumer expertise. *Journal of Consumer Research, 13,* 411–454.

Alba, J. W., Hutchinson, J. W., & Lynch, J. G., Jr. (1991). Memory and decision making. In H. H. Kassarjian & T. S. Robertson (Eds.), *Handbook of consumer theory and research* (pp. 1–49). Englewood Cliffs, NJ: Prentice-Hall.

Ashcraft, M. H. (1978). Property dominance and typicality effects in property statement verification. *Journal of Verbal Learning and Verbal Behavior, 17,* 155–164.

Barsalou, L. W. (1983). Ad hoc categories. *Memory and Cognition, 11,* 211–227.

Barsalou, L. W. (1985). Ideals, central tendency, and frequency of instantiation as determinants of graded structure in categories. *Journal of Experimental Psychology: Learning, Memory, and Cognition, 11,* 629–649.

Boush, D. M., & Loken, B. (1991). A process-tracing study of brand extension evaluation. *Journal of Marketing Research, 28,* 16–28.

Collins, A. M., & Loftus, E. F. (1975). A spreading-activation theory of semantic processing. *Psychological Review, 82,* 407–428.

Collins, A. M., & Quillian, M. R. (1969). Retrieval time from semantic memory. *Journal of Verbal Learning and Verbal Behavior, 8,* 240–248.

Estes, W. K. (1991). Cognitive architectures from the standpoint of an experimental psychologist. *Annual Review of Psychology, 42,* 1–28.

Farquhar, P. H. (1989). Managing brand equity. *Marketing Research, 1,* 24–33.

Farquhar, P. H., Han, J. Y., Herr, P. M., & Ijiri, Y. (1992). Strategies for leveraging master brands. *Marketing Research, 4,* 32–43.

Farquhar, P. H., & Herr, P. M., (1992). *Play it again, Sam: The strength of associative models in evaluating brand extensions* (working paper). The Claremont Graduate School, Claremont, CA.

Farquhar, P. H., Herr, P. M., & Fazio, R. H. (1990). A relational model for category extensions of brands. *Advances in Consumer Research, 17,* 856–860.

Fazio, R. H. (1987). *Category-brand associations and their activation from memory.* Unpublished report, Ogilvy Center for Research and Development, San Francisco, CA.

Fazio, R. H. (1990). A practical guide to the use of response latency in social psychological research. In C. Hendrick & M. S. Clark (Eds.), *Review of Personality and Social Psychology, 11,* 74–97.

Fazio, R. H., Herr, P. M., & Powell, M. C. (1992). On the development and strength of category-brand associations in memory: The case of mystery ads. *Journal of Consumer Psychology, 1,* 1–13.

Fazio, R. H., Powell, M. C., & Williams, C. (1989). The role of attitude accessibility in the attitude-to-behavior process. *Journal of Consumer Research, 16,* 280–288.

Fazio, R. H., Sanbonmatsu, D. M., Powell, M. C., & Kardes, F. R. (1986). On the automatic activation of attitudes. *Journal of Personality and Social Psychology, 50,* 229–238.

Herr, P. M. (1989). Priming price: Prior knowledge and context effects. *Journal of Consumer Research, 16,* 67–75.

Herr, P. M., Farquhar, P. H., & Fazio, R. H. (1992). *Using dominance measures to evaluate brand extensions* (working paper). The Claremont Graduate School, Claremont, CA.

Herr, P. M., & Fazio, R. H. (in press). The attitude-to-behavior process: Implications for consumer behavior. In A. A. Mitchell (Ed.), *Psychology and advertising: Ad exposure, memory, and choice.* Hillsdale, NJ: Lawrence Erlbaum Associates.

John, D. R., & Loken, B. (1990). *Diluting brand equity: The negative impact of brand extensions* (working paper). University of Minnesota, Minneapolis, MN.

Keller, K. L., & Aaker, D. A. (1992). The effects of sequential introduction of brand extensions. *Journal of Marketing Research, 29,* 35–50.

Loftus, E. F. (1973). Category dominance, instance dominance, and categorization time. *Journal of Experimental Psychology, 97,* 70–74.

Loken, B., & Ward, J. (1990). Alternative approaches to understanding the determinants of typicality. *Journal of Consumer Research, 17,* 111–126.

Luce, R. D. (1986). *Response times: Their role in inferring elementary mental organization.* New York: Oxford University Press.

Mervis, C. B., & Rosch, E. (1981). Categorization of natural objects. *Annual Review of Psychology, 32,* 89–115.

Meyer, D. E., & Schvaneveldt, R. W. (1971). Facilitation in recognizing pairs of words: Evidence of a dependence between retrieval operations. *Journal of Experimental Psychology, 90,* 227–234.

Murphy, G. L., & Medin, D. L. (1985). The role of theories in conceptual coherence. *Psychological Review, 92,* 289–316.

Nedungadi, P. (1990). Recall and consideration sets: Influencing choice without altering brand evaluations. *Journal of Consumer Research, 17,* 263–276.

Posner, M. I., & Snyder, C. R. R. (1975). Facilitation and inhibition in the processing of signals. In P. M. A. Rabbit & S. Dornic (Eds.), *Attention and performance.* New York: Academic Press.

Raaijmakers, J. G. W., & Shiffrin, R. M. (1981). Search of associative memory. *Psychology Review, 88,* 93–134.

Rangaswamy, A., Burke, R. R., & Oliva, T. A. (1992). *Brand equity and extendibility of brand names* (working paper). Wharton School, University of Pennsylvania, Philadelphia. (To appear in the *International Journal of Research in Marketing,* 1993)

Ries, A., & Trout, J. (1986). *Positioning: The battle for your mind* (1st rev. ed.). New York: McGraw-Hill.

Rosch, E., & Mervis, C. B. (1975). Family resemblances: Studies in the internal structure of categories. *Cognitive Psychology, 7,* 573–605.

Smith, E. E., & Medin, D. L. (1981). *Categories and concepts.* Cambridge, MA: Harvard University Press.

Tauber, E. M. (1981). Brand franchise extension: New product benefits from existing brand names. *Business Horizons, 24,* 36–41.

Tauber, E. M. (1988, August–September). Brand leverage: Strategy for growth in a cost-control world. *Journal of Advertising Research, 28,* 26–30.

Tversky, A., & Gati, I. (1978). Studies of similarity. In E. Rosch & B. B. Lloyd (Eds.), *Cognition and categorization* (pp. 79–98). Hillsdale, NJ: Lawrence Erlbaum Associates.

Part V

Perspectives on Brand Extensions

Advertising Claims and Evidence as Bases for Brand Equity and Consumer Evaluations of Brand Extensions

Kent Nakamoto
Deborah J. MacInnis
Hyung-Shik Jung
University of Arizona

Much of the literature examining brand equity has focused on the bases for its transfer to brand extensions, and the underlying question is how the brand can capitalize on existing equity (e.g., Aaker & Keller, 1990). Although there is some uncertainty regarding the detailed process, one requirement for successful transfer is some linkage between the two product categories—a reason other than brand name for consumers to suppose that their liking for the brand's existing products should apply to the brand extension (Boush et al., 1987; Chakravarti, MacInnis, & Nakamoto, 1990; Farquhar, Herr, & Fazio, 1989; MacInnis & Nakamoto, 1991; Park, Jaworski, & MacInnis, 1986). In particular, given the competitive setting of product evaluation, it seems that the connection between the two categories should be relevant to the basis for competitive advantage enjoyed by the brand's existing products (cf. Tauber, 1988).

This need for relevance suggests the importance of understanding the nature of the competitive advantage of the existing product. However, few analyses have considered how brand equity is formed or how that formation process affects the nature of equity and its transfer to brand extensions. In particular, the question of how consumer exposure to the brand's existing products and advertising might frame their perceptions of the brand's competitive advantage, and thus limit or enhance the transfer of its equity to brand extensions, remains to be examined. Yet, it is clear that not all brands are equal in their transfer potential, even within a category. Calvin Klein, for example, has successfully extended its line from clothing to such diverse products as perfume and underwear, whereas Levi's, an equally dominant name, was unable to extend even from jeans to suits. In this chapter, we consider how the genesis of brand equity—through advertising and experience (or evidence)—may influence the types of product categories to which brands extend.

In developing these ideas, let us first consider the nature of *brand equity*. Central to this concept is the notion that brand equity is closely tied to the development of long-lived competitive advantage in the eyes of the consumer, hence, a generalized preference for the brand. This competitive aspect is central to the idea of brand equity. It is not enough that a brand is good; it must be better in some sense than the alternatives that contribute to equity. Competitive advantage has been the focus of several recent studies including those by Carpenter and Nakamoto (1987), who suggested that consumers develop naive theories about the basis of performance in a product category as a function of advertising claims and experience. For example, Vaseline was originally introduced in the 1880s and advertised as a wound preparation of great purity, a claim linked to its clear translucent color compared to black coal tar alternatives. Sampling Vaseline, buyers presumably found that the wounds healed and, generalizing from this observation, inferred the importance of purity as reflected in its color. Thus, these perceptions, which emerge from the consumer's exposure to advertising and product experience, frame category preferences as well as specific brand perceptions, giving rise to competitive advantage, as shown by Carpenter and Nakamoto (1989). Presumably, then, advertising and experience provide important bases for brand equity.

More detailed studies of the interaction of advertising and evidence or experience in the evaluation of products were conducted by Deighton (1984) and Hoch and Ha (1986, Ha & Hoch, 1989). These authors suggested that the consumer would learn about a product and its potential benefits through advertising. However, because of the low credibility of advertising, the veracity of these claims would likely be tested, either through experience or through a search for credible evidence (e.g., reviews in *Consumer Reports*). Of particular interest to these authors was the case of ambiguous evidence, where the evidence or experience would be essentially uninformative to the consumer or difficult to interpret. In this case, an interaction between evidence and advertising was found. Alone, neither advertising nor evidence had an impact on product evaluation. However, when advertising preceded evidence, a significant increase in evaluation was noted (Deighton, 1984; Hoch & Ha, 1986). The evidence was interpreted by consumers as validating the advertising claims. When clear, unambiguous evidence was presented, however, the advertising had little effect; evaluation was driven by evidence alone.

Although this research has examined how advertising and evidence frame consumers' perceptions of an original brand, our interest lies in: (a) how these factors may also influence consumers' perceptions of a brand extension, and (b) how or whether they limit or enhance the kinds of categories to which such brands may extend. In other words, if advertising and evidence are factors which promote brand equity, they may also shape the transfer of this equity to novel product categories (see Fig. 18.1).

In the present study, we apply this learning framework to examine the limits of brand equity in supporting brand extensions. In particular, we suggest that the type of information presented in advertising and evidence will affect the basis for the brand's reputation and, as a result, affect its transfer potential to brand extensions. A reputation (and, therefore, competitive advantage) built on a generalized image (e.g., durability of Maytag, sophistication of Liz Clayborne, reliability of Timex) may extend to many product categories. In contrast, a reputation built on a specific attribute (e.g., richness in Haagen Dazs ice cream, whitening power of Clorox, decay prevention of Crest), may be more limited in the types of categories to which it can extend.

ADVERTISING CLAIMS AND EVIDENCE

The development of brand equity relates to the brand's original products. As noted, we suggest that this equity emerges from consumer learning about these products through exposure to advertising and evidence (or experience). Whereas studies of advertising/evidence interactions make no specification of the types of claims and their interaction with evidence, other research on advertising proposed various distinctions among types of message or executional content. For example, Stewart and Furse (1986) distinguish executions featuring, among other things, (a) product attributes, (b) user satisfaction, and (c) superiority claims. Aaker and Myers (1987) distinguished positioning strategies (and, thus, advertising objectives), such as: (a) associating the product with a characteristic or benefit, (b) taking a particular position on price–quality tradeoffs (Saks Fifth Avenue vs. Sears), and (c) associating the product with particular cultural symbols. A general distinction here is one between claims that are linked to a *specific attribute* or function of the product versus claims that develop a *general image* of uniqueness, quality, or superiority for the product (see also Gutman & Reynolds, 1979).

The same type of distinction might be drawn between types of evidence or experience. For example, *Consumer Reports* most often gives product ratings along several different attributes. In some cases, these ratings are not aggregated; in others, a global ranking of quality and/or value is also provided. Direct product experience is likely to be quite general—the product worked. In some cases, however, it may be possible to discern the performance of the product on specific dimensions as well. For example, one can certainly ascertain the gas mileage of a car. Thus, evidence or experience, like advertising, may be described as attribute based or based on overall quality.

Our focus is on the interaction of these factors—attribute specific versus general quality claims in advertising, and attribute based versus general quality information in evidence—as they relate to the character of the brand equity that results. However, in assessing the impact of this equity, we look to the ability of the equity to transfer to brand extensions. Thus, we explore how various forms of advertising (attribute based and quality based) and various forms of evidence (attribute based and quality based) frame consumers' evaluations of the brand extension.

In this study, we examine two types of ads: (a) ads making a claim regarding a single attribute (A_1), and (b) ads making a claim of overall quality. We suggest that advertising for a single attribute focuses attention on that attribute, increasing its salience and importance to evaluation. In addition, we examine three types of evidence (see Table 18.1):

1. Attribute evidence in which the brand is superior on attribute A_1 but mediocre on four others.

2. Attribute evidence in which the brand is inferior on attribute A_1 but superior on four others.

3. General quality-oriented evidence in which no data are given on individual attributes, but the brand is shown to be excellent in overall quality.

We suggest that evidence will be evaluated in light of the advertising claims. Given an attribute-specific claim, attribute-level evidence supporting the claim will generate a strong perception of performance (thus, equity) linked to that attribute. Attribute evidence supporting that claim, even if other evidence is contrary, will lead to some level of equity; attribute evidence refuting the claim, even if other evidence is positive, will not give rise to much equity. Evidence of superior general quality will be interpreted to support the attribute-specific claim, but less strongly, so that equity will again be attribute limited, but weaker.

Given a general quality claim in advertising, by contrast, we expect all evidence—attribute or general quality—to be taken into account, so that the impact on brand extensions will be less dependent on any particular attribute. Generally positive evidence will give rise to broad-based equity, as will evidence attesting to superior general quality. Generally mediocre evidence will lead to less positive evaluation and, thus, equity.

These sources of information form the bases for evaluation of the original branded product (Fig. 18.1). However, our primary interest here is in the evaluation of an extension (i.e., another product bearing the same brand name after the original branded product has developed a reputation). In particular, we are interested in the limits of brand equity in adding perceived value to a brand extension.

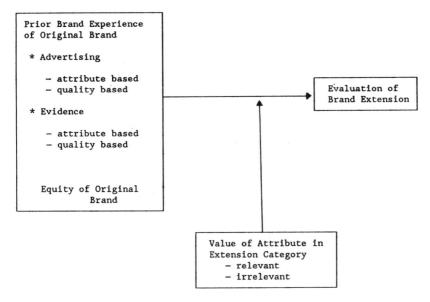

FIG. 18.1.   Conceptual model.

ADVERTISING CLAIMS, EVIDENCE, AND EVALUATION OF BRAND EXTENSIONS

We hypothesize that a brand whose reputation is based on excellence of one attribute (e.g., via attribute-based advertising and attribute-based evidence) will be more limited in the type of extension it can contemplate than one whose reputation is based on image or overall quality (e.g., via quality-based advertising and quality-based evidence). For example, the Levi's brand name has long been synonymous with jeans (durable denim pants). Levi's attempt to expand into suits was disastrous, presumably because the features that made its jeans good were either irrelevant or undesirable for suits. By contrast, Calvin Klein developed a reputation built around a high fashion image. As such, it has successfully diversified into not only jeans and suits but also a variety of other fashion-oriented products, such as perfume. We therefore hypothesize (H) that:

H1.   Brand extensions for products whose equity is based on a specific attribute (e.g., via attribute-based advertising and attribute-based evidence) will benefit only if that attribute is valued (relevant) in the extension category.

H2.   Brand extensions for products whose equity is based on a general quality claim (e.g., quality-based advertising and quality-based evidence) will be more extendible to irrelevant product categories than brands whose equity is based on a specific attribute.

At the same time, we suggest that there is a cost to this generality. Although it is true that a more general reputation can extend further, we suggest that the transfer of value is lessened. This is because the basis for the transfer is less specific and concrete. That is, if a brand's equity is attribute specific and that attribute is valued in the extension category (a type of extension we call *relevant*), then that attribute superiority will be salient in the evaluation of the extension so that transfer will be strong. General quality claims will transfer to a broader array of products but provide less value in the extension because of the lack of focus on specific bases for relevance of the brand's quality in the extension category. If, on the other hand, the attribute is not valued in the extension category (an *irrelevant* extension), the brand whose equity is based on a general quality claim will be enhanced more. Thus,

H3.   Brand extensions for products whose equity is based on a specific attribute will be more extendible to relevant product categories than brand extensions to products based on general quality perceptions.

The above hypotheses deal with situations in which advertising and evidence builds equity, which is clearly based on a specific attribute or overall quality perceptions (i.e., cases when the type of advertising claim and evidence match). It is less clear how equity based on mixed combinations of advertising and evidence (e.g., attribute-based advertising/quality-based experience, quality-based advertising/attribute-based experience) will affect a brand's transfer potential. We therefore treat these cases in a more exploratory fashion, offering limited predictions.

Central to our analysis are the earlier findings of Deighton (1984) and Hoch and Ha (1986) that advertising appears to frame the interpretation of evidence. If advertising is quality based and evidence is attribute based, consumers should evaluate the attribute-based evidence in a holistic fashion, focusing on the global combination of attributes. Because advertising frames a more global interpretation of evidence, we expect a weaker linkage between equity of the brand and any specific attribute. Hence, brands may be more extendible to irrelevant product categories. If, on the other hand, advertising makes a claim of superiority on a specific attribute, then general quality evidence should be treated as confirmation of that claim, so that equity should remain tied to the specific attribute. Thus, in general, we would expect the mixed conditions to mirror those predicted for the two types of advertising.

At the same time, these mixed conditions are likely to be more ambiguous for the consumer when evaluating a brand extension. That is, if the attribute evidence is generally positive, but not uniformly so, the case for a general quality claim in an ad is weaker and the transfer should be weaker than when the evidence supports the general superiority of the brand. Likewise, given a specific attribute claim in advertising, overall quality evidence is ambiguous in the nature of the brand's superiority. Thus, transfer should be weaker than when an attribute claim is supported by validation of that specific claim.

To test these hypotheses, we conducted an experiment in which subjects were exposed to advertising and evidence relating to the quality of a hypothetical branded product. They then evaluated both that product and a brand extension.

STUDY

Experimental Design and Stimuli

Advertising Manipulation. Two types of ads were constructed for the hypothetical brands: (a) one that advertised a specific attribute, and (b) one that made a general quality claim. The base product categories were "yogurt" and "stereo equipment." Advertised attributes were chosen, through a pretest, to be attributes that were not naturally central to evaluation—compatibility with a TV for "stereos" and amount of fruit for "yogurt." For each product class, the two ads used identical graphics but differed in headline and text.

Evidence Manipulation. As noted earlier, three evidence conditions were constructed. A brand attribute rating matrix was used to present the data on five hypothetical brands in each category. Subjects were told the data were drawn from a consumer test organization. Data for four of the brands were held constant for all attributes or overall quality, whichever was presented. Only data for the target brand were varied, as shown in Table 18.1. For the attribute data, each attribute rating was displayed using one to five stars (five stars being better); for overall quality data, a single rating of one to five stars was used. In addition to the focal attributes, the attributes used for stereos were: (a) FM tuner performance, (b) AM tuner performance, (c) convenience, and (d) power output; for yogurt, the attributes were: (a) taste, (b) calories, (c) sodium, and (d) nutritional value.

The advertising and evidence manipulations were crossed, yielding six cells. Each subject was exposed to both product categories. For one of the base categories, the subject saw the attribute ad; for the other category, the subject saw the general quality ad. In addition, the evidence condition differed for the two categories.

Extension Categories. Finally, two product categories were used as extension categories for each base category. In the case of stereos, the extension products were "VCRs" (similar extension category) and "electronic keyboards" (dissimilar extension category). For yogurt, they were "fruit preserves" (similar extension category) and "mayonnaise" (dissimilar extension category).

TABLE 18.1
Evidence Conditions for Stereos (Original Category)

Brand	Attribute Evidence Conditions					Overall Quality Condition

Example of Evidence Data Format Experimental Conditions[a]

Brand	FM Tuner Performance	AM Tuner Performance	Interface with TV	Convenience	Power Output	Overall Quality
SPEX	**	**	*	***	*	*
Banner	***	**	*****	****	***	***
TXNAD	****	***	****	****	**	****
Schugan	***	***	***	****	**	**
Techaji	*****	****	****	*****	****	*****

Evidence Data for Experimental Conditions

Specific Attribute Superiority

Banner	***	**	*****	****	***	

Specific Attribute Inferiority

Banner	*****	****	*	*****	****	

Overall Superior Quality

Banner						*****

Note. [a]Brand shown in bold was target brand; shaded attribute was advertised attribute in attribute-specific ad conditions. Other brands and ratings were held constant. (Overall Quality data column was not included in attribute evidence conditions, and vice versa.)

Subjects evaluated each extension in the same experimental session as their exposure to the attribute/evidence condition. Each subject rated all four extensions. Given the attribute-specific ad, we expected that the attribute targeted in the attribute-specific ad (TV interface capability for "stereos" and amount of fruit for "yogurt") would be relevant and valued for "VCRs" and "fruit preserves," but not for "electronic keyboards" and "mayonnaise." This was verified through manipulation checks. Ten subjects were assigned to each of the 12 cells of the design.

Measures

All brand evaluations were provided using three 7-point semantic differential scales anchored by: (a) *very bad quality–very good quality*, (b) *very dislikable–very likable*, and (c) *very unfavorable–very favorable*. The Cronbach alpha for both "stereos" and "yogurt" were .94. Thus, the scores on the three items were averaged to form an evaluation.

RESULTS

Development of Equity Perceptions

The brand evaluations for the base product category which serve as manipulation checks and a baseline for evaluation of the extensions are reported here. Because the results were similar for the two categories, the results are combined for ease of presentation. In an analysis of variance, the interaction of type of evidence and type of advertising is significant ($F_{12,13}$ = 12.14; $p <$ .001) (more detailed analyses of the evaluations of the original products is presented in Jung, 1991; here, we consider only data and results relevant to the present study). As expected, for the attribute-specific superiority condition, compared to the quality ad, the attribute-ad-enhanced brand equity (X = 4.96 vs. 4.39), even though the brand's performance on other attributes was mediocre (t_{113} = 1.65; $p <$ .05; one-sided). On the other hand, when the claim was disconfirmed (attribute-specific inferiority condition, $\bar{X}$ = 3.87), equity was not enhanced; the evaluation was greatly reduced relative to the general quality claim ($\bar{X}$ = 5.35), even when performance on the other attributes was very good (t_{113} = 4.27; $p <$ .01). For the general quality ad, evaluation in the various attribute evidence conditions followed the general pattern of evidence. Finally, for the overall superior quality evidence condition, there was no significant difference in evaluation between the two ads, as expected given the unambiguous nature of the evidence. These results are consistent with the ideas that: (a) advertising and evidence work together to influence consumers' perceptions of a brand's equity, and (b) the nature of the equity depends on the nature of the advertising and evidence.

Test of the Hypotheses

The next step in the analysis involved a test of the experimental hypotheses. We use two sets of analyses for hypothesis testing:

1. We examine overall evaluations of the brand extension across the 12 advertising/evidence and relevance conditions (see Table 18.2). These global judgments indicate the overall intensity of equity inherent in the brand extension.
2. We examine the difference between the evaluation of the original brand and the evaluation of the brand extension across the 12 conditions (see Table 18.3). These results show the actual transfer of equity from the original brand to the brand extension.

Positive scores indicate that the brand extension is evaluated more favorably than the base product—hence, some equity is transferred to the extension.

TABLE 18.2
Evaluation of Brand Extensions

	Ad Condition for Original Brand			
	Attribute Ad		Quality Ad	
Evidence Conditions for Original Brand:	Relevant Extension	Irrelevant Extension	Relevant Extension	Irrelevant Extension
Specific Attribute Superior	5.10	3.59	4.78	3.42
Specific Attribute Inferior	3.55	3.62	4.12	4.25
Overall Superior Quality	5.38	4.03	5.26	4.26

Negative scores indicate that the evaluation of the extended brand is less than that of its base product. Hence, equity built into the base product has been lost by the extension. From a managerial perspective, one would desire a situation in which the equity of the original brand (a) transfers to the brand extension, and (b) is high (intense) in the extension product category.

Using overall evaluations of the brand extension as the dependent measure, a repeated measures analysis of variance, with relevance of the extension as the repeated measure, revealed a main effect of type of evidence ($F_{2,114}$ = 5.79; $p < .01$) and an interaction between evidence and relevance ($F_{2,114}$ = 15.6; $p < .01$). Our interest, however, focused on specific contrasts reported in Table 18.2.

H1 proposes that brand extensions for products whose equity is based on a specific attribute claim will benefit only if that attribute is valued (relevant) in the extension category. The results support this hypothesis; when advertising presented an attribute claim which was supported by evidence, the evaluation of the extension is 5.10 for relevant extensions, but only 3.59 for irrelevant ones (t_{114} = 5.80; $p < .01$). Equity of the brand extension therefore appears to be tied to the attribute on which the original brand's equity is based. Furthermore, even a relevant extension will not be favorably evaluated ($\bar{X}$ = 3.55)

TABLE 18.3
Difference Between Evaluation of Brand Extensions and Base Products

	Ad Condition for Original Brand			
	Attribute Ad		Quality Ad	
Evidence Conditions for Original Brand:	Relevant Extension	Irrelevant Extension	Relevant Extension	Irrelevant Extension
Specific Attribute Superior	+0.14	-1.37	+0.40	-0.97
Specific Attribute Inferior	-0.32	-0.25	-1.23	-1.10
Overall Superior Quality	-0.42	-1.77	-0.07	-1.07

if the equity one tries to establish by advertising is disconfirmed by evidence. Note that this occurs even though the evidence on other attributes is positive.

This latter result suggests that if advertising is attribute oriented, it prompts a search for evidence regarding that attribute. Equity is based on the brand's value on that attribute. If advertising did not frame evidence, the value of the brand extension should be higher in the cases where the value of the specific attribute was disconfirmed, but the brand was superior on other attributes. This was not the case. Thus, advertising and evidence combined influence the transfer of brand equity to relevant and irrelevant product categories, with advertising framing perceptions of evidence and, hence, the nature of brand equity.

The results in Table 18.3 also suggest that when perceptions of the original brand are clearly attribute based (attribute ad and attribute evidence), equity will transfer from the original brand to the brand extension only when the extension is relevant ($\bar{X} = .14$), but not when it is irrelevant ($\bar{X} = -1.37$). Hence, attribute-based advertising and attribute-based evidence not only frame equity of the original brand around that attribute, they influence the brand's transfer potential to relevant product categories and the intensity of the equity associated with the brand extension. These results support H1.

H2 proposes that brand extensions for products whose equity is based on general quality perceptions (e.g., quality-based advertising and quality-based evidence) would be more extendible to irrelevant product categories than brands whose equity is based on a specific attribute. The results generally support this hypothesis. When advertising and evidence are both quality-based, the equity of the brand is not so clearly built around a specific attribute. Therefore, compared to brands whose equity is based on attributes, brands are evaluated more positively in cases where the attribute is irrelevant ($\bar{X} = 4.26$ vs. $\bar{X} = 3.59$) ($t_{114} = 1.85$; $p < .05$; one-sided). Thus, equity in the brand extension is more intensely positive in irrelevant extensions when equity in the original brand is based on overall quality, as opposed to specific attributes. The results in Table 18.3 also indicate that brands whose images are based on overall quality are more extendible to unrelated product categories ($\bar{X} = -1.07$) compared to brands whose images are based on a specific attribute ($\bar{X} = -1.37$). However, this effect is only directionally consistent with H2.

H3 proposes that brand extensions for products whose equity is based on a specific attribute will be more extendible to relevant product categories than brands whose equity is based on general quality perceptions. However, the results in Tables 18.2 and 18.3 provide mixed support for this hypothesis. In contrast to H3, the results in Table 18.2 suggest that equity is equally intense for relevant extensions, whether the original brand's equity is based on a specific attribute ($\bar{X} = 5.10$) or a general quality perception ($\bar{X} = 5.26$; see Table 18.2). However, as shown in Table 18.3, the differences between consumers' evaluations of the original brand and the brand extension indicate that the attribute ad with confirming attribute evidence leads to a small increase in the evaluation of a relevant extension ($\bar{X}$ = .14); the quality ad, quality evidence case gives a small decrease ($\bar{X}$ = −.07). Furthermore, the decay in support for moving from a relevant to an irrelevant extension is smaller for the general quality case ($\bar{d}$ = .667 for the general quality case vs. $\bar{d}$ = 1.12 for the attribute-specific case). This difference, although consistent with H3, is, however, only marginally significant.

Additional Analyses

Although we offered no explicit hypotheses regarding the mixed advertising–evidence conditions (i.e., attribute-advertising/quality evidence or quality advertising/attribute evidence), their effects are analyzed here for exploratory purposes (Table 18.3). We had anticipated that in these mixed conditions the extendibility of the brand would be framed by advertising. However, the results offer mixed support for this effect.

Quality Ad/Attribute Evidence. When advertising for the original brand was oriented to general quality and evidence was attribute-oriented, subjects appeared sensitive to the relevance of the key attribute in evaluating the relevant extension. When the brand was superior on the attribute, the evaluation of the extension actually rose relative to the evaluation of the original product ($\bar{X}$ = 0.40). When the brand was inferior on the attribute, however, the evaluation of the extension fell ($\bar{X}$ = −1.23; see Table 18.3). These results suggest that the evidence condition was more salient than any framing effect of the advertising; consumers focused on naturally salient attributes of the products in generating equity for the original brand and used these attributes in evaluating transfer potential in the brand extension. In the case of the irrelevant extension, the evaluation of the extension fell regardless of the rating on the key attribute ($\bar{X}$ = −.97 and −1.10).

Attribute Ad/Quality Evidence. When advertising for the original brand was oriented toward a specific attribute, the general quality evidence resulted in a rating for the extension (Table 18.2) that was higher for both relevant and irrelevant extensions than that in the matching attribute evidence condition, seemingly contradicting our expectations. However, looking again to the difference between the rating of the extension and base products (Table 18.3), the means are consistent with expectations. The general quality evidence appears to leave some ambiguity in the source of quality; evaluations fall for both relevant and irrelevant extensions and irrelevant extensions much more than in the case of attribute evidence ($\bar{X}$ = −0.42 vs. +0.14 for relevant extensions and −1.77 vs. −1.37 for irrelevant ones). In this case, then, the advertising appears to have had the predicted framing effect.

The contradiction noted in the results for the overall evaluations and the differences in evaluation of base and extension products is instructive. The analysis of differences between extension and base product addresses specifically the issue of transfer of equity from an existing product to an extension. However, the overall evaluations depend on both the transfer and the amount or intensity of equity (as reflected in the evaluation) of the base product. In the cases we examined, it appears that, on balance, the advantage gained through an attribute-oriented ad and general quality evidence was strong enough that the evaluation of the extensions was quite strong, despite the relatively poor transfer of equity. This is not surprising, given that the evaluation of the base product appeared to be driven largely by this type of evidence due to its unambiguous positive nature. Thus, in addressing the competitive impact of brand equity transfer to brand extensions, it is important to consider both the nature and amount of the equity.

DISCUSSION

Our experiment is rather preliminary. Clearly, the development and extension of brand equity progresses over much longer periods than we have studied here. However, our results are highly suggestive of the importance of understanding the source of equity. Combined, the results suggest that both advertising and evidence influence the equity consumers have for a brand and the extendibility of that equity to relevant and irrelevant product categories. Advertising can sometimes frame perceptions so that attention is focused on specific attributes or general quality, but advertising alone does not influence equity perceptions of the original brand. The nature of the evidence also affects equity perceptions.

The results also suggest that brand equity based on advertising and evidence influences consumers' evaluations of a brand extension. If the basis for a brand's competitive advantage is closely tied to a particular attribute, its ability to capitalize on that advantage through brand extensions is likely to be limited to products that share the same basis for competition. A more general image is likely to transfer more widely to unrelated product categories, but provides less leverage in relevant product categories. Obviously, this distinction is not a dichotomy but more a dimension—bases for competitive advantage can be more or less specific with a corresponding tradeoff in intensity.

The results also suggest the presence of asymmetric effects in the transfer of equity perceptions when advertising and evidence for the original brand is mixed. In general, equity is more transferable to new product categories when advertising for the original brand is quality oriented and evidence is attribute oriented than the other way around. The attribute advertising has a framing effect on perceptions of the original brand, but in addition, the extension category itself can cue specific attributes when specific attribute evidence is available.

Managerial Implications.   The results also offer several managerial implications for brand equity–brand extension decisions. From a brand extension perspective, equity based on general perceptions of brand quality offers the firm more flexibility in extending to both related and unrelated product categories than brand extensions based on attributes. However, because the transfer of a quality image is less effective than the transfer of a specific attribute claim, the quality image must be a strong one to provide a strong base for extension.

This limitation highlights the importance of the intensity of equity developed around the original brand. Intensity is likely to be linked to a variety of other competitive factors. For example, the unique strength of the association of any attribute or image to a brand (regardless of generality) must be considered. Certain product variants are so strongly linked to some brand names that, similar to the present argument, the brands are rather limited in their ability to extend to other variants. At the same time, this may convey a tremendous advantage in a particular category. In pilot data, we have found that Coke, for instance, cannot extend successfully to either lemon-lime or orange soda. On the other hand, consumers have no trouble accepting all of these variants from Shasta. At the same time, the Shasta brand name provides little competitive advantage for these variants, whereas Coke dominates the ''cola'' category for many consumers. Thus, from a competitive standpoint, it may be that strong equity in a narrow range of products is more valuable than weaker equity in a broad range. It is this trade, of course, that would guide the formulation of product and consequently advertising strategy.

If equity perceptions are based on advertising/evidence combinations and influence the transfer potential of the brand to novel categories, one might ask how controllable brand equity is from a managerial perspective. Managers have some control of brand equity through the nature of their advertising and some control of evaluations of brand extensions through the type of product category (relevant or irrelevant) they select for extensions. However, equity perceptions are not completely controllable because they are also affected by consumers' brand experiences and the evidence they evaluate. Because the results suggest that the most viable strategy is to develop quality evidence, the question becomes how evidence can be kept at an overall quality level. What factors should influence evidence based on quality?

One factor influencing overall quality evidence perceptions is prior knowledge. Low-knowledge consumers may evaluate a brand on a more general holistic basis, as opposed to a basis which decomposes the brand into its value on specific attributes. This is so because they may not have the attribute-based knowledge to allow such decomposition.

Research Issues. Although the above study generates preliminary insight into the nature of equity and its transfer to other categories, a number of additional issues regarding equity development should be examined in future research:

1. The study here deals with situations in which attribute advertising and attribute evidence match by presenting information on the same attribute. However, it is unclear from this research what happens to equity perceptions when advertising and evidence are still attribute oriented but (a) report on different attributes, or (b) report on the same attributes, but at different levels of generality (e.g., advertising focuses on size, MPG, body weight, etc. and evidence focuses on "economy," or vice versa). Additional research on these different attribute conditions would be interesting.

2. This study deals with advertising that focuses on only one attribute. This type of advertising is generally appropriate when the firm is attempting to clearly differentiate the brand from competitors (e.g., a unique selling proposition strategy), but not all advertising has such an objective. Advertising may be conducted to establish general superiority of the brand on multiple attributes. The present study focuses on attribute advertising when only one attribute was advertised. However, it is not clear how multiattribute advertising affects equity perceptions and, hence, a brand's transferability to other product categories. As the number of attributes in advertising increases, attribute advertising becomes more like overall quality advertising, except that the basis for equity is now more specific and less ambiguous. In essence, advertising along more attributes may build broader equity and provide more bases for extensions to other categories. Thus, one might hypothesize that the impact of attribute advertising on extension potential is moderated by the number of attributes advertised. Further research that studies this potential moderating factor is needed.

3. A general conclusion of the above results is that advertising frames evidence perceptions. This makes sense in the present experiment because advertising always preceded exposure to evidence. This framing interpretation has also been suggested elsewhere (e.g., Deighton, 1984), where advertising framed brand perceptions only when it preceded evidence. However, more direct evidence for the framing interpretation for the present results might be gained by replicating the above study, manipulating whether advertising or evidence comes first.

The generality of the above results may also depend on the prior knowledge of consumers. Specifically, the nature of the advertising (attribute based vs. quality based) and the nature of the evidence (attribute based vs. quality based) may be less important to high-knowledge versus low-knowledge consumers because they have more flexibility is transferring from one to the other. Thus, when presented with quality advertising or evidence, high-knowledge consumers may immediately infer values on specific attributes, which low-knowledge consumers may not do. Similarly, when presented with attribute evidence, high-knowledge consumers may compute the implications of these attribute values for overall quality; low-knowledge consumers may not. Furthermore, the impact of specific attribute advertising or evidence on the perceptions of high-knowledge consumers is likely to depend on the match between the attributes presented and those high-prior-knowledge consumers know are important indicators of quality.

4. Although this study found that extension potential is clearly influenced by the nature of brand equity, it also shows that extendibility is based on relevance. Additional work on how relevance perceptions are generated and whether marketers can control consumers' perceptions of relevance is important.

In summary, we suggest that, in order to understand the nature of brand equity and its application to brand extensions, we need to consider the basis of equity for consumers because it is this basis that will provide value in the brand extension. This points to the need to focus on the processes leading to brand equity as well as those involved in its transfer between categories, particularly the role of advertising in defining competitive position.

REFERENCES

Aaker, A., & Keller, K. L. (1990). Consumer evaluations of brand extensions. *Journal of Marketing, 54*(1), 27–41.

Aaker, D., & Myers, J. G. (1987). *Advertising management.* Englewood Cliffs, NJ: Prentice-Hall.

Boush, D., Shipp, S., Loken, B., Gencturk, E., Crockett, S., Kennedy, E., Minshall, B., Misurell, D., Rochford, L., & Strobel, J. (1987). Affect generalization to similar and dissimilar brand extensions. *Psychology and Marketing, 4*(3), 225–237.

Carpenter, G. S., & Nakamoto, K. (1987). Market pioneering, learning, and preference. In M. Houston (Ed.), *Advances in consumer research* (Vol. 15, pp. 275–279). Provo, UT: Association for Consumer Research.

Carpenter, G. S., & Nakamoto, K. (1989). Consumer preference formation and pioneering advantage. *Journal of Marketing Research, 26*(3), 285–298.

Chakravarti, D., MacInnis, D., & Nakamoto, K. (1990). Product category perceptions, elaborative processing, and brand name extension strategies. In R. Pollay, M. Goldberg, & G. Gorn (Eds.), *Advances in consumer research* (Vol. 17, pp. 910–916). Provo, UT: Association for Consumer Research.

Deighton, J. (1984). The interaction of advertising and evidence. *Journal of Consumer Research, 11*(3), 763–770.

Farquhar, P. H., Herr, P. M., & Fazio, R. H. (1989). *Extending brand equity to new categories* (working paper). Center for Product Research, Carnegie-Mellon University, Pittsburgh, PA.

Gutman, J., & Reynolds, T. J. (1979). An investigation of the levels of cognitive abstraction utilized by consumers in product differentiation. In J. Eighmey (Ed.), *Attitude research under the sun* (pp. 128–150). Chicago, IL: American Marketing Association.

Ha, Y., & Hoch, S. J. (1989). Ambiguity, processing strategy, and advertising—evidence interactions. *Journal of Consumer Research, 16*(3), 354–360.

Hoch, S. J., & Ha, Y. (1986). Consumer learning: Advertising and the ambiguity of product experience. *Journal of Consumer Research, 13*(2), 221–233.

Jung, H. (1991). *The impact of advertising and evidence on consumer judgments: An extension of research on hypothesis testing.* Unpublished doctoral dissertation, University of Arizona, Tucson.

MacInnis, D. J., & Nakamoto, K. (1991). *Examining factors that influence the perceived goodness of brand extensions* (working paper). University of Arizona, Tucson.

Park, C. W., Jaworski, B. J., & MacInnis, D. J. (1986). Strategic brand concept-image management. *Journal of Marketing, 50*(3), 135–145.

Stewart, D. W., & Furse, D. H. (1986). *Effective television advertising: A study of 1,000 commercials.* Lexington, MA: Lexington Books.

Tauber, E. M. (1988). Brand leverage: Strategy for growth in a cost-controlled world. *Journal of Advertising Research, 28*, 26–30.

Chapter 19

Brands as Categories

David M. Boush
University of Oregon

Brand managers commonly think about how brands compete within product categories. They strive to build the dominant brand in categories like "frozen foods," "personal computers," and "airlines." Marketing academics have reflected this notion of categories in writing about competitive positioning (Carpenter & Nakamoto, 1989; Sujan & Bettman, 1989) as well as consumer perceptions of categories (Loken & Ward, 1987, 1990; Nedungadi & Hutchinson, 1985; Ratneshwar & Shocker, 1991; Ward & Loken, 1986). In this context, an important issue is which brand (such as Hershey's) is most typical of, or dominant in, a particular product category (such as "candy bars"). However, it is useful to think of brands and categories in another way, as well. A brand can represent a category that consists of the products it makes. In this new context, a brand name such as Hershey's is the label for a category of products that are sold under that name. The category "Hershey's products" includes chocolate bars, candy kisses, and chocolate milk.

Thinking of such brand categories does not preclude thinking of brands as competing in product categories. Rather, the notion of a brand as a category complements the more conventional use of the term *category* and helps to shed some light on questions that are of interest to brand managers as they think about building brand equity. Among these questions are:

1. What kinds of brand extensions are likely to be helped most by an existing brand name?
2. What kinds of brand extensions are most likely to help an existing brand (i.e., make the brand name stronger)?

3. What kinds of brand extensions are most likely to hurt an existing brand name (i.e., to make the brand name weaker)?

4. What characteristics of a multiproduct brand give each product the best competitive position?

We should note at this point that all the above questions deal with concerns of brands that represent, or may someday represent, a variety of products. Examining the structure of a category with only one member is not very fruitful. Consequently, the treatment of brands as categories is probably not a useful perspective for brands that never plan to extend beyond a single product.

This chapter addresses these questions through the explication of propositions concerning brand categories, which revolve around the issue of brand category structure. Following the discussion of these propositions, some more specific implications will be described for advertising and brand extension strategies, and suggestions for further research will be discussed. First, however, it is necessary to explain what it means to say that a brand comprises a category.

WHAT IS A CATEGORY?

According to Mervis and Rosch (1981), "A category exists whenever two or more distinguishable objects or events are treated equivalently. This equivalent treatment may take any number of forms, such as labeling distinct objects or events with the same name, or performing the same action on different objects" (p. 89). Historically, categories were considered to be determined by necessary and sufficient criteria. Any object that fit the definition of the concept was considered as good an example as any other. However, more recent research has demonstrated that category members are not completely equivalent. Even though people perceive members of the same category as being equivalent in some sense, they also perceive most naturally occurring categories as varying in their degree of typicality, or representativeness, of those categories. For example, a cow is perceived as more typical of the category "mammal" than a whale. The range in category representativeness from the most representative members of a category to the nonmembers that are least similar to the category is called *graded structure* (Mervis & Rosch, 1981).

If a group of products that share the same brand name is considered to be a category, then graded structure implies that some products are more representative of a brand category than others. The alternative to this proposition is that family-branded products comprise an unordered list. All the members of such a list would be equally associated with a brand name. For example, if the category "Hallmark products" does not have graded structure, then a Hallmark greeting card would be no more typical than a Hallmark Christmas tree ornament. There are a number of possible bases for typicality.

Shared Features

One basis of typicality is the number of features that objects share with each other. Both the notion of family resemblance and the contrast model describe typicality among category members as a function of the number of features they share. For example, according to both models, the relative similarity of tomato soup, tomato paste, and tomato juice could be measured by having people list the features that come to mind for each product. Note that these characteristics could change based on the context. For example, in the context of "cooking," tomato soup might seem more like tomato paste because both could be ingredients, whereas in the context of "eating," tomato soup might seem more like tomato juice because both could be part of a meal in their present form. Although previous research in categorization has most commonly looked at physical features, such as color or shape, features such as the situation in which an object is used can also be important in determining categories (Barsalou, 1983; Ratneshwar & Shocker, 1991).

Family Resemblance. Wittgenstein (1953) first suggested that objects or concepts can be related (i.e., be in the same category) without sharing the same features with all other members. This phenomenon, termed *family resemblance*, is often illustrated using the category "games." It is hard to think of attributes that all or most games share; however, all members share at least one attribute with another category member. The more features a given member shares with other category members, the more typical of the category (Rosch & Mervis, 1975). Family-branded products could be related by family resemblance due to the various different bases for extension (Tauber, 1988). For example, Hershey's bases its extensions on a common ingredient (chocolate) and Coleman bases its extensions on usage context (camping). A brand that changes its basis for extension could include products that are related by family resemblance rather than by any single consistent feature or group of features. It is questionable whether a brand that is extended in a variety of different ways remains meaningful to consumers.

The Contrast Model. Tversky (1977) proposed the contrast model of similarity, which suggests that similarity is based on some combination of features that match (i.e., that objects share) and features that are distinctive (i.e., that objects do not share). Specifically, the similarity between objects A and B is a function of the features they have in common minus both the distinctive features of A and the distinctive features of B. Tversky described typicality as a special case of similarity—the similarity of one object to a class of objects. Note that distinctive features are important in the contrast model, whereas distinctive features are irrelevant in determining family resemblance. Loken and Ward (1990) found that distinctive features helped to explain typicality of products in categories like "types of candy" but were not as important as shared features.

Extreme Values

Barsalou (1983, 1985) extended principles of categorization to sets of objects, such as "foods you should not eat when you are on a diet," that are related because they fulfill a particular goal. These sets, termed *ad hoc* or *goal-directed* categories, are like more common categories in that they have both graded structure and prototypical exemplars. However, the most typical members of goal-directed categories are determined not by the number of shared or distinctive features but by extreme values on a single critical dimension. For example, the most typical members of the category "foods you should not eat when you are on a diet" are the ones with the most calories. Barsalou noted that goal-directed categories generally appear to violate the correlational structure of the environment, frequently including some members from each of several common taxonomic categories. For example, foods you cannot eat on a diet include ice cream, candy, and french fries. Barsalou's findings emphasized the flexibility of categorization processes and the ease with which certain categories can be generated for a particular purpose.

Familiarity

Another possible determinant of an object's typicality is the frequency with which it is encountered. Early work in categorization found no relationship between frequency and typicality (e.g., Rosch, Simpson, & Miller, 1976); however, later studies using more sensitive measures sometimes found such a relationship (Ashcraft, 1978; Malt, 1989; Malt & Smith, 1982). As Loken and Ward (1990) noted, the empirical evidence concerning the relationship between familiarity and typicality is confusing and dependent on the particular definitions of familiarity and the methods used to measure it. In the context of brand categories, if familiarity determined typicality, then we would expect that the product most often associated with the brand name would be the one judged most typical. For example, if a consumer encountered Campbell's tomato juice more often than Campbell's soup, then the memory associations between "Campbell's" and "tomato juice" would become stronger than those between "Campbell's" and "soup," so the former would become more typical.

PROPOSITIONS

The preceding discussion provokes a number of questions about the relationship between brands and their various product and feature associations. This section explores each question and suggests a proposition in response to it. In some cases, the proposition is supported by existing findings; in other cases, it remains to be verified.

Is a Brand a Category?

The first requirement of a category is that its members be equivalent in some way. Brand categories seem to fulfill this requirement because the use of a common brand name signals some kind of equivalence to consumers. For example, the phrase "It's a Sony" implies a kind of equivalence in expectations among Sony products. In Mervis and Rosch's (1981) definition, a brand category takes the form of labeling distinct objects with the same name. Applying a common brand name to products differs from the way names are applied to objects in common taxonomic categories because a branded product is linguistically categorized as a member of the brand category from the outset. Categorization of objects in common taxonomic categories more frequently involves making the categorization decision (That's a bird) after observing its characteristics (feathers, ability to fly). When consumers see a branded product (Atari fax machine), they are essentially told that it is a member of a brand category (products made by Atari); then they may consider what features or benefits it is likely to have.

Brand categories also fulfill the requirement of having graded structure as opposed to being members of an unordered set. Existing and potential family-branded products have been shown to occupy a continuum, from extremely representative of a brand to extremely unrepresentative of a brand (Boush & Loken, 1991). Note the key word *continuum*. The evidence is that branded products are not judged to be simply "bad" or "good," but rather they range in the extent to which they represent the brand category. Similarly, some products are prototypical (most typical) of their brands. For example, greeting cards and soup are prototypical of the brands Hallmark and Campbell's, respectively. Leaving aside for the moment the question of why one product is more typical of the brand category than another, we can assert the following:

Proposition 1a. Family-branded products vary along a continuum in the extent to which they are typical of the brand.

Proposition 1b. Brand categories have prototypical products.

What is the Basis of Brand Category Structure?

The structural basis of brand categories is, as yet, an unanswered empirical question. From the previous discussion, it seems likely that both shared and contrasting features play a role. In addition, brand categories arguably have some of the properties of goal-directed or ad hoc categories. In particular, as Barsalou described, "Many goal-derived categories include some members from

TABLE 19.1
Examples of Brand Categories

The Hershey Brand Category

Brand concept definition: Made with chocolate.

Partial List of Hershey Products:
Chocolate bar
Chocolate kisses
Chocolate syrup
Chocolate milk

The Hallmark Brand Category

Essential characteristics: Gift-associated, high quality.
Contributing characteristics: Combination of pictures and words.
Accidental characteristic: Made of paper.

Partial List of Hallmark Products:
Greeting cards (the brand prototype)
Gift wrap
Posters
Plaques
Party accessories
Christmas ornaments

Brand Subcategory: Hallmark "Shoebox" Greetings
Products: Greeting cards aimed at a younger market

---

each of several common taxonomic categories, but never all the members from a given one. . . . Other goal-derived categories contain subsets of one particular taxonomic category. For example, someone with a back problem might be interested in chairs that provide good back support'' (1985, p. 632).

The quotation seems to describe many multiproduct brand categories. For example, Gerber puts its name on a variety of products for babies. Gucci products include luggage, gloves, and shoes, but not all kinds of luggage, gloves, and shoes. Rather than capitalizing on the natural correlational structure of the environment, ad hoc categories are based on extreme values on a few related salient features. The structure of brand categories seems to share this reliance. For example, the most typical product carrying a brand like Gucci probably has the most to do with "fashionable leather." The typicality of Hallmark products may be based on similarity to greeting cards, the dominant exemplar (see Table 19.1). Barsalou's research on ad hoc categories particularly emphasized the flexible, constructive nature of the categorization process. Ad hoc categories can be constructed on demand.

Proposition 2. The easiest brand category for consumers to accept is one in which typicality is based on extreme values on a few related salient features.

Matching and Distinctive Features. The categorization literature provides mixed evidence on whether distinctive features impact similarity or typicality judgments. The concept of family resemblance treats distinctive features as irrelevant, whereas Tversky's (1977) contrast model posits that distinctive features decrease perceived similarity. Both common sense and experience with failed extensions indicates that inconsistent features can render a particular extension inappropriate. Gerber ketchup, for example, would resemble baby food in many ways, but it is an inappropriate extension because of Gerber's association with babies exclusively. Therefore, it seems reasonable to consider distinctive features as relevant in determining typicality.

Similarity Asymmetry. Perhaps the most significant implication of Tversky's (1977) contrast model is that it predicts asymmetries in similarity judgments. For example, Tversky found that subjects rated North Korea more similar to Red China than Red China was to North Korea. This purportedly occurred because of "the relative salience of the stimuli; the variant is more similar to the prototype than vice versa" (p. 328). Family-branded products are frequently (if not usually) characterized by extension from relatively representative (prototypical) products to less representative variants. For example, Hallmark has extended from greeting cards to other products involved with "social expression," such as posters and paper party goods. Asymmetry in similarity judgments implies that a Hallmark poster would be more similar to a Hallmark card than a Hallmark card is to a Hallmark poster. Johnson (1986) demonstrated that the contrast model applies in similarity judgments for consumer products; Boush (1991) reported instances where brand names produced asymmetries in judgments of similarity between pairs of products.

Proposition 3. Pairwise similarity judgments between products that share the same brand name may be asymmetrical. Specifically, the less typical product will be perceived as more similar to the typical product than the reverse.

Defining and Accidental Features. Not all brand characteristics are of equal importance. Specifically, it is useful to consider some characteristics as essential, some as contributing, and some as accidental features of the brand image. (For example, the characteristics "well-engineered," "stylish," and "for yuppies" may be, respectively, essential, contributing, and accidental features of the BMW brand image.) Theoretical support for a taxonomy of category features is well established, although the terminology differs from that expressed earlier. It has been suggested that some features are defining and some are accidental (Smith & Medin, 1981; Smith, Shoben, & Rips, 1974).

Proposition 4. Not all brand features are of equal importance in determining brand category structure.

Feature Salience.   When people categorize an object, not all of its attributes necessarily come to mind (Barsalou, 1983; Herr, 1986; Higgins, Bargh, & Lombardi, 1985). Some subset of attributes may be activated by the context. A basketball would probably be described as "round" regardless of the context, but the attribute "able to float" would only come to mind in particular contexts. Context bias (priming) has been shown to alter typicality judgments by making some category members more accessible than others. For example, Roth and Shoben (1983) showed that a statement like "the bird walked across the barnyard" made "chicken" more typical of the category "bird" than is "robin."

Particular product features can be made salient in a variety of ways. Gerber's advertising slogan, "Babies are our business, our only business," made the attribute "for babies" salient. Boush (in press) demonstrated experimentally that advertising slogans can prime features of extensions, so that some are judged to be more or less typical than they would be without the slogans. The primary effect of this kind of priming was to limit the range of acceptable extensions.

Proposition 5.   Typicality of brand category members depends on feature salience.

Which Brand Extensions Will be Helped by the Brand?

Transfer of attitude from existing products to a new product does not occur in an "all or nothing" fashion. Rather, it is a linear function of the degree to which a product is perceived to represent the brand (Boush et al., 1987; Boush & Loken, 1991). Negative reaction to an extremely unrepresentative brand extension goes well beyond the failure of positive attitude to transfer. Such products (e.g., a Sony handbag or a Kraft radio) are perceived as "wrong" for the brand and are evaluated negatively. Recent findings concerning the importance of manufacturer credibility and expertise (Aaker & Keller, 1990) are consistent with this. Park, Milberg, and Lawson (1991) found that consumers take into account not only the product-level feature consistency between the extension and the brand's existing products, but also the consistency between the new product and the brand concept.

Proposition 6a.   Attitude follows typicality. The more typical of a brand a product is perceived to be, the more the attitude toward the brand will be associated with the product.

An earlier proposition (3b) posited that similarity may be asymmetrical. If that notion is combined with Proposition 6a, it implies that attitude may not always transfer symmetrically. For example, attitude may transfer more readily from a Hallmark card to a Hallmark poster, or from Campbell's soup to

Campbell's pork and beans, than will the reverse. Asymmetry in the flow of attitude suggests that advertising for prototypical products would be likely to help less typical products more than the reverse. For example, advertising for Campbell's soup may help Campbell's pork and beans more than advertising for Campbell's pork and beans helps Campbell's soup.

Proposition 6b. The transfer of attitude between products represented by a brand may not be symmetrical. Specifically, attitude toward a prototypical product will transfer more readily to a less typical product than will the reverse.

Which Brand Extensions Will Help or Hurt the Brand?

The brand is the cue to a variety of product aspects, including: (a) the level of quality that may be expected, (b) product origin, (c) attributes, and (d) benefits (e.g., Erickson, Johansson, & Chao, 1984; Jacoby, Olson, & Haddock, 1971). In addition, some brands convey added benefits to consumers through their association with beliefs or feelings transmitted by advertising. The key to a strong brand is to have it mean something. In categorization terms, a brand (or any other cue) has meaning (validity) when it is relatively consistent within category members and distinctive from members of other categories. That is, a brand is meaningful when its products and the benefits they convey are similar within the brand and importantly different from other brands. The brand name, the label of the brand category, then serves as an informative cue to consumers making purchase decisions. The brand is strong as well as meaningful when it serves as a cue to meanings that help to sell the product.

Proposition 7a. Brands have utility to consumers because they convey meaning about products in the brand category.

Consistent extensions arguably strengthen the brand in two ways:

1. They increase the number of associations in memory between the brand name and the characteristics that give the brand meaning.
2. The effect of additional consistent associations may produce a higher level belief about the brand.

Two particularly important beliefs may be that: (a) the brand is trustworthy, and (b) it has expertise in the production of a particular product (Keller & Aaker, 1992). Strengthening brands in this manner is consistent with the fortification stage of brand concept-image management, described by Park, Jaworski, and McInnis (1986).

A related concept is that of *brand breadth*, which refers to the variability among product types represented by a brand name. Brand breadth appears to be a result of the typicality of brand extensions. If brand managers consistently extend the brand by offering new products that are very much like (i.e., typical of) existing ones, then a narrow brand results. If brand extensions are very different from existing products, then a broad brand results. It seems clear, furthermore, that as new products become established, people's beliefs about what is "typical" of the category will change. Brand breadth has been shown to influence typicality and attitudinal judgments of brand extensions (Boush & Loken, 1991). For example, if a brand made televisions exclusively, it might gain greater credibility in manufacturing expertise if it extended into products such as stereo components. Later electronic line extensions would then be evaluated more favorably than before.

Proposition 7b.   Meaning about branded products is enhanced by extension to products with the same defining features as the original brand category.

Inconsistent extensions can change the meaning of the brand category in two ways:

1. Inconsistent extensions obscure the original brand category meaning. This happens by direct implication for both the contrast model of similarity and any model based on extreme values.

2. Inconsistent extensions may also convert the meaning to a new—and usually broader—one. For example, extending the Hershey's brand to another product that does not contain chocolate redefines the Hershey's brand definition from "products containing chocolate" to something else, such as "things that are sweet." This is consistent with Ries and Trout's (1981) criticism of brand extension strategies.

Proposition 7c.   Brand extensions that are inconsistent with a defining feature of the brand change the meaning of the brand category.

A brand extension strategy based on a single feature or set of related features reinforces the same salient characteristic repeatedly, giving the extension a position in every market it enters. For example, Planters is a brand name that is closely associated with peanuts. Or, to put it a bit differently, "real peanut taste" is a characteristic that can be leveraged in any product category in which that characteristic is relevant to product choice. Planters peanut candy has a natural position as the candy with real peanut taste, even without promoting that belief. Other Planters products that contain peanuts, such as peanut butter, have an immediate position. Planters microwave popcorn is not, however, based on the same salient characteristic as all other Planters products. Instead, it seems to be based on similarity to roasted peanuts as a snack food. Planters microwave popcorn, therefore, does not enter the market with an instantly recognizable position.

Proposition 8. A brand whose typicality is based on *a consistent defining feature* or set of related characteristics has a salient feature in every market entered, without promotion.

Subcategory Signaling. Brand managers frequently signal product differences and similarities by the use of secondary brand names (Nabisco "Classic" crackers, Hallmark "Shoebox" greetings) and corresponding visual cues. These cues are particularly interesting because they represent a clear attempt to manipulate categories of consumer knowledge. For example, if you look at a grocery store display of crackers, it seems that the "Classic" line is positioned against Pepperidge Farm's "Distinctive" crackers. Such cues should be reflected in consumer product evaluations.

Proposition 9a. Brand subcategories can signal competitive positioning.

In cases where brand extensions contain characteristics that contrast with nondefining features of the original brand, subcategories can be usefully employed to signal the consumer that the extension is a differentiated member of the brand category. Examples of this tactic include Hallmark "Shoebox" greeting cards and Jockey "For Her" underwear. Ideally, the manipulation of brand structure in this manner would allow the positive brand attitude to transfer to the brand extension without compromising the definition of the original brand category. The propositions developed to this point would argue that brand subcategories will compromise the original brand definition if they include features that are inconsistent with a brand category's essential features. In this context, Hallmark "Shoebox" greetings are acceptable because they contrast with other Hallmark cards only because they are slightly less conventional. Jockey "For Her" offers a more complicated example. Perhaps the Jockey brand category is structured around functional clothing attributes and "masculinity" is not an essential feature for Jockey. Note that both Hallmark and Jockey employ brand subcategories based on products aimed at target markets that are different from that of the original brand.

Proposition 9b. Brand subcategories can signal differences from the original brand.

SUMMARY

Managerial Implications

This chapter takes the perspective that a brand serves as a cue to: (a) product quality, (b) product attributes, and (c) expected benefits. The most important implication for managers is that this cue must be as meaningful as possible.

Therefore, the consistency of the brand category is a key consideration. Consistency must be maintained in every communication with the consumer that involves the brand: (a) advertising, (b) packaging, (c) associated distribution characteristics (i.e., the store characteristics where the products are sold), and (d) the products themselves. In building a consistent brand image, it is useful to consider: (a) which features are essential to brand identity, (b) which contribute to brand identity, and (c) which are accidental associations with the brand. If brands are structured according to consumer perceptions of one or a few related salient characteristics, it seems crucial to find and protect the essential features of a brand. In this context, brand extensions would more likely be helped by the brand if they are based on one or a set of related essential brand features. Extensions that are based on a feature shared with only one existing product may not have effective leverage in the market and may obscure what the brand category means.

Two additional implications are suggested for managing brand category structure:

1. Certain features of the brand can be made more salient. Advertising can play a key role in focusing attention on essential brand features to make the relationship among family-branded products clear. Obvious examples include Hershey's emphasizing chocolate or Gerber's emphasizing babies. A more subtle example might be the way General Electric alludes to electricity in its slogan "We bring good things to life."

2. Brand categories can be manipulated to include subcategories. Brand subcategories can protect the original brand definition and position a particular product against one or more specific competitors.

Future Research

One area for future research is to examine the structure of actual brand categories. Interesting empirical issues involve the similarity relationships between brand associations and the rules that govern brand category construction (see Proposition 2). Leavitt (1989) proposed that brand images can be divided usefully according to whether they have a simple or complex structure. The categorization perspective outlined here suggests ways that the concept of brand image complexity may be further developed. For example, a complex structure may be defined in a variety of ways, including: (a) the total number of brand associations, (b) the number of different brand associations, and (c) the number of brand subcategories.

A related area for future research is the effect of brand category structure on the consumer beliefs and attitudes that partially comprise brand equity. Aaker (1991) discussed five dimensions of brand equity: (a) name awareness,

(b) perceived quality, (c) brand associations other than quality, (d) customer base, and (e) other proprietary brand assets. The brand category perspective suggests relationships between some of these dimensions. For example, the previous discussion suggests that brand associations can be described in structural terms (i.e., complexity) and that complexity should improve name awareness because of the number of associations in memory. Complexity can also lead consumers to infer that the branded products are made by a company with considerable expertise (Aaker & Keller, 1990), which may improve perceptions of quality. Finally, many of the propositions stated in this paper concerning brand structure (2, 6b, 7b, 7c, 8, 9a, 9b) require empirical support. Of particular interest are: (a) the propositions concerning extension to products that either do or do not have the same defining features as the brand category (7b and 7c), (b) the proposition that a brand with a consistent definition has a salient feature in every market entered (8), and (c) propositions concerning the effect of brand subcategories (9a and 9b).

REFERENCES

Aaker, D. A. (1991). *Managing brand equity: Capitalizing on the value of a brand name*. New York: The Free Press.

Aaker, D. A., & Keller, K. L. (1990). Consumer evaluations of brand extensions. *Journal of Marketing, 54*(1), 27–41.

Ashcraft, M. (1978). Property norms for typical and atypical items from 17 categories: A description and discussion. *Memory and Cognition, 6*(3), 227–232.

Barsalou, L. W. (1983). Ad hoc categories. *Memory and Cognition, 11*(3), 211–227.

Barsalou, L. W., (1985). Ideals, central tendency, and frequency of instantiation as determinants of graded structure in categories. *Journal of Experimental Psychology: Learning, Memory, and Cognition, 11*(4), 629–648.

Boush, D. M. (1991, October). *Brand name effects on product similarity judgments*. Paper presented at the Association for Consumer Research conference, Chicago, IL.

Boush, D. M. (in press). How advertising slogans can prime evaluations of brand extensions. *Psychology and Marketing*.

Boush, D. M., & Loken, B. (1991). A process tracing study of brand extension evaluation. *Journal of Marketing Research, 28*(1), 16–28.

Boush, D., Shipp, S., Loken, B., Gencturk, E., Crockett, S., Kennedy, E., Minshall, B., Misurell, D., Rochford, L., & Strobel, J. (1987). Affect generalization to similar and dissimilar brand extensions. *Psychology and Marketing, 4*(3), 225–237.

Carpenter, G. S., & Nakamoto, K. (1989). Consumer preference formation and pioneering advantage. *Journal of Marketing Research, 26*(3), 285–298.

Erickson, G. M., Johansson, J. K., & Chao, P. (1984). Image variables in multi-attribute product evaluations: Country of origin effects. *Journal of Consumer Research, 11*(3), 694–699.

Herr, P. M. (1986). Consequences of priming: Judgment and behavior. *Journal of Personality and Social Psychology, 51*, 1106–1115.

Higgins, E. T., Bargh, J. A., & Lombardi, W. (1985). Nature of priming effects on categorization. *Journal of Experimental Psychology: Learning, Memory, and Cognition, 11*, 59–69.

Jacoby, J., Olson, J. C., & Haddock, R. A. (1971). Price, brand name, and product composition characteristics as determinants of perceived quality. *Journal of Applied Psychology, 55*, 570–579.

Johnson, M. D. (1986). Consumer similarity judgments: A test of the contrast model. *Psychology and Marketing, 3*, 47-60.

Keller, K. L., & Aaker, D. A. (1992). The effects of sequential introduction of brand extensions. *Journal of Marketing Research, 29*(1), 35-50.

Leavitt, C. (1989). *The structure and maintenance of well-established brand images* (working paper No. 89-7). College of Business, The Ohio State University, Columbus, OH.

Loken, B., & Ward, J. (1987). Measures of attribute structure underlying product typicality. In M. Wallendorf & P. F. Anderson (Eds.), *Advances in consumer research* (Vol. 14, pp. 22-28). Provo, UT: Association for Consumer Research.

Loken, B., & Ward, J. (1990). Alternative approaches to understanding the determinants of typicality. *Journal of Consumer Research, 17*(2), 111-126.

Malt, B. C. (1989). An on-line investigation of prototype and exemplar strategies in classification. *Journal of Experimental Psychology: Learning, Memory, and Cognition, 15*(4), 539-555.

Malt, B. C., & Smith, E. E. (1982). The role of familiarity in determining typicality. *Memory and Cognition, 10*(1), 60-75.

Mervis, C. B., & Rosch, E. (1981). Categorization of natural objects. *Annual Review of Psychology, 32*, 89-115.

Nedungadi, P., & Hutchinson, J. W. (1985). The prototypicality of brands: Relationships with brand awareness, preference, and usage. In E. C. Hirschman & M. B. Holbrook (Eds.), *Advances in consumer research* (Vol. 12, pp. 498-503). Provo, UT: Association for Consumer Research.

Park, C. W., Jaworski, B. J., & MacInnis, D. J. (1986). Strategic brand concept-image management. *Journal of Marketing, 50*(4), 135-145.

Park, C. W., Milberg, S.; & Lawson, R. (1991). Evaluation of brand extensions: The role of product-feature similarity and concept consistency. *Journal of Consumer Research, 18*(2), 185-193.

Ratneshwar, S., & Shocker, A. D. (1991). Substitution in use and the role of usage context in product category structures. *Journal of Marketing Research, 28*(3), 281-295.

Ries, A., & Trout, J. (1981). *Positioning: The battle for your mind.* New York: McGraw-Hill, Inc.

Rosch, E., & Mervis, C. B. (1975). Family resemblances: Studies in the internal structure of categories. *Cognitive Psychology, 7*, 573-605.

Rosch, E., Simpson, C., & Miller, R. S. (1976). Structure bases of typicality effects. *Journal of Experimental Psychology: Human Perception and Performance, 2*(4), 491-502.

Roth, F. M., & Shoben, E. J. (1983). The effect of context on the structure of categories. *Cognitive Psychology, 15*, 346-378.

Smith, E. E., & Medin, D. L. (1981). *Categories and concepts.* Cambridge, MA: Harvard University Press.

Smith, E. E., Shoben, E. J., & Rips, L. J. (1974). Structure and process in semantic memory: A featural model for semantic decisions. *Psychological Review, 81*, 214-241.

Sujan, M., & Bettman, J. R. (1989). The effects of brand positioning strategies on consumers' brand and category perceptions. *Journal of Marketing Research, 26*(4), 454-467.

Tauber, E. M. (1988). Brand leverage: Strategy for growth in a cost control world. *Journal of Advertising Research, 31*(3), 26-30.

Tversky, A. (1977). Features of similarity. *Psychological Review, 84*(4), 327-350.

Ward, J., & Loken, B. (1986). The quintessential snack food: Measurement of product prototypes. In R. Lutz (Ed.), *Advances in consumer research* (Vol. 13, pp. 126-131). Provo, UT: Association for Consumer Research.

Wittgenstein, L. (1953). *Philosophical investigations.* New York: Macmillan.

Chapter 20

Fit and Leverage
in Brand Extensions

Edward M. Tauber
Tauber Research

IF YOU COULD SEE HER THROUGH MY EYES

When you look at me standing here today, you see someone very different from what I see when I think about myself. You may see a short guy with glasses who is a marketing researcher, but I know that I play guitar in a rock-and-roll band! In fact, I know millions of things about myself that you cannot know. As a result, there is a huge gap between what you perceive about me and what I perceive about myself.

This is the essence of brand extension research. The company that makes a product has one database from which it perceives its brands; the consumer has a far different and more personalized data base that he or she uses to form impressions about these brands.

Our role as researchers is to help management understand their brands through the eyes of the consumer.

Without exception, in every brand extension study I have ever conducted, there has always been a huge difference between what management believed the consumer thought and what the consumer actually thought about their brands.

THE CONCEPTS OF FIT AND LEVERAGE

A brand can successfully be extended to new categories only if: (a) the consumer believes the brand is a logical *fit*, and (b) the brand conveys some benefit wanted in the new category—what I call *leverage*. In my experience, some brands

313

cannot be extended at all; very few have broad extension potential and most can be extended to a very limited number of categories.

The limitations that restrict a brand's extension are varied:

1. Some brands are tied so closely to a product or product class that the consumer rejects the name on anything else. A Coke is a soft drink—period.
2. Some brands convey a narrow or special expertise from the company that manufactures them. This precludes the brand from having credibility in other areas. Hershey makes chocolate. Anything not chocolate is not Hershey.
3. Some brands own attributes or benefits that are tied to the parent product. For example, anything with the Clorox name on it probably can't be delicate or mild. Anything from Contadina better be Italian.

Most brands begin life as the name of a single product, as the name of a company, or both. The meanings and associations that accrue to the brand over its life come from three sources:

1. What the company communicates—the brand's positioning, advertising, and implied communications (e.g., the type of stores where it is sold, whether there is heavy discounting, and so on).
2. The consumers' experience with the product and company. Does it deliver unique benefits or engender special feelings? What type of people does the consumer think are primary buyers of the product?
3. Borrowed associations. Sometimes these are inherent in the brand name. Sometimes they are associations from when the product was used, early memories of use, what other products were used with it, what my mother said about the product, and so on.

CONSUMERS PROTECT "THEIR" BRANDS

Management does not always protect its brands, but the consumer does. If a brand extension is a non sequitur, or is somehow offensive to the consumer, they will reject it.

This can happen precisely because many companies have a false impression of how the consumer sees their brand.

When I conducted a study for Carnation, management saw themselves as a huge multiproduct company with leading-edge food technology. The consumer saw Carnation as a canned milk company, with all the related associations and expectations of that type of product.

Duracell management saw their brand as associated with a variety of types of consumer electronics. The consumer said this company would not know how to make electronic gadgets like Sony, but maybe they could make flashlights.

Citicorp management knew it was a huge financial powerhouse that could offer any service from Citicorp or Citibank. Consumers outside of New York saw a credit card company.

Dole knew they were a broad-based, fruit-and-vegetable company. Consumers thought pineapple and sunny Hawaii.

My examples are intentionally simplified to protect confidentiality, but they reflect the reality that extension opportunities are dictated by the perceptions of consumers—some of these formed years ago and hard to change.

Academic researchers often want to make brand extension research a science—measurable in controlled experiments and quantifiable in multivariate studies. In my opinion, this can never be. When we force brand extension into this type of research, we lose the richness of the meanings and associations of brands. We reduce it to a few dimensions and provide management with another false impression to substitute for the one they already have. Brand extension research is an art that requires a depth of insight and lots of creative thinking. That's the only way we can truly see the brand through the consumers' eyes.

HAVE WE BECOME OVERDEPENDENT ON FIT?

Turning to the papers given at the 10th Annual Conference of the Society for Consumer Psychology, I found myself asking whether some of the papers might not be on the wrong track. As I suggested to Dave Aaker several years ago, when he was developing his thinking about brand extensions, it is my impression that the field is concentrating on fit rather than on leverage. In my view, fit is a relatively trivial concept, easily measured and, in some ways, even deceptive.

In fact, there is probably an inverse relationship between leverage and stretchability. In other words, if a brand name can be stretched with the consumer (i.e., if the consumer will allow the brand to appear on a very broad range of products), it probably has very little inherent leverage.

Conversely, a brand with a great deal of associated meaning probably cannot be stretched very far at all.

FAMILIARITY VERSUS LEVERAGE

Let us consider General Mills' Betty Crocker, an example of a very broadly based brand.

Betty Crocker is very well known and has a great reputation, but—and this is the point, of course—it doesn't stand for anything very specific. In fact, it is very hard to think of an exact category for Betty Crocker. It is on a lot of different things.

The reverse of this is the case of another General Mills brand—Total. General Mills decided to enter the oatmeal category against Quaker Oats, a brand that is very specific and narrow in meaning. General Mills knew they must fight an uphill battle against the brand that "owned" the category. Clearly, when a marketer such as General Mills enters a category that is dominated by a brand like Quaker, there are options. One possibility would have been to use Betty Crocker. However, the risk was that Betty Crocker was just another well-known brand, prominent in a number of categories. Quaker, on the other hand, was a synonym for the category itself.

Using the Total brand, a more specific, cereal-oriented leverage could be developed. To be sure, Betty Crocker would have been accepted by the consumer, but the idea of Betty Crocker Oatmeal has very little leverage.

The name Total, on the other hand, instantly communicated how the brand was different from Quaker, based on the carry-over from advertising for the brand in the cold-cereal category. In my view, that's a good example of how effective leverage can work. Of course, the next question is, "Do consumers want a Total Oatmeal?"

LEVERAGE AS MEANING TRANSFER

Leverage means that when I tell a consumer there is x-brand of this category, the consumer can instantly figure out what the differentiation is and what the attributes are likely to be. In other words, the brand brings something important as well as differentiating to the category.

If that concept were not important in thinking of brand extendibility, literally any well-known brand name would be fine—and there are thousands of brand names around.

Thus, a marketer could enter any category as long as there was a well-known brand name available. Clearly, that is not possible. The reason: More often than not, we are trying to extend into an established, or perhaps a new but rapidly growing, category. In the majority of cases, another brand dominates the category. Our product, although not deficient, is most likely to be "me too" or, at best, marginally superior.

Therefore, our best chance of taking on the competitor is through some leverage that our brand brings to the marketplace—that is what brand extension is really all about.

LEVERAGE IS THE PLACE TO START

I suggest that we are spending far too much time starting with the idea: "We have this brand that we own. Let's see the maximum numbers it will fit."

My view of the starting point is very different. I start with leverage and then work toward fit.

When we do a study, we try to determine the definition of the brand as perceived by the consumer. I have found that, with almost every brand, if I understand that definition, I can predict exactly what products the consumer will allow me to place under the brand's umbrella. I try to determine the essence of the brand. By knowing its leverage, I can then predict what products the consumer will allow. Although we test it, I have found that if I understand the brand from the consumer's viewpoint, I can predict the leverage without asking about it. For example, take the brand Bounty. For Bounty, absorbency is one of its characteristics and also one of its boundaries. Of course, there could also be other boundaries; the consumer won't allow a product under the Bounty brand simply because it is absorbent. Once I understand these other characteristics, I can ask consumers about other categories where they want the benefits of this cluster of attributes. Once we understand this, we know what the other brand-leverage opportunities are.

WHY FIT IS LESS HELPFUL THAN LEVERAGE

To use the Betty Crocker example again, there may be 100 product categories that the consumer will allow the brand to fit. Perhaps none of these are very good as brand extension opportunities. The important thing that is lacking is an understanding of leverage. Leverage—more than fit—determines which categories really represent opportunities for brand extension.

If, on the other hand, fit were the key, all we would need is to own a good brand; then we could enter virtually any product category. Clearly, that is not the case.

I reached this conclusion about the relative importance of fit versus leverage the hard way. After doing many of these studies, I began to realize that I kept hearing similar things. I categorized these as seven types of leverage, described in an earlier paper.[1] In fact, in all the studies of this type that I have ever conducted, I have found only seven types of leverage in total.

This led me to suggest to some clients that it might be useful to predict which types of leverage a brand might have.

OWNERSHIP OF A PROPERTY BY A BRAND

For those of you who are not familiar with my earlier work on this topic, I am referring to the kinds of properties a brand can own.

---

[1]Tauber, E. M. (1988). Brand Leverage: Strategy for Growth in a Cost-Control World. *Journal of Advertising Research, 28*(4), pp. 26–30.

For example, some brands own ingredients; others own a benefit; still others might own a flavor or an association.

Ownership suggests that the brand is inextricably tied to the characteristic in the way that Hershey is linked to chocolate. To be able to successfully line extend, Hershey has to leverage this characteristic along with some other characteristics.

In closing, I suggest that the focus should be away from the determination of fit, which in my mind is rather trivial. The fact that something fits doesn't mean that it is a good brand extension. Instead, the focus should be on understanding leverage, and that will take us way beyond where we are right now.

Part VI

Case Studies
and a Commentary

The Role of Corporate Advertising in Building a Brand: Chevron's Preconversion Campaign in Texas

Lewis C. Winters
Chevron Corporation

When Chevron acquired Gulf in 1985 for $13.2 billion, it was the biggest merger in history. This merger marked the starting point of a huge business challenge for Chevron, involving the integration of two corporate giants—their assets, their personnel, their "cultures," and their brand "personalities." Marketing was an important aspect of this integration; specifically, the corporation now held two viable brands of gasoline—Chevron and Gulf. However, the terms of the merger necessitated divestment of assets such that there was little overlap remaining between Chevron and Gulf's major markets. The Chevron brand was widely known in the Southeast and Pacific regions. Gulf, on the other hand, was a major gasoline brand in the Southwest region, especially in the state of Texas, where Chevron was a virtual unknown.

To build a single strong brand, and for efficiency's sake, Chevron's management decided that the company would market a single brand coast-to-coast. This decision meant converting 3,000 Gulf stations to the Chevron brand in the four-state area including Texas, Louisiana, Arkansas, and New Mexico. Management was determined that the conversion would yield more than a change in identity or signage at Gulf service station outlets; Chevron would commit $50 million to introduce itself to the region and to create a personality and presence for the Chevron brand.

To direct the marketing aspect of the total brand conversion challenge, Chevron's management appointed a committee with representatives from marketing, advertising, public affairs, and research. This chapter chronicles the elements of one small aspect of the comprehensive brand conversion plan which the committee conceived and carried out. Specifically, it discusses the role of corporate advertising during the period of time in advance of the sign change at Gulf stations. This time period has been labeled *the preconversion*. Although in budget terms the corporate advertising effort constituted only about 2% of the total conversion investment, data suggests that corporate advertising made a considerable contribution to the development of the Chevron brand in this region. Moreover, corporate advertising today still plays an important role for the considerable success of the brand in this market. This success may be measured, among other ways, by the 7% market-share increase that Chevron has experienced in Houston since the brand conversion was completed. The efforts of the San Francisco offices of J. Walter Thompson on the corporate-advertising side and Young & Rubicam on the product-advertising side contributed greatly to this success.

To fully understand the corporate-advertising role in the brand conversion program, it is necessary to go back to the early 1980s in California. During that time, research uncovered three main belief factors that predicted overall attitude toward Chevron: (a) marketing beliefs, (b) socially conscious beliefs, and (c) beliefs about Chevron's contributions. Of the three belief factors, the one with the highest weight in predicting overall attitude was the marketing factor. However, there was one segment of the California market, VALS Inner-Directeds,[1] that placed more weight on Chevron's social conduct—especially its environmental conduct. These Inner-Directeds were a fairly hostile group when it came to attitudes toward oil companies.

A campaign that eventually became known as Chevron's "People Do" campaign was developed and successfully pretested. The "People Do" campaign became one of the most successful campaigns ever for Chevron (Winters, 1988). Even though the Texas market was different psychologically, the question remaining was "Would the 'People Do' campaign convey the 'good company' image that was needed as a platform before introducing specific 'good brand' advertising about Chevron?"

THE GULF BRAND AND ITS CUSTOMERS, CIRCA 1986

The brand conversion was a risky proposition. In 1985, Gulf had about 11% market share in Texas. Chevron's research indicated that Gulf had an unusually loyal following for their brand of gasoline, but that this franchise was eroding.

---

[1]VALS Inner-Directeds are a segment of the market identified by SRI International. Unlike Outer-Directeds, who psychologically identify with the "establishment" values, the Inner-Directeds march to their own drummer. They are more likely to focus on people and processes for doing things, rather than on objects and output. Inner-Directeds comprise about 20% to 25% of the U.S. adult population.

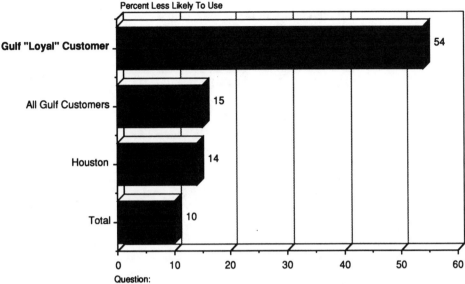

Percent Less Likely To Use

Gulf "Loyal" Customer — 54

All Gulf Customers — 15

Houston — 14

Total — 10

0   10   20   30   40   50   60

Question:
If Gulf Oil stations started to look like Chevron stations, with Chevron signs and colors, selling Chevron gasoline, would it make you more likely, less likely, or make no difference in your likelihood to buy at these stations?

Source: Chevron Market Research
1987 Study By Winona MRB, Inc.

FIG. 21.1.   Likelihood of using Chevron.
N = 600 gasoline purchasers: Houston, Dallas, and New Orleans.

Moreover, in September, 1987, Chevron's research found that 54% of loyal Gulf users would consider defection if Gulf changed its name to Chevron (Fig. 21.1). In other words, 54% of our customers did not like what was about to be done to them. In addition, it was going to cost $50 million. Usually, you would like to increase customer satisfaction if you spent $50 million. Since the four-state area represented 25% of Chevron's total U.S. volume (1.3 billion gallons of branded gasoline annually), there would be significant economic consequences if this type of customer attrition were to occur. It was also expected that Gulf's primary competition would try to capitalize on the fragility of the brand and seize the opportunity to capture new customers during the brand conversion. Research showed that 41% of Gulf's customers used multiple brands (Fig. 21.2). There was some evidence that this was already happening; according to AutoFacts,[2] Gulf's market share fell from 10.7% in the first quarter of 1986 to 9.5% by the first quarter of 1987.

---

[2]AutoFacts is a marketing research service that polls people about their gasoline purchasing habits, including brand bought last (a commonly used index of market share).

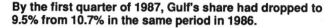

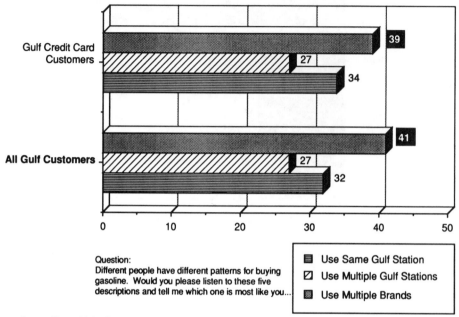

FIG. 21.2. Gulf customers' waning loyalty—1987.
N = 600 gasoline purchasers: Houston, Dallas, and New Orleans.

Furthermore, qualitative and quantitative research conducted by Chevron uncovered some interesting lore about the Gulf brand. Gulf, it seemed, had become a part of Texas' history and people felt a longstanding connection to the brand. Thus, the marketing problems associated with converting the brand went beyond utilitarian dimensions associated with brand preference and loyalty (e.g., "high quality," "good service," "conveniently located," "low price") to more emotional issues like "caring" and "pride of Texas." Research suggested that consumers were especially desirous of more information about Chevron and what the company stood for. It seemed Chevron was little known and perceived as an outsider (Fig. 21.3).

Other research was conducted to understand more about the people in the new region. Findings suggested that the lifestyle composition of the region was very different from Chevron's other major markets. Using the SMRB database of the media and VALS classification of a sample of 20,000 people, it

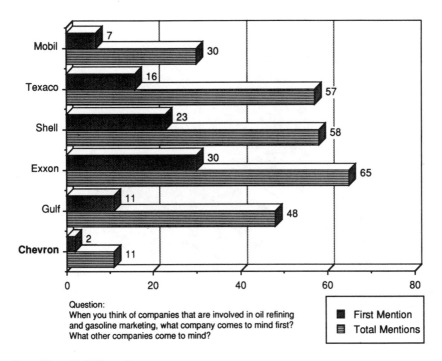

Question:
When you think of companies that are involved in oil refining
and gasoline marketing, what company comes to mind first?
What other companies come to mind?

■ First Mention
▤ Total Mentions

Source: Chevron Market Research
1987 Study By Winona MRB, Inc.

FIG. 21.3.   Gasoline brand awareness—1987.
N = 600 gasoline purchasers: Houston, Dallas, and New Orleans.

was discovered that these states had a high concentration of VALS Belongers,
a lifestyle group (part of the Outer-Directeds) that values security, conformi-
ty, tradition, and major established brands. Simply put, Belongers were ad-
verse to change. They were not looking for new and different brands; they
were looking for trustworthy and familiar brands. Gulf had been the Belongers'
brand in this respect (Fig. 21.4).

COMMUNICATIONS OBJECTIVES AND AD PRETESTS

With this knowledge, Chevron's foremost goal during the preconversion period become customer retention, rather than share building. It was felt that a
slow, evolutionary approach to conversion was needed to establish a positive
awareness and image for the Chevron brand and to avoid alienating customers.
Chevron would call the preconversion strategy its "drip, drip, drip" approach.

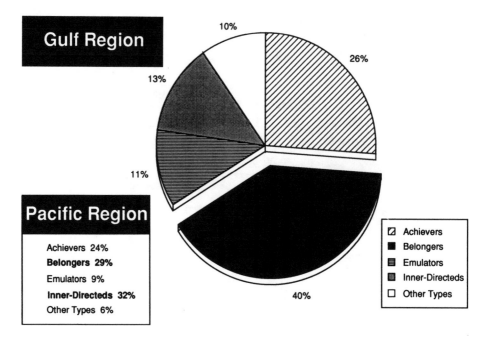

FIG. 21.4.   Customer psychographics/lifestyle segmentation.

The possible value of corporate advertising seemed apparent. Given the low awareness between Chevron and Gulf at the retail level, and what was known about Belongers, Chevron's communications strategy was to use the time between late 1987 and 1989 to build a comfort level with Chevron—first, as a company and then, as a brand—using publicity, point of sale, and corporate and marketing advertising.

Chevron had a corporate campaign using an environmental message that had been running in California for about two years. This campaign, called ''People Do,'' had proven extremely effective in building brand favorability. However, given the already described differences in the markets, it was unknown whether ''People Do'' could effectively introduce Chevron to the Gulf region. To learn whether ''People Do'' would be effective, or whether alternative campaigns might be better suited, commercial pretests were arranged. The McCollum-Spielman mall intercept pretest method was employed to test three alternative executions, including a ''People Do'' commercial from the California campaign. Tests were undertaken in three markets: (a) New Orleans, (b) Dallas, and (c) Houston. The McCollum-Spielman procedure provides several measures of a commercial's effectiveness, including: (a) clutter/awareness, (b) message communications, (c) overall reaction to the commercial, and

(d) commercial effect on attitudes and future purchases. The commercial that was tested was called *Eagle*, scripted here:

- This eagle could land in trouble.
- The high point he might decide to rest on could be dangerous.
- Unaware that 13,000 volts await him, he heads toward it and lands, unharmed.
- Wooden platforms above power lines now keep him above danger.
- They were developed and put there by a lot of people whose work brings them to this remote area.
- Do people really reach that high to protect a natural wonder?
- People do.[3]

The research demonstrated that the existing ''People Do'' campaign should be quite effective in introducing Chevron to the region's residents and beginning to build a well-regarded company. In terms of potential awareness, *Eagle* scored slightly below average. On correct message communication, it scored slightly above average. It also got above average scores on descriptors like ''imaginative,'' ''believable,'' and ''interesting.'' People thought of it as entertaining. Most importantly, the *Eagle* commercial received very high persuasion scores. Compared to the norm of + 15, *Eagle* got a score of + 34, meaning 34% of the respondents said that the commercial made them feel more favorable toward Chevron as a company. Unlike the earlier telephone research that found less likelihood of buying Chevron gasoline following the brand conversion, after seeing *Eagle* there was a 3-to-1 margin of people saying that they would be more likely to buy Chevron.

To summarize Chevron's preconversion strategy, it was decided to first build *company* image and subsequently establish *brand* image. This would be logical to the consumer. Corporate advertising, along with public relations, would be the best tools for establishing a positive company image. Incidentally, research also showed what was required to build a positive brand image, namely a high-quality product. This makes sense, considering that some people in the region thought Chevron might be an ''off'' brand.

IMPLEMENTATION

The ''People Do'' campaign began running in each conversion market nearly three months before any physical station changes took place. Houston was the

[3]A videotape of Chevron's ''People Do'' commercials to date is available upon request. Please write to: Chevron Corporation, Public Affairs Strategy and Opinion Research, P.O. Box 7753, San Francisco, CA 94120–7753.

first market to be converted. In Houston, "People Do" advertising ran in several 3- to 4-week flights[4] at 115 to 150 GRPs[5] per week. As mentioned earlier, in addition to the corporate advertising produced by J. Walter Thompson, brand advertising was created by Y&R. For example, a print ad that ran in Houston ("I heard Gulf stations are changing to Chevron. What's that mean to Houston?") provided information about the conversion.

POSTWAVE ATTITUDES AND USAGE STUDY, 1989

In mid-1989, a second wave of awareness and attitude research was conducted for comparison to the 1987 study. Although it is not possible to attribute the improvements that were found by this study to any single communications program, several measures indicated that the comprehensive communications program had increased the awareness of the Chevron-Gulf merger (Fig. 21.5). Also, the number of customers that would defect from Chevron stations had decreased to virtually nil (Fig. 21.6).

ANNUAL EFFECTIVENESS MEASUREMENTS, 1989

Perhaps the ultimate "report card" for advertising at Chevron comes at the end of each year, when the company conducts its advertising effectiveness research. For years, Chevron has used the Communicus methodology for this research. The Communicus procedure compares the same respondents' attitudes and self-reported behavior before and after the advertising. In the reinterview, respondents are shown edited commercial clips (about 10 s for each 20-s television spot) and asked whether or not they have ever seen the commercial. If they say that they have seen the commercial, they are asked if they know which company sponsored it. The group that has seen an ad and correctly identified the sponsor is then compared to the group that was unable to do so. The difference between the groups is referred to as the *index of ad effect*. In Houston, during the first year of the "People Do" campaign, Chevron received good marks on this annual report card, despite being a new brand in the market. Two ads, *Eagle* and *Kit Fox*, scored very well on awareness and correct sponsor identification. The campaign also did well at targeting poten-

---

[4]*Flights* are periods of the year when the advertising is on (separated, of course, by periods when the advertising is totally off the air).

[5]*GRPs* stand for gross rating points, or the multiplicative product of the percentage of households likely to be exposed to the campaign in a week times the average number of potential exposures to the campaign during the week. Thus, for example, 75% of the households exposed to the campaign an average of two times in the week equals 150 GRPs.

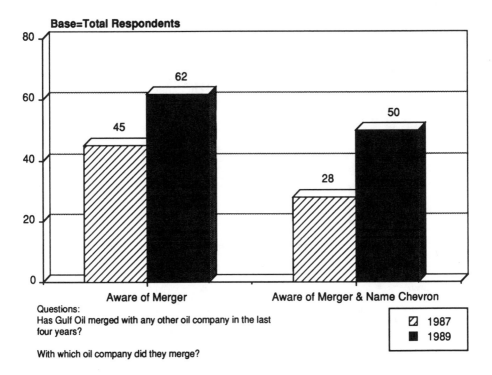

Base=Total Respondents

Questions:
Has Gulf Oil merged with any other oil company in the last four years?

With which oil company did they merge?

| ▨ | 1987 |
| ■ | 1989 |

Source: Chevron Market Research
1987 & 1989 Studies By Winona MRB, Inc.

FIG. 21.5.   Merger awareness: Houston
N = 600, 750 gasoline purchasers: Houston, Dallas, and New Orleans.

tially favorable people and making them even more favorable toward Chevron (Fig. 21.7).

BRAND TRACKING, 1989–1991

In August, 1989, Chevron began a continuous tracking study in Houston to trace the relationship between advertising and sales. This research included both marketing and corporate advertising. Fifty interviews were conducted each week and the results were accumulated on a 4-week rolling average basis. Several self-reported behavioral measures, as well as attitude and belief measures, were collected.

Results from the Houston tracking study indicated Chevron was the one oil company most likely to be mentioned as trustworthy to handle an environmentally sensitive project in a responsible manner (Fig. 21.8). In addition, Chevron was the brand of gasoline that was first in terms of overall favor-

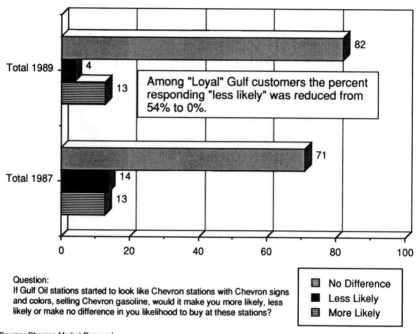

Total 1989

82

4

13

Among "Loyal" Gulf customers the percent responding "less likely" was reduced from 54% to 0%.

Total 1987

71

14

13

0   20   40   60   80   100

Question:
If Gulf Oil stations started to look like Chevron stations with Chevron signs and colors, selling Chevron gasoline, would it make you more likely, less likely or make no difference in you likelihood to buy at these stations?

▒ No Difference
■ Less Likely
☰ More Likely

Source: Chevron Market Research
1987 & 1989 Studies By Winona MRB, Inc.

FIG. 21.6.   Impact of conversion on purchase intent.
N = 600, 750 gasoline purchasers: Houston, Dallas, and New Orleans.

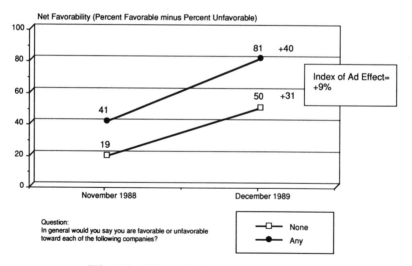

Net Favorability (Percent Favorable minus Percent Unfavorable)

100

80

81   +40

60

50   +31

Index of Ad Effect=
+9%

41

40

19

20

0

November 1988   December 1989

Question:
In general would you say you are favorable or unfavorable toward each of the following companies?

─□─ None
─●─ Any

FIG. 21.7.   "People Do" ad effects scores: Texas.

330

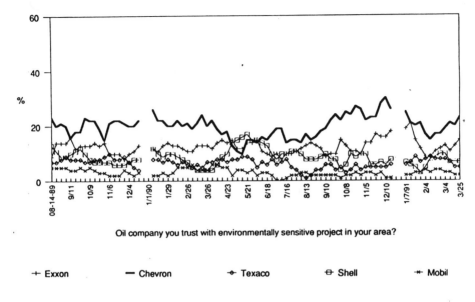

Oil company you trust with environmentally sensitive project in your area?

-+- Exxon   — Chevron   -*- Texaco   -θ- Shell   -*- Mobil

Base=Houston

FIG. 21.8.   Trust with environmentally sensitive project. Source: Chevron tracking survey. Reprinted by permission.

ability (Fig. 21.9). After the Exxon Valdez accident, attitudes toward oil companies started heading downward. However, Chevron bucked that trend in
Houston. The combined efforts of many people, especially Chevron's advertising and marketing people, put Chevron's market share in the Houston market
near the top, at 18%. This effort earned Jim Gordon, Chevron's advertising
manager, and the marketing people at Chevron the honor of "Marketer of
the Year" for 1990, awarded by the San Francisco chapter of the American
Marketing Association.

SUMMARY

During the conversion of Gulf to Chevron in the Southwest, the "People Do"
campaign built a company image, a platform from which the brand could
"launch itself." Given the consumer psychographic profile in that region, it
may well be that without this activity the brand conversion effort would not
have been as successful. Certainly, all of the credit cannot go to corporate advertising. However, it can be said that the "People Do" campaign was a viable contributing member to the preconversion and conversion successes. The
research that was performed—from pretesting, to the postwave, to the advertising tracking and effectiveness studies—all support this hypothesis. To bor-

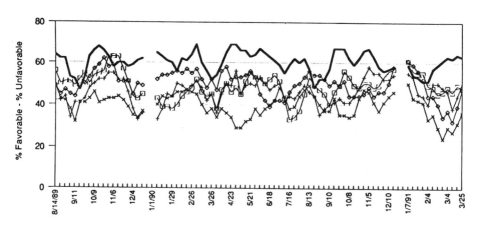

Are you favorable or unfavorable toward the following gasoline brands?

+ Exxon   — Chevron   ◆ Texaco   ⊟ Shell   ✱ Mobil

Base=Houston

FIG. 21.9.   Overall favorability. Source: Chevron tracking survey. Reprinted by permission.

row a phrase, as far as Chevron's "People Do" campaign is concerned, when Chevron ventures from California, "we will not leave home without it."

REFERENCE

Winters, L. C. (1988). Does it pay to advertise to hostile audiences with corporate advertising? *Journal of Advertising Research, 28*(3), 11–18.

Chapter 22

Are Brand Equity Investments Really Worthwhile?

David A. Aaker
University of California at Berkeley

Gaining organization support and resources for brand-building activities is often difficult, even with a consensus that brands are strategically important to the organization. Two explanations can be postulated:

1. There are enormous pressures on the organization, and on the involved brands, to deliver short-term profit results.
2. Demonstrating the long-term value of brand building is exceptionally difficult (Fig. 22.1).

Short-Term Profit Pressure

There is no shortage of informed observers of Japanese and U.S. managers who would agree with the MIT Commission on Industrial Productivity, which concluded that there is a tendency for American business to be preoccupied with short-term results (Dertouzos, Lester, & Solow, 1989). One reason may be the fast-track job movement so common in U.S. firms, which is designed to challenge and reward high-energy managers. One by-product is that brand managers often have a 1- to 3-year time horizon and little incentive to make strategic brand-building investments. But the primary cause, in my view, is the pressure generated by shareholders for positive quarterly earnings news.

The goal of maximizing shareholder wealth has been legitimized by economic and finance theorists and by the attitudes of business managers. We

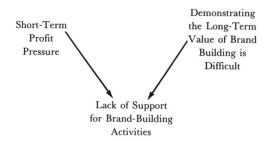

FIG. 22.1.   Difficulties in sustaining brand-building activities.

have been taught that a society that maximizes shareholder wealth will have all sorts of good things happen to it (e.g., people will have meaningful incentives, capital will be available, resources will be optimally allocated, etc.). Most U.S. managers have been exposed to these theories in school and have accepted their validity. In one illuminating study, U.S. and Japanese managers were asked to rate the importance of various objectives (Kagono, Nonaka, Sakakibara, & Okumura, 1985). U.S. managers put ROI at the top (2.4), stockholder capital gain second (1.1), and market share third (.7), with new products a poor seventh (.2). In contrast, for Japanese executives market share was first (1.4), followed by ROI (1.2) and new products (1.1); stockholder capital gain was of zero importance (0.0).

Theoretically, there is nothing wrong with maximizing shareholder wealth; the problem arises in its application. Shareholders of U.S. firms who need to estimate the future profit stream lack information. They are not usually privy to a firm's internal strategic plan. They lack information about the off-balance-sheet intangible assets. For example, shareholders of Kraft were unaware that the Kraft brands had a value of nearly $13 billion, over 600% over its book value. To cope, the shareholder basically hunkers down to a simple model— focus upon quarterly earnings and assume that they predict the future. U.S. management systems and styles have adapted to this short-term pressure. They are good at delivering short-term results and weak at building assets, such as brands, for the future.

Problems in Demonstrating Brand Equity Value

As a field, we have been remarkably unsuccessful at measuring/modeling the long-term value of advertising and other brand-building activities. In particular, there are at least four major problems with efforts to estimate long-term value:

1. The available independent variables in most historical data sources do not usually tap brand-equity dimensions (e.g., advertising expenditures might be tracked instead of brand associations, perceived quality, or awareness).

2. There is rarely any meaningful change in a brand strategy. It is hard to determine the impact of a strategy that does not change. For example, an experiment showing that repositioning V-8 Cocktail Vegetable Juice from "better tasting than tomato juice" to "a healthy drink useful for weight control" increased sales 20% is all too rare (Eastlack & Rao, 1986).

3. The period in which changes are monitored is rarely long enough to observe long-term effects, which usually involve years rather than months.

4. It is difficult to translate the results that are detected (such as a change in awareness or attitude) to bottom-line numbers that relate to shareholder value.

In sharp contrast to efforts to show long-term value of marketing activities, there is the amazing ability of models using scanner data to provide detailed documentation of the dramatic short-term impact achieved by promotion expenditures. One review of studies that measured both price and advertising elasticity involving 260 data points concluded that the median ratio of price to advertising elasticity is over 16 (Sthuraman & Tellis, 1991)! It is difficult to sell a promise tomorrow for a sure thing today.

The Role of Case Studies

Our challenge is to demonstrate convincingly (both internally to top management and externally to investors) that investments in brand equity do lead to sustainable competitive advantages and, thus, to long-term value. The value of brand-equity elements needs to be established. People have to accept the premise that an asset such as brand equity can be a key to future performance.

A possible approach is to develop case studies that will illustrate the value of brand equity, using historical analysis of actual brands over a long time period. The idea is to examine brand decisions, or sets of decisions, that have a direct link to shareholder value. Such case studies could act as role models to help managers articulate a strategy, both internally and externally. A key is the link to shareholder value. A significant problem is that we do not communicate well to financial types inside or outside the firm, in large part because they are used to dealing with profit streams and shareholder value instead of conceptualized strategies. We need to bridge the gap.

FOUR CASE STUDIES

Four case studies are offered here to illustrate the power of brand equity.[1] Each provides an estimate of shareholder value involved, which is in the area of $1 billion. Each also involves one of the four dimensions of brand equity that

---

[1]For a more complete treatment of each, see Aaker (1991, chapters 2, 3, 4, & 5).

is included in this definition: Brand equity is the set of brand assets and liabilities linked to the brand, its name, and symbol, that add or subtract value to a product or service for a firm and/or its customers (Aaker, 1991, chapter 1).[2] The assets and liabilities on which brand equity is based will differ from context to context. However, they can be grouped into four major categories: (a) name awareness, (b) perceived quality, (c) brand associations in addition to perceived quality, and (d) brand loyalty. Three of the studies show how brand equity can be damaged; one shows the value of creating brand equity.

Awareness—The Datsun-to-Nissan Name Change

In 1982, Nissan decided to change the name of its U.S. entry from Datsun to Nissan, the name by which the car was marketed in Japan. During the years from 1982 to 1984, the change was implemented. During this period, some models actually carried both brand names. By 1984, the Datsun name had completely disappeared. Establishing the Nissan name involved replacing the long running and successful "Datsun: We are Driven" advertising campaign with the "Major Motion: The Name is Nissan" campaign, for which over $240 million was spent.

Despite this investment in the Nissan name, in the spring of 1988 a national survey conducted by Landor Associates found that the recognition and esteem of the Datsun name was essentially the same as that of the Nissan name—the Nissan name was no stronger than a brand name that had been dead for 5 years.

It seems likely that the name change resulted in extra spending of well over $200 million on advertising that was much less effective than prior advertising. In addition, $30 million was spent just on changing dealer's signs. The biggest cost, likely to have been many hundreds of millions over the course of the 1980s, was the lost sales caused by name confusion.

Of course, it is impossible to document exactly how sales were affected by the name confusion; a lot happened in the automobile market during the 1980s, such as import restrictions, some Nissan quality problems, and the Honda effort. However, we do know that the Nissan share dropped from 5.9% in 1982, to 5.5% in 1983, to 4.5% in 1984, a rather dramatic loss of 1.4 share points during a period in which Toyota, for example, lost only 0.9 share points. It is probable that the name confusion was a major contributing factor. It is likely that brand recall and image suffered years later because of the name change. Certainly, the strength of the Datsun name in 1988 suggests a dilution in awareness equity that surely affected sales. In total, the name change surely cost over $500 million and very likely it was a decision involving well over $1 billion.

---

[2]Aaker, op. cit. chapter 1.

Brand Loyalty—The WordStar Case

An example of the value of a customer-installed base is provided by Word-Star, the word-processing pioneer (until recently named MicroPro) that lost position, in large part, because it turned its back on its installed base. Word-Star, introduced in 1979, was the first reliable, full-featured word-processing program. It dominated the market for serious word-processing users in the early 1980s. With clever use of keystroke pairs, a touch typist could do a wide variety of word-processing tasks extremely quickly.

In 1983, WordStar faced its first real competition—WordPerfect and Microsoft Word. These two programs, unlike WordStar, used the function keys of the IBM personal computer introduced in 1981. Despite the competition, WordStar sales exploded from $22 million in 1982, to $44 million in 1983, to $67 million in 1984. In 1983, WordStar dominated the market and, more importantly, developed an installed base of nearly 1 million users.

However, sales fell to $42.6 million in 1985 and then remained flat through 1989. Market share fell precipitously to 12.7% by 1987 and to 7% by 1990. The value of the stock in 1990 was under $10 million. In contrast, the upstart WordPerfect went from zero share in 1982 to over 70% by 1990, when its value (had it been publicly traded) would probably have exceeded $1 billion.

WordStar, throughout this period, failed to support its existing customers. As late as 1987, WordStar was deservedly known as being indifferent to its customers. Customers called MicroPro with problems, at their own expense, and could not get through. Within the industry, the firm had the nickname "WordStar-please-hold." Further, customers were often referred to dealers who were unwilling or unable to help. The frustration level was high. In contrast, WordPerfect developed an unlimited access, toll-free phone-in user-support service, which became one of their points of differentiation.

Perhaps a worse blunder was making a follow-on product that was incompatible with the original WordStar. In November, 1984, WordStar started to shop WordStar 2000, which was eagerly awaited by WordStar users who wanted to upgrade the program they loved. However, WordStar 2000 involved learning a new set of instructions and forced the WordStar touch typists to use the function keys. It was no easier to switch to WordStar 2000 than to WordPerfect or Microsoft Word. At last, in February, 1987, WordStar Professional, a backward compatible upgrade to the original WordStar, was finally shipped, but it was confused with WordStar 2000 in the minds of dealers and customers and was years late.

Brand Associations—The Weight Watchers Case

In 1978, the H. J. Heinz Co. bought the Weight Watchers weight control program and frozen dinner business for approximately $120 million. At the time, observers questioned the judgment of buying such a mature, unexciting business. Two years later, they purchased Camargo Foods, a Weight Watchers licensee for nonfrozen foods. By 1989, the Weight Watchers area of Heinz had revenues of $1.3 billion and its operating income was over $100 million, close to the total acquisition price of the three companies. Further, Heinz called the Weight Watchers line its "growth engine for the 1990s."

Of interest to Heinz in 1978 was the potential of the Weight Watchers association with a professional approach to weight control, coupled with its links to health and nutrition. The Heinz vision was that these associations would provide the basis for a sustainable competitive advantage, not only in the core frozen dinner area but in numerous other extensions as well. During the 1980s, Heinz exploited these associations by relentlessly extending the name to new products. By 1989, they had 60 frozen and over 150 nonfrozen food items. Each extension not only exploited the Weight Watchers name and associations but reinforced them as well.

In most of the food categories, most notably frozen entrees, the two salient dimensions in the low calorie/health segment, in which Weight Watchers was competing, were taste and weight control. Gaining a strong, convincing position on either dimension was difficult. Hence, the value of the Weight Watchers name. O'Reilly, the president of Heinz, noted, in 1990, "You can say light and you can say very light and you can say extra light and trimline or slimline, but at the end of the day, Weight Watchers has an authority about it, and a cogency and a simplicity, in that if the product is good and tastes good, the consumer will take it."

However, in the early 1980s, Weight Watchers had a problem with respect to the taste dimension, partly because of its association with hard-core dieting and partly because its products were inferior. The image of inferior taste needed to be addressed, particularly for frozen entrees. In response, Weight Watchers (a) dramatically improved the product, (b) created a more upscale, quality package, and (c) softened the hard-core-diet Weight Watcher image with the introduction of frozen desserts. The advertising was changed from poking fun at dieters who cheated to a more uplifting, positive campaign featuring Lynn Redgrave and the tag line, "This is living." These efforts paid off; in 1988, Weight Watchers passed Lean Cuisine to become the top-selling, low-calorie frozen-entree line.

Weight Watchers was one of the big winners of the 1980s. However, in the 1990s there was a shift in consumer focus from weight control to overall health. Weight Watchers was attacked by Healthy Choice, a brand well positioned by name and product to exploit this new interest. Some fascinating questions arise. Can Healthy Choice replicate the Weight Watchers success story using a similar strategy? What response can and should Weight Watchers make to the changing conditions facing them?

Perceived Quality—The Schlitz Case

Through the 1960s and early 1970s, Schlitz beer was a strong number two beer brand, supported by the well-regarded gusto campaigns, such as "You only go around once in life—so grab all the gusto you can." In the mid-1970s, however, Schlitz's perceived quality was damaged and its fortunes tumbled.

Sales of the Schlitz brand went from over 17.8 million barrels in 1974, to 12.9 million in 1978, to 1.8 million in 1984, to 0.6 million in 1988 when it was on the verge of disappearing. In contrast, from 1978 to 1984 Pabst only fell from 12.7 to 6.8 and Coors actually gained from 12.1 to 12.6, even though both were subject to the same competitive pressures from Miller and Budweiser.

The value of the brand name as measured by the stock market value (prorated by the percentage of firm sales represented by the Schlitz brand) fell from over $1 billion in 1974 to $75 million only 6 years later. Over 93% of the brand equity was lost. The Schlitz value fell three times more than that of Coors during the 1975 to 1980 period when Coors was publicly traded.

In 1974, Schlitz management, aiming to develop a strategic cost advantage (during a time in which the BCG matrix was very influential), converted to a fermentation process which took 4 days instead of 12 and substituted corn syrup for barley malt. Although the taste was apparently unaffected, the word on the street was that Schlitz was making "green beer" and was using "cheap" ingredients. The image problem was compounded when Schlitz promoted heavily and Anheuser-Busch announced that they would retain premium ingredients.

In 1976, the worst happened. "Flaky," "cloudy" beer appeared on the shelves. Several months later, it was finally traced to a new foam stabilizer introduced in January. Worse, in early summer, one attempted fix caused the beer to go flat after time on the shelf. In the fall of 1976, 10 million bottles and cans of Schlitz were "secretly" recalled and destroyed, and Schlitz became something of a joke.

Beginning in 1975, a series of advertising campaigns attempted to address the perceived quality problem. In 1980, in desperation, Schlitz spent $4 million on five live taste tests in which 100 drinkers of a competing brand—either Budweiser, Miller, or Michelob—engaged in a blind taste test on live television. On average, nearly 50% selected Schlitz, an impressive result. However, nothing convinced customers that Schlitz was back, even though the physical product had, since 1978, been based on the old formula and process.

A remarkable aspect of this story is that the loss in perceived quality turned out to be irreversible and resulted in a decay that extended over a 10-year period. During that period, positive word of mouth probably dried up and negative comments left Schlitz vulnerable. Correcting the product was not enough to affect the changed perceptions, despite the enormous sums that were spent on advertising. Some consumers were simply impossible to convince. An effort to make a small improvement in margins may have cost $1 billion in brand equity.

It should be easy to generate additional examples of how changes in perceived quality made a difference to shareholder value. In fact, many firms have developed quality programs involving changes in their culture and strategy to alter their perceived quality. Ford, with its "Quality is Job 1," is not alone. The Baldgridge quality award, now established in the United States, is a sought-after award. The value of perceived quality has been shown rather convincingly by PIMS studies involving over 3,000 businesses (Jacobson & Aaker, 1987). In particular, the lowest 20th percentile businesses, with respect to perceived quality, had around 17% ROI, whereas those in the top 20th percentile earned nearly twice as much.

Some Lessons

These four $1 billion case studies provide some food for thought:

1. The Datsun Case. Creating name awareness can be costly; a new name needs to be established and linked to a product class. If you buy a name and automatically consider changing it, think about Datsun and the diversion from the marketing program that occurred when it was changed.

2. The WordStar Case. Brand loyalty should not be taken for granted. Investing in your customers to keep them happy can pay off. Watch switching costs—build them up, not down.

3. The Weight Watchers Case. Enhancing brand-name associations and awareness by investing in quality can pay off, especially if the brand name can be used to enter new product classes.

4. The Schlitz Case. Perceived quality is fragile. Once lost, it is hard to reverse. Don't tinker with the product.

A Final Observation

Given our financial system, there is a need to get investors into the loop by, when appropriate, communicating brand strength and strategy to them. If investors are convinced of the power of brand names, there will be more tolerance and patience for brand-building activities, including advertising. In addition to having the will to communicate to shareholders, it is important to have a clear idea of what the brand strategy is and to develop credible measures of the strategy.

First, there is a need to develop and employ a crystal clear brand identity or vision. This is a statement about what the brand stands for (e.g., What is the customer benefit that it delivers? What are the most important associations which it builds?). Such a statement communicates strategy internally as well as externally. It provides guidance to managers in making decisions about which actions will enhance the brand and which have the potential to damage. It sounds like something that organizations should do as a matter of course. Surely firms know what their brands stand for. No! In reality, this is the rare exception.

Weight Watchers, for example, had a vision that the associations of weight control and nutrition could create a competitive advantage in important markets and a lever to enter a host of others. These associations, as much as the product, provided the basis for a competitive advantage. WordPerfect believed that customer service and product upgrades would cement customer loyalty and provide the basis for competitive advantage. The vision and its implementation in each case was clear and well articulated.

A second need is to develop credible indicators that the brand strategy is in place, being monitored, and working. Investors should be convinced that brand equity is a real driving force in providing a sustainable competitive advantage and, thus, long-term financial performance. This often means that tracking studies on equity dimensions (e.g., perceived quality, awareness, associations, and loyalty/satisfaction) will be needed. It also means that well-articulated programs to enhance these dimensions will be part of the communication package.

REFERENCES

Aaker, D. A. (1991). *Managing brand equity*. New York: The Free Press.

Dertouzos, M. L., Lester, R. K., & Solow, R. M. (1989). *Made in America: Regaining the productive edge*. Cambridge, MA: The MIT Press.

Eastlack, J. O., & Rao, A. G. (1986). Modeling response to advertising and pricing changes from "V-8" cocktail vegetable juice. *Marketing Science, 5*(3), 245–259.

Jacobson, R., & Aaker, D. A. (1987). The strategic role of product quality. *Journal of Marketing, 51*(4), 31–44.

Kagono, T., Nonaka, I., Sakakibara, K., & Okumura, A. (1985). *Strategic vs. evolutionary management—A U.S.-Japan comparison of strategy and organization*. New York: North-Holland.

Sthuraman, R., & Tellis, G. J. (1991). An analysis of the tradeoff between advertising and price discounting. *Journal of Marketing Research, 28*(2), 160–174.

Chapter 23

Brand Equities, Elephants, and Birds: A Commentary

William D. Wells
University of Minnesota

THE ELEPHANT FALLACY

Critics of our research methods like to tell the story of the blind men and the elephant: Different men examine different parts of an elephant, and each is sure that the whole elephant is a trunk, a leg, a side, a tail, or an ear. This story is popular because it illustrates a common fallacy in research. In all too many cases, researchers generalize from one atypical segment to the whole beast.

On the academic side, this fallacy is evident in generalizations from college students to all consumers, from one advertisement to all advertising, and from one laboratory experiment to the whole world. On the practitioner side, this fallacy is evident in generalizations from isolated test markets to nationwide new-product introductions, from people-meter readings to television-commercial audiences, and from attitude-change scores to final sales.

THE BIRD FALLACY

A second parable is also worth considering. In this parable, a researcher averages ostriches and robins and draws conclusions about the nature of all birds. This parable has its own analogy. In study after study, researchers pool two (or more) separate entities, calculate averages or percentages, and misrepresent the aggregate in major ways.

Here is an example of the bird fallacy at work. Advertisements for fur coats, perfume, and expensive automobiles are pooled with advertisements for floor

343

wax, life insurance, and underarm deodorant in a study that asks, "Should brand image and user image be the same?" If, as Lannon suggests in chapter 11, the answer to that question is "yes" for the first class of products and "no" for the second, the answer for the total pool is "maybe"—wrong for both.

Here is a second example. Home computers, compact disc players, microwave ovens, athletic shoes, and frozen yogurt are pooled in a study of early adopters of new brands. Because early adopters of those products have so little in common, averages calculated across products are virtually certain to misrepresent each one.

Here is a third example. Respondents from five different countries are pooled in a study of a worldwide brand. If, as Moore suggests in chapter 3, brand images differ sharply from country to country, a worldwide average misrepresents every place the brand is sold.

Examples could be multiplied indefinitely; the principle is always the same. When researchers merge sharply different segments, they lose critical insight into how each segment works.

TAXONOMIES

The best defense against either the elephant fallacy or the bird fallacy is a relevant taxonomy. If researchers divide objects into truly different categories and analyze those categories separately, they avoid generalizing from one atypical segment to the entire population and averaging across segments which differ in too many ways.

Of course, the taxonomy must be relevant. No one could isolate every category that anyone could possibly invent. The question, then, is which categories are most likely to be helpful when planning brand equity research?

The four taxonomies which follow have helped our understanding of attitudes toward brands. Although they may seem obvious, researchers have neglected them more often than they should. When researchers have neglected them, insight and precision have diminished as a direct result.

After the four tested taxonomies, the discussion will turn to three relatively new divisions proposed elsewhere in this book. No one can be sure that the new will be as useful as the old, but all are worth careful thought.

Salience Versus Trust

The first old taxonomy divides salience and trust. Marketers know that well-known brands develop "personalities" that are analogous to human personalities in many ways (see Biel's discussion in chapter 5, Blackston in chapter 8, and Batra, Lehman, & Singh in chapter 6).

These personalities add two qualities to brands:

1. They confer salience—they make the brand stand out from the crowd.
2. They inspire trust. They provide favorable continuity that crosses product categories and encourages repeat purchase time after time.

Salience and trust are similar in spirit to share of mind and esteem in the Landor ImagePower® survey in chapter 2.

The point at issue here is that salience and trust are very different entities, and much is lost whenever that distinction is not made. This point is critical because, unlike the Landor survey, many studies fail to divide salience from trust. Instead of retaining them as separate dimensions, they merge them, as though high salience could make up for low trust, and the other way around.

If this seems like a trivial issue, consider the late but not lamented Isuzu campaign. In that long series of humorous commercials, "Joe Isuzu" told enormous lies about Isuzu cars. This campaign may have generated salience, but it could hardly have done much for trust. Salience is not a substitute for trust; the two are not at all the same.

Consider the consequences of using day-after recall as a surrogate for sales effects. Because recall responds to salience, not trust, advertisers who used recall produced "Ring Around the Collar," Mr. Whipple, and hundreds of other advertisements that consumers hate. By ignoring the difference between salience and trust, these advertisers derogated their own brands.

So, when equity is the issue, salience and trust should not be interchanged. Like ostriches and robins, they are separate entities. When they are averaged, much potential insight is thrown away.

Definition Versus Redefinition

The second old taxonomy bears on an equally old question: "How does advertising work?" Early advertisements hit people over the head. A typical early newspaper advertisement insisted that Scott's Emulsion was "a cure for consumption, scrofula, bronchitis, coughs, and colds" and "as palatable as milk." An early Coca-Cola poster declared that Coca-Cola was "the most refreshing drink in the world."

When consumers (and government regulators) demanded proof of such unvarnished claims, advertisers turned to symbols and metaphors. The Prudential Insurance Company became "as strong as the Rock of Gibraltar." The Standard Oil Company "put a tiger in your tank." And the Green Giant Company portrayed a valley where only the very finest vegetables were raised.

Advertisers found that symbols and metaphors had two wonderful advantages over blatant claims:

1. Symbols and metaphors made advertising more captivating, more vivid, and more fun.
2. Symbols and metaphors were harder to pin down. Advertisers could now imply properties they could not prove in court.

It is important to note that the Rock of Gibraltar, the Tiger in the Tank, and the Jolly Green Giant were still "information" about current attributes of brands. Their creators had accepted current attributes as given, and they depicted those attributes in novel and intriguing ways.

Marketers soon discovered that advertising can do more than that. Marlboro did not rely on current attributes. Instead, Marlboro imported a new attribute—masculinity—and thereby revised the basis on which equity could be derived. Similarly, Rolex imported success. As Biel notes in chapter 5, Wells Fargo imported traditions of dependability and commitment from the Old West.

Unlike the Rock of Gibraltar, the Tiger in the Tank, and the Jolly Green Giant, these symbols and metaphors did not take current attributes as given. Instead, they introduced new attributes. They changed the rules of competition by changing the dimensions on which brand decisions were made.

One of the great advantages of this new kind of advertising was that it added dimensions which advertisers could preempt. As Biel points out, "Bank of America and Security Pacific may be locked in combat about who offers the best rates and points on mortgages. However, they cannot today 'own' the spirit of the West."

Once marketers appreciated the value of new dimensions, they flocked to this new trend. In category after category, advertisers tried to change the content of the decision process by adding attributes which had not previously been there.

Advertising which added attributes, and thereby transformed the decision process, also transformed the experience of using the brand. Marlboro smokers felt "masculine." Rolex wearers felt "successful." Wells Fargo patrons felt "safe." Advertising of this type—which added new attributes and thereby transformed both the decision process and the experience of using the brand— came to be known as *transformation advertising*.

As transformation advertising developed, two confusions emerged:

1. The first was confusion between transformational advertising and *emotional advertising*. Although much transformational advertising was, and is, indeed emotional, emotion is neither necessary nor sufficient to change the way decisions are made. The content of the decision process and the experience of using the brand, can be changed by changing the product itself—a new ingredient, a new convenience, or a new price structure, for instance. The advertising which describes the change may be emotional, or it may not.

2. A second confusion stemmed from the assumption that *informational advertising*—which describes current attributes—is necessarily cognitive and

"hard." Although early information advertising was indeed just that, the symbols and metaphors of later information advertising allowed it to become "energetic," "inspired," "playful," "affectionate," "hopeful," "sentimental," or "warmhearted"—to quote just a few of the adjectives used in chapter 13 by Edell and Moore. The rock of Gibraltar, the Tiger in the Tank, and the Jolly Green Giant presented information about current attributes—safety, power, and quality, respectively. They were effective because they presented that information in a more engaging way.

Because information advertising can be emotional and transformation advertising can be factual, emotion, cognition, information, and transformation have become hopelessly entangled at this point in time. Therefore, it might be better to change terms.

From here on, advertising that accepts present attributes as given and either claims superiority with unvarnished facts or implies superiority via symbol and metaphor will be called *definition advertising*. As Blackston notes in chapter 8, definition advertising "favors the strengths of the brand."

By contrast, advertising which does not accept current attributes as given, but rather attempts to redefine the product category by adding new dimensions to choice, will be called *redefinition advertising*. When redefinition advertising works as intended, it redefines both the experience of using the product and the basis upon which consumers decide how to behave.

The distinction between definition and redefinition advertising is critical because these two types increase brand equity in quite different ways. When definition advertising works, it favors the (present) strengths of the brand. When redefinition advertising works, it first alters the basis of comparison, then establishes superiority on some dimension that had been unimportant before the change.

One consequence of this distinction is a new way of thinking about copy research. Most current methods assume that advertising conveys information about present attributes of brands. When the advertisement is a definition advertisement, that assumption is exactly right.

When the advertisement is a redefinition advertisement, that assumption is exactly wrong. When the advertisement is a redefinition advertisement, the fundamental questions are: "Can this message add a new attribute? Can it change the rules of the game?" If, and only if, the answer to these questions is "yes," the question becomes, "Will the brand win the game as redefined?" Most current copy testing undervalues redefinition because it misses that point.

More generally, a failure to distinguish between definition and redefinition carries over to most academic analysis of choice. As Haughtvedt, Leavitt, and Schneier observe in chapter 16, "Most academic studies of choice begin by providing the subjects with the alternatives to be evaluated, as well as the attributes on which the evaluation is made.'' When attributes are predesignated, redefinition is impossible because it is assumed away.

A similar omission inhibits attempts to measure deception and truth. When an advertisement is intended to favor the strengths of the brand, objective evidence can determine whether it is true or false. When an advertisement is intended to redefine the product category, the very same advertisement is false before it is disseminated and true by definition once it has had its intended effect. That seeming contradiction leaves regulators at a loss.

Thus, definition advertising and redefinition advertising differ in important ways. Like ignoring the differences between ostriches and robins, ignoring the differences between definition and redefinition reduces the value of anything we find.

Customers Versus Noncustomers

Although advertisers aim their messages at potential customers, they often miss. Ads for cake mix reach people who never bake. Ads for gasoline reach people who never drive. Ads for travelers' checks reach people who vacation in their backyards.

In some product categories, the number of potential customers is very small. Of those who see commercials for the U.S. Army, for example, few are ever likely to enlist. Of those who see Jaguar or Mercedes advertising, few will ever own a car in that price class.

Even when a brand is not exotic, its messages reach many who have little interest in the advertiser's pitch. Not everyone cares about nail polish, vitamins, or beer.

The distinction between customers and noncustomers is important because those two segments have different stakes. (Hereafter, the segment *customers* includes both present customers and potential customers.) To customers, an advertisement provides guidance as to whether or what to buy. To noncustomers, the same advertisement is a part of the environment—a source of entertainment, annoyance, or incidental information that has no direct connection with the sponsor's aims.

Customers are therefore more likely to process information about the brand. As Kirmani and Zeithmal say in chapter 10:

> When consumers are familiar with the product class, they have the knowledge required to interpret concrete product attributes. For instance, consumers familiar with cars can understand horsepower information and evaluate the concrete information to form their own quality assessments. Consumers with low familiarity with cars, on the other hand, may find the horsepower information meaningless. . . . Highly involved consumers require more concrete information because they are either more knowledgeable or more motivated to seek in-

formation. . . . As shown in the elaboration likelihood model . . . high involvement increases the motivation to process an ad; low involvement decreases this motivation.

Further, customers have had experiences which mediate attempts to change their minds. In the Schlitz case, for example, personal experience with "flaky," "cloudy" beer produced attitudes that millions of dollars in advertising could not affect (Aaker, chapter 22).

By contrast, noncustomers are not interested in copy points. The most involving aspect of the advertisement may be a costume or a setting, a hair style, a celebrity, a bit of background music, a catch phrase, or some other matter unrelated to the marketer's intent. The advertisement is only a source of amusement, entertainment, enjoyment, diversion, boredom, annoyance, aggravation, or offense.

Differences between customers and noncustomers are particularly important in copy testing because most copy-testing services do not separate those two groups. The venerable Starch test, for example, polls readers who "read or looked through" the test magazine. The Video Storyboard survey polls a sample of "TV viewers." For each campaign evaluated, some respondents are customers and others (often many others) are not.

In those two surveys, and in all other studies which do not separate customers from noncustomers, reactions to each advertisement depend upon the number of customers the sample happens to contain. When the sample contains many customers, the quantity and quality of product information has major impact on the outcome of the test. When the sample contains few customers, the outcome is determined by respondents the advertiser did not want to reach.

The way to solve this problem, of course, is to separate customers from noncustomers ad by ad, and to base findings only on those who might care about the brand. Neither the Starch test nor the Video Storyboard test does that. Like most copy-testing services, they base findings on all parties, interested or not.

Academic research faces a parallel threat. Typically, academic researchers ask respondents to rate collections of advertisements for varieties of brands. Some of the brands have many customers among the raters, and some have few or none. As in the Starch test and the Video Storyboard test, advertisements with many customers in the sample are rated by respondents who are interested in the brand; advertisements with few customers are rated by respondents who have little reason to process the brand-specific content of the ad. To those raters, the advertisement is at most a source of incidental information, an aesthetic or entertainment event.

This means that the effects of information, entertainment, relevance, warmth, attitude toward the ad, attitude toward the brand, and any other content-related variable will always be confounded with the interests of the particular respondents who happen to have been employed. As a consequence, different mixtures of products, services, and respondents will produce different results. As a further consequence, experiments which employ college students will produce outcomes which differ from the outcomes of parallel experiments in the real world.

Again, the remedy is well known. For each brand in the study, customers should be separated from noncustomers; for each brand in the study, customers and noncustomers should be treated as separate groups.

As ostriches are different from robins, customers are different from noncustomers. Ignoring this difference produces outcomes which are incorrect for both.

Brand Loyal Versus Open to Change

In some product categories, buyers develop strong allegiances to short lists of brands. These allegiances come from first-hand experiences, side comments, outside experts, past advertising, and so on. Such loyalties can be very hard to change.

Even within those categories, however, some customers are less committed than others. For one reason or another, they are not locked into their old standbys and are willing to consider change.

In other product categories, especially new ones, commitment is comparatively low. Consumers have not had the relevant experience—or, having had experience, they have detected few real differences among brands.

The distinction between brand loyals and all others is important because it tells us where to expect change. Change will be difficult in product categories where loyalties are strong. Within those categories, change will be less difficult among respondents who are on the move. Change will be easiest of all in product categories where loyalties are weak or not yet formed.

If all this seems perfectly obvious, consider attitude change tests of advertisements for mature brands. Even though everyone should know that one communication is most unlikely to effect a real change in a well-established attitude, advertisers persist in looking for—and expecting to find—such changes, and are surprised and disappointed when they fail.

What advertisers should do, of course, is to separate brand-loyal respondents from the remainder of the sample and to look for change only among respondents who might be moved. Although that segment may be tiny, it is the only segment where the advertisement has a reasonable shot.

What advertisers most especially should not do is to compare change scores across samples, without regard to how many brand loyals each sample might contain. When different samples contain different proportions of brand loyals, outcomes depend more upon the equities in the samples than upon the merits of the ads.

On the academic side, failure to recognize the impact of brand loyalty reduces the validity of much brand-equity research. In an effort to make sure that everything else is equal, researchers eliminate brand loyalty altogether by employing fictional brands. Considering the great power of brand loyalty and the many ways this powerful variable interacts with almost every other influence on consumer choice, it seems especially shortsighted to generalize fictional brand findings across the board.

Brand loyal consumers are different from consumers who, for one reason or another, are relatively open to meaningful change. Findings based on one of those two segments cannot safety be generalized to the other. When the segments are merged, the findings may well be wrong for both.

Here we have four taxonomies which have been neglected in both academic and applied research: (a) salience versus trust, (b) definition versus redefinition, (c) customers versus noncustomers, and (d) brand loyal versus open to change. All four of those taxonomies can add insight and validity to almost any study of the equities of brands.

We now turn to three relatively new taxonomies, proposed in other parts of this book. All three seem likely to contribute to our understanding of brand equity and to increase our knowledge of how marketing and advertising really work.

Memory-Based Versus Stimulus-Based Decisions

In their discussion of mature brands, Haugtvedt, Leavitt, and Schneier (chapter 16) draw attention to two quite different kinds of purchasing decisions. Some decisions are stimulus based, as when diners choose from a menu. Others are memory based, as when decision makers call up alternatives from memory, and also call up the criteria they will use.

As those authors point out, most of our current research methods are stimulus based. They provide menus of criteria and ask respondents to choose among predesignated brands. To the degree that stimulus-based procedures exclude elements that would have been considered, or promote consideration of elements that would not have been considered, they misrepresent the process through which memory-based decisions take place.

One of the unintended consequences of stimulus-based research methods is overemphasis on what Haugtvedt, Leavitt, and Schneier call *evaluative extremity*. If all the decision maker needs to do is to apply predesignated criteria to predesignated alternatives, then any obvious superiority will determine choice. Under those highly simplified conditions, stark messages which hammer away at one of the predetermined criteria are likely to be more "effective" than more complex messages which link brand images to multiple aspects of the decision maker's life.

When the decision is memory based, different criteria and alternatives may be called up by the very same decision maker under different circumstances at different times. Under those conditions, any single-minded message may be too narrow to be right; richer, more complex images, with complex connections to many situations, may include what is needed to carry the day.

The distinction between stimulus-based and memory-based decisions is related to the distinction between definition advertising and redefinition advertising. Definition advertising focuses singlemindedly on present strengths. Redefinition advertising adds new associations between brand images and consumers' needs. The distinction between stimulus-based and memory-based decisions is also related to the distinction between salience and trust. Salience requires stark, simplistic repetition. Trust requires intimate association over time.

If most real purchasing decisions are memory based, rather than stimulus based, findings from stimulus-based experiments may be largely wrong. We don't know how many consumer decisions are memory based rather than stimulus based. We also don't know how critical the differences between them will turn out to be.

The evidence presented by Haugtvedt, Leavitt, and Schneier—and the distinctions between definition and redefinition and between salience and trust—all suggest that memory-based and stimulus-based decisions are not at all alike. If so, we should not continue with the pretense that they are the same.

The Five Faces of Loyalty

In chapter 15 of this volume, McQueen, Foley, and Deighton demonstrate that grocery product purchasers can be divided into six loyalty groups: (a) Long Loyals, (b) Short Loyals, (c) Rotators, (d) Deal Selective Rotators, (e) Name Brand Price Driven, and (f) Store Brand Price Driven.

From the academic point of view, this taxonomy suggests that the traditional distinction between Loyal and Nonloyal conceals much useful information. Within Loyals, for example, Long Loyals seem almost immune to advertising; Short Loyals seem much easier to persuade. Within Nonloyals, Deal Selective Rotators, Name Brand Price Drivens, and Store Brand Price Drivens are, in fact, loyal; they are simply loyal to specific brand groups in specific ways. Thus, any simple-minded distinction between Loyal and Nonloyal is likely to merge purchasers of very different types.

From the applied point of view, the McQueen, Foley, and Deighton taxonomy suggests a solution to a difficult problem in advertising copy research. As noted earlier, most copy-testing services fail to separate essentially unmovable respondents from those who might be open to some change. McQueen, Foley, and Deighton's findings suggest that copy-test respondents should be divided into loyalty segments, and the segments should be matched when comparing ads. Even if the matches were not perfect, this procedure would surely be more sensitive and valid than any procedure which assumes respondents are all alike.

Dividing respondents into loyalty segments can be helpful in other ways. Consider, for example, the Schlitz case described by Aaker in chapter 22. As the Schlitz franchise began to deteriorate, loyalty segmentation could have provided clues as to the reasons for the brand's decline. Given that Schlitz was then a leading brand, the resources to collect such data would surely have been available. Perhaps the data were collected, but not analyzed in that way.

The McQueen, Foley, and Deighton approach can be extended past the grocery cart. A bank researcher might classify customers into Long Loyals, Short Loyals, Deal Selective Rotators, and Name Brand Price Drivens for each service the bank provides. This classification would be the first step toward measuring the lifetime value of each segment. Tracked over time, it would also yield diagnostic measurements of change.

In the durable goods area, loyalty segmentation sheds light on customer retention and customer loss. As the Compaq case in chapter 22 demonstrates, marketers pay a heavy price when they focus exclusively on present sales.

Like ostriches and robins, loyalty segments differ in major ways. The details of those differences provide useful insights that aggregations hide.

What Advertising Is

The final new taxonomy, from Lannon in chapter 11, tracks advertising's evolution over time. This taxonomy suggests that advertising has taken five steps: (a) the manufacturer speaks, (b) the target group consumes with pleasure, (c) hyperbole and exaggeration dramatize product benefits, (d) brand appropriates symbols, metaphors to express personality, and (e) brand creates own language code. Although these steps depict "increasingly sophisticated visual literacy," examples of all five can still be found today.

This taxonomy is useful because it guards against the elephant fallacy and the bird fallacy. It tells us once again that findings derived from just one advertisement, or one type of advertising, cannot be generalized to all the rest. It demonstrates that studies which merge different types of advertising will overlook important details of the mechanisms through which advertising works.

The first three of Lannon's phases—the manufacturer speaks, the target group consumes with pleasure, and hyperbole and exaggeration dramatize product benefits—are subcategories of definition advertising. They are similar in that the advertiser takes existing benefits as givens. They are different in that, as the steps progress, the message becomes increasingly abstract.

The fourth step—brand appropriates symbols, metaphors to express personality—incorporates the shift from definition advertising to redefinition advertising. Because this shift is so consequential, this category might be more informative if divided into subtypes.

Lannon's fifth step—brand creates own language code—represents a further qualitative shift. In this step, product attributes vanish altogether, and *brand language* becomes the sole basis for brand choice. As Lannon notes, campaigns based on this philosophy have so far met with limited success: "By excising all product references and concentrating solely on brand language . . . communications run serious risks and few examples truly come off. By giving insufficient information and offering inadequate clues, they assume too much and are merely insulting and irritating." Only time will tell whether this step represents a wave of the future or merely a passing fad.

As we move through this taxonomy, advertising takes a more important role. In the first category—the manufacturer speaks—advertising conveys information about the attributes that mark the brand. As the categories progress, execution becomes more critical, and advertising becomes a greater fraction of what the brand connotes. When we get to symbols and metaphors, advertising becomes the major carrier of equity. At the point where advertising becomes most important, traditional information-processing models become least adequate for understanding how advertising works.

Lannon's taxonomy captures critical aspects of advertising's diverse effects. It points to oversights in current models and consequent omissions in current work. Research will be stronger whenever those insights are incorporated, and weaker whenever they are left out.

CONCLUDING COMMENTS

These seven taxonomies—four relatively old, three relatively new—are certain to be useful when planning brand equity research.

Given the dangers of vacuous generalization, one might wonder why these safeguards have been so neglected in the past. One possibility is that academic consumer research, which tends to set the theoretical research agenda, has been too willing to condone both the elephant fallacy and the bird fallacy in the name of grand theory: Too much emphasis on the consumer equivalent of $E = MC^2$, and too little emphasis on discovering how real things really work.

In discussions of theory versus reality, researchers like to quote Lewin, to the effect that nothing is as practical as a good theory. They should notice, however, that Lewin said "a good theory," meaning a theory that really predicts how real people really behave. No matter how charitably interpreted, theories based on the elephant fallacy and the bird fallacy can never be expected to be good in that way.

As a safeguard against premature generalization, the field would be better served by closer inquiry and greater care. This more patient strategy would require that things be divided into parts, and that those parts be examined closely and seriously, one at a time. Instead of disregarding the sharp divisions surveyed in this chapter and elsewhere in this book, this strategy would require that each segment be examined in detail and in its own right. It would ignore high-level, abstract generalizations, and would celebrate low-level, valid discoveries of how real things really work.

Admittedly, this strategy would not lead to $E = MC^2$ any time soon, but this more truly scientific agenda would be productive in two important ways:

1. It would preserve the richness and detail of the real behavior of real consumers.
2. It would penetrate more deeply into the complex processes by which consumers respond to brands.

About the Contributors

David A. Aaker is the J. Gary Shansby professor of marketing strategy at the Haas School of Business, University of California at Berkeley. He is the author of over 75 articles and nine books on branding, advertising, and business strategy. His recent books include the influential *Managing Brand Equity* (Free Press) and *Developing Business Strategies*, 3rd edition (Wiley).

Rajeev Batra is associate professor of marketing at the University of Michigan at Ann Arbor. His research interests center on the role of emotion in advertising, optimal advertising budgeting issues, and the effect of advertising on brand image development. He received his PhD from Stanford, and his MS in advertising from Illinois.

Alexander L. Biel is the former executive director of the Ogilvy Center for Research & Development and presently heads the consulting firm of Alexander L. Biel & Associates in Mill Valley, California. He has published over 40 articles on advertising research, market segmentation, and more recently, on brand equity and customer satisfaction. He serves as an outside director of a major international research firm.

Max Blackston is worldwide director of advertising and branding research for Research International, based in New York. He is currently engaged in developing and applying research methodologies designed for the measurement and understanding of brand equity. Mr. Blackston was a researcher and consultant in the United Kingdom and Italy for 20 years before joining Ogilvy & Mather New York, where he was head of planning and research for 5 years.

David M. Boush is an assistant professor of marketing at the University of Oregon. His research interests center on consumer evaluation processes and consumer knowledge structure. His work on brand extensions has appeared in the *Journal of Marketing Research* and *Psychology and Marketing*. He is a member of the American Marketing Association, the Society for Consumer Psychology, and the Association for Consumer Research.

Dipankar Chakravarti is professor of marketing and psychology at the University of Arizona. He holds a PhD from Carnegie-Mellon University. His research examines consumer and managerial judgment and decision making in marketing contexts. He is acting editor of the *Journal of Consumer Psychology* and a member of the editorial review boards of the *Journal of Consumer Research* and the *Journal of Marketing Research*.

John Deighton is associate professor of marketing at the Graduate School of Business, University of Chicago. He studied marketing at the Wharton School and taught at Dartmouth College before moving to Chicago. His research is published in the *Journal of Marketing*, the *Journal of Consumer Research*, *Organizational Behavior and Human Decision Processes*, *Sloan Management Review*, *Psychology and Marketing*, and in various books and conference proceedings. He teaches in Chicago's MBA program in the areas of marketing management and services marketing, in the university's executive education programs in financial services marketing, and for service firms such as Citicorp, Sears Roebuck & Company, Harris Bank, and BancOne.

Julie Edell received her PhD from Carnegie-Mellon University in 1982. She came to Duke University from Carnegie and is currently an associate professor at the Fuqua School of Business. She is currently researching the role of advertising in the development and maintenance of a brand's equity and is currently a member of the editorial boards of the *Journal of Consumer Psychology* and the *Journal of Consumer Research*. She recently edited a book, *Emotion in Advertising: Theoretical and Practical Explorations* (with Stuart Agres and Tony Dubitsky). Her research appears in *Journal of Consumer Research*, *Journal of Marketing Research*, *Advances in Consumer Research*, and *Advertising and Consumer Psychology*.

Peter H. Farquhar is professor of management at the Peter F. Drucker Graduate Management Center and director of the Product Strategy Institute at the

Claremont Graduate School. His current research focuses on brand strategy and product design. Dr. Farquhar has been involved in launching over 20 new products and is a management consultant to many leading companies throughout the world.

Carol K. Foley is vice-president and group research director at Leo Burnett. At Burnett since 1974, she has developed a theoretical framework regarding the role of emotion in consumer behavior and a lexicon of emotion words and phrases used in research studies for Burnett clients. She also has developed and operationalized a model for uncovering patterns of buying behavior in scanner data that is reported in this book.

Curtis P. Haugtvedt is an assistant professor of marketing at Ohio State University. His research focuses on attitude persistence and resistance, the role of personality variables in persuasion, and order of presentation effects in persuasion. He teaches undergraduate and MBA courses in consumer behavior and PhD level seminars in consumer psychology. Professor Haugtvedt holds MA and PhD degrees in social psychology from the University of Missouri, Columbia and BA and BS degrees in sociology and psychology from North Dakota State University.

Paul M. Herr is associate professor of marketing at the Graduate School of Business Administration at the University of Colorado at Boulder. His research work has examined important topics in social psychology, advertising, branding, and marketing research. He received his PhD in psychology from Indiana University and is a principal for the BEARS Group.

Hyung-Shik Jung received his PhD from the Marketing Department at the University of Arizona. His dissertation focused on the impact of advertising and evidence on consumers' evaluations of products. He currently manages a family business in Korea.

Amna Kirmani is an assistant professor of marketing at the Fuqua School of Business at Duke University. She received her PhD in marketing from Stanford University. Dr. Kirmani's research focuses on how consumers make judgments of product quality and how they process advertisements.

H. Shanker Krishnan is assistant professor of marketing at Indiana University, Bloomington. He holds a PhD in business administration from the University of Arizona. His research examines issues in the processing of advertising information, specifically how ad executions impact on consumer memory and the role of implicit memory in consumer behavior.

Judie Lannon runs her own consultancy after 20 years with J. Walter Thompson, most recently as research & development director, J. Walter Thompson, Europe. She works primarily with multinational companies specializing in developing integrated marketing and communications strategies on a European or global scale. She designs and runs courses for all levels of management in social trend forecasting, developing corporate and brand communications and all aspects of consumer research. She is a member of the faculty at Management Centre Europe, a frequent speaker at international conferences, and regular contributor to professional journals. Her clients include Nestlé, De Beers, Visa International, Unilever, and Heineken.

Clark Leavitt is currently professor of marketing at Ohio State University. He was visiting scholar at the Ogilvy Center for Research and Development in 1985 and 1986. His interests include the relationship of consumer knowledge structures, particularly brand images, and marketing strategy.

Donald R. Lehmann is professor of marketing at Columbia University Graduate School of Business. He has a BS from Union College and an MSIA and PhD from Purdue. His research interests include choice modeling and the adoption of innovations.

Deborah J. MacInnis is currently an associate professor in the Marketing Department at the University of Arizona. Her research interests center on the impact of marketing communications on brand images, imagery, memory, emotion, and persuasion. Dr. MacInnis serves on the editorial board of the *Journal of Marketing Research*, *Journal of Consumer Research*, and the *Journal of Marketing*, and her work has appeared in each of these journals.

Grant McCracken holds a PhD in anthropology from the University of Chicago. He was a Killam Post-Doctoral Fellow at the University of British Columbia and visiting scholar at the University of Cambridge. He is the author of many articles and two books: *Culture and Consumption* (Indiana University Press) and *The Long Interview* (Sage). He has advised many organizations including Eastman Kodak, Chrysler Corporation, Coca-Cola, Landor Associates, and Young and Rubicam. He was the founding director of the Institute of Contemporary Culture and is now curator in the Department of Ethnology at the Royal Ontario Museum.

Josh McQueen joined Leo Burnett in 1974 as an assistant research analyst. In 1978, Josh was named Associate Research Director of Burnett's U.K. office, and, in 1980, Research Director of the Australia/Asia offices. Josh returned to the United States in October, 1984 and in February, 1985 was promoted to Director of Research. He was made senior vice president in July of that year and executive vice president in August, 1988. He has BS and MS degrees from the University of Illinois.

Jeri Moore is an executive vice president at DDB Needham Worldwide, where she has been for the past 14 years in positions of market research, strategic planning, and account management. Her present job involves developing strategic models and research techniques for the agency's United States and international advertising clients. Prior to joining DDB Needham, she held market research positions at Communicus, Inc. and Haug Associates.

Marian Chapman Moore is an associate professor of marketing at the Fuqua School of Business at Duke University. She received her PhD from the University of California at Los Angeles. Her research on the role of affective reactions to ads has appeared in the *Journal of Marketing Research*, the *Journal of Consumer Research*, and *Advances in Consumer Research*. In addition to her research on advertising, Dr. Moore has published in the areas of strategic management and competitive analysis. She serves on the editorial board of the *Journal of Marketing* and is a member of the Marketing Science Institute's Marketing Strategy Steering Committee.

Kent Nakamoto is currently an assistant professor in the Marketing Department at the University of Arizona. His research interests include consumer learning and decision making, behavioral issues in competition, and psychological measurement. His papers have appeared in *Management Science*, *Journal of Marketing Research*, and *Marketing Science*.

Stewart Owen is the vice-chairman of Landor Associates, the world's leading consulting firm in the areas of identity, design, and branding. Prior to joining Landor, he was a principal in the Matrix Research Group focusing on communications research issues. At Landor, he has done consulting work with such major corporations as Ford, the General Electric Company, IBM, AT&T, Coca-Cola, Japan Airlines, Fuji Film, 3M, and British Airways. In addition to his client-based work, Mr. Owen is a noted speaker in the United States and throughout Asia on marketing and research issues.

Michael L. Ray is the first John G. McCoy–Banc One Corporation professor of creativity and innovation and professor of marketing at Stanford University's

Graduate School of Business. Professor Ray's early work contributed to the body of knowledge on consumer information processing. He developed one of the most widely used models in the field and edited two of its first books. Among his over 100 publications are the text *Advertising and Communication Management*, the anthology *Measurement Readings for Marketing Research*, and his co-authored books *Creativity in Business* and *The Path of the Everyday Hero*. He also co-authored the companion book to the PBS series, *The Creative Spirit*, and co-edited *The New Paradigm in Business*.

Wendy L. Schneier is a doctoral candidate in the Department of Marketing at Ohio State University. She holds a BA in psychology from Tulane University and an MBA from Ohio State University. Her research interests focus on motivational factors associated with consumer and managerial information search and information use.

Dipinder Singh is currently manager of consumer research at Duracell USA in Bethel, Connecticut. He was previously associate research director at Ogilvy and Mather in New York, which he joined after receiving his PhD from Columbia University; he has also worked as a product manager with Richardson-Vicks in India. He is a member of the American Marketing Association and serves on committees of the Advertising Research Foundation.

Norman Smothers is an associate professor of strategy and new ventures at the California State University, Hayward. He consults with firms such as Apple Computer, AT&T, and others in developing customer-focused, market-responsive strategies. Dr. Smothers holds BS and ME degrees in electrical engineering from the University of Kansas, and PhD and MBA degrees in business administration from the University of California at Berkeley.

Hiroshi Tanaka is an associate marketing director at Dentsu Inc. in Tokyo and is currently working with leading western advertisers. He received his MA in journalism from Southern Illinois University, Carbondale and completed doctoral coursework in business at Keio University (ABD). Tanaka coauthored an award-winning book (*Advertising Psychology*) and has published over 10 papers in academic journals. He teaches marketing at several universities as a visiting lecturer.

Edward M. Tauber is president of Tauber Research, a marketing consulting firm founded in 1981. The company focuses exclusively on brand extension research and counsel. Dr. Tauber has conducted over 50 brand extension studies. Ten successful new products are currently in the marketplace which evolved from these studies. They are generating retail sales in excess of 750 million dollars.

Brian Wansink is assistant professor at the Amos Tuck School at Dartmouth College. Prior to earning his PhD at Stanford, he worked as a marketing consultant with the Small Business Administration. His research projects focus on the impact that advertising and other marketing variables have on a person's consumption rate of a package good that he or she is already favorable toward. He serves on the Editorial Review Board of the *Journal of Advertising Research*.

William D. Wells is Mithun Land Grant Professor of Advertising in the School of Journalism and Mass Communication at the University of Minnesota. He is the co-author or editor of several books including *Advertising: Principles and Practice*, *Consumer Behavior* and *Lifestyle and Psychographics*. He has published over 60 articles on advertising, consumer behavior, and research methods. Dr. Wells earned a PhD in psychology from Stanford University and is on the editorial boards of several consumer behavior and marketing journals.

Lewis Winters received his PhD in social psychology from the University of Delaware. He started his marketing research career in 1964 at Associates for Research in Behavior (ARBOR) in Philadelphia. From 1967 to 1972 he was manager of behavioral research in the Corporate Marketing Research Department at Du Pont. Currently, he is at Chevron Corporation, where he is Manager of Strategy and Research in the Corporate Public Affairs Department. He also teaches part time in the MBA program at Santa Clara University. From 1986 until 1991 he was on the faculty at Stanford University, where he taught the marketing research course in the Stanford MBA program. He has been an active contributor of articles in the *Journal of Advertising Research* and is the editor of the new technologies section of the American Marketing Association's journal: *Marketing Research Management and Applications*.

Valarie Zeithaml is currently a partner in Schmalensee Zeithaml Associates, a firm specializing in strategy and measurement of service quality. She was formerly an associate professor at the Fuqua School of Business at Duke University.

Author Index

A

Aaker, D. A., 2, 5, *8*, 83, 86, 87, 88, 90,
  95, 99, *110*, 143, 144, 151, 158, *159*,
  177, *193*, 195, 196, *210*, *211*, 213,
  214, *229*, *230*, 235, *245*, 263, 264,
  268, *276*, 281, 283, *296*, 306, 307,
  310, *311*, *312*, 335, 336, 340, *341*
Achenbaum, A. A., 33, *48*
Ahtola, O. T., 90, *95*, 145, *159*
Ajzen, I., 185, *193*, 253, *259*
Alba, J. W., 153, *159*, 217, *229*, 250, 251,
  259, 265, 272, *276*
Allen, C. T., 94, *95*
Anderson, N. H., 84, 87, 88, *95*
Anderson, R. E., 151, *159*
Andrews, I. R., 147, 148, *159*, *161*
Areni, C. S., 215, *229*
Ashcraft, M. H., 267, 268, *276*, 302,
  311

B

Badenhop, S. B., 146, *160*
Bagozzi, R. P., 216, *229*

Baldwin, B. M., 93, *95*
Ballachey, E. L., 254, *260*
Ball-Rokeach, S. J., 47, *48*
Bargh, J. A., 306, *311*
Barsalou, L. W., 180, *193*, 267, 268, *276*,
  301, 302, 303, 304, 306, *311*
Barwise, P., 213, *229*
Bass, B. M., 100, 101, *110*
Batra, R., 56, *62*, 90, *95*, 99, *110*, 144,
  160, 192, *194*, 195, *210*
Bearden, W. O., 148, *159*
Belk, R. W., 85, *95*, 104, *110*, 179, *193*
Bennett, D. R., 76, *82*
Berger, P., 100, *110*
Berry, L., 76, *82*, 148, *161*
Bettman, J. R., 299, *312*
Beyer, J. M., 100, 101, *111*
Biehal, G., 251, *259*
Biel, A., 143, *159*, 163, 175, *176*
Birdwell, A. E., 84, *95*
Bjork, R. A., 216, 217, 221, *231*
Blackston, M., 114, *124*
Blattberg, R. C., 236, *245*
Blaxton, T. A., 218, *231*
Bloch, P. H., 182, *194*
Blount, S., 98, 99, 106, *110*
Bonnal, F., 172, *176*

Booker, J., 220, *231*
Boulding, W., 148, 149, *159*
Boush, D. M., 213, *229*, 273, *276*, 281, *296*, 303, 305, 306, 308, *311*
Bowers, J. S., 220, *229*, *231*
Brewer, W. F., 197, *211*
Brock, T. C., 249, *261*
Brown, C. W., 76, *82*
Brown, P. K., 151, *159*
Brucks, M., 148, *159*
Buesing, T., 236, *245*
Burke, M. C., 99, *111*, 195, 199, *211*
Burke, R. R., 251, *259*, 267, *277*
Burnett, J., 198, *211*
Busato-Schach, J., 147, *160*

C

Caballero, M. J., 52, *63*
Cacioppo, J. T., 153, 157, *161*, 248, 249, 255, *259*, *260*
Calder, B. J., 114, *124*, 197, *211*
Campbell, C., 104, *110*
Carpenter, G. S., 282, *296*, 299, *311*
Chakravarti, D., 213, 215, 218, 227, *229*, *230*, 251, *259*, 281, *296*
Challis, B. H., 216, 218, *231*
Chao, P., 307, *311*
Chattopadhyay, A., 251, *259*
Chestnut, R. W., 186, *194*, 236, *245*
Childers, T. L., 223, *230*
Chiu, J. S., 147, *161*
Churchill, G. A., 215, *231*
Cialdini, R. B., 249, *259*
Clemons, D. S., 255, *261*
Cohen, J., 215, *229*
Cohen, J. B., 227, *229*
Cohen, M. J., 218, *231*
Cole, C. A., 222, *229*
Collins, A. M., 265, 266, 267, 269, 270, 272, 273, *276*
Conger, J. A., 100, 101, *110*
Cooper, P., 114, *124*, 171, 172, *176*
Craik, F. I. M., 224, *229*, *230*
Crockett, S., 213, *229*, 281, *296*, 306, *311*
Crowder, R. G., 251, *259*
Crutchfield, R. S., 254, *260*

D

Dallas, M., 217, 224, *230*
Daser, S., 32, *48*

Davis, K. E., 180, 181, *194*
de Chernatony, L., 165, *176*
DeFleur, M., 47, *48*
Deighton, J., 94, *95*, 195, *211*, 257, *259*, 282, 286, 295, *296*
Dertouzos, M. L., 333, *341*
Deshpande, R., *193*, *194*
Digman, J., 84, *95*
Dobni, D., 143, 146, *159*
Dodds, W. B., 147, *159*
Dowd, K. M., 32, *48*
Duboff, R. S., 97, *110*
Duncan, C. P., 85, *95*
Dunkan, T. R., 51, *63*
Durgee, J., 97, *111*

E

Eastlack, J. O., 335, *341*
Edell, J. A., 99, *111*, 195, 196, 199, *211*, 223, *229*
Englis, B. G., 197, *211*
Erickson, G. M., 307, *311*
Estes, W. K., 265, *276*
Etgar, M., 148, *159*
Etzioni, A., 100, *111*
Eysenck, H. J., 84, *95*

F

Fahey, L., 60, *63*
Farquhar, P. H., 33, *48*, 196, *211*, 213, *229*, *230*, 264, 265, 267, 268, 272, 273, 274, 275, *276*, 281, *296*
Fazio, R. H., 196, *211*, 213, 228, *230*, 250, 252, *259*, *260*, 265, 268, 269, 272, 273, 274, *276*, 281, *296*
Feldman, J. M., 251, *260*
Fields, G., 56, *62*
Fishbein, M., 185
Fiske, S. T., 179, 180, *193*
Flint, J., 97, *111*
Fodor, E. M., 100, 101, *111*
Ford, G. T., 152, *159*
Ford, T., 94, *95*
Freiden, J. B., 151, *159*
Friestad, M., 197, *211*
Frijda, N. H., 197, *211*
Furse, D. H., 150, *161*, 283, *297*

G

Gardner, D. M., 147, *159*, *160*
Gardner, M. P., 150, *160*
Garvin, D. A., 147, *160*
Gati, I., 266, *277*
Geistfeld, L. V., 146, *160*
Gencturk, E., 213, *229*, 281, *296*, 306, *311*
Gensch, D. H., 83, 84, *95*
Gibson, E. J., 255, *260*
Gillund, G., 219, *229*
Goldberg, M. E., 197, *211*
Golden, L. L., 87, *95*
Goodstein, R. C., 199, *211*
Gorn, G. J., 197, *211*
Graf, P., 217, 218, *230*, *231*
Grathwohl, H. L., 85, *95*
Greenberg, A., 106, *111*
Greenwald, A. G., 249, 256, *260*
Grubb, E. L., 85, *95*
Gruder, C. L., 197, *211*
Guilford, J. P., 84, *95*
Gutman, J. O., 83, 84, *95*, 283, *296*

H

Ha, Y., 257, *260*, 282, 286, *296*, *297*
Haddock, R. A., 147, 148, *160*, 307, *311*
Hagerty, M. R., 99, *110*
Haley, R. L., 93, *95*
Hamman, S. B., 219, *230*
Han, J. Y., 213, *229*, 264, 275, *276*
Harris, R., 104, *111*
Hasegawa, K., 52, 53, *62*
Haugtvedt, C. P., 250, 255, 256, 257, *260*
Heckler, S. E., 223, *230*
Heide, M. P., 197, *211*
Herr, P. M., 196, *211*, 213, *230*, 250, *259*, 264, 265, 267, 268, 272, 273, 274, 275, *276*, 281, *296*, 306, *311*
Herren, T., 251, *260*
Herzog, H., 146, *160*
Higgins, E. T., 306, *311*
Higson, C., 213, *229*
Hirschman, E. C., 99, *111*, 178, *193*
Hoch, S. J., 257, *260*, 282, 286, *296*, *297*
Holbrook, M. B., 33, *48*, 99, *111*, 144, 150, *160*
Holden, A. C., 32, *48*
Holmberg, E. R., 53, *62*

Holmes, M., 114, *124*
Hong, J. W., 52, *62*
House, R. J., 100, 101, *111*
Houston, M. J., 222, 223, *229*, *230*
Hovland, C. I., 249, *260*
Howard, D. J., 216, *230*
Huber, J., 94, *95*
Hutchinson, J. W., 217, *229*, 250, *259*, 265, 272, *276*, 299, *312*
Hutchinson, W. W., 153, *159*

I

Ijiri, Y., 213, *229*, 264, 275, *276*
Isen, A. M., 215, *230*
Ishii, J., 58, *63*

J

Jacobson, R., 340, *341*
Jacoby, J., 84, *95*, 146, 147, 148, *160*, 186, *193*, 236, *245*, 307, *311*
Jacoby, L. L., 217, 224, *230*
Jamieson, L. F., 84, *96*
Janis, I., 249, *260*
Jatusripitak, S., 60, *63*
Jaworski, B. J., 97, *111*, 143, 154, *161*, 281, *297*, 307, *312*
Jenkins, J. J., 220, *230*
Johansson, J. K., 307, *311*
John, D. R., 264, *276*
Johnson, M. D., 147, *160*, 305, *312*
Jolibert, A., 147, *161*
Jolson, M. A., 151, *159*
Jones, E. E., 180, 181, *194*
Jones, J., 163, 171, *176*
Jung, H., 153, *160*, 182, *194*, 289, *297*

K

Kagono, T., 60, *63*, 334, *341*
Kardes, F. R., 94, *95*, 265, *276*
Keller, K. A., 264, *276*
Keller, K. L., 83, 86, 87, 88, 90, *95*, 158, *159*, 177, *193*, 195, 198, *211*, 213, 220, 225, *229*, *230*, 252, *260*, 264, *276*, 281, *296*, 306, 307, *311*, *312*

Kelley, H. H., 180, *194*
Kelly, H. H., 249, *260*
Kennedy, E., 213, *229*, 281, *296*, 306, *311*
Kernan, J. B., 87, *95*
King, S., 120, 122, *124*
King, S. H. M., 73, *82*
Kirmani, A., 148, 149, 150, 151, 152, *159*, 160
Kishii, T., 52, *63*
Knox, S., 165, *176*
Kohn-Berning, C. A., 147, *160*
Kosaka, H., 51, *63*
Kotler, P., 60, *63*
Krech, D., 254, *260*
Krishnan, H. S., 215, 218, *230*
Krugman, H. E., 216, *230*

L

Landler, M., *230*
Lannon, J., 114, *124*, 171, *176*
Lawson, R., 213, *231*, 306, *312*
Lazer, W., 51, *63*
Leavitt, C., 70, *82*, 251, 256, *260*, 310, *312*
Leerhsen, C., 107, *111*
Lester, R. K., 333, *341*
Leuthesser, L., 213, *230*
Levine, J., 107, *111*
Levitt, T., 51, *63*, 101, *111*
Lewis, H. S., 97, *111*
Light, L. L., 222, *230*
Likierman, C., 213, *229*
Linville, P. W., 253, *260*
Loftus, E. F., 265, 266, 267, 268, 270, 271, 272, 274, *276*, *277*
Loken, B., 213, *229*, 264, 267, 273, *276*, *277*, 281, *296*, 299, 301, 302, 303, 306, 308, *311*, *312*
Lombardi, W., 306, *311*
Luce, R. D., 269, *277*
Luckmann, T., 100, *110*
Lutz, R. J., 180, *194*, 248, *260*
Lynch, J. G., 217, *229*, 250, 251, *259*, *260*
Lynch, J. G., Jr., 94, *96*, 265, *276*

M

MacInnis, D. J., 97, *111*, 143, 154, *161*, 213, 223, *229*, *230*, 281, *296*, 297, 307, *312*

MacInnis, D. L., 153, *160*
MacKenzie, S. B., 150, *160*
MacMaster, N. A., 52, *63*
Madden, C. S., 52, *63*
Malhotra, N. K., 148, *159*
Malt, B. C., 302, *312*
Manabe, K., 54, *63*
Mandler, G., 217, 219, *230*
Marmorstein, H., 250, 251, *260*
Marquez, F. T., 53, *63*
Marsh, P., 213, *229*
Martin, D. N., 257, *260*
Matsui, M., 53, *63*
Matsukubo, S., 52, *63*
Mazursky, D., 147, *160*
McAlister, L., 236, *245*
McCann, J., 94, *95*
McCracken, G., 94, *95*, 125, 126, 127, 129, 130, 132, *139*
McGuire, W. J., 257, *260*
McQueen, J., 94, *95*
Medin, D. L., 265, 270, 273, *277*, 305, *312*
Merikle, P. M., 220, *230*
Mervis, C. B., 267, 268, 269, 273, *277*, 300, 301, 303, *312*
Meyer, D. E., 265, *277*
Meyers-Levy, J., 223, *231*
Milberg, S., 213, *231*, 306, *312*
Miller, R. S., 302, *312*
Minshall, B., 213, *229*, 281, *296*, 306, *311*
Mischel, W., 84, *95*
Misurell, D., 213, *229*, 281, *296*, 306, *311*
Mitchell, A. A., 150, 151, *160*
Miyashita, M., 54, *63*
Mizerski, R. W., 87, *95*
Mol, H., 104, *111*
Monroe, K. B., 147, *159*, *161*
Moore, M. C., 199, *211*
Morgan, R., *82*
Moriarty, S. E., 51, *63*, 198, *211*
Mudderrisoglu, A., 52, *62*
Mueller, B., 52, 53, *63*
Murata, S., 51, *63*
Murphy, G. L., 270, 273, *277*
Myers, J. G., 283, *296*
Myers, J. H., 145, *160*

N

Nakamoto, K., 153, *160*, 213, *229*, 281, 282, *296*, 297, 299, *311*

Nathanson-Moog, C., 97, *111*
Nedungadi, P., 215, *231*, 252, *260*, 273, 277, 299, *312*
Nelson, J. E., 85, *95*
Neslin, S. A., 236, *245*
Newman, J. W., 146, *160*
Nishio, C., 58, *63*
Nonaka, I., 60, *63*, 334, *341*
Nunnally, J. C., 185

O

Oglivy, D., 67, *82*, 93, *95*
Okumura, A., 60, *63*, 334, *341*
Oliva, T. A., 267, *277*
Olson, J. C., 84, *95*, 147, 148, 150, 151, *160*, 307, *311*
Olson, J. G., 144, 146, 147, *160*, *161*
Ostrom, T. M., 249, *261*
Otsuki, H., 54, 55, *63*

P

Page, T. J., Jr., 197, *211*
Pak, S., 219, *231*
Parasuraman, A., 148, *161*
Park, C. W., 97, *111*, 143, 154, *161*, 213, 223, *230*, *231*, 281, *297*, 306, 307, *312*
Peacock, P., 236, *245*
Pedhazur, E. J., 91, *95*
Percy, L., 150, 151, *161*, 178, *194*
Peterson, R., 147, *161*
Petty, R. E., 153, 157, *161*, 248, 249, 250, 255, 256, 257, *259*, *260*, *261*
Pincus, S., 148, *161*
Plummer, J. T., 83, *95*, 99, *111*
Posner, M. I., 265, *277*
Powell, M. C., 250, 252, *259*, *260*, 265, 272, *276*
Preston, I., 33, *49*
Puto, C. P., 257, *261*

Q

Quillian, M. R., 265, 269, 272, 273, *276*

R

Raaijmakers, J. G. W., 265, *277*
Rachman, S., 84, *95*
Raju, P. S., 147, *161*
Ram, S., 182, *194*
Rangaswamy, A., 267, *277*
Rao, A. G., 335, *341*
Rao, A. R., 147, *161*
Ratneshwar, S., 299, 301, *312*
Ray, M. L., 99, *110*, 192, *194*, 195, *210*
Reed, J. D., 52, *63*
Reingold, E. M., 220, *230*
Reynolds, T. J., 83, 84, *95*, *96*, 146, *161*, 283, *296*
Richardson, J., 93, *95*
Richardson-Klavehn, A., 216, 217, 221, *231*
Richens, M. L., 182, *194*
Richey, B., 32, *48*
Ridgway, N. M., *194*
Ries, A., 264, *277*, 308, *312*
Rips, L. J., 305, *312*
Rochford, L., 213, *229*, 281, *296*, 306, *311*
Roediger, H. L., 216, 218, 219, *231*
Romer, D., 94, *95*
Rosch, E., 267, 268, 269, 273, *277*, 300, 301, 302, 303, *312*
Rossiter, J. R., 151, *161*, 178, *194*
Roth, F. M., 306, *312*
Rothschild, M. L., 215, 219, *231*
Russo, J. E., 195, *211*

S

Sakakibara, K., 60, *63*, 334, *341*
Sanbonmatsu, D. M., 265, *276*
Sawyer, A. G., 216, *230*
Schacter, D. L., 215, 216, 217, 218, 220, 224, *229*, *230*, *231*
Schiller, Z., *230*
Schneier, W. L., 250, 255, 256, *260*
Schramm, W., 47, *49*
Schumann, D. W., 250, 255, 256, *260*, *261*
Schvaneveldt, R. W., 265, *277*
Scott, W. A., 253, *261*
Segal, R., 98, *111*
Sen, S., 236, *245*
Sherry, D. F., 216, *231*
Sherry, J., 67, *82*

Sherry, J. F., Jr., 104, *110*
Shiffrin, R. M., 219, *229*, 265, *277*
Shils, E., 100, *111*
Shimaguchi, M., 58, *63*
Shimp, T. A., 94, *95*, 148, *159*
Shipp, S., 213, *229*, 281, *296*, 306, *311*
Shoben, E. J., 305, *312*
Shocker, A. D., 145, *160*, 299, 301, *312*
Shoeben, E. J., 306, *312*
Silk, A. J., 216, *229*
Simmons, C. J., 94, *96*
Simpson, C., 302, *312*
Singh, A., 222, *230*
Singh, S. N., 215, 219, *231*
Sirgy, M. J., 84, 85, 87, *96*
Smith, D. B., 152, *159*
Smith, D. C., 213, *231*
Smith, E. E., 265, *277*, 302, 305, *312*
Smith, R. A., 94, *95*
Snyder, C. R. R., 265, *277*
Solow, R. M., 333, *341*
Speller, D. E., 147, *160*
Sproles, G. B., 146, *160*
Squire, L. R., 218, *231*
Srinivas, K., 218, 219, *231*
Srull, T. K., 250, 251, *259*, *260*
Staelin, R., 223, *229*
Starr, M. K., 99, *111*
Stayman, D. M., 56, *62*, 99, *110*, 195, *211*
Stephens, D. L., 195, *211*
Stewart, D. W., 150, *161*, 283, *297*
Sthuraman, R., 335, *341*
Strobel, J., 213, *229*, 281, *296*, 306, *311*
Sujan, M., 299, *312*
Swasy, J. L., 152, *159*
Szybillo, G. J., 147, *160*

T

Tajima, Y., 54, *63*
Tanaka, H., 52, *63*
Taschian, A., 219, *231*
Tauber, E. M., 264, 267, 270, *277*, 281,
        297, 301, *312*, 317
Taylor, S. E., 179, 180, *193*
Tellis, G. J., 335, *341*
Therrien, L., *230*
Thomson, D. M., 225, *231*, 252, *261*
Thorson, E., 197, *211*
Trice, H. M., 100, 101, *111*
Trout, J., 264, *277*, 308, *312*

Tulving, E., 220, 224, 225, *229*, *231*, 252,
        261
Tversky, A., 266, *277*, 301, 305, *312*

U

Ullmann, J. E., 99, *111*

V

Valenzi, E. R., 147, 148, *159*, *161*

W

Wade, S., 47, *49*
Walker, L., 98, 99, 106, *110*
Wallendorf, M., 104, *110*
Wansink, B., 191, 192, *193*, *194*
Ward, J., 267, *277*, 299, 301, 302, *312*
Warren, W. L., 250, 255, 256, *260*
Waters, L. K., 148, *161*
Watkins, M. J., 222, *231*
Weber, M., 98, 100, 101, *111*
Webster, F. E., 236, *245*
Weigold, M. F., 250, 251, *260*
Weldon, M. S., 216, 218, *231*
Wells, W. D., 94, *96*, 198, *211*, 257, *261*
Wheatley, J. J., 147, *161*
White, J. D., 219, *231*
Wildavsky, A., 100, *110*, *111*
Williams, C. J., 250, 252, *260*, 265, *276*
Winters, L. C., 322, 323, 324, 325, 326,
        330, *332*
Winters, P., *194*
Wittgenstein, L., 301, *312*
Woycke, J., 100, 101, *111*
Wright, P., 148, 152, *160*, 179, *194*
Wulf, F., 254, *261*

Y

Yamaki, T., 57, *63*
Yamamoto, M., 55, 56, *63*

Z

Zaichkowshy, J. L., 178, 182, *194*
Zeithaml, V. A., 144, 145, 147, 148, 149,
        159, *161*
Zinkhan, G. M., 52, *62*, 143, 146, *159*

Subject Index

A

Absolut vodka case
concerning product charisma, 98-100
Acquisitions, 12
Ad-induced feelings, 195-196
advertising and brand equity regarding, 196-197
research study on, 197-210
cue effect, 198, 204, 207, 209-210
feelings recall, 197-198, 203-204, 207
future directions for, 210
robust to cue effect, 198, 206-207, 209-210
robust to delay effect, 198, 204-205, 207, 208-209
Advertising
brand equity and, 196-197
role of, in creating, 5-6
two ways of influencing, 196
claims and evidence regarding brand equity and extensions, 281-296
components of, 150-151
definition vs. redefinition, 345-348
effectiveness of alternate strategies in, 157
effect of, on perceived quality, 149-150
direct, 152-153
indirect, 150-152

effects of, on consumers, 169-170
emotional, 346, 347
European Community's increase in, 32
expansion and brand equity, 177-193
five broad categories of, 353-354
brand language, 174-175
hyperbole and exaggeration, 174
manufacturer speaks, 173
metaphors and symbolism used, 174
target groups consume with pleasure, 173-174
hard vs. soft sell in, 172
informational, 346-347
Japan's strategy for, 52-57
likability as an effective measure in, 175-176
links among perceived quality, brand image, and, 153-156
message components in, 214-215
repetition of, 255
role of corporate, in brand building, 321-332
soft vs. hard sell, 52-53, 55
strategies for established brands, 257
styles of, 5
transformation, 346, 347
two basic dimensions of, 172
U.S. vs. Japan regarding, 52-54
varieties of brand memory induced by, 213-229

Age
   brand memory and, 222–223
   brand strength and, 20, 21, 23
Air Jordan brand case, Nike
   and product charisma, 104–106
Ajinomoto brand system, 57
Alcoholic beverages, 22
Anthropological approach. *See Cultural approach*
Apolinaris mineral water
   brand equity measures for, 39
Assimilation, 254
Associations, brand, 7, 71
   associative networks, 265
   asymmetries in strength of, 270–272
   directional, 265–266
      brand-to-associate vs. associate-to-brand, 266–268
   implications for brand management
      brand building, 272–273
      brand leveraging, 273–274
   measuring strength of
      category-dominance, 268–269, 270–271, 272–273, 274–275
      instance-dominance, 269–270, 270–271, 272–273, 274–275
   types of, 263–264
   Weight Watchers case, 337–338, 340
Attitudes, brand, 145, 150, 151, 156
   changes in, 255–256
   cognitive strength and, 248–250
   definition of, 248
   existing positive, 255–256
   taxonomies concerning
      brand loyal vs. open to change, 350–351
      customers vs. noncustomers, 348–350
      definition vs. redefinition, 345–348
      memory- vs. stimulus-based decisions, 351–352
      salience vs. trust, 344–345
Attributes, 285, 291, 292, 295
   and expansion advertising, 180–181
   extrinsic and intrinsic, 146–148, 149–152, 155, 157–158
      distinguished from central-peripheral processing, 157–158
      effects on perceived quality, 148–149
   hard and soft image, 71, 73–74
Attribute similarity, 89–90
Automobile brands, 21–22

B

Beer brands
   and cultural meaning, 129–130
      college years, 130–132
      female reaction, 133–134
      postcollege years, 134–137
      regarding competition, 133
   masculinity and, 130–138
Bird fallacy, 343–344
Bottled water
   use of, in five European countries, 41
Bottom-up information processing, 55–57
Brand affinity, 3
Brand associations. *See Associations, brand*
Brand attitudes. *See Attitudes, brand*
Brand awareness, 35
   Datsun-to-Nissan name change case, 336, 340
   variations in countries, 26
Brand breath, 307–308
Brand concepts, 154–156
Brand equity, 1–2
   ad-induced feelings and, 195–210
   advertising and, 196–197
      claims and evidence regarding, 281–296
      expansion, 177–193
      role of, in creating, 5–6
      two ways influenced by, 196
   brand image concerning
      distinguished from, 69, 143
      driven by, 70–71
   brand personality and, 4–5
   building of, 215–216
   company vs. managerial views on, 2
   converting image into, 67–81
   and culture, 3
   definition of, 2, 33, 69
   in Europe, 33–48
   five dimensions of, 144
   investments, 340–341
      four case studies on, 335–340
      problems in demonstrating value, 334–335
      short-term profit pressure of, 333–334
   quantification of, 77–78
   three different perspectives on, 6–7
Brand extensions. *See Extensions, brand*
Brand goodwill (BG)
   brand personality component of, 83–94
   transferability, 86–93

Brand identity. *See Identity, brand*
Brand image. *See Image, brand*
Brand language, 354
Brand loyal consumers. *See Loyal buying behavior*
Brand name. *See Name, brand*
Brand personality. *See Personality, brand*
Brand relationships, 4, 113–117
  cultural differences within Europe, 31–48
  researching, 117–118
    corporate brands, 120–123
    credit card brands, 118–120
  three dimensions of, 35, 43–46
  two types of, 122–123
Brands
  of beer and cultural meaning, 129–137
  building of, 31–48, 263–264, 272–273
    difficulties in sustaining activities, 333–334
    global view on, 3
    role of corporate advertising in, 321–332
  as categories, 7, 299–311
  consumer buying patterns for, 235–244
  consumption of, 190, 191
    and expansion advertising, 182–183, 188–189
  consumers protecting, 314–315
  definition of, 33, 69
  established
    cognitive strength of, 247–259
    increasing frequency of use for, 5–6
  expansion advertising of, 177–193
  factors related to performance of, 33
  five different ways to use, 241
  in Japan
    strategies of, 51–62
    use of corporate, 57–62
  metaphor standing for functions of, 166
  multinational, 36–40
  preference for, 78–81
  strong, 1–2, 3, 6–7, 11–30, 70, 73, 81, 163–164
  three classes of, 36–40
  three sources of meanings and associations for, 314
  value of, 125–139
  versatility of, 182, 188, 189
  weak, 3, 69
Brandscape
  and personal brandspace, 67–68

Brand strength, 11–30
  and age, 20, 21, 23
  factors influencing
    continuity, 18
    efficiency, 19
    longevity, 16
    media support, 18
    personality and imagery, 18
    product category, 16
    quality, 16, 18
    renewal, 19
  and gender, 20–21
  measurement of, 13–14
  regional differences in, 20
Breakfast cereal
  use of, in five European countries, 43, 44
Buyer types, 6, 236, 238–239, 242–244
  deal selectives, 240
  long loyals, 239–240
  name brand price driven, 241
  rotators, 240

C

Categories, brand, 299–300
  basis of structure for, 303–304
    defining and accidental features, 305
    feature salience, 306
    matching and distinctive features, 305
    similarity asymmetry, 305
  and brand extensions, 306–309
    subcategory signaling, 309
  contrast model of similarity regarding, 301
  examples of, 304
  extreme values of, 302
  familiarity and, 302
  family resemblance in, 301
  future research regarding, 310–311
  goal-directed, 302, 303–304
  influence on brand strength, 16
  managerial implications for, 309–310
  shared features of, 301
  similarity of, 91
Category dominance
  definition of, 268
  four possible combinations of instance and, 271–273, 274–275
  methods of measurement, 270–275
    facilitation, 269
    latency, 269
    naming, 268–269

Category salience, 48
  in five European countries, 40–43
Celebrity endorsement, 151, 155, 215
Central processing, 157–158, 255–256
Cereal, breakfast
  use of, in five European countries, 43, 44
Charisma, product. *See Product charisma*
Chevron's preconversion campaign, 321–332
  annual effectiveness measurements of,
    328, 330
  brand tracking, 329, 331
  communications objectives and ad pretests
    for, 325–327
  Gulf brand customers regarding, 322–325
  implementation, 327–328
  postwave attitudes and usage study for,
    328, 329, 330
Cognitive responses, 185–186, 249
  impact on brands, 181–182, 187–188
Cognitive strength, 247–248, 258–259
  attitudinal correlates of, 248–250
  creating and maintaining strong images,
    256–258
  development of structure
    multiplexity, 255, 256–258, 259
    simplexity, 254, 256–258, 259
  existing positive attitudes and, 255–256
  role of, in stimulus and memory-based
    choice, 250–252
  structural approaches to, 253–254
Competition
  beer and, 133
  Europe and United States' environment
    for, 163–164
Consumer-brand relationships, 113, 115–117
  corporate brands and, 120–123
  with credit card brands, 118–120
Consumer franchise, 69
  future research priorities concerning,
    243–244
  structure of, 235–239
    application to brands, 241–242
    attitudinal correlates, 239–241
    management of brands, 242–243
Consumers
  brand-loyal, 180, 186–187, 192, 236, 238,
    242, 244
    categories of, 352–353
    definition of, 186–187
    long loyals, 239–240
    product charisma and, 105–106

  versus open to change, 350–351
    WordStar case, 337, 340
  buying patterns of, 235–244
    Japanese, 54–55
  describing advertising, 172–176
  effects of advertising on, 169–170
  familiarity of, 152–153
  five types of, 6
  high- vs. low-knowledge, 295–296
  Japanese
    behavior of, 54–57
    marketing system of, 51–62
  level of involvement of, 152–153
  and selecting products, 165–166
  use of brand personalities, 166–167
Contrast model of similarity, 301
Copy, advertising, 150
  testing of, 347, 349, 352–353
Corporate advertising
  role of, in brand building, 321–332
Corporate brands, 76
  brand relationships
    extending the concept of, to, 120–122
    influence of, on, 122–123
  Japan's use of, 57–62
Credit card brands
  consumers' relationships with, 118–120
Cues, 197, 252
  effect of, on recall, 198, 201, 203, 204,
    206–207, 209–210
  extrinsic and intrinsic, 146–149, 149–152,
    155, 157–158
Cultural approach, 125–139
  beer brands and cultural meaning,
    129–130
    college years, 130–132
    female reaction, 133–134
    postcollege years, 134–137
    regarding competition, 133
  limitations and advantages of, 128–129
  three key research questions regarding,
    125–127
Culture
  advertising and, 53, 94
  brand equity and, 3
  and differences in brand relationships in
    Europe, 31–48
Customers
  Chevron's preconversion campaign and
    Gulf, 322–325
  versus noncustomers, 348–350

D

Datsun-to-Nissan name change, 336, 340
Deal selectives, 240
Decision making
    Japan and in-store, 54–55
Definition advertising, 347–348
Differentiation, brand, 35, 43–46
Directional associations, 265–268
Direct marketing, 75, 124
Direct tests of memory, 218–219, 220, 221,
        222, 224–225, 227, 228
    recall, 218–219, 221, 222, 224–227,
        228–229
    recognition, 219, 221, 222, 224–227
Disrespect relationship, 123
Dominance, 268
Dove brand, 263

E

Elaboration, 224–225, 226, 227, 256
Elaboration Likelihood Model (ELM), 255
Elderly
    brand memory for, 222–223
Elephant fallacy, 343
Emotional advertising, 346, 347
Employees
    and image communication, 76–77
Encoding, 221, 222, 224–225
Europe
    Eastern
        strongest brands in, 23–26
    strongest foreign brands in, 23
    versus U.S. on different research styles,
        171–172
    Western
        strongest brands in, 22–23
European Community (EC)
    creation of trading bloc and marketing
        changes, 31–32
    cultural differences in brand relationships
        within, 31–48
Evaluative consistency, 253
Evaluative extremity, 351
Evian mineral water
    brand equity measures for, 36–40
Executional elements, 215
Expansion advertising

    attributions and, 180–181
    and brand consumption, 182–183,
        188–189
    definition of, 178
    impact of cognitive responses on brands,
        181–182, 187–188
    leveraging brand equity through, 177–179
    managerial implications regarding,
        190–192
    research studies on, 183–189
        future directions for, 190, 192–193
        limitations of, 190
    risks involved in, 178–179
    situation- and product-specific beliefs con-
        cerning, 179–180, 181–182, 183, 186,
        187–188, 189, 190–192
Experiential brand concepts, 154, 155–156
Explicit memory, 217–218, 221
    intentional vs. involuntary, 217
Extensions, brand, 7–8, 12, 85–86, 158,
        213–214
    advertising claims and evidence regarding
        brand equity and, 281–296
    brand categories and, 306–309
    fit and leverage in, 313–318
    limitations that restrict, 314
    strategies regarding, 308
Extrinsic attributes, 146–148, 149–152, 155,
        157–158
    effects on perceived quality, 148–149

F

Facilitation methods, 269, 270
Familiarity, 14, 90, 152–153, 302
    corporate, 61
    relationship between typicality and, 302
    versus leverage, 315–316
Family resemblance, 301
Fit, 8
    concepts of leverage and, 313–314
    lack of, 180–181
    as less helpful than leverage, 317
    overdependence on, 315
Food, fast, 21–22
Food, frozen
    use of, in five European countries, 42–43
Foreign brands, 23, 26–27
Functional brand concepts, 154–155

G

Gender
  and brand strength, 20–21
Gender meaning
  beer and masculinity, 130–138
Global assessment
  of brand strength, 11–30
Global branding strategies, 3
Goal-directed categories, 302, 303–304
Graded structure, 300
Gulf brand. *See Chevron's preconversion
  campaign*

H

Hierarchy of effects concept, 169
Humor, 215

I

Identification, 85, 122–123
Identity, brand, 26
Image, brand, 4, 7, 67–81, 83–84, 164,
    251–252
  brand equity driven by, 70–71
  and brand positioning, 77
  creating and maintaining strong, 248,
    256–258
  definition of, 69, 71, 146
  distinguished from brand equity, 69, 143
  effect of perceived quality on, 144–146
  influence on brand strength, 18
  links among perceived quality, advertis-
    ing, and, 153–156
  perceived value as basis for, 146
  in relation to behavior, 78–81
  simplex vs. multiplex, 254–255
  three components of
    hard and soft attributes, 73–74
    personality and character, 71–72
    sources of imagery, 74–77
    visual representations, 73
ImagePower Survey, Landor, 3, 11–30
Image similarity, 88–89
  definition of, 86
Implicit memory, 6, 215–216, 217–218, 221, 227
  brand equity and, 216
  operational issues in inferring, 219–220
Indirect tests of memory, 218–219, 220, 221,
    222, 224–225, 227, 228

Inference, 94
Informational advertising, 346–347
Information processing
  central and peripheral, 157–158
  during encoding, 224
  Japanese, 55–57
  top-down vs. bottom-up, 55–57
  U.S. vs. Japan regarding, 55–57
Instance dominance
  definition of, 269
  four possible combinations of category
    and, 271–273, 274–275
  measurement of, 269–270, 270–275
Intrinsic attributes, 146–148, 149–152,
    157–158
  effects on perceived quality, 148–149
Involvement
  consumers' level of, 152–153
  of long loyals, 239–240
  of rotators, 240

J

Japan
  advertising in, 3
  branding in, 51–62
    advertising strategy, 52–57
    using corporate brands, 57–62
  compared to U.S. regarding
    advertising, 52–54
    information processing, 55–57
    product purchasing, 54–55
  launching new products in, 58–61
    reasons for, 59–61
    use of corporate branding system, 59
  popularity of foreign brands in, 26–27
  strongest brands in, 26–27

K

Kao brand system, 58
KIRIN brand system, 57

L

Landor ImagePower Survey, 11–30
  measuring brand strength in, 13–14
  methods for conducting, 14–15
  reasons for conducting, 11–13
Latency methods, 269, 270

Leveling, 254
Leverage, 8
  concepts of fit and, 313–314
  as meaning transfer, 316
  as more helpful than fit, 317
  versus familiarity, 315–316
Leveraging, 264, 265, 273–274
  brand equity through expansion advertis-
    ing, 177–179
  definition of, 267–268
  importance of directional associations in, 267
Levissima mineral water
  brand equity measures for, 39–40
Lifestyles
  and product usage, 42–43
Linear sequential models, 169, 170
Logos, corporate identity
  Japan's use of, 57–62
Longevity
  influence on brand strength, 16
Loyal buying behavior, 35, 43–46, 180,
    186–187 192, 236, 238, 242, 244
  categories of, 352–353
  definition of, 186–187
  long loyals, 239–240
  product charisma and, 105–106
  versus open to change, 350–351
  WordStar case, 337, 340

M

Marketing, direct, 124
Markets
  building brands across, 31–48
Marlboro cigarette case
  concerning product charisma, 98
  cultural meaning and, 126–127
Masculinity
  beer and, 130–138
Meaning transfer, 5, 126
  leverage as, 316
  model, 128–129
    applied to beer brands, 137–138
    weak vs. strong brands, 129
Means-end chains, 146
Measurement
  for ad-induced feelings and brand equity
    attitude toward ad and brand, 200–201
    claims recall, 200
    feelings inventory, 199–200

of brand memory, advertising-induced,
    218–220
of brand strength, 13–14
regarding expansion advertising, 185
Media, 47
  advertising, 74–75
  European Community's increase in, 32
  ineffectiveness of traditional, 12
  support and influence on brand strength, 18
Memory, semantic, 271–272
Memory, brand, 196–197, 213–216, *see also*
    Recall
  advertising-induced
    measurement of, 218–220
    varieties of, 216–218
  age and, 222–223
  cognitive strength in relation to, 250–252
  direct and indirect tests for, 218–219, 220,
    221, 222, 224–225, 227, 228
  explicit, 217–218, 221
  four categories of determinants of
    encoding factors, 221, 224–225
    individual viewer, 220, 222–223
    retrieval factors, 221, 225–226
    stimulus characteristics, 220, 223
  implicit, 6, 215–216, 217–218, 221, 227
    operational issues in inferring, 219–220
  role of, in consumer choice, 251–252
  theoretical accounts
    activation view, 217–218
    multiple memory views, 218
    processing views, 218
Memory-based decisions
  versus stimulus-based decisions, 351–352
Mergers, 12, *see also Chevron's preconversion
    campaign*
Message components, 214–215
Metaphors, 73, 164, 174, 345–346, *see also
    Symbolism*
  standing for brand's function, 166
Mineral water
  multinational brands of, 36–40
Motivation, 152–153
Multinational brands, 36–40
Multiplexity, 7, 256–258, 259
  development of, 254, 255

N

Name, brand, 75, 215
  change in, example of, 336

Name, brand *(Cont.)*
  as an extrinsic cue to perceived quality,
    147
  transferability of, 85-94
Naming methods, 268-269, 270
New products
  Japan and launching of, 58-61
Nike Air Jordan brand case
  and product charisma, 104-106

P

Packaging, 76
People Do campaign. *See Chevron's preconver-*
    sion campaign
Perceived quality, 5, 90, 143-159
  antecedents of, 146-149
  definition of, 144-145
  distinguished from perceived value, 145
  effect of, on brand image, 144-146
  effects of advertising on, 149-150
    direct, 152-153
    indirect, 150-152
  effects of concrete attributes on, 148-149
  links among advertising, brand image,
    and, 153-156
  model, 145
  Schlitz case, 339-340
Perceived value, 5, 145-146, 156
  as basis for brand image or positioning,
    146
  definition of, 145
  distinguished from perceived quality, 145
Peripheral processing, 157-158, 255-256
Personal brandspace
  and brandscape, 67-68
Personality, brand, 71-72, 165, 344-345, *see*
    also Product charisma
  advantages of, 73-74
  and brand equity, 4-5
  brand name transferability as a conse-
    quence of
    analysis and results, 91-93
    hypotheses regarding, 86-87
    method of study, 88-91
    prior literature, 85-86
  consumers' use of, 166-167
  definition of, 83-84
  dimensions of, 84
  influence on brand strength, 18

measurement of, 167-168, 169
  research issues concerning, 93-94
Personality similarity, 88-89
  definition of, 86
Persuasion
  central vs. peripheral route to, 255-256
Pilot/Locator micromodel, 78-81
Positioning, 77, 309
  definition of, 77
  perceived value as basis for, 146
  strategies for, 283
Preference, brand, 78-81
Price sensitivity, 148-149, 236, 240-241
  and long loyals, 240
Proactivity, 121
Product category. *See Categories, brand*
Product charisma, 97, 107-110, *see also Per-*
    sonality, brand
  definition of, 100-101
  famous cases of
    Absolut vodka, 98-100
    Marlboro cigarettes, 98
  reasons for usefulness of, 109
  relevance of theory regarding, 101-105
  resulting in buyer loyalty and motivation,
    105-106
Products
  expansion advertising of, 177-193
  Japan vs. U.S. on
    launching new, 58-61
    purchasing, 54-55
  lack of true differentiation of, 13
Product-specific (PS) beliefs, 6, 179-181,
    181-182, 183, 186, 187-188, 189,
    190-192
Profit Impact of Market Strategy (PIMS), 5
Promotion, sales, 75
Public relations, 76
Purchasing patterns, 235-244
  Japanese, 54-55

Q

Qualitative research, 114, 118
Quality
  dimensions of product, 147-148
  influence on brand strength, 16-17
Quality, perceived. *See Perceived quality*
Quantitative research, 114

Questionnaires
  used in researching brand relationships,
    117–118

R

Recall, 197–198, 203–204, 207, 268–269,
    345, *see also Memory*
  effect of delay on, 198, 204–205, 207,
    208–209
  role of cues in, 198, 204, 206–207,
    209–210
  tests of, 218–219, 221, 222, 224–227,
    228–229
Receptivity to brands, 45–47, 48
Recognition
  tests of, 219, 221, 222, 224–227
Redefinition advertising, 347–348
Research studies
  advertising claims and evidence regarding
    brand equity and extensions, 286–293
  on beer brands and cultural meaning,
    129–137
  on brand categories
    future directions for, 310–311
  brand equity
    in Europe, 33–48
    and image, 77–81
  brand image, 117
    limitations on, 114
  brand name transferability, 85–94
  on brand relationships, 117–123
  differences in styles of
    U.S. vs. Europe, 171–172
  on expansion advertising and brand equi-
    ty, 183–189
  future, 190, 192–193
  limitations of, 190
  quantitative vs. qualitative, 114, 118
Risk aversion, 35, 43–46
Rotators, 240

S

Sales promotion, 75
Salience versus trust, 344–345
Satisfaction with brands, 121
Schlitz case, 339–340
Semantic memory, 271–272

Semantic relatedness, 265
Shareholders
  maximizing wealth of, 333–334
Sharpening, 254
Shopping habits
  Japanese, 54–55
Simplexity, 7, 256–258, 259
  development of, 254
Situation-specific (SS) beliefs, 6, 179–180,
    181–182, 183, 186, 187–188, 189,
    190–192
Soviet Union
  strongest brands in, 23–26
Staff
  and image communication, 76–77
Standardization, 51
Stimulus characteristics, 220, 223
Stimulus-based decisions
  versus memory-based decisions, 351–352
Stockholder demands, 59
Strong brands, 1–2, 3, 6–7, 11–30, 70, 73,
    81, 163–164
  meaning transfer model regarding weak
    and, 129
  of the world, 18–20
    Japan, 26–27
    Soviet Union and Eastern Europe,
      23–26
    United States, 20–22
    Western Europe, 22–23
Subcategory signaling, 309
Supportiveness, 122
Symbolic brand concepts, 154, 155
Symbolism, 73, 94, 99, 102–103, 105–106,
    107, 109, 126, 166, 174, 214,
    345–346, 353–354, *see also Metaphors*

T

Tea
  use of, in five European countries, 41–42
Top-down information processing, 55–57
Trademark logos, corporate
  Japan's use of, 57–62
Trading bloc
  European Community's creation of, 31–32
Traditionalism
  four indicators of, 46–47
Transferability, 85–94, 286, 291
  factors influencing, 92–93

Transformation advertising, 346, 347
Transportation models, 169, 170
Trust, 46–47
    in brands, 121
    versus salience, 344–345
Typicality, 300–302, 305–306, 308
    definition of, 267
    relationship between familiarity and, 302

U

United States
    compared to Japan regarding
        advertising, 52–54
        information processing, 55–57
        new product launches, 58–61
        product purchasing, 54–55
        use of corporate brands, 57–62
    strongest brands in, 20–22
    versus Europe on different research styles,
        171–172

V

Value, perceived. *See Perceived value*

Versatility, brand, 182, 188, 189
Visual representations, 73
Vittel mineral water
    brand equity measures for, 36, 38

W

Wa, 58
Water, bottled/mineral
    multinational brands of, 36–40
    use of, in five European countries, 41
Weak brands, 3
    meaning transfer model regarding strong
        and, 129
Weight Watchers case, 337–338, 340
Women
    reaction to beer, 133–134
    working
        and breakfast cereal usage, 43, 44
        and frozen meal use, 42–43
WordStar case, 337, 340
World
    most powerful brands in the, 18–30